Old Families of Louisiana

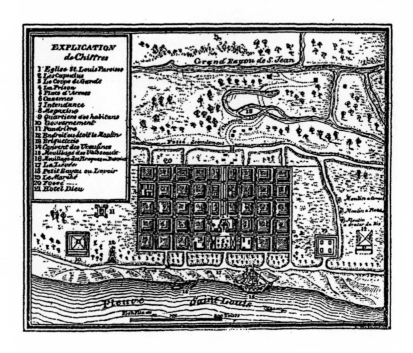

THE VIEUX CARRÉ

or "Old Square"

New Orleans in 1723 as laid out
by Adrien de Pauger, engineer

Old Families of Louisiana

by

Stanley Clisby Arthur
Editor and Compiler

George Campbell Huchet de Kernion
Collaborator and Historian

A FIREBIRD PRESS BOOK

PELICAN PUBLISHING COMPANY
Gretna 1998

Manufactured in the United States of America

Published by Pelican Publishing Company, Inc.
1000 Burmaster Street, Gretna, Louisiana 70053

Avant-Propos

OLD FAMILIES OF LOUISIANA has been compiled in response to a demand in book form of a comprehensive series of genealogical records of the foundation families of the state. Families whose ancestors settled with Bienville in New Orleans at the time the famous old city was laid out in the cresent bend of the Mississippi river. Also of those who came to · Louisiana when the golden lilies of France, the castellated banner of Spain, the Union Jack of Great Britain, or the flag of fifteen stars and fifteen stripes waved over the land.

As originally projected the present work was to have been a continuation and augmentation of the genealogical series on *Louisiana Families* written by Charles Patton Dimitry in 1892, and published in weekly installments in the old New Orleans *Times-Democrat.*

The Dimitry genealogical series in the age-yellowed files of a newspaper published forty years ago, has been, with the exception of Miss Grace King's delightful *Créole Families of New Orleans*, the sole source of printed information concerning the root or foundation families of French and Spanish descent whose names have been indelibly associated with the history of Louisiana and New Orleans for hundreds of years. Unfortunately, this admirable collection of genealogical sketches has been neither easy to procure nor simple of access.

It was in response to many requests, and at the suggestion of Mr. Robert Usher, librarian of the Howard Memorial Library, that the publisher of this volume determined to reprint the Dimitry series. Mr. Leonard Nicholson, of the present *Times-Picayune*, kindly extended the necessary permission.

In the compilation of the original data it became apparent that the present book would be greatly augmented in interest and value by the addition of genealogical records of other prominent foundation families besides the French and Spanish. For such reason has been included English, Scottish, and Irish lineages whose representatives now form an integral part of the present-day population of Louisiana. It was also recognized that the Dimitry series and Miss King's compilation of family histories did not include many French and Spanish foundation families who, by reason of their importance in the early colony, should appear in a work of this character.

The compiler and the publisher of this volume were fortunate in having associated with them a recognized student of Louisiana genealogy and history, Mr. George Campbell Huchet de Kernion, a descendant of one of the important early families, who very kindly volunteered to act as collaborator and historian. Through Mr. Kernion's intimate knowledge of old families it was possible to make extensive corrections and additions to the Dimitry data as it originally appeared, and to include in this publication histories of a number of other prominent first families.

The families treated by Mr. Dimitry in his series in the *Times-Democrat* have been grouped in Part One of this volume. As all of his genealogical sketches have been scrupulously edited, corrected, and amplified with more recently obtained data, a footnote at the conclusion of each article gives the page and issue of the newspaper in which the original article appeared. Use was not made of the Dimitry sketch on the St. Martin family, including data on the Perret family, which appeared August 7 and 14, 1892, it having been found necessary that a descendant of both families, Mr. St. John Perret, write two entirely new histories.

It was likewise found necessary for Mr. Kernion to write as separate chapters the genealogical records of the Juchereau de Saint Denys family and those of the Chauvin de Léry, and de Beaulieu families rather than make use of the data found in Mr. Dimitry's articles of October 9 and 16, 1892.

The work of compilation has necessarily been long and arduous, but it was desired to make the work as correct and complete as possible. The compiler has received much outside assistance and gratefully acknowledges the generous cooperation that has permitted the examination of many family records.

The editor is indebted for assistance to Mr. Robert Usher, of the Howard Memorial Library; Miss Josie Cerf, of the

Louisiana State Museum; Miss Carrie Freret, of the Louisiana Historical Society's library; and Mr. St. John Perret, who compiled the histories of the Perret and St. Martin families, and supplied valuable data and statistics on the Derbigny family and that of the Chevalier Charles Frédèric d'Arensbourg, thus permitting us to publish for the first time accurate data on this celebrated Louisianian.

Acknowledgments are also due Miss Louise Butler, of West Feliciana parish, for the Butler genealogy; Miss Lise Allain, who corrected and supplied data for the Le Blanc, Allain, Tounoir, and Jarreau chapter; Mrs. Josie Landry Stirling, for data on the Landry, Alston and Stirling families; Mr. J. Hereford Percy, of Baton Rouge, for assistance in the Percy, Johnson, and Hereford compilations; Miss Louise de Hault de Lassus, who supplied family data; Miss Tennessee Robertson, of West Baton Rouge parish, for assistance in the Johnson genealogy; Mr. Trist Wood, who supplied details on the Bringier family; Mr. Charles A. Favrot, for his compilation on the Favrot chapter; Mrs. David I. Norwood, of West Feliciana parish, for the Barrow family history; Mr. J. E. Ducros, who supplied accurate data on the la Ronde and Chalmette families; Mr. Charles S. Waggaman, who was of assistance in supplying new and correct data on the Arnoult, Sauvé, and Waggaman families; Mrs. James Wilkinson, for data on General Wilkinson's family; Miss Marie Breazeale of Natchitoches, for data on the Breazeale, Prudhomme, and Benoist families; Mrs. Henry Grady Price, who furnished the Plauché-Dart genealogy; Miss Zoé Posey, for her assistance with the Bermudez family; Miss Justine Godchaux, for her search of old Spanish and French documents in the Cabildo; Mr. George Ferrier Jr., for data on the Forstall and Cruzat families, and many others. Acknowledgement is also due Miss Ethel Hargroder for her reading of the final proofs.

Mr. Kernion's special thanks are due Messrs. Arthur A. de la Houssaye, William H. de la Houssaye, René J. Le Gardeur, Mr. W. O. Garic, Dr. A. E. Fossier, Dr. J. E. Doussan, and Col. C. Robert Churchill, and Mmes. Augustus H. Denis, Louis F. Anaya, Guy B. Lawrason, and the Misses Mary Tennant, Barrow, Rubie de la Lande, and many others. Much valuable genealogical information of old Louisiana families of Canadian origin was also gathered by him from the works of the eminent Canadian genealogists, l'Abbé Tanguay and Mr. Pierre George Roy.

The *OLD FAMILIES OF LOUISIANA* has exceeded the original scope intended. In order to set a limit to its range, it was agreed that only those families settling in Louisiana before and up to the time of the beginning of the American domination in 1803, should be included. Whereas the original plan was to issue a genealogical record of 368 pages, the finished result totals 432 pages. It is to be regretted that records of a number of families, including the Randolph, Beauregard, Lewis, Guion, de Reggio, Bouligny, and others of equal importance do not appear in these pages, due to exigencies of space or the inability to secure necessary data from descendants.

It had been planned also to include in this work a roster of the famed Orleans Battalion and a list of the first inhabitants of New Orleans. But it developed the list of Plauché's soldiers secured did not differ from that published in this compiler's *The Battle of New Orleans*, issued by the Louisiana Historical Society in 1915. Likewise, the first census of New Orleans had been published in the Historical Society's quarterly in 1920. It was thereupon concluded the space these two lists would have employed could be used to better advantage for the publication of additional family biographies, rather than the repetition of names already printed.

There is no question of precedence in this record of family histories, the genealogies having been printed in the order in which they were written or received by the compiler. Every precaution has been taken to guard against errors in names, places, and dates, and in each instance, as far as practicable, manuscripts and proofs have been turned over to descendants for checking and correction.

STANLEY CLISBY ARTHUR.

CONTENTS

Part One

Part Two

OLD
FAMILIES
of
LOUISIANA

VUE DE LA NOUVELLE ORLEANS EN 1719

Part One

"LOUISIANA FAMILIES" [1]

THE history of a nation, a state, or a community is not comprised in a record of its fauna, its flora, or its geographical or geological conditions; that which composes history is the stories of the lives of the men and women who have had more or less to do with its affairs.

In a series of genealogical sketches of Louisiana families, which for over a year appeared in the columns of the *Times-Democrat* in 1892-93, my readers and I retraced by many paths, through the lives of individuals, the romantic and many-hued story of Louisiana from its earliest settlement by the French to our day.

In preparing those sketches I endeavored, where the material was at my command, to impart to them the interest that is associated with the memories of the old days of Iberville, of Bienville, of Vaudreuil, and the line of successors, as governors of the colony and state, under the French, Spanish, and American dominations. I hope my readers then were pleased in the perusal of those records of families whose names have been so long a time familiar to the ears of Louisianians, as I hope, also, especially, to have secured the satisfaction of those immediately concerned to many of whom I am indebted for whatever measure of success I may have achieved in recalling past episodes in French and Louisiana history, and in tracing the stories, directly or indirectly, of hundreds of Louisiana's colonial families and the families of the first decades of this century.

It is true that in the honorable company of Louisiana's ancient population other hundreds of families of merit and distinction remained to be chronicled. But for the series of these family sketches, the limit was reached, and so, on that

---

1. The concluding article by Charles Patton Dimitry in his genealogical series, which is now used, with slight changes in tense, as a foreword to his revised, reedited, and corrected family biographies printed in Part One of the present work.

crowded stage of Louisiana's past—a past closely linked with the present, however—the curtain was rung down.

The records of the families of which I have had the honor to be the chronicler show that while many of the ancestors of the older families of Louisiana came hither directly from France, and many from San Domingo, others by the way of American cities more to the northward of us, the majority, probably (although of French ancestory) arrived in the colony as officers of the Infantry of the Marine (the Louisiana colonial troops) from Canada. There is also the Spanish element, which from 1769, when the Spanish rule in Louisiana became established, added the infusion of Castillian blood to the old population. Ireland, too, sent many branches of her ardent families to give variety to the human mosaic of the peoples whose representatives, gathered together from afar, had laid the foundation of Louisiana society, giving to it its exceptional tone and qualities—its elegance, chivalry and courtesy, and, it may be added, in all truth, its exemplary sense of honor and self-respect.

Leading the list of provinces of France which gave to Louisiana the elements of the majority of the families whose stories and generations I have recorded in *"Louisiana Families,"* is Brittany, a land of chivalry, of poetic and romantic memories, of a people pious, of brave soldiers and sailors. Normandy, the dwelling place of knights and seigneurs of old, whence went with William, their duke, the barons whose names are read in the roll of the Battle Abbey—Normandy, forever associated with the memories of the rearing of the structure of English laws and English society, and of the bringing to perfection and completeness the English language —Normandy, mingling in the land of conquest with the strong Saxon blood that had preceded the going thither of her sons and producing a people great at home and not less great in their English-speaking progeny of the United States —Normandy sent many.

Others came from Provence, from Dauphiné, from Lorraine, from Burgundy, from Champagne, Alsace, Poitou, the Bourbonnais, and some came from the cities of Paris, Marseilles, Nantes, and Bordeaux, and from the towns of Grenoble, La Rochelle, Noémy, Estampes, and Brie. Some came with the titles of ancient nobility, with commissions signed by the three Louises of France, as Knights of the Order of Saint Louis, as officers of the army, while others, bearing no titles, came to Louisiana breathing the free and ennobling air of which constituted for them and their posterity a liberal and sufficient patent of nobility.

In following the lineages of some of our Louisiana families of greater or less antiquity there is a reopening of doors, as it were, and strange and picturesque historical vistas appear before the mental vision. The characters, men and women of forgotten days—days almost as extinct as if they had never been—come trooping before us. The crusader is there with face stern and martial in expression, and yet, in repose, illuminated with the light of faith and a pious zeal. The *chatelain* looks from the castle-turret over his broad domain, and the men-at-arms cross the drawbridge according as the varying trumpet sounds the departure or the return. The marches of armies are again revealed; from Italy they return to France singing songs of victory and bringing with them the civilizing lessons from Padua and Mantua and Florence and wonderful tales of the mighty civilizations, the embers of whose greatness still smoldered on the shores of the Mediterranean sea.

The *mousquetaire gris* or the *mousquetaire noir*, like that Chevalier de la Marjolaine, "*toujours gai*," crosses the scene with his pretty embroidered cloak, his high russet boots, his perfumed ringletty hair, and his steel-sheathed rapier. Among those who appear and disappear, filling the intervals of the generations, are King's Councillors, Councillors of the Parliment, officers in the households of the Kings and in their military and naval services, chevaliers, some so born and some so appointed, men adorning the civil and unofficial walks of life. There are there, also, the glint of jewels, of coronets, of gold and silver decorations and ornaments, and the garbs of silk and satin, velvet and cloth.

In a palace of the Scottish Kings a man out of Italy (David Rizzio was his name) with dark, languishing eyes, in his composition something of the troubadour, the *improvisatore*, the professor, but most of the lover, reclines on a rude flooring of damask of the weavery of the looms of Venice, at the feet of a royal patroness, a beautiful queen, the azure of whose eyes, the ruddy hue of whose hair, and the pink and white of whose satin cheeks are repeated in the eyes and hair and cheeks of the fair maids of honor who surround her. They, sitting at their spinning wheels, are listening mute while the troubadour touches with suave fingers the strings of his mandolin, singing for their delectation love songs. Love songs of the Arno and gay barcaroles of the lagunas of Venice. When not singing he relates the legends of spectre-haunted halls of gray Florentine palaces, the story of the riches of the Medics, the traditions of the Viviadis, the Grimaldis, and the Dorias, of Genoa, the tale of the two lovers of Verona—Messer Romeo Montesche and sweet Madame Giulletta Capoletto—The two who died for love and were entombed together in the tomb of the Capoletti in the Campo-Santo of the old Italian city! and the quaint sayings of Ser Riggoletto, the Duke's jester of Mantua.

And so, as the nearer doors open and more modern vistas appear, the vistas revealed are vistas of Louisiana—the fairest scene of all—her forests, her prairies, her dark and odorous lagoons, Bienville, with light helmet decked with feathers, and clad in half-armour, walks in the *Place d'Armes* with his officers, while the rolling of the drums that beat a salute at morn to the flag of the *fleur-de-lys* blends with the hymn that is sung in the old convent in Condé street by the pious sisterhood of the Ursuline nuns.

Sometimes a pedestrain wending his way late at night along a city's streets will hear, coming from a dwelling in one of the streets, the sounds of music, the murmur of many voices, the echoes of merry laughter. If he will pause for a while at the window and gaze at the scene he will behold a goodly company, gallant men and graceful women. But there must come a time when the merriment is over and silence and quiet prevail where was bustle and motion. And so, the lights are extinguished, and like visions wrought by the imagination out of enchanted materials, the company vanishes, the gallant men and the graceful women disappear, and are seen no more.

CHARLES PATTON DIMITRY

[20]

MORANT—ST. AVID—PICHOT Families

AMONG the prominent citizens of New Orleans at the beginning of the nineteenth century was Vincent, Chevalier de Morant, the son of the Marquis de Morant, a French nobleman who came to New Orleans in the early days of the eighteenth century. The Chevalier de Morant, who was born in New Orleans and died there, was a younger brother of the Marquis Charles de Morant, and the last of his line who bore the family name were his three daughters.

The Morants were from Normandy, and among the Norman gentlemen, who in the year 1096 followed the banner of Robert Courte-Heuzé to Palestine, were members of this family. Later, as is shown by the records of the Church of Saint-Laurence in Paris, Thomas de Morant, Marquis d'Estreville, and Count de Montignac, acquired in 1621 the estate of du Mesnil in Normandy, which was erected into a *marquisate*, and the title of Marquis de Morant was conferred on its overlord. The Morant family, in the seventeenth century, contracted matrimonial alliances with the Dampierres and with the princes de Beauffremont. In 1620 one of the name founded a monastery for the use of the Dominicans on the estate of du Mesnil. Other titles borne by the de Morants were Count de Pences and Baron de Thénon, some of whom were *maréchaux de camp* of the king's army, and gentlemen ordinary to the king.

In the year 1735, or 1745, Antoine, Marquis de Morant, obtained from Louis XV a concession of land outside New Orleans, which was later known as the *Faubourg Tremé*. Under the Spanish domination the military authorities of the city erected fortifications on this tract, thus giving the present name of Rampart street to the thoroughfare. Although the Spanish government recognized the pecuniary obligation for the land thus used, the money due was never paid, because, so it was then alleged, of the poverty of the Spanish Crown. At a later period a suit was instituted against the city of New Orleans for the value of the land, and Etienne Mazureau, a celebrated lawyer of his time, was counsel for those bringing suit. The case was lost in the courts, but had the descendants of de Morant succeeded in their suit they would have realized a large fortune. The three heirs who entered suit were Charlotte de Morant, who became Mrs. James Hepburn; Marie de Morant, who married Adolphe W. Pichot, and Pépita, who became the Baroness de Saint-Avid, the daughters of Chevalier de Morant by his second marriage.

Vincent, Chevalier de Morant, was twice married. His first wife was Constance Volant, who as family traditions relate, was attracted to him by his wit, his handsome face, and agreeable presence, heightened as it was when he appeared before her one day wearing a coat of blue moiré embroidered with silver. This lady, when the chevalier married her, was the widow of Pierre Marquis, one of the French patriots shot by order of the Spanish governor, Don Alessandro O'Reilly. After the death of his first wife, de Morant married Marguerite Françoise Chauvin de Léry des Islets, daughter of Antoine Chauvin de Léry des Islets and Charlotte Faucon du Manoir, descended from a noble family of Brittany, the founder of which, named Falconieri, went from France to Italy in the train of Charles VIII, on the return of that monarch after the conquest of Naples. The second Mme. de Morant was a widow of eighteen at the time of her marriage to Chevalier de Morant, her first husband having been Jean Balthazar Esnould de Livaudais. Her father was of a distinguished colonial family of Canada.

The ancestors of the second Mme. de Morant, after their arrival in France with Charles VIII in 1495, were known as Marquis de Charleval, Count de Bacqueville, together with other titles. From the marriage of Antoine Chauvin de Léry de Islets and Charlotte Fançon were born: first, Jean François de Léry des Islets, who married Marthe Bienvenu and left a numerous posterity; second, Charlotte, who married Jacques Esnould de Livaudais in 1763; third, Louise Constance, who married René Huchet de Kernion; fourth, Jeanne, married to François Beaumont de Livaudais; fifth,

Judith, who married Count de McNamara, and sixth, Marguerite Françoise, who married the Chevalier de Morant.

Mme. Marguerite de Morant was born in 1761 and during her life occured most of the important events in the early history of the colony. She was a mere child when the conspiracy of Marquis took place, but she knew all the particulars in which Pierre Marquis, her uncle Nicholas Chauvin de Lafrénière, and her cousin Jean Baptiste Payen de Noyan, acted a conspicuous and, to them, fatal part, and in which her brother des Islets was also concerned. She died in 1850, and during her lifetime Louisiana was given up to Spain, retroceded to France, and sold to the United States. Most of her relatives were engaged in the war of 1812, stood with Jackson on the Plains of Chalmette and helped beat back the British attack on the memorable Eighth of January. She was handsome, of fair complexion, and looked so much younger than her years that at a ball given by the governor a gentleman who admired her requested an introduction to "that pretty young lady sitting next to the governor's wife." The request was made to no less a person than her husband, the Chevalier de Morant. "That pretty young lady is my wife," replied the husband to the admiring stranger, "and she has had no less than seventeen children!"

Of this numerous family, however, only three daughters survived, and they were regarded as foremost among the many handsome women of their day in old New Orleans. The oldest, Pépita de Morant, married, first, the Sieur de Villechaise, and after his death married Jean Martin de la Selve, Baron de Saint-Avid, and passed the greater part of her life in Paris where she died. The second daughter, Charlotte Mathilde de Morant, married James Hepburn of Philadelphia, whose grandfather went to Pennsylvania from England with William Penn. He was of the Hepburns, Earls of Bothwell of Scotland, whose blood was mingled with that of the royal house of Scotland when James, Earl of Bothwell, married the unfortunate Mary Queen of Scots. Mr. Hepburn died in 1862 at the age of seventy-four.

Marie Clémentine de Morant, the third of the lovely de Morant sisters, married Judge Adolphe W. Pichot. In addition to her personal charms she was known for her refined intelligence, was an excellent musician, and showed a decided talent for painting.

A celebrated daughter of Old Louisiana was Judith Chauvin de Léry des Islet, fifth child and fourth daughter of Antoine Chauvin de Léry des Islets and Charlotte Faucon du Manoir, and a sister of Mme. de Morant, the second. Judith married the Comte de McNamara, born in Ireland, who settled in Louisiana, where he followed the occupation of a planter, naming his plantation *Mérieult*. Where the McNamara acquired his title of "Count" is a genealogical mystery.

Mme. de McNamara-Mérieult was a handsome blonde and lived in Paris. She had a handsome head of hair, so long and thick and golden as to arouse general admiration. It is related at that time Napoleon Bonaparte was anxious to secure a political alliance with Turkey and the report came to him that the Sultan would like to present his Sultana with a blonde wig. Napoleon did not know where to procure a suitable one. The Empress Joséphine's hairdresser told her that he attended a lady who possessed a *chevelure* of the kind desired by the Emperor, but that the lady was high-born and might not choose to part with her beautiful hair. Josephine told Napoleon of the golden-haired beauty so he sent an emissary to fair Louisiana and offered her a castle in exchange for her hair. As much as Countess McNamara wanted the castle the exchange was refused and the Sultana did without her blonde *péruque*. Her granddaughter, Françoise Georgine Blanche Ogden, married Célestin de Pontalba, son of Micaela and the Baron de Pontalba. The family of Chauvin de Léry (or Delery, as it is usually written at the present time) to whom the father of Comtesse McNamara belonged, dates in Louisiana from the first settlement of the colony.

Jean Martin de la Selve, Baron de Saint-Avid, born in Limousin, France, was a nephew of Baron de Pontalba. While on a visit to Louisiana he met, wooed and won for his wife, Pépita, oldest of the three daughters of Chevalier Vincent de Morant, by his second marriage with Marguerite Chauvin de Léry des Islets. At that time Pépita (which is a Spanish diminutive of Joséphine) was the widow of

[24]

Sieur de Villechaise, a wealthy French merchant of New Orleans. After the marriage, the baron and his charming bride went to Paris where the Louisiana baroness won instant social success by her unusual beauty and grace and became a favorite at the court of Louis Philippe. In 1848, after her titled husband's death, Mme. de Saint-Avid lived in Paris until her death 1874.

In the posterity of Vincent, Chevalier de Morant by his first marriage with Mme. Constance Volant Marquis, widow of the martyred Pierre Marquis, was born a daughter Constance de Morant named for her mother. She was twice married. Her first husband was M. Landier, whose daughter, Mme. Fierville Bienvenu, was the mother of Charles Bienvenu, former head of the United States Mint; Placide Bienvenu, Mme. Chastant, Mathilde Bienvenu, and Eliza Bienvenu. By her second marriage, Constance de Morant Landier, became Mme. Guichard, and had a daughter who married Mélicour Bienvenu, thus becoming the mother of Mrs. Louise Crawford, Mrs. Archibald Montgomery, Guichard Bienvenu, Mrs. Boucher, and Amanda Bienvenu.

Judge Adolphe Wencelas Pichot, who married into the de Morant family, came to Louisiana early in 1800. He was descended from a wealthy French family of magistrates in Normandy. His father was an exception, giving preference to the sword over the advocate's gown, and became an officer of rank in the armies of Napoleon I. Among his intimates in this service was a Polish officer, a General Wenceslas, after whom he named his son. The latter, to retrieve a fortune impaired by his father's prodigalities, came to the United States and endeavored to establish himself in Texas. Disappointed in these expectations, he was on his way back to France when he passed through New Orleans and one night attended a ball where he met Mlle. Clémentine de Morant, fell in love, studied law in his loved one's native city under Pierre Bourguignon Derbigny, and married her.

In 1827, in partnership with John Gibson, an early journalist of the Crescent City, he founded the New Orleans *Bee*, or as it was called, *l'Abeille de la Nouvelle Orléans*. But as his law practice increased and his views of paper management did not coincide with that of Gibson, he withdrew from the newspaper and devoted himself wholly to the law. He was elected a member of the legislature, and became one of the directors of the Citizen's Bank. Later, the governor appointed him a judge of one of the Lafourche courts and it was during his term on the bench that he became involved in an altercation which resulted not only in a duel but in Judge Pichot's death.

One daughter, Léonie Pichot, under the *nom-de-plume* of "Guy de Morant," contributed a number of papers to *Le Correspondent* of Paris, and the *Athénée Louisianais*. She was an ardent Southern patriot during the war between the States, displaying on all occasions her love for the Stars and Bars of the Confederacy. It is related that after New Orleans had been captured by Farragut and General Ben. Butler became its military commander, Léonie Pichot purposely displayed, while passing some Federal soldiers in Canal street, a handkerchief showing in its corner an embroidered Confederate flag. Being asked to surrender it, the young woman bit off the treasured corner and swallowed it. Brought before General Butler, she said she had no apology to make and being held as an enemy of the United States, she was sent a prisoner to Fort Jackson.

The original Dimitry article on the Morant family appeared in the New Orleans Times-Democrat January 10, 1892, p. 13.

Coat of arms of the Duc d'Orléans

ALMONESTER—
DELFAU DE PONTALBA Families

IN the historic St. Louis Cathedral in Chartres street, New
Orleans, lie the remains of Don Andres Almonester y
Roxas by whose piety and through the expedient of
whose money, the sacred structure was founded and
given to the Catholic clergy and laity of the city. A tablet on
which is inscribed a commemorative epitaph marks the spot
where Don Andres lies buried, and the lines are an epitome
of his life, of his dignities, and of his benefactions. They tell
him who reads them that beneath the tablet is buried Andres
Almonester y Roxas, a native of Mayrena, in the kingdom
of Andalusia, and that he died in New Orleans April 26,
1798. He was born November 6, 1725.

Concerning his dignities, it is told that he was a knight of
the Royal Order of Charles III of Spain, colonel of the
militia of the department of New Orleans, and alderman
and royal lieutenant of that corporation. Regarding his chari-
ties, the reader is informed that he was the founder and
donor of the cathedral in which he now lies, founder, also,
of the Royal Hospital of Saint-Charles and of its church;
of the hospital for lepers, of the Ursuline Convent, of the
school for the education of girls, and of the courthouse—
the old Cabildo—which still rears its bulk of masonry and
concrete on the uptown side of the cathedral.

Don Andres' father, Miguel Almonester, and his mother,
Doña Juan Maria de Estrada y Roxas, belonged to
ancient Hispanic houses, numbered among those of the
grandee class. In 1769, when Don Andres reached Louisiana
in the train of Alessandro O'Rielly, he was only a notary
or escribano. He had buried his first wife, Doña Maria
Martinez, in Andalusia. A widower at forty-four, he had
come to the Louisiana land to build up a fortune.

[27]

He was an able man for shortly after his arrival O'Reilly appointed him *Alfarez Real*, or Royal Standard Bearer, in the Cabildo. He eventually became a colonel of militia and in the last days of his life his king rewarded him with the Cross of Charles III. Almonester possessed keen business acumen and accumulated a great fortune in New Orleans by judicious investments and by the careful management of his commercial ventures. So anxious was he to acquire land and wealth in his new found home, that the thought of remarrying did not cross his mind until he reached the age of sixty. But when he did decide to give up his celibacy, he proved as wise in choosing his second mate as he had been in selecting his many parcels of real estate.

The beautiful Louise de la Ronde, baptised in New Orleans August 2, 1758, became his second wife on March 20, 1787. She was twenty-nine, one of the richest heiresses in New Orleans, and the oldest daughter of the Chevalier Pierre Denis de la Ronde, a knight of Saint-Louis, and Madeleine Broutin, (the widow of Sieur de Lino de Chalmette,) who had married de la Ronde in 1756.

From the illmated union of Don Andres Almonester and Louise de la Ronde was born on November 6, 1795, a daughter Micaëla Leonarda Almonester. She was educated at the Ursuline Convent in Condé street, (now Chartres street), and as was customary in those early days, she was betrothed, by an arrangement between the parents, to Joseph Xavier Célestin Delfau de Pontalba, the son and heir of the baron Joseph Xavier Delfau de Pontalba, a royal musketeer, and Jeanne Louise Le Breton des Chappelles.

The Delfau de Pontalbas were wealthy. The future father-in-law of Micaëla having been an officer in the Spanish army and at one time commandant of the *Côte des Allemands*, or German Coast, on the Mississippi river above New Orleans. The younger Pontalba, at the time he was betrothed to the daughter of Don Andres Almonester, was living in France where he had become an officer in the French army. For that reason, as the bride-to-be could form no idea of the personal appearance of the *fiancé* she had never seen, his portrait was painted on ivory and sent to Micaëla. This pictured proxy of her future husband so pleased the fair heiress of Almonester's millions, so it is related, that she fell in love with the original from an inspection of the miniature.

The large fortune which Don Andres Almonester acquired, which at his death descended by inheritance to Micaëla his only child, resulted not only from his perspicacity in the matter of land values but also from the fact he was his own architect and contractor. He had spent fifteen years of his life erecting numerous buildings in New Orleans. They were valued at more than a million and half *livres*. They had cost, nevertheless, considerably less to the astute Spaniard. For he employed in their construction none other than his own slaves numbering over a hundred. They were carefully trained as masons, carpenters, cabinet-makers, and blacksmiths. Most of his materials, such as lumber and brick, came from his own forests and kilns. Iron was about the only thing he had to buy, but even this rough metal was converted by his own skillful blacksmiths into most exquisite iron lace.

When, on March 21, 1788, during the administration of Governor Miro, occurred the disastrous fire in New Orleans that destroyed eight hundred and fifty-six buildings, including the parish church of Saint-Louis, Almonester was already known as a philanthropist. The Hospital of San Carlos, built in 1779, was due to his munificence. The Ursulines enjoyed a home he had given them. The *leprosarium* of San Lazaro, constructed in 1785, had been paid with his *pesos*. And now that the parish church had been wiped out by the flames, Don Andres came, as the Balm of Gilead, with the gift of a splendid new cathedral, to soothe and heal the wounds of the afflicted community.

Don Andres died in 1798. Six years later, on March 17, 1804, his young wife, Louise de la Ronde, became the bride of M. Castillion, the dapper young French consul in New Orleans. The bride, being much older than the groom, the provoking burghers of the city gave vent to their disapproval of the match by treating the pair to a *Charivari*, the customary seranade of rattling tin pans, blowing whistles, and horns, calculated to make the night hideous with a cacophony of nerve-racking sounds.

Pére Antoine, the venerable and well-loved pastor of the Saint Louis Cathedral, officiated at the marriage, October 23, 1811, which joined the Pontalba and Almonester names and money, in a ceremony which for brilliancy and *éclat*, together with the wealth of the contracting parties, and their conspicuousness in the community, eclipsed any like ceremony in the history of the city. Among the witnesses were: M. de Saint-Avid, the Chevalier de Macarty, Ignace de Lino de Chalmette, and Mme. Bernard de Verges de Saint-Sauveur. And, representing Marshal Ney, the famed soldier of Napoleon I, Colonel Bernard de Marigny de Mandeville gave away the bride (her father having passed away a dozen years before) in the presence of the brilliant assemblage of the flower of New Orleans' aristocracy.

It was under particularly bright auspices that young Pontalba and his bride Micaëla, shortly after sailed for France to take up their abode in Paris. The elder Pontalba soon followed his son and daughter-in-law to France and took up his residence in the chateau *Mont l'Eveque*. Four children were born to the marriage of Micaëla and Célestin. While the marriage at first appeared to be a happy one, it was not long before matrimonial complications arose and the couple separated, Célestin making the charges. The daughter of Don Almonester retained possession of the children but it was agreed and understood that their paternal grandfather, the old Baron de Pontalba, should be consulted on all matters that appertained to their education. It was while Micaëla was on a visit to his chateau on business concerning the children, that she was attacked by her father-in-law, the Baron, and seriously wounded before the Baron de Pontalba committed suicide by shooting himself with the pistol he had used on his daughter-in-law.

Micaëla recovered from her wounds and, subsequently, Célestin applied for and was given a divorce by the *Cour de Cassation* and so the matrimonial difficulties of the Pontalbas ended. Micaëla, freed of her husband and in the enjoyment of her large income from the New Orleans properties left her by her father, erected a splendid and costly *hotel* or city residence in the rue Saint-Honoré, in the Faubourg Saint-

Germain, in which magnificent entertainments and a profuse hospitality marked the years of her residence there, until the day of her death, which occured in Paris, April 20, 1874. Her former husband outlived her four years.

Micaëla revisited the city of her birth a number of times and has left several mementoes of her return to the old New Orleans that gave her her wealth. About 1850, the revolution of 1848 having caused her to leave France, she took steps that led to the improvement and beautification of the historic *Place d'Armes*, the name of which, at her insistence, was changed by the city council to "Jackson Square," in honor of General Andrew Jackson and his services in beating back the British hosts in 1815. She gave a substantial sum towards the erection of the Clark Mills equestrian bronze statue of Jackson and his rearing horse that is today a feature of the square.

At this same time she erected the two red brick apartment houses that flank the square to the north and south, on the rues Ste. Anne and St. Pierre, which are still designated as "the Pontalba Buildings."

One son of her marriage, named for his father, Célestin de Pontalba, married Blanche Ogden, who was a grand-daughter of the Comtesse McNamara-Mérieult, who in turn had been Judith Chauvin de Léry des Islets. The issue of the Pontalba-Ogden marriage now reside in Paris. Another son of Micaëla Leonarda and Célestin Pontalba was Alfred Pontalba who married, first, Cecile Henriette Marie de Parseval and left a son by this marriage, named Michel de Parseval de Pontalba. His second wife was Louise d'Estrées from whom he left no issue. The last son of the baroness Micaëla was named Gaston de Pontalba. He died unmarried November 1, 1875.

The Dimitry article on the Almonester-Pontalba genealogy, in its original form, appeared in the Times-Democrat, January 17, 1892, p. 12. The above chapter, rewritten by Mr. Kernion, corrects a number of printed errors and amplifies all previous genealogical sketches of these two families by important additions of fact and historical data.

ALPUENTE Family

AFTER the merciless exhibition of the purpose of Spain to really rule her newly acquired colonial territory of Louisiana, as manifested by the stern and cruel punishment inflicted by O'Reilly, the Spanish general and governor of the colony, in the year 1769, upon the native Louisiana patriots Marquis, Lafrénière, Noyan, Milhet, Carresse, Villeré and others who had conspired against the authority of Spain, the settlers of Spanish nativity or descent began to arrive in New Orleans in considerable numbers. This new element of the population of the city, from whom have sprung a number of our most honorable Louisiana families, were, many of them, from Spain proper, and others from the Canary Islands, Catalonia and from the Spanish Antilles.

Among the officers of the early Spanish forces that arrived with O'Reilly to govern and occupy New Orleans was Don Mathias Francisco de Alpuente. Don Mathias was a man of ancient lineage and of a Castillian family. He was born in the city of Madrid in the year 1740, and at the time of his arrival in Louisiana was about thirty years of age, of dignified bearing, with much of the characteristic gravity of his people.

For sometime after his arrival Don Mathias retained his commission as an officer of the Spanish army, but he finally resigned from that service to enter the pursuits of civil life, as did many of the Spanish military officers of his day who were stationed in New Orleans, and became a merchant. Don Mathias was twice married. His first wife was Marguerite du Plessis, and it is from this marriage that are descended the members of the Alpuente family of New Orleans, a family long well known and esteemed.

By his second marriage, Don Mathias de Alpuente became the spouse of Mlle. de Chouriac, granddaughter of the

[32]

Comte de Chouriac of France, a lady noted for her beauty. There was but one child born of this marriage, a son, who died early in life.

Don Francisco Bonaventura de Alpuente, son of Don Mathias by his first marriage, was born in New Orleans, June 21, 1783, in a house that stood on the corner of Rampart and Dumaine streets for many years, occupying the site of a previous residence erected by his father, and it was in this same house that Don Francisco died in 1841. In this house was born Dr. Francisco Ruiz Alpuente and the latter's daughter, Mathilde Alpuente Bailey.

Don Francisco married Doña Catarina Millon, daughter of Santiago Millon, an officer of the Spanish army, who was stationed in that part of old Louisiana now given over to the state of Nebraska. M. Millon was of a French family and had married Jane Wet, daughter of an English officer, whose acquaintance he had made at Pensacola.

During the War of 1812, Don Francisco Bonaventura de Alpuente raised a company of volunteers for service in the campaign of 1814-15 against the English army then threatening New Orleans. An autographed letter of General Jackson orders Captain de Alpuente to English Lookout, in the vicinity of the Rigolets, as a "forlorn hope," with instructions to hold it at all hazards until reinforcements could be sent. But the English advance against the city was made from below, and the historic battle was fought without giving Captain de Alpuente the opportunity of taking his men into action to participate in that wonderful and glorious victory.

Dr. François Ruiz Alpuente was born on a day historic and memorable in the annals of the United States—the fourth of July, 1814. He received his education at St. Joseph's college, Bardstown, Kentucky, and then went to Paris to study medicine. On his return to New Orleans he began his practice in his native city and soon rose to the front rank in his profession. He married Mathilde Antoinette Hepburn, daughter of James Hepburn and Mathilde de Morant, and granddaughter of Vincent, Chevalier de Morant. The issue of this marriage was Mrs. Mathilde Alpuente Bailey; Louise Alpuente, who married Alfred Colomb;

Bertha Alpuente, and Henry Alpuente. After the death of his first wife, Doctor Alpuente married Zoé le Breton des Chapelles, and by this union became the father of Gabriel Alpuente, Marie Alpuente, who married Edward Michel; Odette Alpuente, who married Jules Michel, and James Almirault du Plessis Alpuente. Doctor Alpuente died May 15, 1875.

The Dimitry article on the Alpuente family appeared in the **Times-Democrat** January 24, 1892, p. 12.

General Jackson's headquarters in Royal Street

LE BLANC—ALLAIN—TOUNOIR
JARREAU Families

THE early records of the parishes of West Baton Rouge and Pointe Coupée during the early eighteenth century bear witness to the residence in that part of Louisiana of many of the best known families of the state, names honorably familiar in her annals. Among them we find such names as Le Blanc, Allain, Tounoir and, related to them by marriage and blood, such equally well known names as Jarreau, Duralde, Lobdell, Dubroca, Lacour, Morgan and others of equal importance.

Most of these important early families had their start in Louisiana from a celebrated, picturesque, and romantic figure —Louis Paul Balthazar Le Blanc de Villeneuve, a native of France, who became commandant of the Opelousas country, and from another native of far-off France, François Allain of Brittany, who settled in the Pointe Coupée district, became the progenitor of the distinguished Allain branch, and, when a son of Le Blanc de Villeneuve and a daughter of Allain married, the families were united in a tie of blood that survives to this day.

Of the many families of West Baton Rouge and Pointe Coupée that form a part of the extensive Le Blanc-Allain connection are to be numbered those named Culbertson, Coulon, Wright, Janin, Cusachs, Lobdell, the Morgans of *Morganza*, Dubroca, Favrot, Lacour, Blancq, Eustis, Woodlief and others.

Commandant Louis Paul Balthazar Le Blanc de Villeneuve, progenitor of the LeBlanc family so frequently mentioned in Louisiana genealogical records, came to Louisiana from Villeneuve, in the south of France, holding the rank of officer in the French military service during the first half of the eighteenth century. His wife was Jeanne Avart.

[35]

After being appointed commandant of the Opelousas country, M. Le Blanc de Villeneuve spent many years among the Indians of that district and a family portrait represents him clothed in an Indian costume of that day which he habitually wore when with the Opelousas. This costume, almost dropping to pieces with age, together with his tomahawk, the handle of which forms a pipe, was in the possession of the family for years.

It was not only as commandant among the Opelousas that the name Louis Paul Balthazar Le Blanc de Villeneuve finds a permanent place in the history of colonial Louisiana. He is noted also as having been the author of the first literary work produced in the colony. This was an epic poem written in 1753 and entitled *La Fête du Petit Blè* ("The Feast of the Young Corn") founded on the Indian festival which celebrated the sprouting of the growing corn. He also wrote *Le Grand Soleil* ("The Great Sun"), and *Poncha Houma*, an Indian tragedy. As the first produced on the soil of Louisiana, the writings of this gentleman must always have an interest of their own as the initial contribution to the literary annals of the state.

After retiring from military service Commandant Le Blanc de Villeneuve took up his residence on a plantation in Pointe Coupée parish, where he lived until his death, which occured at an advanced age. His son, Alexandre Paul Balthazar Le Blanc de Villeneuve married Charlotte Allain, thus uniting two important families, and the two became the parents of numerous children. A son of Alexandre and Charlotte, and a grandson of the first Commandant Le Blanc de Villeneuve, was Joseph Le Blanc de Villeneuve who was born in West Baton Rouge in 1794. He married Desirée Tounoir, of another important Point Coupée family, and lived on his plantation, *Hard Times*, until his death in 1852. In the course of time the name de Villeneuve was only used by the family as a given name and for this reason we find his grandson being set down in records as Joseph de Villeneuve Le Blanc.

Among the well known members of the Le Blanc family of former days were Charles Octave Le Blanc and Pakenham Le Blanc, who were sons of Octave Le Blanc and Mlle. Fabre d'Aunoy, of the family descended from General d'Aunoy, who was an officer under His Catholic Majesty during the Spanish domination of Louisiana. When Spain relinquished her hold on the colony, General d'Aunoy returned to his native land with his Spanish troops and subsequently distinguished himself, becoming in the course of time Viceroy of the province of Andalusia. His only son died early in life and with his end the French d'Aunoy family in Spain became extinct.

The Allain family is descended from François Allain of Brittany, a colonel in the French army, who played a conspicuous and distinguished part at the Battle of Fontenoy in 1745, where he bore, as colonel of his regiment, the standard of France—the *fleur-de-lys* of the Bourbons. For his bravery the king bestowed upon him a sword of honor. Later he came to Louisiana with his regiment, was commandant of the Attakapas Post and subsequently established himself as a planter in the parish of Pointe Coupée. He had two sons, François and Augustin, who were the progenators of the several Allain families of this state. Both of them were officers under Galvez, and fought against the British at the taking of Baton Rouge. Charlotte Allain, as already recorded, married the son of Commandant Le Blanc de Villeneuve.

François Allain married a Miss Ricard, and their son, Pierre Allain, married Manette Du Plessis, of a Louisiana family which traces its affiliations and descent from the Du Plessis family to which belonged the Cardinal de Richelieu and Maréchal, Duc de Richelieu, in the days of the Regent of Orléans and Louis XV. Pierre Allain was the father of Théophile Allain. One of the daughters of François Allain, the second, was named Pauline Allain and she married Charles Janin, a lawyer and notary of New Orleans. The three sons of Pierre Allain were François, Fergus, and Théophile. The latter, the youngest of the three, married Aspasie Le Blanc, daughter of Joseph Le Blanc. He had several children: (a) Villeneuve François Allain, who married Sarah Lobdell of West Baton Rouge; (b) Aline Allain, who married James Fréret of New Orleans; (c)

Alexander Pierre Allain, who married Jeanne Georgine Proctor; (d) Pauline Allain, (e) Lise Allain, (f) Théophile Allain, (g) Charles Allain, who married Alice Haggerty; (h) George Allain, who married Lizzie Stevenson; (i) Lina Allain, who married Mr. Sawyer of Norfolk, Virginia, and (j) Ida Allain.

Aline Allain, who became Mrs. James Fréret, had five daughters and two sons, one daughter marrying Louis Montégut of St. John the Baptist parish; another marrying Charles Favrot, and a third becoming Mrs. Alfred Livaudais. The two sons married into the Delery and Lange families of New Orleans. The grandchildren of Aline Allain thus constituted the seventh generation from their ancestor, M. Le Blanc de Villeneuve, commandant of the Opelousas.

Augustin Allain, son of the original François Allain of Brittany, and brother of François Allain the second, was a captain of grenadiers, and became the head of the numerous Allain family of New Orleans. He had two sons, Valérien and Sosthème Allain. Valérien Allain married Céleste Duralde, a daughter of Martin Duralde, a Spanish officer stationed at a post in the Illinois country and a founder of St. Louis, Missouri, and a Mlle. Perrault of Canada, the latter being a descendant of Charles Perrault, author of Cendrillon, the Cinderella of "glass" slipper fame, and other immortal fairy stories. Martin Duralde, it may be mentioned here, was the father of other daughters, one marrying John Clay, brother of Henry Clay; Louise Duralde becoming the wife of Guy Joseph Soniat du Fossat, and Clarisse Duralde, marrying William C. C. Claiborne, first American governor of Louisiana.

Valérien Allain and Céleste Duralde had one son and three daughters. The son, named for his father, was born in 1799; a daughter, Célestine Allain, became Mme. Ursin Soniat. Another daughter married Valérien Dubroca, and the youngest daughter was wedded to George Eustis. Mrs. Eustis became the mother of Allain Eustis, who married Anais de Saint-Manat; James Eustis, who became ambassador of the United States to France, and George Eustis, who married Louise Corcoran.

[38]

Valérien Allain, son of Valérien Allain and Céleste Duralde, was educated in France. On his return to New Orleans he married Armantine Pitot, a daughter of Jacques Pitot de la Beaujardiére, the first mayor of New Orleans in the American domination.

Sosthème Allain, second son of Augustin Allain, had a very pretentious plantation near Baton Rouge, where he lived in the generous style of that period.

The members of the Jarreau family, according to Dimitry, were originally from Pointe Coupée parish, the first of that name being Jacques Jarreau, a navigator who commanded a merchantman plying between France and the various ports of the United States. During one of his visits to New Orleans, and the country above this port, Captain Jarreau met and wooed Hélène Tounoir.

From this marriage were born two sons, Bruno Jarreau, who died at an early age, and Jean Ursin Jarreau, who married Octavine Le Blanc and lived in princely style on his extensive plantation on the island of False River. This couple had a number of children, including Jean Ursin Jarreau, Jr., Helene Ida Jarreau, Marie Alice Jarreau, and Leon Jarreau. Leon had for his second wife Helen Virginia Le Blanc. The brothers and sisters of Mrs. Jean Ursin Jarreau, the first, were Augustin Le Blanc, Villeneuve Le Blanc, Octave Le Blanc, Terence Le Blanc, and Valérien Le Blanc.

In continuing the record of the Allain, Le Blanc, and Jarreau families, Dimitry included a brief sketch of Etienne Mazureau, the distinguished attorney of the first quarter of a century of New Orleans' history. He was a native of La Rochelle, France, being born about the middle of the nineteenth century and the first of his name to come to Louisiana where, taking up the law he won for himself an undying name in criminal law practice. He married Alice Grima, granddaughter of Alfred Grima, and their children were Edward Mazureau, Adolphe Mazureau, Polyxene Mazureau, wife of Emile Reynes; Stéphanie Mazureau, and Clara Mazureau. Etienne Mazureau died May 25, 1848.

Adolphe Mazureau, his second son, followed his father in

the profession of the law and married Joséphine Le Blanc, granddaughter of M. Le Blanc de Villeneuve, and his two daughters were Rosa Mazureau, who married J. U. Jarreau, Jr., and Corinne Mazureau, who died without issue.

The Morgan family, whose plantation on the Mississippi river was well known in connection with Morganza levee, which yearly was the cause of so much solicitude to the people in the interior back of it, are of descent from Colonel Charles Morgan, the original, or one of the original proprietors of *Morganza*. He was a prominent planter of his day, and a member of the first legislatures convened in the newly-formed state of Louisiana. For twenty years he kept a day by day journal showing the conditions of the weather, and the daily rise or fall of the river in front of his plantation. During the Civil War, *Morganza* was occupied by Federal troops as a military position, and a fort was built upon its levee. Colonel Charles Morgan married Augustine Allain.

A descendant of the Dubroca and Allain families residing in West Baton Rouge was Alzire Dubroca, daughter of Valéntin Dubroca and Alzire Allain. In the same parish resided Mrs. Augustin le Blanc, widow, who was the daughter of Joseph Le Blanc, and mother of Mrs. Leon Jarreau of New Orleans.

The Dimitry article on the Le Blanc-Allain families appeared in the New Orleans Times-Democrat February 14, 1892, p. 13.

Seal of the Territory of Orleans 1803

CENAS Family

FOR a number of generations the name of Cenas has been known in New Orleans and Louisiana as that of a family of high reputation and consideration in the community. The first of the name who came to this country was Blaize Cenas, a native of Marseilles, France, who took up his residence in Philadelphia shortly before Louisiana was purchased from Napoleon. He married Paulina Baker, daughter of Hilary Baker, then the mayor of William Penn's celebrated Quaker City, and to them was born Hilary B. Cenas, Dr. Augustus H. Cenas, and Peter Cenas, all prominent citizens of New Orleans in their day. As New Orleans offered many opportunities to enterprising men of his day, Blaize Cenas moved to New Orleans, became sheriff, and later postmaster. Following the death of Blaize Cenas, his widow married George W. Christy, a well known notary and writer of political campaign songs that were popular among the Whigs of that day. He died in 1891..

The three sons of Blaize Cenas were students at the famous classical academy of Doctor Hull, familiarly known as "Parson Hull," who was the first clergyman of the Episcopal Church established in New Orleans, among the other pupils were the Hunters, the Lewises, including General John B. Lewis, the Dimitrys, Alexander Dimitry being a student there in 1814 at the age of nine, the Conrads, Kenners, Sterretts, Lavillebeuvres, and the sons of other equally well known families of the city and state.

Hilary Breton Cenas, the oldest son, adopted the profession of notary, and became prominent in the affairs of the city. He married Margaret O. Pierce, by whom he had several children, the survivors being, first, Héloise Cenas, who became the head of a flourishing academy in Baltimore,

Maryland; second, Clarisse Cenas, head of the institute founded by her mother at the corner of Claiborne and Esplanade avenues; third, Anna Cenas, who married John Poitevent of Pearlington, Mississippi, a brother of Mrs. E. J. Nicholson, better known as *Pearl Rivers*, a charming lyrical writer of the gay nineties and later publisher of the old *Picayune*. She was the mother of Leonard and Yorke P. Nicholson, now identified with the *Times-Picayune;* fourth, Alice Cenas, who married Judge R. T. Beauregard; fifth, Frances Cenas, and, sixth, Louis Eugene Cenas, who married Leonide May, stepdaughter of John G. Gaines, a former president of the Citizens' Bank.

Dr. Augustus H. Cenas, who was born in New Orleans in 1807, married, in 1838, Minerva C. Carmick, born in 1815, daughter of Major Daniel Carmick of the United States Marine Corps, a native of Philadelphia, whose grandfather was Lord Carmick of Scotland. Major Carmick participated in the Battle of New Orleans and died in that city a few years later. Doctor Cenas received his medical education in Philadelphia, went to Europe in 1837, where he perfected his knowledge of his profession, and returned to his native city to practice, becoming professor of obstetrics in the University of Louisiana, now Tulane, of which institution he was one of the founders. By his marriage with Miss Carmick he had two sons and two daughters. (a) Blaize Cenas, the elder son, was killed at Murfreesboro during the Civil War while serving with the Confederate army; (b) Edgar Cenas met an accidental death in New Orleans after the close of the war; (c) Georgine Cenas, the eldest daughter, married Henry Denis, a New Orleans attorney, while (d) Corinne Cenas married George Dick Nicholls of Natchez, Mississippi and died without issue.

The children of Georgine Cenas by her marriage to Henry Denis were (a) Augustus H. Denis, who married the Widow Ossuma, she being the daughter of Nelville Soulé, and a granddaughter of Pierre Soulé, the celebrated lawyer. Augustus H. Denis was the father of four children, and became the owner of an orange grove near Tampa, Florida. (b) George Denis, the second son of Georgine Cenas, studied law and practiced his profession in Los Angeles, California.

Peter Cenas, the youngest son of Blaize Cenas and Paulina Baker, was born in New Orleans in 1810 and married a Miss St. John. He entered the real estate and auctioneering business and was a member of the firm of Hewlitt & Cenas. His death occured in 1845. He had two sons, the first, George Cenas, died without issue, and Richard B. Cenas, who married the widow of W. R. Adams. She was a Miss Ranney, daughter of Asa Sage Ranney, and her uncle was Major Ranney, a former president of the old Jackson Railroad, later a part of the Illinois Central System. By her first marriage she had one child, May V. Adams. By her second marriage to Richard B. Cenas, she had five daughters, Augusta B. Cenas, Georgie M. Cenas, Mathilde Cenas, Clara P. Cenas, and Pearl Estelle Cenas.

The Dimitry article on the Cenas family appeared in the New Orleans Times-Democrat, March 6, 1892, p. 13.

Old Court Building in Royal Street

FORTIER Family

AMONG the older colonial families of Louisiana there is none perhaps that includes a larger posterity and a more numerous family connection than that of the Fortiers, a family which originated in France and dates back in Louisiana from a period anterior to the middle of the eighteenth century. The descendants of Michel Fortier are very numerous and among them are also members of the esteemed families of Labranche, Augustin, Aime, and others who, for many decades have been conspicuous in the annals of the city of New Orleans and the state of Louisiana.

According to family traditions, Francois Fortier of St. Malo, Brittany, was the father of Michel Fortier who, born in 1725, was the first of the name to come to Louisiana. When Michel arrived in the infant colony about 1740, he established himself in New Orleans as *armurier du roi*. He married Perrine Langlois, daughter of a distinguished Créole family, and he not only made arms for the king's soldiers but he used them as well, for we find him, a colonel, accompanying Galvez in his campaign against the British and helping the Spanish governor haul down the Union Jack from the fort at Baton Rouge. Michel Fortier, the first, died in 1785.

By his marriage to Perrine Langlois, Michel Fortier had seven sons; Michel Jr., Jacques, Honoré, who was lost at sea; Norbert, Eugene, Adélard, and Ludger Fortier. Michel Jr., and his brother Jacques married the sisters Durel. A daughter, Louise Fortier, married Michel Labranche, a son of Jean Labranche (Zweig) and Suzanne Marchand.

Michel Fortier, the second, was born in 1750 and died September 19, 1819. He married Marie Rose Durel, and became a merchant and ship owner. In 1803, when the double-transfer of Louisiana took place—from Spain to

France and from France to the United States—Laussat, the French *préfet*, appointed him a member of the municipal council. By his marriage he had two sons, Michel, the third, and Edmond Fortier. His one daughter married François Aime, a planter, became the mother of the princely planter and philanthropist, Valcour Aime of St. James parish, who owned the most magnificent sugar plantation of his time in Louisiana, where a profuse hospitality welcomed friends and strangers continually. Valcour Aime was the benefactor of Jefferson College which, after years of usefulness, was recently closed. After the death of Valcour's father, his widowed mother married Adélard Fortier.

Edmond Fortier, the second son of Michel Fortier and Marie Rose Durel, was born in 1784 and lived until 1849. He was a successful planter of St. Charles parish and married Félicité Labranche of a family distinguished not only for its antiquity in Louisiana, but for its personal worth and for the services rendered by several of its members. He became a prosperous planter in St. Charles parish. His oldest son, also named Edmond, married Mathilde Labranche. Of the many children born to them, three sons died of yellow fever in 1858; Mathilde Fortier, one of his daughters, married Adolphe de Blanc, who died of the fever scourge in 1858, one of the two sons born to them was accidently drowned in 1868, and the other, Michel M. de Blanc, lived in New Orleans where he married Eugénie Garcia and had three children.

François Fortier, another son of Edmond Fortier and Mathilde Labranche, died in 1885. He married Louise Augustin, daughter of Donatien Augustin (q. v.), and was noted for his valor while serving in the ranks of the Confederacy. Marie Micaëla Fortier, sister of François, married Judge Donatien Augustin, brother of Louise, and had a family of eighteen children, among them being James M. Augustin and George Augustin, noted journalists of New Orleans in their day.

Florient Fortier, second son of Edmond Fortier and Félicité Labranche, and brother of Edmond, Jr., was born on his father's plantation in St. Charles parish in 1811, and died in 1886. After his marriage to Edvige Aime, daughter of Valcour Aime, he went to St. James parish and established a plantation which, like many of the other old plantations, passed out of his possession. He resided in New Orleans with his son Alcée. Florient Fortier and Edvige Aime had several children. One of them, Louis Fortier, served with the Confederates during the Civil War at the age of 17 and died soon after the close of hostilities. A daughter, Nathalie Fortier, married Nelvil Leboeuf and became the mother of Dr. Louis Leboeuf, a physician at one time coroner of Jefferson parish. Another daughter, Amélie Fortier, married Edward Roman and four children were born of this union. Joséphine Fortier, the third daughter, became the wife of Alfred Fortier and was the mother of eight children. The youngest daughter of Florient Fortier, was named Marguerite and she married Edward Le Breton by whom she had six children.

Alcée Fortier, one of the three great historians of his native state, author, educator, lecturer, renowned for his researches into French history and literature, especially for his *History of Louisiana* in four volumes, and a number of other very valuable works on Louisiana, was the youngest son of Florient Fortier and Edvige Aime. Professor Fortier was born in St. James parish, June 5, 1856, and died February 14, 1914. In the year 1881 he married Mlle. Lanauze, daughter of a prominent French merchant and niece of M. Feraud-Giraud, an eminent jurist of France. Four sons and one daughter were born to the union: Jeanne Fortier, who married Paul Cox; Edward Joseph Fortier, who married Miss Tricou and followed in the educational footsteps of his father becoming a professor in Columbia University, dying in 1918; James Joseph Alcée Fortier, born July 15, 1890, who married Marie Rose Gelpi, and became a New Orleans attorney and president of the Continental Bank, and Gilbert J. Fortier, New Orleans business man.

Septime Fortier, another son of Edmond Fortier and Félicité Labranche, was born in St. Charles parish in 1816, and married Emma Aime, a daughter of Valcour Aime and sister to Edvige who married Florient Fortier. Twelve children were the result of this union. The eldest son, Captain Michel Jean Fortier served with distinction in the Civil War. Born in the lap of luxury, this Michel Jean Fortier was born on the plantation of his princely grandfather, Valcour Aime, in St. James Parish. This plantation, on account of its opulence and beauty, was known throughout the state as *Le Petit Versailles de la Louisiane.* The early days of Michel Jean were spent amid such pleasant surroundings and at the age of nine he was already studying under one of the most famous pedagogues of the time—Monsieur Elisé Reclus, a noted French geographer residing in Louisiana.

At the age of twelve he matriculated at the Brookland School, in Albemarle, Virginia, where he remained, as a student, until June 1859. Illness compelled him to return to Louisiana. On recovering he became a student at Jefferson College, in St. James Parish, then owned by a corporation in which his grandfather, Valcour Aime, was the principal stockholder. The war between the states shortly thereafter began. Jefferson College, like many other institutions, was forced to close its doors as every student strong enough to shoulder a musket was rushing to a recruiting station to enlist and do his part. Michel Jean Fortier was not a laggard among them. Though only seventeen years of age, he enlisted as a private in the Louisiana Artillery, Fourth Battalion, St. Mary's Cannoneers and served to the end of the war.

No man was ever more ready to fight than Captain Fortier. Long associated with the Louisiana National Guard, he became lieutenant of Battery C, Louisiana Field Artillery and participated with it in the battle fought on that memorable 14th day of September 1874 when the white men of New Orleans and the surrounding country made a supreme effort to dislodge the negroes and Carpet Baggers who had assumed an insolent ascendency over the Caucasian race and were riveting shackles of steel on its best white citizens, he marched his command into the very muzzles of sputtering Metropolitan Police rifles and cannon. Captain Fortier was treacherously murdered in the late eighties while serving, as a representative of General Ogden, at a poll in the Seventh Ward of New Orleans, during the Ogden-McEnery gubernatorial campaign. He had married twice, his first and second wives being sisters and first cousins of his. They were Françoise Jeanne and Félicité Amynthe Fortier. By the first-named he had only one daughter, Félicité Fortier who did not marry. By his second spouse he left four children, namely: Michel Jean Fortier, who married Stella Le Bon and has issue; Marie Joséphine, Marguerite Marie and Haydée Michael Fortier, still living and unmarried.

After the fall of New Orleans, Valcour Aime, anticipating that the victorious Federals might seize Jefferson College, of which he was the principal stockholder, and convert its buildings into a negro arsenal, bought out the shares of the other stockholders and, though the war had already cruelly ravaged his personal fortune, he presented this College, in which so much of his money had been invested, as a gift to the Marist Fathers, in order to save it from falling into the enemy's hands.

Other children of Septime Fortier were: Alfred Fortier, a St. Mary parish planter; Gustave Fortier, a New Orleans merchant; Gabriel Fortier, a planter of Vermilion parish; Anna Fortier, who did not marry; Alice Fortier, who married Agricole Grevemberg; Louise Fortier, who married Henry Ganucheau; Emma Fortier, who married Edward Bérault; Félicité Fortier, who became the wife of Charles Ganucheau; Effie Fortier, who married Gustave Lallande; Edvige Fortier, who married George Blois, and Nathalie Fortier, who became the wife of Ben Brou.

Several daughters were born to Edmond Fortier by his marriage to Félicité Labranche. One married Michel Aime, another became the wife of M. Piseros, still another married Edmund Ganucheau. Octavie Fortier married Gustave Bouligny, (she became the mother of Arthemise Bouligny, who married Albert Baldwin; Mrs. John Wood, Mrs. Jumonville and Mrs. Smythe). The youngest daughter of Edmond and Félicité Fortier, Félicité, married Dominique Bouligny and the oldest daughter, married Oscar Villeré, a planter of the lower coast. She was the mother of a large family. Mathilde Fortier married Adolphe de Blanc, and her three daughters were named Constance, Léontine, and Léonide de Blanc.

The Dimitry article on the Fortier family appeared in the New Orleans Times-Democrat March 20 and 27, 1892, p. 14.

AUGUSTIN Family

THE French Revolution of 1796 was followed by the equally terrible and sanguinary outburst of the negro slaves of San Domingo in 1803, when so many thousands of French inhabitants of that island, particularly in the part now known as Haiti, were victims of their former black vassals. A few hundreds of the French population did not meet death, and their escapes, sensational in many instances, were due in almost every case to the devotion and fidelity of some among their many slaves. Several of these families came to New Orleans and their posterity became prominent among the more famed foundation families, either by direct descent of the male line or through marriage.

Among the better known and more notable was the Augustin family. The first of that name in Louisiana was Jean Augustin, a native of Sarigny, near Chénon, Tourraine, in France, where he was born in 1764. He married Marie Sauton, a native of Lyons in 1782. The disorders bred in France by the Revolution induced M. and Mme. Augustin to leave their native land. They fled to San Domingo where they purchased a plantation. There they were living when the negro uprisings began on the island. They effected their escape to Cuba through the agency of a faithful slave named Circé, who accompanied them on their flight. Jean Baptiste Donatien Augustin, their first-born, was then about a year old. In San Iago de Cuba, where the family resided for about ten years, three other children, Clara, Clémence, and Marie Delphine, were born. The family came to New Orleans in 1811 where Joseph Numa Augustin, the last child, was born.

Several years of Jean Augustin's life were devoted to the profession of educator. He occupied for a long time a professor's chair in the famous *College d'Orléans*. Otherwise his life was quiet and uneventful up to the day of his death which occured in 1832. He outlived his wife by two years.

Jean Baptiste Donatien Augustin, his first child, was born in Port-au-Prince, July 4, 1802, and died in New Orleans in 1876. He married Elizabeth Mélanie Labranche. The daughters of this union were, the eldest, who married Pierre Adolphe Schreiber; Clémance Augustin, who married Thomas Toby, and Delphine Augustin, who became the wife of Daniel Frederich. The sons of J. B. Donatien Augustin were, James Donatien Augustin, whose wife was Marie Micaëla Fortier, daughter of Edmond Fortier, the second, and Mathilde Labranche, and John Alcée Augustin, who married Emilie Dupré. James Donatien Augustin had four daughters, one of them, Louise Augustin, marrying François Fortier.

M. and Mme. Pierre Adolphe Schreiber had four children. Two daughters, Adéle and Anaïs, died unmarried; and a son, Pierre A. Schreiber Jr., the eldest child, born October 11, 1825, married Hélène Forstall, while Josephine Schreiber married Joseph Beugnot. The nine children of Clémence Augustin and Thomas Toby, were: two sons, Simeon Toby, married, first, to Leona Parmley, second, to Rose Wilkinson, and Edward Toby, married, first Martha Fuller, and then Pauline Matthews. The four married daughters became Mmes. George C. Bogert, Harry Charles, Richard Charles, and W. S. Campbell, while three daughters died unmarried.

Eleven children were the issue of Joseph Numa Augustin, the youngest child of Jean Augustin and Marie Sauton, who married Elizabeth Marie Adeline Thibaut. Their sons were Jean Adolphe Augustin, who married Gabrielle Pascal; Louis Alphonse Augustin, Joseph Arthur Augustin, and Joseph Donatien Augustin, three brothers who never married; and Joseph Numa Augustin, the second, who married Marie Delphine Dolhonde. The married daughters were: Mmes. Leopold Henrionuet and Ludovic Lafargue. Three other daughters died unmarried.

Jean Baptiste Donatien Augustin, the first-born of Jean Augustin and Marie Sauton, studied and practiced law in New Orleans, became one of the leaders of the bar, was elected to the bench, and at one time served as sheriff of the parish. He was one of the founders of the famous Orleans Battalion, an expert and adroit fencer and, being exceedingly tenacious of his personal integrity, became involved in several duels—not, however, as a duelist but because sufficient provocation had been given him. His home at Esplanade and St. Claude streets was built under his direction and here all his children were born. The house was in his day a famous landmark, with its peculiar features of architecture, its terrace, its tower that rose sixty feet in the air surmounted with a weather-cock which faithfully pointed out to passers-by the direction of the wind. But the picturesque old Augustin house has long since passed away.

James Donatien Augustin, the eldest son of Jean Baptiste Donatien Augustin and Elizabeth Labranche, was born December 16, 1834, and died February 1, 1888. James received his education at Spring Hill college, and followed his father in the practice of the law. In 1875 he moved to the country and practiced in the parishes of St. John the Baptist, St. James, and St. Charles, being elected judge in the latter parish. As a result of his marriage to Marie Micaëla Fortier, twelve children were born. Of this family James M. Augustin married, in 1884, Cora M. Chapotin; Paul Sumpter Augustin, in 1885, married Noemi Barbot; the other children, Alice, George, Edmond, Alfred, Henry, Eric, Josephine and Mathilde Augustin did not marry.

James M. Augustin, eldest son of Judge James Donatien Augustin, became a well known and accomplished journalist. He was born March 31, 1858, was educated at the Jesuit's College, was in the cotton business a short while but deserted business to become a reporter on the old *Democrat* in 1877, when his uncle, John Augustin, was its city editor. Later he studied law and practiced in St. Charles parish but returned to New Orleans to be engaged in a journalistic capacity on the *City Item* and *Daily States.* By his marriage to Cora Chapotin he had five children, Lillian Augustin, born December 13, 1884; Fernand and Edna Augustin, twins, born November 19, 1885; James Augustin, born August 5, 1889, and Cora Augustin, born August 20, 1891.

George Augustin, the fourth son of Judge Augustin and Micaëla Fortier, born February 22, 1867, was a pupil of

Mrs. Virginia Dimitry Ruth. He had a flair for poetry and chose a literary career, dedicating his first work, *Romances of New Orleans*, to his teacher. He entered into a partnership with Judge J. L. Bossier in the publication of the *Figaro*, a sprightly literary magazine of the early '90's, and became its editor.

The five other sons of Judge Augustin entered various pursuits. Edmond and Henry became planters in St. Mary's parish. Alfred was associated with the law firm of Howe & Prentiss. Paul Sumpter Augustin entered the post office service, as did Eric Augustin, the youngest son.

John Alcée Augustin was born in 1838 and, like his brother Judge J. D. Augustin, was educated at the Jesuit's College, Spring Hill, Alabama. He was in the mercantile business in New Orleans when the war between the states broke out and enlisted in the Orleans Cadets, commanded by Captain Charles D. Dreux. When the cadets were mustered out of service in 1862, their twelve months of service having expired, they, with others of the First Independent Louisiana Battalion, organized Fenner's Battery. It was to this outfit that John Alcée Augustin belonged, and when he was not fighting the Yanks he was writing poetry. When the war was over he published these verses under the title of *War Flowers*. Later he became a reporter on the old New Orleans *Crescent*, and then went to the *Democrat* as its city editor, a position he also filled when the *Times* and the *Democrat* combined. For a time he held down the city desk on the *Daily States*. When he retired in 1887 he became minute clerk of the Louisiana Supreme Court and died February 8, 1888.

The youngest son of Jean Augustin, and brother of J. B. D. Augustin and John Alcée Augustin, was Colonel J. Numa Augustin who, after finishing his education at the Orleans College, was cashier of the Canal Bank branch at Donaldsonville, where he founded the *Donaldsonville Cannoneers* and was its first captain. When he returned to New Orleans to enter the brokerage business he organized the city's militia and in 1860 was elected colonel of the Orleans Guard Regiment, which he resigned to become a member of General Beauregard's staff. He participated in the Battle of Shiloh, where he was mentioned for bravery. He was the cashier of the New Orleans bank when he died in 1872. His son, J. Numa Augustin, Jr., was a lawyer. He was twice a state senator, and later was made secretary of the New Orleans Slaughter House. From his marriage with Marie Delphine Dolhonde he left several children, three of them still living and well known in New Orleans. They are Hattie Augustin, unmarried; James Augustin, also single, and Corinne Augustin, wife of Sydney St. John Eshleman, a prominent businessman of New Orleans. The eldest son of Joseph Numa Augustin, the second, and Miss Dolhonde, was Joseph Numa Augustin, the third, who married Alice Palmer. A graduate of West Point Military Academy, he fell in action while leading, as a lieutenant, his company of regulars in the attack on San Juan Hill, during the Spanish-American War. His funeral was one of the largest ever held in New Orleans.

The eldest son of Col. J. Numa Augustin, the first, was Adolphe Augustin, born in 1835, who became a member of the Orleans Guard regiment, commanded by Captain Roman. He died September 1862. He had married Gabrielle Pascal in 1860, and his daughter, Marietta Augustin, became the wife of Raoul Armant and mother of Henry Armant.

One of Colonel J. Numa Augustin's daughters married Leopold Henrionnet. Three children blessed this union, one becoming a priest, l'Abbe Louis Henrionnet, attached to the diocese of Paris, France. Another daughter married Ludovic Lafarge. Lillian Augustin, his oldest daughter, attracted attention as a graceful writer and journalist. She was of the fifth generation from Jean Augustin who came to Louisiana from San Domingo.

The Dimitry article on the Augustin family appeared in the New Orleans Times-Democrat, April 3 and 17, 1892.

MORPHY Family

IN the old days of Irish chieftainry—in the days when Ireland made history of her own—the prowess of the Omurphu family was sung in castle and baronial hall by the Irish bards, as they told also of the achievements of Brian Boru, of the McDermott, the O'Connell, and the Nial. Thus Charles Patton Dimitry prefaced his review of a Louisiana family made immortal by the achievements of one of its sons, Paul Morphy, the celebrated chess player.

Transformed with the passing of the centuries, the family name of Omurphu became in time O'Murphy and finally Murphy. Established in their native land around Cork and Londonderry, and other cities of Ireland, from their early habitations many of the branches of the family found homes in other countries.

For the past one hundred and fifty years the annals of continental Europe have been dotted with the names of brilliant Catholic Irish families that have helped to make history for their times. These families were of the self-exiled class, some Stuart Royalists, some republicans departing from Ireland for their opinion's sake, at various periods from the time of the downfall of the royal house of Stuart and throughout the different unsuccessful rebellions since that period against English rule. Thus we find in history the names of General Count O'Reilly, the Spanish warrior and governor of the colony of Louisiana in 1769; Marshall O'Donnell, also in the Spanish service; Count Dillon, Marechal Mac-Mahon, O'Neill, and Vicomte de Tyrone, of the ancient Irish earls of Tyrone, in France, and O'Higgins, of South American fame.

Among the Irish families which thus within nearly two centuries have left Ireland because of political troubles, was a branch of the Murphy family, posterity of Omurphu, and the ancestors of the Morphy family of Louisiana. Spain was their destination, and there they acquired the prestige of Spanish nomenclature and associations which attaches to the name.

On a reverse of a card displaying the Morphy coat-of-arms—quarterly *argent* and *gules;* four lions rampant interchanged; over all on a fesse *sable* three garbs *or,* and with a lion rampant *gules* holding a garm *or,* as a crest.—which descended to D. E. Morphy, and preceding the description of the heraldic devices was written "Morphy, alias Curphy, alias Omurphu."

In Madrid, where dwelt the parents of Don Diego Morphy, Sr., the first of the name in Louisiana, the Spaniards found it easier to pronounce the name Murphy with the "u" changed into "o"—wherefore the name Morphy, pronounced in Spanish and French as if written "Morfee," with the accent on the last syllable. But the relationship and connection with the other members of the Murphy family, who also emigrated to Spain or her colonies, and who retained the original spelling, were maintained by Don Diego Morphy and his family, for in a letter handed down through the years, it is shown that Don Diego informed his son in 1813 that he was anxious for him to form a business connection "with his cousin Matthew Laurence Murphy of Havana."

Don Diego Morphy, Sr., arrived in New Orleans in the latter part of 1803. He was born in Madrid but became a resident of Cap Français, on the island of San Domingo. The Cap, as it was called, was inhabited largely by Spaniards and while there Don Diego married Mollie Creagh. Their child, named for the father was a month old when the negro outbreaks took place. In order to preserve his wife and child from persecution, and perhaps death, Don Diego had his spouse place the infant in a market basket and covered him with cabbage leaves. The mother, with basket on her arm, and under the pretext of wanting to sell vegetables to the captain of an English vessel at anchor in the harbor, succeeded in boarding the ship. A few weeks later she and her child landed in Philadelphia. It was several months later before Don Diego was able to leave the island and go to Charleston, South Carolina. He joined his wife in the Quaker City and returned to Charleston, where he lived for several years. There his second son, Ernest Morphy, and two daughters, Matilde and Eléonore, were born. After the death of his first wife, Don Diego married Louisa Peire, daughter of an old Huguenot family of Charleston. By his second wife he had Alonzo Morphy, who became a sumpreme court judge of Louisiana, and three daughters. They were Mrs. James Ross, Mrs. William Taylor, and Emma Morphy, who married David Hincks of New Orleans, and they became the parents of Edgar Hincks, former secretary of Tulane and Newcomb Universities.

Before coming to New Orleans, Don Diego Morphy, Sr., was vice-consul for Spain, and in New Orleans, up to the day of his death in 1814, he served as Spanish consul. Don Diego, Jr., who was made vice-consul after his father's death, in 1818, was sent to Natchez as consul. When he returned to New Orleans he devoted himself to teaching Spanish and making translations, being a man of high intellectual attainments, a scholar, and author. He compiled several works, among them a book on Spanish idioms and a dictionary of the French, Spanish, and English languages. Don Diego Morphy, Jr., married Eulalie Dubord, daughter of Don Lorenzo Troisville Dubord and Eulalie Beaumont de Livaudais. Don Diego, Jr. died in New Orleans in 1865. His son was Diego E. Morphy.

Judge Alonzo Morphy, a son born of the second marriage of Don Diego Morphy, Sr., studied law in New Orleans and was admitted to practice January 7, 1819, by the supreme court then composed of Justices Mathews, Derbigny, and Martin. He was appointed to the supreme bench by Governor Roman, August 31, 1839, but became attorney general of Louisiana in 1829 before going to the high court. Alonzo Morphy married Telcide Le Carpentier, daughter of Joseph Le Carpentier and Modeste Blache, the latter being the daughter of Don Louis Carlos Blache and Marie de Tournade. Joseph Le Carpentier had four children; Aménaïde, who married Edouard Fortin; Telcide, who married Judge Morphy, and Amélie and Charles Le Carpentier who died unmarried.

Four children were the issue of Judge Morphy's marriage. —two sons and two daughters. Edward Morphy, the elder son; Paul Morphy, who became the world's greatest chess player; Malvina Morphy, who married J. C. Sybrandt, a cotton merchant and consul for Sweden. Helena Morphy, the other daughter, died unmarried. The Sybrandt children were: Edward Sybrandt, who became a Jesuit priest; Alonzo Sybrandt, who moved to Savannah and died unmarried; John Sybrandt, unmarried, lived in New York, and Marie Sybrandt who did not marry.

Diego Eugéne Morphy, son of Diego Morphy Jr. and Eulalie Dubord, was born in New Orleans, March 15, 1817, and became well known in banking and auctioneering circles. He married Louise Emily Grivot, who died in 1884, leaving two sons, Albert Morphy, who did not marry, and Captain E. A. Morphy, and two daughters: Ophelia Morphy married to C. W. M. Friedlander who, after her death, married her sister Camille, and lived on the Rhine, in Germany. Captain Alfred E. Morphy married Mary Eliza Seip, daughter of John Seip and Eliza Martin of Rapides parish, and their children were Albert, Eugene, Adelia Seip, Mary Elise, and Clifford Charles Morphy.

Edouard Morphy, who lived in St. Peter street, was the head of one branch of the Morphy family long identified with New Orleans. He was the son of Judge Alonzo Morphy and Telcide Le Carpentier, and the brother of the celebrated Paul Morphy. Edouard was born in New Orleans December 13, 1834, and married, November 20, 1860, Alice Percy, daughter of E. S. Percy, of a family of English lineage established in Louisiana for four generations. E. S. Percy was president of the New Orleans Water Works, and his wife was Julie Blache, of an old New Orleans family. Arthur Blache, who married a Miss Trémoulet, was a nephew of Mrs. E. S. Percy, and the father of Edgar Blache and Octave Blache. Two of Mrs. Edouard Morphy's brothers were Henry F. Percy and Léonce Percy. Others of the Percy family lived in West Feliciana parish and in Mississippi.

The children of Edouard Morphy and Alice Percy, were a son and a daughter. This son was Edward S. Morphy who married Emma Merlin. They had three children: one of the daughters being, Juanita Morphy. The son was named Paul after his famous uncle, and an adopted daughter was Ida Magnon. Régina Morphy, the daughter of Edouard Morphy, married George Voitier.

Paul Morphy, renowned in the annals of chess playing, and noted for the possession of a peculiar mental organization which is usually attributed to genius, was the younger son of Judge Alonzo Morphy, and the only brother of Edouard. He was born in New Orleans, June 27, 1837. Very few men have lived in any epoch of the world's history who achieved the celebrity at the age of twenty-one that marked the experiences of Paul Morphy when he first came before the world as the incomparable chess player of his or any other time. Perhaps his accomplishment as a chess player and calculator was inherited, although developed by him to the highest degree, from his maternal grandfather, Joseph Le Carpentier. His father, Judge Alonzo Morphy, and his uncle, Ernest Morphy, were also devotees of chess and players of strength. Paul began playing chess at the age of ten. At twelve he played against the best chess experts of New Orleans. When he was thirteen he was ranked among the best players in the United States having, in 1850, defeated the celebrated Hungarian champion, Lowenthal. He went abroad and defeated the best of all countries, frequently playing blindfolded against four, and sometimes eight, opponents. When there were no more champions to triumph over, he returned to his native city.

Paul Morphy never married. He lived in the old home, 80 Royal street, now known as the *Patio Royal*, and one hot day, 1884, he was found dead in the bath room. It was said that he had taken a shower when overheated and the shock to his system produced a congestion of the brain.

The Dimitry article on the Morphy family appeared in the New Orleans Times-Democrat, April 24 and May 1, 1892.

DE LA VERGNE—VILLERÉ—
BERMUDEZ Families

AMONG Louisiana families of ancient chivalry is that of the de la Vergnes. It is of remote French origin and had its beginning in the provinces of Limousin and Quercy. Records and family traditions show that the de la Vergnes were Crusaders, that for centuries they were considered a race of courageous, brave, and loyal knights, and that among them were men who bore the title of marquis, count, vicomte, baron, and chevalier. Among those of this name were sailors, ministers of the church, and patriots.

The Seigneurs de la Vergne, de la Mauriange, and de Saint-Exupery lived in the twelfth century. The family *fiefs* are situated near Exupery, between Bost and Ussel, in Limousin. They rendered the military services of knights of approved valor, and their marriages were contracted with the best houses of France—the de Turenne, the d'Aubusson, the de Cosmac d'Abzac, de Clermont, and many others of equal rank and dignity. Records from the year 1248 to 1330 give the names of members of this family in connection with various contracts of marriages and otherwise, or as witnesses to the will of Bernard VI, Sire de la Tour, in the month of April, 1256.

The first of the name de la Vergne in Louisiana was the Count Pierre de la Vergne, chevalier de Saint-Louis. He came to the colony about 1766, or a year later, as lieutenant in some military company, and settled in New Orleans. He was descended from an ancient branch of the family, that of the de la Vergnes, Seigneurs de Juillac, des Paillus, Viscomptes de Turenne. There were two other main branches of the family, all descended from the Seigneurs de la Vergne of the crusading days. The manor or chateau of the house

[59]

of de Juillac is situated near Beaulieu, in the department of Correze, in France, and belongs to the family in question.

Count Pierre de la Vergne was born in the city of Brive la Gaillard, in Limousin. His grandfather was named Daniel de la Vergne, and his parents were Jean de la Vergne and Marguerita de Billeron, also of a noble family. On his arrival in Louisiana, Count Pierre endeavored to Americanize his patronymic and signed his name "Lavergne." He was married in New Orleans, October 29, 1780, to Marie Elizabeth (or Isabella) du Vergier Marié, widow of Joseph Fides. She was born in New Orleans August 14, 1763, where she died August 27, 1807. Her parents were Guillaume Duverjé de Marié and Rose Busson de la Marinière, the latter born in New Orleans July 10, 1733, and who died there January 5, 1794, and was the daughter of Nöel Busson de la Marinière of Rennes, Brittany, and Marie de Bertin of the province of Normandy. Guillaume Duverjé was a native of Rennes and married Rose de la Marinière in New Orleans November 3, 1751. He died December 11, 1780. His parents were Bertrand du Vergier de la Tour de Marié, a native of Dolac, Brittany, and Julienne Hubert, of Rennes. The family Duverjé (the name having been spelled originally du Vergier) held for a long time a high position in Louisiana. The site of the town of Algiers, opposite New Orleans, was once the property of that family.

Pierre de la Vergne, after having rendered many years of faithful service to his country, died in New Orleans January 31, 1813. One child was born of his marriage to Elizabeth Duverjé—a son Hugues, upon whom was conferred every educational advantage that wealth and accomplished teachers could afford. With the aim of entering the *Polytechnique* School of Paris, he devoted his time chiefly to the study of mathematics. The dream of the young man's life was to cross the ocean, reach Paris and enter this school.

After a year in Paris the youth returned to New Orleans —he was then nineteen—with a tale of remarkable adventures in the capital of France. He had not entered the *Polytechnique*. He did not spend his days as a student locked in a schoolroom—he spent most of his time as an inmate of the prison *La Force*, and some of the other political goals. This was due to the treachery of a false friend, a former French army officer Hugues had met in Philadelphia when on his way to France. The motive for the latter's action appears to have been to obtain easy possession of several thousand francs, which he had secured from the young Louisianian who, he thought, imprisoned on a false charge of conspiring against the Emperor Napoleon's authority, never would be heard of again. Through the efforts of the Marquis de Lafayette and other friends, young de la Vergne was released after a year's incarceration and the end of 1812 found him again in New Orleans.

Hugues de la Vergne, on October 13, 1813, married Marie Adéle de Villeré, daughter of General Jacques Philippe de Villeré and Jeanne Henrietta de Fazende, both members of the oldest families in Louisiana. When the troops of Pakenham's army began their movement against New Orleans in the winter of 1814, Hugues de la Vergne was appointed by General Jackson as aide-de-camp on his staff with rank of major. When the defeated troops of Pakenham retired from the scene of their inglorious discomfiture, Major de la Vergne was appointed chief of a committee to repair to l'Isle-aux-Viessaux (Ship Island) to claim the negro slaves of the sugar planters who had been debauched from their fidelity by the English invaders.

From that moment Hugues de la Vergne conceived the idea of having the loss suffered by his fellow-countrymen properly indemnified. He had a list made of all the slaves found in the English ships of war and an exact valuation of each colored man set down, which served as a basis for a settlement with the English government some years later. In 1816, his father-in-law General Jacques Villeré, then elected governor of Louisiana, appointed Hugues de la Vergne his private secretary, and, in 1820, made him secretary of state. A year later he became a notary public and had his office with Moreau L'Islet, a jurist of celebrity. On April 3, 1826, he was admitted to the bar. Later he was instrumental in having the Congress confirm many of the early French and Spanish concessions made to citizens of Louisiana. In 1833 he became cashier of the City Bank and two years later its president. He died February 16, 1843.

[61]

Through his marriage with Marie Adéle Villeré, the de la Vergnes became affiliated with the celebrated family of that name. The Rouer de Villeré family is said to belong to the house of Rouer or la Rovere, one of the most important and illustrious in Europe, which rendered many services to Italy and furnished a number of doges to the Republic of Genoa, and many knights to the most distinguished orders of Europe, as well as Romish Popes. The first Villeray (as the name was spelled originally) to come to America was Louis Rouer de Villeray, who settled in Canada. He was descended from a branch of that family established at Touraine, France. He held a position as the first Councillor of the Supreme Court of Canada for thirty years, and left a large posterity, among whom was Joseph Rouer, or Roy, de Villeray.

Joseph Roy de Villeray was the second of the name to come to Louisiana, and was the son of Etienne Rouer de Villeray, who preceded him to New Orleans, and Catherine Nepveu, daughter of Jacques Nepveu and Michelle Chauvin de Léry. Joseph de Villeré, was married October 21, 1759, to Marguerite Louise de la Chaise, born in New Orleans, the daughter of Jacques de la Chaise Jr. and Marguerite d'Arensbourg, and a granddaughter of Chevalier d'Arensbourg of the German Coast. (q. v.)

Joseph Roy de Villeré (to give him his surname in its present form) in 1750 was appointed *écrivain de la marine* or "marine notary" in Louisiana, and in 1768 he was commissioned as captain of militia of the *Côte des Allesmands* or "German Coast." It was while occupying this position that he met his death—an event written in blood-red letters in the annals of Spanish Louisiana. Always a prominent man in the colony, he was one of the leaders in the movement to establish independence when France sold Louisiana to Spain. This resistance, coupled with the expulsion of the timid Governor Ulloa, roused the Spanish crown and resulted in Don Alesandro O'Reilly being sent to the new Spanish colony to crush the French "rebels." And so Villeré, together with Marquis, Lafrénière, Noyan, Caresse and Milhet, met his doom. The others were officially executed, but Villeré's death was pure murder. According to one version, which is

[62]

believed correct, he was seized by Spanish soldiers at the Tchoupitoulas Gate when he came to New Orleans, bayonetted when he resisted arrest and mortally wounded, he was hurried aboard a Spanish frigate. When his wife in a skiff approached the ship lying in the river to visit him, the Spanish soldiers threw the gallant Louisianian's blood-stained shirt into his wife's skiff—mute but terrible evidence of her husband's death. Years later, Louis XV of France, as some compensation for this cruel martydom, ordered that Villeré's son Jacques should be educated at the monarch's expense.

In 1780 Jacques Philippe Villeré, after serving as a page at the king's court, at the age of eighteen, was presented with a sword by the monarch and commissioned a captain of artillery in the colonial army serving in San Domingo. After a few years service on that island young Villeré returned to New Orleans, his return hastened by the death of his mother, resigned his commission and married Jeanne Henriette de Fazende, and lived on his plantation *Conseil*.

The Fazende family was one of the oldest and most esteemed in the state. Jeanne, who became Mme Jacques Philippe de Villeré, was born in New Orleans in 1765, being the daughter of Jean René de Fazende, who was sent from France as member of the first council established in the colony, and Charlotte Dreux de Gentilly, the marriage taking place in 1760. Charlotte was born in New Orleans in 1745, and died June 6, 1835. Her parents were Mathurin Dreux de Gentilly and Claude Francoise Hugo. Jean René de Fazande was the son of Jacques de Fazande and Helene de Morrière.

A number of children resulted from the union of Jacques Philippe de Villeré and Jeanne Henriette de Fazende, among them being a daughter named Marie Adéle de Villeré, who became the wife of Hugues de la Vergne as already narrated. During the campaign of 1814-15, when Pakenham's forces endeavored to capture New Orleans, Jacques Villeré was major general of the state militia and in command when they fought under Jackson at the famous battle on the Chalmette plantation. In 1816 General Jacques Philippe Villeré was elected governor of his native state, being the first Créole to occupy the chief executive's chair. He died in New Orleans March 7, 1830.

Jules de la Vergne, the elder son of Hugues de la Vergne and Marie Adéle de Villeré, and the only son that left a descendant bearing the family name, was born October 7, 1818. He married on September 4, 1866, Emma Joséphine Bermudez, daughter of Joaquin Bermudez and Marie Bonne-Emma Troxler. Young Jules de la Vergne was educated at the institute conducted by Gabriel Boyer, and later entered the law offices of Charles Bourguignon Derbigny, son of Governor Derbigny, who at that time was president of the state senate. Jules was admitted to the bar June 10, 1840, and about that time became identified with the Barataria and Lafourche Canal company, of which he was later made president. In 1844 he was elected to the state legislature and when the Native American, or "Know Nothing," Party appeared in national politics he espoused its cause and in 1845 was the candidate of that party for state senator from his district and was duly elected. When the Civil War broke out he enlisted as an ardent supporter of State Rights and with his own fortune erected a fort in the Barataria section known as "The Temple," a shell mound on Boutté Island, once the rendezvous of Jean Lafitte and his merry crew of freebooters. He was placed on the staff of Governor Moore, holding the rank of lieutenant colonel. At the close of hostilities between the states, Jules de la Vergne retired to his plantation home *Concord* on the west bank of the Mississippi river in Plaquemines parish, but like other southern planters he was practically ruined by the long struggle between the North and the South. He died in New Orleans April 12, 1887.

The only son of Jules de la Vergne and Emma Joséphine Bermudez, was Hugues Jules de la Vergne, born July 1, 1867. His mother, at the time of her marriage to Jules de la Vergne, was the widow of Charles Méloncy Soniat du Fossat, by whom she had four children: Joseph M. du Fossat, who married Eugénie de Reggio; Emma du Fossat, who married her cousin Théodore Soniat du Fossat; Edward J. du Fossat, and Amélia du Fossat, who married Judge Charles F. Claiborne.

Hugues Jules de la Vergne married Marie Louise Schmidt, daughter of Charles Edward Schmidt, one of the most eminent lawyers of New Orleans, and Léda Hincks, and by this union with Miss Schmidt left several sons and daughters, among whom are numbered the Contesse Boni de la Vergne and Mrs. H. C. St Paul. After the death of Hugues Jules de la Vergne his widow Marie Louise Schmidt married Henry J. Landry de Fréneuse de Saint-Aubin, who was the son of Alexandre Landry de Fréneuse and Léontine de Bouligny.

This account shows the close relationship of the de la Vergne, the Villeré, the Fazende, and the Bermudez families by marriage, therefore it is proper time to say something more specific about the descendants of an old Louisiana family whose members have borne themselves before their countrymen with honor and dignity,—the Bermudez.

The Bermudez family must ever attract the attention of the muse of history as she calls out the list of families of that state whose names should be inscribed in the Golden Book of Louisiana's annals as Venice of old wrote in her *Libro d'Oro* the names of her senators and patricians. It is said of the Bermudez family that it is of royal descent—coming down from the kings of Asturias in Spain. In the old days the name was spelled Bermud, and the immediate progenitors of the Louisiana branch of the family were of the class known as grandees of Spain.

Joaquin Bermudez, father-in-law of Jules de la Vergne, a man of irreproachable character and a judge at once firm and just, was born in New Orleans, May 20, 1796, and was baptised in the cathedral October 3rd. His parents were Juan Bautista Bermudez and Marie Emelia Saunhac (or Soniat) du Fossat, who were married in August, 1795. Doña Bermudez was the daughter of Guy de Saunhac du Fossat, a descendant from the French barons du Fossat, and Claudine Dreux de Gentilly, a daughter of Mathurin Dreux de Gentilly and Claude Francoise Hugo, and sister of Mme. Jean René Gabriel de Fazende, great-grandmother of Hugues de la Vergne.

Don Juan Bautista Bermudez, was a native of Havana, Cuba, and the first of the Bermudez family in Louisiana.

[65]

His father was Don José Antonio Bermudez, a native of Jaen, in the province of Andulasia, Spain, and his mother was Doña Constanza Gomez de Sylva, native of Setuba, in Portugal. The son Joaquin was educated at the *College d'Orléans* and was a student there when the British under Pakenham invaded the state and advanced on New Orleans. He left his books to bear arms under Jackson in the famous battle of January Eighth. Taking up the study of law, young Bermudez early attracted attention by his abilities and was elected, first, justice of the peace, then elevated to the bench of the city court, where he soon bcame presiding judge. Later he was selected to preside over the Court of Probate, and throughout the rest of his life Judge Bermudez held a high position in the esteem of his fellow-citizens of New Orleans. He died September 11, 1866, his wife preceding to the grave on May 9, 1852.

Judge Joaquin Bermudez's wife was Marie Bonne-Emma Troxler, whom he married October 26, 1824, in the parish of St. Charles. She was the daughter of Pierre Troxler and Marie Pelagie Melanie Bossier, the latter a daughter of Jean Baptiste Bossier, a native of St. John the Baptist parish, and Marie Manon Beauvais of New Orleans. Marie Bossier was born in Natchitoches December 21, 1787.

A daughter of Joaquin Bermudez and Marie Troxler, named Emma Joséphine Bermudez, married Jules de la Vergne September 4, 1866. A son of Judge Bermudez, born January 19, 1832, was baptised Edward Edmond Bermudez, April 26, 1832, at the Church Ste. Marie. His *parrain* was Edward D. White and Dame Eulalie Félicité Laure Dreux, wife of Pierre A. Rousseau, was his *marraine*..

Edouard Edmond Bermudez, on January 20, 1853, married Elizabeth Amanda Maupassant. She was the daughter of Henri de Maupassant, a native of del Moll, San Domingo, and Louise Isabel Clara Casalis, a native of Baracoa, Cuba. The parents of Doña Casalis were Lusi Casalis and Luisa Alzire de Sonty. Henrique de Maupassant, as his name was set down in the records, was the son of Pierre Francois Valentin de Maupassant and Rosa Masson de Bettignac. Armanda Maupassant, for she was known best by this name, was born May 20, 1829, and became the mother of a number of children. They were:

1.—Joachim Joseph Edouard Bermudez, born November 24, 1853, died April 20, 1896.

2.—Edmond Henri Octave Fernand Bermudez, born April 6, died May 8, 1902.

3.—Jean Léonce Camille Bermudez, born September 21, 1856, died young.

4.—Marie Louise Emma Alzire Bermudez, born October 16, 1857. She married in 1883 a French lieutenant of artillery, Henri Farjas.

5.—Marie Elizabeth Armanda Bermudez, born October 25, 1859, died young.

6.—Joseph Pierre Martin Henri Bermudez, born May 3, 1861.

7.—Marie Paul Gustave Zéa Bermudez, born February 2, 1886, died young.

8.—Jeanne Marie Bermudez, born November 29, 1867. She married, in 1897 Henri J. Ledoux.

The marriage of Edouard Edmond Bermudez and Amanda Maupassant was a very happy one. The wife died January 30, 1897, mourned by her children and grandchildren. In a record book presented to his intended before their marriage, Edouard Bermudez set down their family motto: "*Espérance!! Patience!! Courage!! Fidélité!!*" and on September 22, 1852, four months before their wedding, wrote the following verse to her:

Amanda!!

A tes voeux, Amanda, je ne puis qu'obéir . . . .
Ma force est audessous de mon ardent désir.
Apollon de ses feux ne sait bruler mon âme,
Ni verser en mon coeur sa poétique flamme!
Dans ces vers décousus ou nul art n'apparait,
Ange, fille du Ciel, ton nom seule est parfait.

The original Dimitry article on the de la Vergne-Villeré family appeared in the New Orleans **Times-Democrat**, May 8, and 27, 1892. This account has been considerably simplified by the Editor.

L'HOMME—DE GLAPION—HICKMAN—
LINCOLN Families

IN the middle of the eighteenth century the de l'Hommes, a French family of ancient distinction, resided in New Orleans. Charles de L'Homme, of this family, was an infantry officer in the *Regiment détachée de la Marine*, as some of the French troops that composed the garrisons of colonial Louisiana were then termed. About the same time among the residents of New Orleans was the family de Glapion, from Normandy, and like the de l'Hommes, they enjoyed high consideration in the colony. Christophe, Chevalier de Glapion was one of them.

Charles de l'Homme had a son, Edmé Joseph de l'Homme, born in New Orleans in 1754. His mother, previous to her marriage to his father, was Laurence Chauvin de Léry. Somewhat later was born to the Chevalier de Glapion and his wife, whose maiden name was Jeanne Antoinette Rivard, a daughter named for her mother. Mlle. Rivard was the daughter of Antoine Rivard Jr., from Canada, and Jeanne Antoinette de Mirebaize de Villemont, of a noble family from Poitou.

The contract of marriage between Edmé Joseph de l'Homme and Jeanne Antoinette de Glapion was drawn up and witnessed in the parish of St. Charles before François Simars de Bellisle, commandant of the *Côte des Allemands*, January 14, 1777. The witnesses, of whom most, if not all, have left descendants in Louisiana, were: the father of the groom and the mother of the bride; Jean François Huchet de Kernion, step-father of the bride; François de l'Homme, des Islets de Kernion, Fagot la Garcinière, Glapion du Menil, and George Glapion, *fils*.

The de Glapions, in Normandy, bore the titles of Seigneurs de Mesnilganchie and were also lords of Rosnay, Boitron, Gaultier, Huardière and other places in their native province.

[68]

In 1667 they were duly recognized, in a judgement rendered by the commissioners of the king of France, as being of ancient nobility. This decree was given in the district of Evreux. Their escutcheon shows on a field *azure* three winged fasces *or*, bordered with *gules*. Saint-Allais, the famous genealogist of Normandy, includes the de Glapions in his *Nobiliaire de Normandie*.

The first Glapions in Louisiana were the Chevalier Christophe de Glapion, Seigneur de Mesnilganchie, and his brother, Charles de Glapion, Sieur du Mesnil. Both of them were distinguished French colonial officers. Their father, Charles, Seigneur de Mesnilganchie, and their mother, Jeanne Thiboust, lived in the parish of Saint-Escolasse, in the bishopric of Scé, in Normandy.

The Chevalier Christophe de Glapion, sometime after his arrival in Louisiana, married Jeanne Antoinette Rivard on June 18, 1757. Her mother, Jeane Antoinette de Mirebaize de Villemont, was then a widow of Antoine Rivard junior, who was born at the Natchez post, and whom she married on February 30, 1730 in New Orleans. He died on his plantation facing the Bayou St. John, September 27, 1735. His widow, being then only twenty, married, on October 4, 1736, Jean François Huchet de Kernion, a young military officer in the colony. By her first marriage to Antoine Rovard *fils*, she had two daughters, Jeanne Antoinette Rivard, born in New Orleans, February 17, 1732, who died the same year, and Jeanne Antoinette Rivard, second of the name, born in New Orleans during May, 1734, who married Chevalier Christophe de Glapion and became, by this marriage, the mother of Jeanne Antoinette de Glapion, wife of Edmé Joseph de l'Homme.

Several children were born of the marriage of Edmé Joseph de l'Homme and Jeanne Antoinette de Glapion. They were: (a) Alexandre de l'Homme, who married Adéle Trouard; (b) Chevalier de l'Homme, who married Mlle. de Clouet, of the family from which sprang a distinguished son of Louisiana, General Alexander de Clouet; (c) Octave de l'Homme, who married Mlle. Hardy de Boisblanc; (d) Constance de l'Homme, married to Achille Trouard; (e) Suzette de l'Homme, who married John

Hickman; (f) Adelaide de l'Homme, who did not marry; (g) Céleste de l'Homme, who married Pierre Trépagnier, and (h) Arsene de l'Homme, who married Mlle. de Fleuriau de Bellmare.

In Dimitry's sketch of the de l'Homme family, he followed the genealogical line of the descendants of John Hickman and Suzette de l'Homme down to the family of Helluin and the posterity in Louisiana of Pierre Helluin and Virginia Hickman. He proceeded, by way of a preliminary, with some account of the Hickman family, an old established one of Virginia, later a noted family of Kentucky, (giving the name to the town of Hickman in that state), and then of Louisiana.

The Hickman family, of which Virginia Hickman (Mme. Pierre Firmin Helluin, granddaughter of Mme. Suzette de l'Homme Hickman of Assumption parish and mother, among other children, of Suzette Helluin and of Adrienne Helluin, first wife of Major L. L. Lincoln of New Orleans) was a member, was numbered among the pioneer settlers of Kentucky. The first of the name who went to Kentucky from Virginia, his native state, was a contemporary of many of those adventurous men the Daniel Boones, the Kentons, the Simon Girtys and others—who left the grand mountains and the valleys of the Old Dominion to develop into civilization "the dark and bloody ground" of "the far West." This gentleman was the Reverand William Hickman, a clergyman of the Baptist church, who removed to Franklin county, Kentucky, in the year 1784, when he was thirty-seven years old. He was the father of John Hickman, who married Suzette de l'Homme of Assumption parish, Louisiana, from whom are descended the children and other descendants of Pierre Firmin Helluin, a native of Picardy, in France, who in the year 1816 came to Louisiana, and having married Virginia Hickman, founded the Helluin family in that state.

Reverand John Hickman was the son of Thomas Hickman and Sarah Sanderson of King and Queen county, Virginia, where he was born February 4, 1747. His parents died young, leaving him and his sister Elizabeth, who married a member of the Broaddus family, as their entire issue. Before taking his departure for Kentucky, William Hickman

[70]

married, in Virginia, Elizabeth Shackleford. The families of Sanderson, and Shackleford of Virginia, are all families well known and of established reputation in that state. From the marriage of the Reverand William Hickman and Elizabeth Shackleford were born thirteen children, seven daughters and six sons, and one of these sons, John, married Suzette de l'Homme.

Two children were the issue of the union of John and Suzette: Virginia Hickman and Franklin Augustus Hickman. The son married Angelina Rieson of Assumption parish, and died childless. He was for several terms sheriff of his native parish and later a New Orleans merchant, a member of the firm of Riviere & Hickman. Virginia Hickman when she was fifteen married Pierre Firmin Helluin, a native of France who came to Louisiana in 1816. The Helluin family in Picardy were landed proprietors and farmers. Pierre Helluin settled in Napoleonville, Louisiana, as a merchant, later becoming postmaster, and owner of a saw mill that shipped lumber to New Orleans. Several children were born of the marriage. One son, Edgar Helluin, a planter of Assumption parish, became like his uncle Franklin Hickman, sheriff of the parish. He married Louisiana Himel, daughter of Drauzin Himel, a planter of the parish, and they became the parents of three boys and three girls.

One of the daughters of Pierre Helluin and Virginia Hickman married Henry B. Foley, an Assumption parish planter, and left a large family when she died in New Orleans in 1875. Stéphanie, the oldest daughter of Pierre Helluin, married A. D. Bougère, a planter of St. Charles parish, and later moved to the parish of St John the Baptist, and became the mother of four sons and two daughters. Adrienne Helluin, the youngest child of Pierre and Virginia Helluin, married Major L. L. Lincoln of New Orleans in 1870. At her death seven years later, she left two children, Rixford J. Lincoln, and Mary Lincoln, who were reared by their Aunt Suzette Helluin. Major Lincoln was a Confederate veteran and well known in New Orleans journalistic circles.

The original Dimitry articles on the l'Homme family appeared in the New Orleans Times-Democrat, June 5 and 12, 1892.

LE BRETON Family

THE records in France of the LeBreton family, that
came from that kingdom to Louisiana, go back to a
remote period. The family name was originally
d'Envrich, Knight and Seigneur du Mesnil-Boulé in
Normandy, whose arms were, on a field *azure*, three pigeons
argent, two pigeons *en chef* opposite each other. This Seigneur du Mesnil-Boulé was the father of Nicholas d'Envrich,
who left the paternal home when quite a youth, and went
to Vannes in Brittany, to reside. Marrying there he became
the father of Denis d'Envrich, an only son, and this Denis
d'Envrich it was who first took the name of Le Breton, now
borne by one of the most honorable families of Louisiana,
included among the members of which are the Le Bretons
des Chapelles and the Le Bretons d'Orgenois, or Dorgenois,
as the name is spelled today.

It is an interesting fact in connection with the assumption
of the name of Le Breton by Denis d'Envrich that it was
bestowed upon him by Charles VIII of France, "the affable
and courteous," who had been witness of his soldierly conduct
at the battle of Fornoue in Italy, fought July 6, 1495, by
that monarch in his war against Naples. A captain in the
regiment of Piennes, Denis d'Envrich during the battle served
near the French king's person. In the following year, Charles
the Eighth, who had married Anne of Brittany, thus cementing the royal authority in that duchy, conferred on the cadet
of Envrich, who had distinguished himself at Fornoue, a
patent of nobility in which it was expressly declared that he
and his posterity should continue to bear the name Le Breton,
which the king conferred on him. In the *Letters-Patent* it was
set down: "We have the said Le Breton rehabilitated, and
we rehabilitate him, declare, and we declare him, Gentleman
sprung from noble lineage and, as far as it may be necessary,
we have enobled, and we enoble, him and his children—the

said Le Breton, his children and his successors not to change
the name of Le Breton in the future, only causing to be added
to the arms borne by the Seigneurs du Mesnil-Boulé a golden
star, as a mark of his worth and his virtue."

Since that day the Le Breton coat-of-arms has displayed
in the heart of the escutcheon the single star granted by royal
favor as a living testimonial to the courage exhibited by their
immediate ancestor at the battle of Fornoue, the valorous
cadet d'Envrich. The manner in which Denis d'Envrich received the name Le Breton, and the fact that a king of
France bestowed it, may be a source of legitimate pride to
the Le Bretons of Louisiana, for by the selection of this
name by Charles VIII, Denis Le Breton and his posterity
have been made, so far as a king's edict can prevail, to stand
forth through the generations of men that have followed, as
the continuing types and representatives of the Bretons of
France, dwellers in Brittany, that land of half fable and
half romance, whereon, in the purple dawn of unrecorded
civilization, the fair Armoric knights of the Round Table,
Sir Launcelot, the brave, and Sir Galahad, the good, cara-
colled on prancing steeds, when white-bearded Arthur, the
King, drew from its golden sheath, his mighty sword *Excali-
bur*, and the silver trumpets pealed the sally-forth from
Camelot.

The Le Breton family, established in Louisiana, was one
of the richest and most distinguished in this French colony.
The first of the name to settle there was Louis Césaire Le
Breton, born in Montereau-faut-Yonne, now in the department of Seine-et-Oise, in the district of Fontainebleau. He
died in Dijon, France, in the parish of Saint Philibert on
June 10, 1776, in his sixty-fourth year.

This Louis Césaire Le Breton, *écuyer*, Sieur des Chapelles,
lord of Charmeau, in the parish of Villeroy, department of
Cote d'Or, formerly Burgundy, was also seigneur of Civry,
la Poterie, and Basson-sur-Yonne. He had acquired the last
named *fief* as well as that of Charmeau, with his wife,
Jeanne Marguerite Chauvin de la Frénière, for 150,000
livres, from Louis François de Neufville, duke of Villeroy,
peer of France, by notarial act passed in Paris, July 28,
1759.

[73]

This Louis Césaire Le Breton des Chapelles etc., born in Montereau-faut-Yvonne, November 13, 1711, was the son of Messire Anne Francois Le Breton, Sieur de la Maugerie, in the county of Perche, Normandy, perpetual mayor of Montereau, and of Marie Gatien de Salmon, born in Montereau, December 31, 1681, who was, in turn the daughter of Edmé Gatien de Salmon, member of the Superior Council of Louisiana and *Commissaire Ordonnateur* of that province, later on appointed *Procureur du Roi* and perpetual mayor of Montereau-faut-Yonne.

Messire Anne François Le Breton de la Maugerie, father of Louis Césaire, the progenitor of all the Louisiana Le Bretons, was, on April 1, 1700, Commissioner of Police in Montereau. He became royal notary in that city April 1, 1703, and on November 13, 1711, was made its perpetual mayor and Comptroller for the King. From his marriage with Marie Gatien de Salmon issued seven children, namely: Anne François Gatien, Joseph Simon, Jacques Nicholas, Louis Césaire (who came to Louisiana), Jacques, Antoine François, and Antoine Le Breton.

From the family papers of the Louisiana Le Bretons, it appears that in September, 1787, the French king, through Louis Pierre d'Hozier, judge of arms for the kingdom, granted to Louis Césaire Le Breton des Chapelles and his legitimate descendants, a special escutcheon described as being: "On a field *argent*, three palms sinople arranged two and one." In 1774 this same Louis Césaire, as a further mark of his monarch's esteem, was appointed Honorary Councillor in the *Cour des Monnaies* of Paris.

Louis Césaire Le Breton des Chapelles married twice. His first nuptial contract with Jeanne Marguerite Chauvin de la Frénière, attested by Henry, royal notary in New Orleans, was passed on February 7, 1738. The marriage ceremony was celebrated on March first of the same year. The bride was the daughter of Nicholas Chauvin de la Frénière and Marguerite le Sueur, and a sister of Nicholas Chauvin de la Frénière, victim of O'Reilly in 1769. At the death of his first wife Louis Césaire married again and Anne Thérese Berthelin was his second spouse. From this last union was born only one child, a son named François Marie

Le Breton de Saint-Mesme, who died unmarried, October 16, 1785.

Four children were born from the marriage of Louis Césaire Le Breton and Jeanne Marguerite Chauvin de la Frénière. They were:

1.—François Joseph Le Breton d'Orgency, born in New Orleans and baptised October 10, 1750. He died September 21, 1814. He had married Anne Marguerite Harang, daughter of Don Louis Harang and Dona Barbara Harang, by whom he had six children: (a) Louis Gatien Le Breton d'Orgenoy, who married Marie Josephine Harang and moved to San Domingo where he was in 1782 and 1790 *sénéchal* in Saint-Marc. He died in 1785, leaving a son, the Comte des Chapelles, and a daughter, the Comtesse Gomer. His son the count who moved to France where he resided permanently, was a famous chess player and a formidable opponent of the French master, Philidor; (b) Louis Gassien Le Breton d'Orgency, who married Marie Josephine Harang; (c) Louis Joseph Le Breton de Préfontaine, unmarried; (d) Marie Le Breton, who became the wife of Sébastian Morière Fazende; (e) Marie Françoise Le Breton, who married Jean René Fazende, and (f) Marie Anne Genevieve Le Breton, who became the wife of the Sieur Dusseau de la Croix.

2.—Louise Marguerite Le Breton des Chapelles, born July 17, 1742 or 1752, who died in France in 1780, married in that country the Comte Etienne de Mermity, from Pont Bernard in the township of Montmancou, in the canton of Pontailler-sur-Saone, from which marriage was born a son, François de Mermity.

3.—Louis Nicolas Gassien Le Breton, *cornette* of cavalry in the Regiment of Volunteers of Clermont, was born in New Orleans between 1745 and 1755, and died in France in October 1805. He married Mademoiselle Héremie de la Cartouzière, and from her had three children, to-wit: (a) Stanislas Xavier Le Breton des Chapelles, who lived in Batignolles Monceaux near Paris and was official verifier of property belonging to the king; (b) Louise Antoinette Le Breton who married the Sieur de Lyvet d'Arantot; (c) Mademoiselle Le Breton who became the wife of the Count O'Haguerty, marshal in the French army in Paris, their issue being Joseph O'Haguerty, esquire of the Duke of Bordeaux, Charles O'Haguerty, esquire of the Duchess of Angouleme, and Marie Augustine O'Haguerty, wife of Ferdinand de Parceval, *chambellan* of the King of Bavaria and Colonel in the Prince Charles Regiment of Cuirassiers, living in Munich, Bavaria.

4.—Jean Baptiste Césaire Le Breton des Chapelles, born in New Orleans between 1747 and 1757. He was a *Mousquetaire Noir* in the King's own body-guard, and later became a captain in the Spanish colonial army in Louisiana. He was commandant of militia at the German Coast and was murdered by his slaves in 1771. He married Jeanne Françoise de Macarty, daughter of Barthelemy de McCarty, knight of St. Louis, and Hélene Pellerin. From this marriage issued two children: (a) Barthelemy François Le Breton des Chapelles, who first married Marguerite de Boré, daughter of Etienne de Boré and Marguerite Marie d'Estréhan des Tours, and secondly took for wife Jeanne Eulalie Robin de Logny. He died on December 27, 1823; (b) Jeanne Françoise le Breton des Chapelles who became the wife of the baron Joseph Xavier Delfau de Pontalba and had one child: Joseph Xavier Célestin de Pontalba married to Micaëla Leonarda Almonester y Roxas. (q. v.)

We have seen from the above that Barthelemy François Le Breton des Chapelles married first Marguerite de Boré, daughter of Etienne de Boré and Marguerite d'Estréhan des Tours. This marriage was celebrated in Paris, where her father resided at the time. Etienne de Boré, was the grandfather of Charles Gayarré, distinguished historian of Louisiana. De Boré served as first and only mayor of New Orleans during the celebrated twenty days that France ruled again over Louisiana after the retransfer of the province by Spain and before the Stars and Stripes were flung above it by William C. C. Claiborne the first American Governor. De

Boré was also first to introduce into Louisiana a successful process of granulating cane juice so as to produce sugar.

Boré made his first crop in 1796 on a plantation that embraced the land that now constitutes Audubon Park. He was born in Kaskaskia, then in the Illinois country, in the year 1748. One of his ancestors had been a King's Councillor in the days of Louis XIV, and he himself had served as captain in the *Mousquetaires du Roi*, or *Mousquetaires Noirs*, so called from their uniforms of black, during the reign of Louis XV. Among the documents at one time in the possession of Charles Le Breton of New Orleans, one of his descendants, were parchment commissions of the de Borés signed by Louis XIV and Louis XV respectively.

The wife of Etienne de Boré, namely Marguerite Marie d'Estréhan des Tours, was the daghter of the Sieur des Tréhans des Tours (as the name was originally written), who had been the Royal Treasurer of the Province of Louisiana but had been sent back to France because he had allied himself with those who opposed Governor Billoart de Kerlerec's policies.

Jean Baptiste Césaire Le Breton des Chapelles, from his marriage with Jeanne Françoise de MacCarthey (or Macarty), who married after his demise a Mr. Conway, had, as already stated, two children, Jeanne le Breton, who became the baroness de Pontalba, and Barthélemy François Le Breton des Chapelles who married first Miss de Boré and then Miss Robin de Logny. This François Barthélemy was born on his father's plantation in 1762, located in what was once called Jefferson Parish but is now a part of Carrollton in New Orleans. After the death of his father, who was murdered by his slaves, young François Barthélemy was sent to receive his education at the *College d'Orléans*, in France, and here he met two son of the Duc d'Orléans, one of whom was known as *Prince Egalité* or *Philippe Egalité*, and who was later the father of king Louis Philippe, representing the younger branch of the Bourbons. His intimacy with the sons of the Duc d'Orléans secured for François Barthélemy, when he left college, a position in the service of that prince, which he resigned, however, shortly afterward to join the Regiment of Aquitaine. He served therein for a few years and gave up his commission to return to his beloved Louisiana. He established himself on his father's plantation in what was once known as Greenville, and it was soon afterward that he married Mademoiselle de Boré.

From this marriage issued two sons, namely: Barthélemy Le Breton, who died unmarried in 1820 at the age of twenty eight and Jean Baptiste François Le Breton, who married first Marie Marthe Melicerte de la Barre, daughter of François Pascalis de la Barre and Charlotte Chalinette du Tillet, and at her death, August 16, 1823, Jean Le Breton married Marie Celestine de la Barre, widow of Pierre Guermeur Huchet de Kernion.

From the second marriage of Barthélemy François Le Breton to Jeanne Eulalie Robin de Logny, who died on December 27, 1823 were born two children: Josephine Eulalie Le Breton, deceased in 1862, who became the wife of Charles Zénon Derbigny (q.v.) and left three daughters: Lucie (Mrs. Courmes), Eulalie (Mrs. LeBreton-Cochrane), and Odile (Mrs. LaBarre); and Noël Barthélemy Le Breton.

This last named Noël Barthélemy, son of Barthélemy François Le Breton and Jeanne Eulalie Robin de Logny died in New Orleans on August 29, 1849. He married three times, his first two wives being sisters, very attractive young daughters of Pierre Bourguignon Derbigny fifth American governor of Louisiana and of Mademoiselle de Hault de Lassus. Noël's third wife being Henriette Ganucheau.

By his first wife he left no issue. One son, Alphonse Romuald Le Breton, was born of his second spouse. By his third, Miss Ganucheau, he left one son, Noël Henri Le Breton, who was killed while serving in the Confederate Army, and six daughters, Marie Henriette, Elizabeth Louise, Jeanne Eulalie, Natalie and Philomene Le Breton, respectively married to Messrs. St. Clair, Fergus Mayronne, Charles Coulon Jumonville, Octave Mayronne and Charles Boudousquié. His last daughter, Marie Antoinette Le Breton, did not marry.

Jean Baptiste François Le Breton, half brother of Noël Barthélemy, and son of Barthélemy Francois Le Breton by his first wife, Jeanne Marguerite de Boré, at the death of his maternal grandfather, Etienne de Boré, the Louisiana sugar king, became half-owner with his aunt, Elizabeth de Boré Gayarré, of the plantation whereon the first sugar had been granulated in the United States. At a later period of his life, he established himself on a plantation five miles further up the river than the Boré plantation, and which formed part of the plantation belonging to his mother-in-law, Madame Pascalis de La Barre. This plantation was purchased in 1851 by his son, Charles Le Breton, who sold it after the Civil War to satisfy his creditors.

Jean Baptiste François Le Breton was educated at the College Lefort in New Orleans. Together with his brothers, Barthélemy Edmond des Chapelles and Noël Barthélemy Le Breton, he served as a soldier in the Battle of New Orleans. He was proficient in mathematics and had a natural taste for civil engineering, and by this knowledge, he was enabled to assist his neighbors and friends very materially. He possessed a fine library and was a great reader, especially of historical books and the classics. He was a profound admirer of Napoleon Bonaparte, though he censured the great emperor's treatment of Josephine. His inclination was for a military life and he often regretted that he had not become a professional fighting man. For a long time he was a member of the *Chasseurs-a-Cheval*, a volunteer cavalry company of Jefferson Parish. At the outbreak of the Civil War, he joined, as a private, the Jefferson Mounted Guards, a company commanded by Captain Guy Dreux. It had been organized under a call issued by Charles Le Breton, his son, who was several times offered its captaincy and finally became one of its second lieutenants. Notwithstanding the advanced age of Jean Baptiste François Le Breton, he would have accompanied his company to the bloody field of Shiloh had not the sudden serious illness of his son Charles prevented both father and son from leaving when the command took its departure for the scene of war. Charles Le Breton, however, recovering, joined his company, but in the capacity of a private, and served as such until the end of the war.

Jean Baptiste François Le Breton married twice. His first wife was Mélicerte de La Barre, daughter of François

Pascalis de la Barre and Charlotte Chalinette du Tillet. She died on August 16, 1823 and thereupon he took as his second wife, Célestine de La Barre, widow of Pierre Guermeur Huchet de Kernion. His second spouse died on April 9, 1845, leaving no issue.

From his first wife, Mélicerte de La Barre, were born three sons, namely: (a) Jean Etienne Le Breton who died in his twenty-fifth year, in 1840, unmarried; (b) Edmond Le Breton, who died on July 31, 1847 in his twenty-eight year and who married Eulalie Bourguignon Derbigny from whom he had a son, Charles Le Breton who became the husband of Mademoiselle Chauvin de Léry, and a daughter, Mélicerte Le Breton, unmarried; (c) Charles Le Breton, born in New Orleans, twice married, and one of the most highly respected citizens of his native city, who died at a very advanced age.

This Charles Le Breton's first wife was Marie Célestine Guermeur Huchet de Kernion, daughter of Pierre Ladislas Guermeur Huchet de Kernion and of Marie Célestine Roseïde Volant de La Barre. Three children issued from this union, namely: (a) Marie Célestine Le Breton, who became the wife of Jules Tuyès, of New Orleans, and left, among other children, Jeanne Tuyès, married to L. A. Wogan of that city; (b) Jean Baptiste Edmond Le Breton, whose wife was Marguerite Fortier, a sister of Professor Alcée Fortier, Louisiana historian and educator; (c) Miss Le Breton who died during childhood.

At the death of his first wife on October 28, 1848, Charles Le Breton married her sister Marie Roseïde Guermeur Huchet de Kernion. This second marriage took place on May 25, 1851. Six children were born from it among whom Louis Césaire Le Breton, and Charles François Barthelemy Le Breton died young. Alice Le Breton did not marry. Roseïde Le Breton, from this second marriage, was wedded to James Knapp and Amelie Le Breton, last child of Charles Le Breton and his second wife, became Mrs. Alphonse Baudéan and left a numerous posterity.

---

¹ The original Le Breton sketches by Dimitry appeared in the New Orleans Times-Democrat, June 19 and 26, 1892 pp. 14. It was found necessary, however, to have numerous changes made and for Mr. Kernion to supply new and corrected data.

ARNOULT—SAUVÉ—WAGGAMAN Families

THE story in Louisiana of the Sauvé Family—a name of honorable associations in the colonial and state annals, takes us back to the year 1769 when Pierre Sauvé, a native of Dunkirk, in France, where he was born in 1749, came to Louisiana and founded the family that still bears his name. This gentleman's father who was also known as Pierre Sauvé, was in the days of Louis XV, a commandant in the French Naval Service. He lost a leg in a sea engagement, and as a reward was presented with a costly sword.

Pierre Sauvé, soon after coming to Louisiana, engaged in sugar planting. At the time the United States took over Louisiana, President Jefferson appointed commissioners to received from Citizen Pierre Clément de Laussat, the French *Préfet*, the province of Louisiana, newly ceded by the First Consul, Napoleon Bonaparte, to the United States. Among the orders issued by the French Commissioner was one by which the Spanish Cabildo or Supreme Council of New Orleans, was replaced by a municipal council which was composed of a mayor, two *adjoints*, and ten members. Etienne de Boré, was named mayor of New Orleans during the short-lived French Domination, with Jean Noël Destrehan and Pierre Sauvé as *adjoints*, while the members of the council included: Messrs. Livaudais, Cavelier, Villeré, Jones, Fortier, Donaldson, Faurio, Allard, and Watkins, with Derbigny and Labatut as secretary and treasurer respectively. Later, when the house of representatives of the new territorial legislature met to nominate ten persons from which the President of the Untied States was to choose a legislative council, Pierre Sauvé was one of the ten named. And when the legislature under the new form of government met in New Orleans, President Jefferson appointed Sauvé, Bellechasse, Destrehan, Macarty, and Jones as members. Sauvé, with Destrehan and

Derbigny, went to Washington to obtain states' rights for Louisiana.

Previous to 1800, Pierre Sauvé married Mlle. Rosalie Second of Marseilles, who died in December 27, 1827. Four children were born to them. They were (a) Adélema Sauvé who married René Trudeau (q.v.) a Jefferson parish planter; (b) Mathilde Sauvé who married William Walter Brock, native of Scotland, in the cotton business in New Orleans; (c) Fanny Sauvé, born 1802, married Edouard Reinhold Hollander, born in November 20, 1786 at Riga, a New Orleans merchant; and (d) Pierre Sauvé, II, born in 1805, who married Telzire Fortier, daughter of Norbert Fortier, and Aimée Hardy de Boisblanc de Beaulieu. They had eight children: (1) Félicie Sauvé married Col. Eugene Waggaman; (2) Dr. Henry Pierre Sauvé did not marry; (3) Valentine Sauvé married Dr. Frank L. Taney; (4) Clemence Sauvé, unmarried; (5) George Sauvé, who married Eugenie Tureaud of St. James Parish, and later moved to Florida—descendants in Tampa and Jacksonville; (6) Felix Sauvé, unmarried; (7) Louis Frederick Sauvé, unmarried; (8) Paul Sauvé, who married Louise Demeritt of Boston.

Valentine Sauvé and Dr. Frank L. Taney were parents of six children: (a) Roger Brooke Taney, named after his paternal granduncle Roger Brooke Taney, Chief Justice of the United States Supreme Court, and who died without issue; (b) Louise Taney who married William Ray of Monroe, Louisiana; (c) Bertha Taney, died young; (d) Leigh Taney, unmarried; and (e) Harold Taney of Seattle, Washington.

Dr. H. Pierre Sauvé was a prominent physician of Hot Springs Arkansas, distinguished for his services at Memphis during a yellow fever scourge. He did not marry.

Paul Sauvé, by his marriage to Louise Demeritt, had four children: Louise and Paul born in Boston, and Arthur and Velma Sauvé born in New Orleans.

Pierre Sauvé II, at the outbreak of the Civil War, was a Louisiana sugar planter. He backed the celebrated Lopez Expedition to Cuba in 1855, which had for its purpose the independence of that island. His plantation *Providence* was noted for its lavish hospitality, and it was here that the great

"Sauvé Crevasse" occured in 1849. When the war between the states broke out he did not subscribe to the popular view of secession, favoring a gradual emancipation of the slaves. However, the conflict meant to him what it meant to so many other Louisiana planters and his rich estates disappeared. At the time of his death in 1867, he was sixty-two.

Col. Eugene Waggaman, who married Felicie Sauvé, was the son of George Augustus Waggaman, a brilliant young lawyer of Maryland, born at Fairview, Dorchester County, Maryland, in 1790. George Augustus Waggaman was a member of a distinguished family of Virginia and Maryland, connected with the first families of America. His father was Henry Waggaman born in Sommerset county, Maryland in 1751, and his mother Sarah Ernnells, of Dorchester county, Henry Waggaman was the first attorney general of Maryland. The young Marylander, soon after his arrival in New Orleans in 1810 married Marie Camille Arnoult, who was heiress to the plantation on the west bank of the Mississippi first called *Tchoupitoulas* but later known as *"Avondale."* An ancient deed under date of March 6, 1769 shows that *Tchoupitoulas* was first owned by Sieur Delille Dupard, who bequeathed it to his daughter, Marie Delille Dupard who married Jean Arnoult, and it then went to their heirs. It was the daughter of this last named couple, Marie Camille Arnoult, born 1795, who married George Augustus Waggaman on June 4, 1818. Besides inheriting *Avondale*, as her husband renamed the plantation, she inherited much city property in New Orleans and a very considerable amount of money in bank for the times. The young Marylander, both accomplished and popular, soon became prominent politically. He participated in the Battle of New Orleans. He was first elected a Federal judge, next secretary of state of Louisiana, and finally, United States Senator. He was intimate with Henry Clay and Daniel Webster, entertaining Mr. Clay at *Avondale*. The old Dupard plantation home was called *Tchoupitoulas* and went to the Soniats through Marie Anne Arnoult, born 1774, who married Joseph Soniat du Fossat. *Avondale*, at 12 Mile Point, was one of the most magnificent plantations in the state. The residence was built in 1840 at a cost of $40,000, and its entertainments were noted for their

[83]

elegance and social importance. Senator Waggaman was an avowed leader of the Whig Party. He became engaged in an altercation with Dennis Prieur, leader of the Democratic faction, and former mayor of New Orleans, which resulted in an *"affaire d'honneur"* under the oaks. Waggaman expressly shot to miss but Prieur's shot struck his antagonist's leg, severing an artery, and Waggaman died March 23, 1843 of gangrene, refusing to allow his leg to be amputated until too late. His wife lived at *Avondale* until her death in 1876.

The children of George Augustus Waggaman and Marie Camille Arnoult were: (a) Henry St. John Waggaman, who studied for the law, married Adele Bujac, and died early in life. He had two sons: George Augustus Waggaman and Henry St. John Waggaman; (b) Christine Waggaman married John Sandfield McDonald, prime minister of Ontario, Canada, who refused the order of knighthood tendered him by Queen Victoria; (c) Eugene Waggaman, educated at Mont St. Mary's College, Maryland, graduating as valedictorian in 1846. At twenty-five, he married Felicie Sauvé. He was distinguished for his Civil War record in the service of the Confederacy, and was designated as the hero of Malvern Hill being Colonel of the 10th Louisiana Regiment, and Commander of Hayes and Stafford's Brigades A. N. V. He commanded a company on the 14th of September, 1874, at Jackson Square; (d) Mathilde Waggaman, who married Judge Henry D. Ogden, had five children: Charles Garner Ogden, Frank D. Ogden, Marie, Louise and Henry Duplessis Ogden who married Lora Horn. The others died unmarried: (e) Eliza Waggaman, who married John R. Conway; and (f) Camille Waggaman, who died young.

Col. Eugené Waggaman was educated as a civil engineer and architect, but practiced neither profession, preferring the life of a planter. He was born in New Orleans, October 17, 1826; married Felicie Sauvé in March of 1852, and died in New Orleans, April 24, 1897. His wife, born on *Providence* plantation October 15, 1831, married young Waggaman in New Orleans in March, 1852, and survived her husband by several years, dying March 23, 1912. Their children were: (a) William Waggaman, who married Sara

Kennedy; (b) Marie Waggaman, who married William Berl of San Francisco, and Willmington, Delaware. (c) Christine Waggaman, who married a distant cousin, Thomas E. Waggaman, of Washington, D. C.; (d) Albert Waggaman, who married Selena Solomon; (e) Charles Spinola Waggaman, who married Laura E. Duggan; and (f) Frank Waggaman, not married.

In following the Sauve-Waggaman line, it proves proper to briefly refer to the antecedants of Marie Camille Arnoult, who married the first Waggaman to come to Louisiana. (1810) Her father, Cyril Honoré Arnoult, born 1770, had married Christine Juana Battista de Brounner. She was the daughter of Jean Rodolpho Baron de Brounner, born in Switzerland in 1700. He was the son of David von Brounner *Patricien de Berne*, and Barbara le Roy of Flanders. Baron de Brounner was the hero of many brilliant achievements at arms, holding commissions as a commanding officer of Swiss troops serving under three kings—Charles Emmanuel, III of Sardinia in 1732; Stanislaus Augustus of Poland; and Carlos III of Spain. He was Lieutenant Colonel of German Mercenaires on *Côte des Allemands*. He married a daughter of Count Ignazio Carbonara and Duchess Maria Teresa Spinola, and came to Louisiana in service of Carlos III, and under Governor Bernardo Galvez was with him at Baton Rouge and Pensacola. His bride, Maria Camilla di Carbonara y Spinola, was the daughter of Captain Paola Spinola, who was related to the Pallavicini, and Doria families of Genoa, and came from a long line of noble and distinguished ancestors. The daughter of this marriage was Christina Battista de Brounner who married Cyril Arnoult; her two sisters, Anna Barbara and Maria Teresa died unmarried. A son, whose godfather was Governor Galvez, died in infancy. The corner of Royal and Customhouse Streets, was a Spanish grant to the Baronne de Brounner.

Jean Arnoult, father of Cyril, came from Poitou, France, and after his arrival in Louisiana, was appointed *Regidor Perpetual du Cabildo*, and lived on his plantation *Tchoupitoulas*. He married Marie Delille Dupard, daughter of Pierre Joseph Delille Dupard and Jacqueline Michel, who in turn was the daughter of Roch Michel, of the Faubourg St.

[85]

Germain, and Louise Phillipau, who were married in 1726. The issue of Jean Arnoult and Marie Dupard consisted of (a) Cyril Honoré Arnoult born 1770, died April 1832, who served as aide to General Andrew Jackson, married Christine de Brounner, as noted above; (b) Marie Anne Arnoult, born 1774, died 1798, married Joseph Soniat Dufossat; (c) Barthelemy Arnoult, born 1766; (d) Jacques Arnoult, born 1767; (e) Marie Magdelena Jacinta Arnoult married Nicolas Louis de la Lande de Ferrière in 1793, and (f) Pierre Arnoult married Céleste Beaumont de Livaudais June 1800.

Charles Spinola Waggaman, third son of Col. Eugene Waggaman, married Laura E. Duggan, daughter of Thomas J. Duggan and Aurore Hortense Morgan, sister of H. Gibbs Morgan. She was also a granddaughter of Philip Hickey and closely related to the Mather and Conrad families of Pointe Coupée and Baton Rouge Parishes. Mr. Duggan was a veteran of Fenner's Battery of Civil War fame.

The genealogical data on the Sauvé family by Dimitry, New Orleans Times-Democrat, July 10, 1892, has been extensively corrected and amplified by the Editor with the assistance of members of the family.

DU TILLET—MONTREUIL Families

IN the days of old when the conquering tread of the Crusader was heard under the walls of Acre and along the banks of the brook of Kedron, when the victorious clarions of Godfrey of Bouillon summoned the Saracen to surrender the Holy Sepulchre into the hands of his Christian soldiers, among those goodly hosts in Palestine that followed the pennants of the kings of Europe and of the sovereign dukes of that hemisphere were the ancestors of many Louisiana families.

A Louisiana family of prominence in the state and colony in early days whose ancestors bore a part in the combats of Palestine between the powers of the True and the False, were the du Tillets. Another family was that of de Montreuil, also of noble descent and of distinction in French annals. Concerning the de Montreuils it should be mentioned that the full name of this family is Gautier de Montreuil, as it is recorded on the family tomb in the St Louis cemetery, and as it is displayed on the family coat-of-arms. But in these days the name as borne by the members of the family is simply Montreuil.

The records of the du Tillets, whose ancient manors and estates were in Normandy, not only go back to the year 1332, when five generations of were recorded, but reach the year 1121, the year wherein Guillaume du Tillet, Crusader and Knight of the Order of Saint John of Jerusalem, lived. Following him came Armand du Tillet, Seigneur du Tillet, Knight of the same order as that of the crusading soldier. In 1240 Pierre du Tillet appears on the scene; in 1296 Guillaume du Tillet is of record, and in 1332 mention is made Hugues du Tillet, of the fifth generation from the first Guillaume.

Raimond du Tillet, Seigneur du Tillet, represents the

sixth generation of that name, and four generations later Jean du Tillet, who was secretary to Francis I, king of France, is of record. Four generations still later in the history of this family, or in the year 1764, is found Charles du Tillet, Marquis de la Bussière, Baron de Pontchevon, and *seigneur* of many estates. Dimitry, in concluding the history of the oldest branch of the du Tillets, records four branches of the family being extant, with the mention of Jean Baptiste du Tillet, Marquis de la Bussière, Comte de Nogent, etc., who flourished in 1687. Both the last named du Tillets were councillors in Parliament.

In the second branch, Elie du Tillet, Knight, Seigneur de Gonais, etc., who died in 1608, was councillor and secretary to Charles IX. About 1647, Jean du Tillet, Seigneur of Gonais, etc., was Master of Requests to Queen Marie de Medicis. In the third generation from this Jean du Tillet, Elie Claude de Tillet de Marsay, of the same branch, having given evidence of his nobility, was appointed, in 1744, colonel of the regiment of the *Gardes-Francaises*, but was killed a few months later at the battle of Richevaux, on the Rhine.

The record of the third branch of the du Tillets begins with Jacques du Tillet, Seigneur de Barre and Vicomte de la Malmaison, who was intendent and lieutenant of Paris. Following him were Charles Claude du Tillet de Montremé, Marquis du Tillet, who died without issue. He was a Chevalier of St Louis and colonel of the Royal Regiment.

Jean Leonard du Tillet, who came to Louisiana in 1765 or 1770 and who was the first of the name in the colony, belonged to the fourth branch of this family. This gentleman was seigneur of Aubévie le Terme, la Salel, etc., a councillor to King Louis XV and his brother, the Comte d'Artois, and was their attorney-general in the administration of the forests and rivers of Angoumois. In the year 1763 he was married in the chapel of his chateau at *La Marguerite* to Marguerite du Tillet. Among the du Tillets of her branch were Simon du Tillet, the king's attorney in the seneschal's court of Angoumois, who was Seigneur de Roussellères and married to Marguerite de Lestanche, their daughter in 1773 becoming the wife of the Comte de Béarn-Brassac; Messire Jean du Tillet, Seigneur de Vergnes, etc., *sénéschal* of Suny, Merieres, Chambon, who, by his marriage with Jeanne Tradieu, became the father of Leonard, Henri, and Joseph du Tillet; and Messire Gabriel du Tillet, Seigneur of Tremé, Aubévie, and Gangemont, who was captain of militia and *sénéschal* of Carrieres.

Reverting to the Louisiana branch, it is found that Pierre Dominique du Tillet de Vilhameur, captain of colonial infantry, married Marie Marest de la Tour, their children being (a) Jeanne du Tillet, married to Jean Robin Lacoste, who died in 1781; (b) Charlotte du Tillet, born in 1759, died in 1847, and married to François Pascalis de La Barre, who died in 1827; (c) François du Tillet de Vilhameur who, in 1782, married Marguerite Adélaide Amelot de la Roussilhe, daughter of Hippolyte Amelot de la Roussilhe and Marguerite Saint Cyr du Breuil de Villars.

From this last named marriage issued seven children: (a) Marguerite Félicité Adélaide du Tillet, born in 1783, died in 1863, who married, in 1800, Francois Léander Lacoste, son of Jean Robin Lacoste and Jeanne du Tillet. (b) Marie Félicité du Tillet, in 1811, married Charles Chauvin de Léry, son of François Chauvin de Léry and Constance Le Sassier. (c) Marie Jeanne du Tillet in 1809, married Barthélemy de Montreuil, son of Gaultier de Montreuil and Marthe de Macarty; the husband died in 1834 and the wife in 1854. (d) Pierre Charles Aubévie du Tillet, who took for his first wife, in 1815, Eulalie de Villanueva, daughter of François de Villanueva and Constance Dreux de Gentilly, and whose second marriage with Emily Elizabeth Elliot took place in 1800. (e) Jeanne du Tillet married, in 1812, Louis Ambroise Garidel, and died in 1860; (f) Célestine Eulalie du Tillet, in 1819, married Francois Gutierrez de Arroyo, son of Francois Gutierrez de Arroyo and Genevieve Massicot, and (g) Claire Estelle du Tillet who married Eugene Willoz.

The family of Hippolyte Amelot de la Roussilhe consisted of three children: (a) Marie Félicité, born in 1753, who married Canon de Tréville, her husband disappearing one month after his marriage; (b) Catherine, married to Marquis de Morant, and (c) Marguerite Adélaide, who married, as stated above, François du Tillet de Vilhameur.

Among the marriages of the children of François du Tillet de Vilhameur and Marguerite Adélaide was that of their daughter, Aimée Félicité to Charles Chauvin de Léry from which were born a son and three daughters. The son, Paul de Léry, married Fanélie de Montreuil, daughter of Barthélémy de Montreuil and Adélaide Modeste du Tillet. Of the daughters, Constance de Léry was married to Armand de Montreuil; Modeste de Léry to Auguste de Montreuil, and Emma de Léry married Juhel Renoy.

As has already been pointed out, the Montreuil family, closely related to the du Tillets, is one of the oldest among the colonial families of French origin in Louisiana. In France, also, its record goes back to early times, its members dwelt in Brittany, stronghold of religion and land of valiant hearts.

Among the comrades of Bienville, coming with him from Canada, was Francois Gautier de Montreuil, an officer of the French Marine service, and a native of France, and the ancestor of the Montreuils of Louisiana. A few years after his arrival he resigned from the service, and as a reward for services rendered to the French government he obtained a grant of land in St. Bernard parish. There, after his marriage to Marie Carrière de Montbrum, he lived in retirement. In the possession of the Montreuil family is a document which grants to Robert Gautier de Montreuil and his heirs all the vacant land extending between the limits of his plantation in St Bernard parish and Lake Borgne, reserving for the king of France the right to the timber necessary for the construction of forts, military stores, and other works that had been ordered to be built, or might be ordered built in the future. Provision was also made for other possible requirements of the crown, such as the preparing of vessels and the building of roads and fortifications. The document is dated New Orleans, June 14, 1766, and is signed by Charles Philippe Aubry, *Chevalier de l'Ordre Royal et militaire de Saint-Louis, commandant à la Louisiane*, and countersigned by Foucault, *ordonnateur* of the province.

Robert Gautier de Montreuil married Marie Marthe de Macarty, whose sisters were Mme. Le Breton, the Countess de Miro, and Mme. de la Jonchère. Three daughters resulted from this marriage: (a) Estelle de Montreuil, who became the wife of Laurent Millaudon, and who died at the early age of eighteen; (b) Elmire de Montreuil, who married her sister's husband, and (c) Desirée Gautier de Montreuil who became Mme François Pascalis de La Barre, (q.v.) and the mother of four children.

Charles Gautier de Montreuil, the younger son, married a Mlle. Bellaumé. That branch of the Montreuils is now extinct, its last male representative being the late Jules de Montreuil, who was secretary of a prominent New Orleans insurance agency, which he joined after his return from service in the Army of the Tennessee during the Civil War. The elder son, Barthelémy Gautier de Montreuil, married Adélaide Modeste du Tillet, daughter of François du Tillet de Vilhameur and Amelot de la Roussilhe. Several children were born to that union, among them Hippolyte, who died in 1832 at the chateau of *Mont l'Evéque*, Senlis, near the chateaux of his aunts, the Comtesse de Miro and the Baroness de Pontalba; Armand de Montreuil, who married Constance Chauvin de Léry, daughter of Charles Chauvin de Léry and Aimée du Tillet, and another son, Barthélemy Jr. who married Mlle A. Lacoste.

Auguste de Montreuil, head of the family in 1892, married Modeste Chauvin de Léry and Aimée du Tillet, and their children were: Joseph, who married Marie Gosset and died without issue, and Marie who, in 1881, married Dr. E. J. Mioton. Auguste de Montreuil was for many years cashier of the Bank of Louisiana and was, with his cousin Jules de Montreuil, connected with New Orleans insurance agencies. Other representatives of the elder branch were George de Montreuil and four sisters, children of Armand de Montreuil, and Joseph and Barthélemy, sons of Barthelémy de Montreuil.

The coat-of-arms of the Gautier de Montreuil family displays on a field *or*, a cross *gules*.

The record of the du Tillet-Montreuil families by Dimitry appeared in the New Orleans **Times-Democrat**, July 17, 1892. The present genealogical sketch has been greatly extended by the Editors.

TRUDEAU Family

THE study of philology, especially in the branch devoted to the investigation of the origins and meanings of family names, is a deep and interesting one, for it often happens that in this pursuit one may be called upon to trace the story of a name in which is involved the story of historical events and of the progress of civilization from very remote periods in the past to the present time. Should one follow closely and accurately through its past generations in France, the history of the Trudeau family in Louisiana, which for generations has been a family of approved merit and of conspicuous service to the colony and state, he would be greatly interested in what he would eventually discover.

Many of the Trudeaus of the past signed themselves Trudeau de Longeuil, thus showing their affinity with the knightly family of de Longeuil of France, who are also of the Le Moynes, from whom came the Ibervilles, the Bienvilles, the Chateaugués, the Sauvilles, and the Ste. Hèlenes, of early Canadian and Louisiana memory, and whose head in France bore, in the eighteenth century, the title of count. Among the conspicuous ladies of the French court in the later days of the Regent d'Orléans and the earlier years of Louis XV, was a Countess de Longeuil, whose name sometimes appears in memoirs of those times.

The old form of spelling the patronymic Trudeau was "Trudo," and so it is spelled even now by branches of the family in France. The name Trudo appears on the original picture of the Trudeau coat-of-arms in conjunction with the quarterings of the family of Longeuil (whose coronet of comte surmounts the escutcheon), the Dreux, Macarty, de Carrière, de Lassize, and others, all connections of the Trudeaus in Louisiana. The distinctive armorial device of the

Trudeau family, shows two battering rams. These battering rams and the significant name of Trudo give hint, clear enough to be interpreted without giving much trouble to the inquirer, of the chain of circumstances by which the Trudeau family obtained its name. Associated intimately wtih a battering ram is a suggestion of the days when that ancient implement of warfare was used in the sieges of walled cities and of moated castles. In one of these sieges, perhaps during the crusades, a cadet of the house of Longeuil penetrated with battering rams the walls of a besieged city, making a breach through which his companions-in-arms entered. Adopting subsequently, in commemoration of this achievement, two battering rams as his device, he assumed also the motto "*Trudo*," a Latin word, meaning simply, "I thrust." Later his posterity added the motto to their family name, styling themselves Trudo de Longeuil, in order to distinguish themselves from others of the de Longeuil family. Therefore, Trudo became Gallicized into its present form of Trudeau And so it is that in this name, as in the family of Le Breton, survives the heroic story of a courageous exploit of a historic past.

According to the records of the Trudeau family of Louisiana, it appears that M. Alexandre Trudeau of Canada, who was married in 1668, had a son named François, who became the spouse of Jeanne Burel and had several sons, one of whom was named Jean. In a letter written by René Trudeau of Jefferson parish to his son Dr. James D. Trudeau, under date of August 6, 1846, a few days before the writer's death, he set down: "My grandfather was a Canadian. His name was Jean Trudeau. He studied for the priesthood, but as that condition did not suit him, he went among the Indians in order to finish his education by learning their language. He came to Louisiana holding the rank of lieutenant or captain, having as companions on the voyage, Messrs. de Villeré, Le Blanc, de la Frénière, and a large number of others who had fought bravely for France.

"Jean Trudeau continued his system of education by living among the Indians, and soon became proficient in Western native languages. He finished his studies in the Indian languages among the Chickasaws and Choctaws, the knowledge thus acquired securing for him the appointment of interpreter general and Indian commissioner.

Jean Trudeau, the Indian agent, took for his first wife a Mlle. de Carrière, a name as well known in Canada as that of Trudeau, by whom he had four sons: Jean Trudeau, named for his father; Carlos Laveau Trudeau, better known by his middle name, who became a surveyor general of Louisiana; De Burel Trudeau, who went to Spain when the Spanish troops left Louisiana and was killed at the siege of Pampeluna while holding the rank of colonel in the Queen's regiment; and Zénon Trudeau, the youngest of the quartette of sons, who became a lieutenant colonel in the Louisiana regiment and at one time, during the Spanish domination, was lieutenant governor of the territory called Upper Louisiana, being one of the two of French birth holding that appointive officer. Jean Trudeau, Sr., took for his second wife a Mlle. de Macarty, by whom he had a son, Felix, and a daughter, Fanchonette, neither of whom married.

Jean Trudeau, the second, who was known in his days as "the Chesterfield of Louisiana," married Félicité du Breuil de Villars, the grandmother of Claude du Breuil de Villars, Gaston de Villars, Paul E. de Villars, and C. A. de Villars. The children of Jean and Félicité were: (a) Jean Louis Trudeau, (b) Félicité Trudeau, who married Louis Dreux de Gentilly; (c) Josephine Trudeau, who married Thomas Power, and (d) Aurore Trudeau, who married her cousin Du Breuil Bernard de Villars. Jean Trudeau II died on his plantation known as the Butler Kenner place.

Carlos Laveau Trudeau, second son of Jean Trudeau and Mlle. de Carrière, married Charlotte Peyraud and they became the parents of four daughters. (a) Caroline Trudeau, who married Thomas Urquhart; (b) Célestine Trudeau, who married General James Wilkinson; (c) Joséphine Trudeau, who became Mme. Andry, and (d) Mannette Trudeau, who married Doctor Kerr.

Zénon Trudeau, fourth son of Jean Trudeau and Mlle. de Carrière, was married in 1781 to Eulalie de Lassize, daughter of Chevalier Nicholas de Lassize. To them were born eight children, among whom René Trudeau, the oldest,

[94]

a planter in Jefferson parish, married Adéle Sauvé, daughter of Pierre Sauvé (q. v.).

The other children of Zénon Trudeau and Eulalie de Lassize were: Felix Zénon Trudeau, Emile Trudeau, Valéry Trudeau, Eulalie Trudeau, who married John Watkins; Aurore Trudeau, who became the wife of George Mather, and Caroline Trudeau, who married Robin de Logny.

René Trudeau's children were: Célestine (Mrs. W. H. Leverich), James de Berty Trudeau, Adelma Trudeau, Zénon Trudeau, and Mathilde Trudeau, all of whom, with the exception of Zénon, left posterity.

James de Berty Trudeau, elder son of René Trudeau and Adéle Sauvé, best known as Doctor Trudeau, but sometimes spoken of as General Trudeau, for he was distinguished in his day in the three-fold capacity of physician and surgeon, officer of artillery, and ornithologist and scientist, was one of the most learned, accomplished, and many-sided man, intellectually, that Louisiana ever produced. To say that he stood in the front rank of his profession as physician and surgeon scarcely gives accurate comprehension of the varied intellectual powers he displayed throughout a long, active, and useful life, which ended in New Orleans May 25, 1887.

Doctor Trudeau was born September 14, 1817. His parents sent him to Europe to receive his education, and he matriculated first at the College of Louis-le-Grand where he remained until sickness necessitated a change of climate. He then finished his education at a military school in Switzerland. Later he began the study of medicine in Paris. He continued his study of medicine in Philadelphia in 1835 under Doctor Pancoast. For several years after becoming a physician he studied in New York and frequently visited Europe. At this time of his career he became acquainted with John James Audubon, the celebrated ornithological artist, and frequently supplied Audubon with rare species of birds, Audubon naming several of these newly discovered species after Trudeau, notably the Trudeau Tern, a species of sea bird taken by the physician at Great Egg Harbor, New Jersey. Doctor Trudeau named a woodpecker he killed near New Orleans in April of 1837, after Audubon. Among Doctor Trudeau's many accomplishments was an ability to paint in watercolors and many of the birds he collected were painted by him. Several specimens of his skill in this direction were for years in the possession of his widow, Mrs. Louise Bringier Trudeau. Audubon's son, John Woodhouse Audubon, painted a full length portrait of Doctor Trudeau in Indian costume for during some of his wanderings in the West Doctor Trudeau spent a number of months among the Osage Indians, who esteemed him highly.

In 1861 Doctor Trudeau was a general commanding the Louisiana Legion in New Orleans, and wrote and published a treatise on the defense of New Orleans. As a brigadier general in the Confederate Army he was severely wounded at the Battle of Shiloh, and in 1863 he was captured by the Federal forces but was paroled to remain on *Houmas* plantation in Ascension parish, then the property of A. S. Bringier. When the war between the states ended he returned to New Orleans where he practiced until a short time before his death.

Doctor Trudeau was twice married. His first wife was Céphise Berger of New York. From this marriage he had a son and daughter, the latter marrying a Doctor Roberts of Brooklyn, New York. His son, Dr. Edward Livingston Trudeau also became a physician of eminence and established and conducted a hospital for those afflicted with tuberculosis in the Adirondack Mountains in New York state. Dr. James de Berty Trudeau's second marriage, which took place in 1863, was with Miss Louise Bringier, the daughter of M. S. Bringier and Augustine Tureaud, who was the daughter of Judge A. D. Tureaud of St. James parish, and Elizabeth Bringier, whose father was the owner of the princely *La Maison Blanche*, usually called "White Hall," plantation in St. James parish, noted for its Italian villa type of architecture. There were no children by this marriage.

Resuming the record of the children of René Trudeau and Adéle Sauvé, it should be noted that their daughter Adelma, sister of Dr. James de B. Trudeau, married Louis Gay-Lussac of France, son of the celebrated chemist and aeronaut Gay-Lussac, whose name is recorded in scientific annals concerning early aeronautics. Their children were: (a) Louise Gay-Lussac, who married a M. Beaumelou of

France; (b) Henry Gay-Lussac, who became a French naval officer and married Mlle. Veviale; (c) Marie Gay-Lussac, who became the wife of Edmond Luner, and Jules Gay-Lussac, who followed his grandfather's profession—that of chemist.

Zénon Trudeau, second son of René Trudeau and Adéle Sauvé, was a distinguished lawyer of New Orleans, having studied abroad with his brother Doctor Trudeau. He died unmarried.

Mathilde Trudeau, second daughter of René Trudeau and Adéle Sauvé, married Colonel Alfred Collard and became the mother of Lucie Collard, Fanny Collard, Therese Collard, and René Collard.

Célestine Trudeau, third daughter and youngest child of René Trudeau and Adéle Sauvé, who married William Henry Leverich. She became the mother of an only child, Adéle Leverich, who married Claude Albert du Breuil de Villars, and her children were: René, Alice, Henry, Albert, Adéle, Marie, Jeanne, Regina, and Adolphe de Villars.

The Trudeau genealogical records as set down by Dimitry are to be found in the New Orleans Times-Democrat, August 21 and 28, 1892. The present data has been considerably corrected.

Trudeau coat-of-arms

LABARRE Family

AT a period during the eighteenth century in the history of the colony of Louisiana when the French still held possession of the land, there came from Canada one Francois Pascalis de Labarre (or de la Barre). This gentleman was the founder of the Louisiana family of that name which has distinguished itself in the annals of the colony and state by producing in its successive generations, courteous and chivalric men, and amiable, graceful and witty ladies.

The Labarre family belongs to a house of ancient nobility in French Flanders, a branch of which established itself circa 1330, at Beauce, to which belong the Louisiana Labarres. In Flanders, previous to the year mentioned, several members of the family were high bailiffs in the city of Ghent, and one of the name attained the dignity of soverign bailiff of Flanders, an office bearing with it, like that of the lawgivers of Athens, or the doges of Venice, almost kingly authority.

The Beauce branch, records of which are given in volume VIII of M. Delachennaye-Desbois' *Dictionnaire de la Noblesse* (Paris, 1774), furnishes a story of equal dignity from the time of its establishment there in 1330, in the person of Guillaume de Labarre, Chevalier and Seigneur de Chauvincourt, who married Robine d'Orval, a lady of noble family, down to Alexis Thibault Gaspard de Labarre of Canada, of the fourteenth generation from the Seigneur de Chauvincourt of Beauce. He was the son of Joseph François de Labarre, Seigneur de Laage in Poitou, Chevalier de Saint Louis, and captain in the regiment of Richelieu in 1731, who married, on January 16, 1738, Marie Jeanne de Blom, daughter of Messire Silvain de Blom, Chevalier and Seigneur de Beaupuy in Poitou. They had four children: (a) Alexis Thibault Gaspard de Labarre, the oldest; (b) Henri Thibault de Labarre de Laage, who attended as a pupil the Royal Military school, and subsequently became a cornet in the regiment of Dragoons of Lamant; (c) Marie Dorothée de Labarre, who became the wife of M. de Véry, Marquis de Villeneuve; and (d) Victoire de Labarre, another daughter who died while a pupil in the Royal Academy of Saint-Cyr: "Alexis Thibault Gaspard de Labarre, Seigneur de Laage," says the mémoire in the *Dictionnaire de la Noblesse*, "first a page to Louis XV, later captain-commandant of the Regiment of Huzzars of Chamborant, married Genévieve Léveque, Américaine." The term *Américaine* here evidently indicates a lady of Canadian birth. Thus Alexis and his wife Genévieve appear to have been the immediate direct ancestors of François Pascalis de Labarre, originally of Canada and, subsequently, established in Louisiana.

It were an interesting task to follow in detail the knightly and chivalric story of this important Labarre family in its three branches in France, to wit, the lines of the Seigneurs d'Arbouville, the Seigneurs de la Chaussée of Nivernois, and the Seigneurs de Laage of Poitou (to which last branch belong the Louisiana Labarres) but, as it is, we can only glance at the fourteen recorded generations from the first Guillaume de Labarre of Beauce, to that of Alexis Thibault Gaspard de Labarre of Canada—generations which, through more than four centuries, included among their members men bearing the titles of marquis and viscount, knights, chevaliers, seigneurs of villages, officers of the army, *mousquetaires* of the king, chamberlains, and other officers of the royal French households.

The arms of the Labarre family are given as: *Argent*, with a bar *azure*, charged with three shells *or*, and accompanied with two blackbirds *sable*, (which would seem to indicate a crusading ancestor) in the chief and at the point. Two lions form the support of the escutcheon.

François Pascalis Labarre, who was the first in Louisiana, held during the Spanish domination the office of *alguazil mayor*, or "high sheriff." He thus was one of the most important members of the administration of colonial affairs appointed by the colony's executive. From his marriage with Charlotte Volant, daughter of the Chevalier Grégoire Volant commanding the fourth company of the Swiss Regiment of

Karly in Louisiana, Volant becoming henceforth a quasi-family name among the Labarres, were born four children. (a) François Pascalis de Labarre, Jr., born about 1760, died in 1815; (b) Pierre Volant de Labarre, born 1762, died 1838; (c) Aimée de Labarre, who married Antoine Bienvenu; and (d) Marie Marthe de la Barre, who married François Joseph la Molère, infantry officer ni Louisiana, and son of Joseph La Molère d'Orville, ancient captain and adjutant major of New Orleans, and Marie Simarre de Bellisle.

François Pascalis de Labarre, Jr., married Charlotte du Tillet, by whom he had four sons and six daughters. His oldest son (who bore the father's and grandfather's name) was born in 1783, and died in 1843. He married Désirée Gautier de Montreuil, a daughter of Robert Gautier de Montreuil and Marthe de Macarty; the second daughter, Uranie de Labarre, born in 1785, died in 1864, married Alexandre Devince Bienvenu; Amédée de Labarre, the third daughter, born 1787, died 1833, was the wife of Ludger Fortier; the fourth daughter, Céleste de Labarre, born 1790, died 1863, married her first cousin François Lacestière de la Barre, son of Pierre Pascalis Volant de Labarre and Mlle. Louise Constance Huchet de Kernion; Marie Mélicerte de Labarre, the fifth daughter, who married J. B. Francois Le Breton, was born in 1791, and died August 16, 1823; the sixth child, a son, Pierre Lacestiere de Labarre, born March 11, 1793, died March 20, 1858, married Aimée Sarpy, daughter of Lille Sarpy and Mlle. Cavalier; Delphine de Labarre, the seventh child, born in 1795, died in 1818 or '19, was also married but left no children; Valsin de Labarre, the eighth child, born 1797, died in 1826, married Virginia Conrotte, to whom was born a son also named Valsin, who died previous to 1890, and by his death this branch became extinct; (i) Adélaide de Labarre, the ninth child born 1799, died 1832, by her marriage with Zénon Foucher, became the mother of a son and three daughters; (j) Edmond de Labarre, the tenth and last child died at the age of sixteen.

Pierre Pascalis Volant de Labarre, second son of the first François Pascalis de Labarre and Mlle. Volant, took for his first wife, on September 5, 1783, Louise Constance

Huchet de Kernion. Two sons were born to them: François Pascalis Lacestière de Labarre, who married his first cousin, Charlotte Céleste de Labarre, from which marriage were born three sons: Pierre Pascalis de Labarre, Murville Volant de Labarre, and Jean Lacestière de Labarre. The second son, Jean Baptiste Volant de Labarre, born in 1790, died in 1843, married Philomise de Léry, and from this marriage were born several children, among them being a son Michel, who died in 1856 unmarried. This branch is now extinct on the male side. Pierre Pascalis Volant de Labarre, at the death of his first wife, Mlle. Huchet de Kernion, married Rosine de Léry, and two sons and three daughters were born of this union. The eldest son, Valcour de Labarre, born 1804, died 1880, married his second cousin, Désirée de Labarre. Of their children, Léontine, the oldest, married M. Maillé; the second daughter became the wife of Senor Alminiana, Spanish consul in New Orleans who later returned to Spain; the third child, a son, Clement de Labarre, married Mlle. Bouligny; the fourth child, George de Labarre, married Virginie Hubbard and died childless, while a fifth child, Alice de Labarre, was not married.

Marie Célestine Roséide Volant de Labarre, second child of Pierre Volant de Labarre and Rosine de Léry, born in 1815, died in 1845, first married Pierre Ladislas Guermeur Huchet de Kernion. To them were born six daughters, three of whom died in their youth. Those surviving were: Marie Célestine de Kernion, who became the first wife of Charles Le Breton; Charlotte Emilie de Kernion, died unmarried, and Marie Roséide de Kernion, who married Charles Le Breton after the death of her sister, his first wife. Marie Celestine Roséide de Labarre, the widow of Pierre Ladislas Guermeur Huchet de Kernion, married J. B. François Le Breton, a son of Barthelemy Francois Le Breton and Jeanne Marguerite de Boré, but had no children by this union.

Aimée de Labarre, third child of Pierre de Labarre and Rosine de Léry, born in 1807, died in 1853, by her marriage with François Joseph Le Breton had several children, most of whom died in infancy. Those surviving were daughters: Adalise Le Breton, the eldest, became the wife of James Hopkins; Eliska Le Breton, married Ovide De Buys; Cécilia Le Breton, married D. H. Hubbard, and the fourth, Léonie Le Breton, became the wife of Onésime Robert.

Nelson de Labarre, fourth child of Pierre de Labarre and Rosine de Léry, born in 1809, died in 1851. He married Estelle Le Breton d'Orgenoy. Two children survived this marriage, a son, Pierre Volant de Labarre, who married a Miss Schmidt, and a daughter, Anais de Labarre, became the wife of Lacestière Volant de Labarre, son of Murville de Labarre and Mathilde Rivard.

The fifth and last child of Pierre de Labarre and Rosine de Léry, Ezilda by name, born in 1823, died in 1849, married James Hopkins, who later married Adalise Le Breton.

Continuing the genealogy of the oldest branch of the Labarre family, namely the posterity of Francois Pascalis de Labarre (the oldest son of the second Francois Pascalis and Charlotte du Tillet) it is found he married Desirée Gautier de Montreuil, from which marriage were born four children, the oldest, Desirée de Labarre, married her cousin Valcour de Labarre. The second child, a son also, François de Labarre, born in 1818, died in 1867, married Delphine Pollock, and had four children: Lélia de Labarre, who married Delphine Mayronne; Marie de Labarre, who married Captain Adolphe Chalaron; Charles de Labarre, who married Jeanne Durel, and died without posterity, and James de Labarre who did not marry.

The second son of François Pascalis de Labarre by his marriage with Charlotte du Tillet, was named Pierre Lacestière de Labarre, who married Aimée Sarpy. Three sons and one daughter reached maturity. The oldest son, Pascalis de Labarre, born May 18, 1817, died in 1880, was twice married, his first union being with Aménaide Labranche, daughter of Louis Labranche and Céphise Piseros, two children issuing from this marriage: Céphise de Labarre, who married Fernand Chalard, and Louis de Labarre, born in 1843, who died a few years after his return from the Civil War. Pascalis de Labarre espoused in second nuptials Célina Le Breton des Chapelles, daughter of Gabriel Le Breton and Zoé Fortier, but left no children by this marriage. Pascalis de Labarre was a resident of St Charles parish for several years and after his removal to Jefferson parish was elected its sheriff.

The second son of Pierre Lacestière de Labarre and Aimée Sarpy was Pierre de Labarre, born in 1820 and died in 1888, who married Louise Labranche, daughter of Similien Labranche and Hénriette Foucher, and of their children who reached maturity, the oldest, Pierre Lacestière de Labarre, married Ronuald Labranche. The second son of Pierre de Labarre and Louise Labranche, named George Pascalis de Labarre, married a Miss Putnam of Vicksburg, Mississippi, and had several children. Hénriette de Labarre, the third child of Pierre de Labarre and Louise Labranche, married a Mr. Dupuy of Iberville and later removed to Florida. Pierre Labarre and Louise Labranche left three other daughters, Amélia, Andrea, and Gabrielle de Labarre. Their third son, Antoine Lacestière de Labarre, born in 1825, married Elina Pollock, a daughter of Thomas Pollock and Arthémise Sarpy. His surviving children were: (a) Edmond de Labarre, born 1847, died 1882, who married Adéle Tuyès, daughter of Jules Tuyès by his first marriage to Célestine Pemberton. He died leaving four daughters: Jennie, the oldest; Marguerite, the *cadette;* Célestine, the third, and Adéle, the youngest. Octave de Labarre, second son of Antoine La Lacestière Labarre, married Clara Massicot, and three children were born of this union. Alphone de Labarre, the third son of Antoine Lacestière de Labarre and Elina Pollock, was unmarried. The daughters of Antoine and Elina were Marie de Labarre and Arthémise de Labarre.

The fourth child of Pierre Lacestière de Labarre and Aimée Sarpy, married her first cousin, Marmand Bienvenu, son of Alexander Devince Bienvenu and Uranie de Labarre, who was the sister of Pierre Lacestière de Labarre. Their five children were Robert Bienvenu, Lacestière Bienvenu, Corinne Bienvenu, who married a Mr. Calonge; Marie Bienvenu, who married Albert Bienvenu, and Alma Bienvenu, not married.

Antoine Lacestière de Labarre was the great-grandson of the first François Pascalis de Labarre by his marriage with Charlotte Volant. He served with the Army of Tennessee in the calvary company commanded by Captain Guy Dreux. Lacestière Volant de Labarre, a cousin of A. L. de Labarre, was of the second branch of the Labarre family. He was born in 1838, and was the great-grandson of Pierre Volant de Labarre, who died in Virginia in the service of the Confederacy. He was the son of Murville Volant de Labarre and Mathilde Rivarde, one of whose sisters married the father of Dr. Frank J. Taney, whose first wife was a Miss Clarkson, and who in second nuptials married Valentine Sauvé. Lacestière Volant de Labarre's father was a lawyer in New Orleans. His wife was Anaïs Volant de Labarre, daughter of Nelson Volant de Labarre, a rice planter of Jefferson parish, and Estelle Le Breton d'Orgenoy. Valcour de Labarre was a brother of Nelson de Labarre and together they operated a brickyard above Gretna, and today, in the lower part of the city, still may be seen the imprint of "Labarre" on many of the bricks composing the aged *banquettes*. Two sons of L. V. de Labarre were: Murville Volant Labarre, a New Orleans merchant of the '90s, and Charles Labarre, who studied law in the offices of Moise & Kahn. Louise Labarre was an unmarried sister of L. V. de Labarre. Another sister, Alice Labarre, married a Mr. Escoffier, and had two sons, Fernand and George Escoffier, and a daughter, Louise, who entered the Order of Marianites of the Holy Cross and became sister Mathilde.

The oldest member of the second (or Volant) branch of the Labarre family in 1892 was François Volant de Labarre, who became a planter of Assumption parish. By his marriage with Euphrosyne Schmidt, daughter of Gustave Schmidt and Mélanie Sèghers, and sister of Charles Schmidt, a one-time well known lawyer of New Orleans, he had several children: Nelson Labarre, Gustave Labarre, Frederick Labarre, Amélie Labarre, who married a Mr. Barlow, and Mélanie Labarre, who became Sister Marguerite Mary at St. Joseph's Convent.

Pierre Lacestière de Labarre and his brother George Pascalis de Labarre were sons of Pierre de Labarre and Louise Labranche. The elder brother married Romuald Labranche, and the younger Miss Putnam of Vicksburg.

The Labarre genealogy, as written by Dimitry, is to be found in the New Orleans Times-Democrat, September 4 and 11, 1892. The present article has been extensively expanded and corrected.

DUBREUIL DE VILLARS Family

THE first of the Villars to come to Louisiana was Joseph Dubreuil (or du Breuil) de Villars, at one time an artillery captain in San Domingo. After his arrival in the colony along the Mississippi river, he was placed in command of a company of colonial militia and later, in recognition of his duties as king's *commissaire* in Louisiana the title of chevalier together with the cross of the Royal and Military order of St. Louis was conferred upon him in 1736.

This gentleman had the further distinction of being known as the "Croesus of Louisiana," having erected in 1752 the first cotton gin in the colony, and also being the first to engage in sugar making, building for that purpose a sugar house on his plantation. But his granulation of the cane juice was too imperfect to produce sugar, and it was not until forty years later, in 1796, that Etienne de Boré successfully solved the granulating problem, when the manufacture of sugar became one of the colony's major industries.

Joseph Dubreuil de Villars, Chevalier de Saint Louis, occupied many important positions both in Louisiana and the French Indies. He was born in Louisiana in 1744, and it is supposed that his parents came to Mobile or Biloxi in 1716 when three of Crozat's ships arived with a body of troops under Rome and Gonis, together with a number of colonists, among whom was one named Dubreuil. Young Joseph Dubreuil de Villars, (the name Claude appearing only on the document that made him a chevalier) was sent to France to be educated and while a pupil in the royal corps of artillery in 1764, he was commissioned by Louis XV a second lieutenant in a company of cannoneers and bombardiers at Boullive-Bonneveaux in Guadaloupe. He was promoted, successively, in the course of thirty years service, from lieutenant to commandant of a regiment of artillery, brevet major, and finally lieutenant colonel of colonial troops stationed at Léogane in San Domingo.

About 1780 he was appointed *commissionaire*, or commercial agent, of France to represent that country in trading matters with the Spanish colony of Louisiana and it was while in this service he received the coveted decoration of the cross of Saint Louis. When disturbances arose in San Domingo as a result of the revolutionary tumult, in France, of 1793, he was sent to Léogane, San Domingo, to assist in preserving order in the disturbed island. His commission as lieutenant colonel, dated Paris, December 20, 1790, signed by Louis XVI, is addressed to the Sieur Joseph Villars Dubreuil. When the Haitian insurrection began, Chevalier de Villars, who adhered to the cause of the fallen house of Bourbon, underwent several exciting experiences during these sanguinary times in San Domingo. He was forcibly banished from the island by two agents of the French Republic (Jacobins, he called them in a lengthy letter describing these events, dated Kingston, Jamaica, 1793) who had been sent to the island to assert the authority of the new-born French republic in San Domingo. Compelled to leave Port-au-Prince on an American ship bound for Philadelphia with two of his children, Eulalie and Dubreuil, he left two others, Villars and Chevalier, on the island. In this enforced exile he was obliged to abandon all his property, including slaves, plantations, etc., to the eventualities of chance.

The voyage to Philadelphia was interrupted by the seizure of the vessel by an English privateersman, which conveyed the captured ship to Kingston, Jamaica. In that town, a short time later, de Villars and others organized an expedition composed of French colonists loyal to the Bourbon cause, the purpose of which was to cooperate with the English when the latter undertook the task of restoring order in San Domingo. The leaders of this expedition were Loppinot, who, by right of office, was commander in chief of the colony, Chevalier de Villars and Montanit, a military officer. Under escort of an English frigate the expedition set sail for a point in San Domingo where the Spanish were established, hoping the latter would aid them in their expedition whose object was, that peace might be restored and confiscated property returned to the French plantation owners. The presence of Loppinot, it was hoped, would cause the remaining white colonists on the island to gather under the white flag of the Bourbons against the *tricolor*, then in the ascendant. The English government at Jamaica supplied them with ammunition.

Chevalier de Villars did not give any details of the after-fortunes of this undertaking, but its promotors shared in the success which eventually gave the English troops temporary control of French San Domingo, as later the Chevalier de Villars acted as member of the Privy Council of the English government at Port-au-Prince. When the English abandoned the island in 1798, de Villars departed with them, going to Louisiana, where lived several of his uncles and aunts. In a letter dated 1798 he mentioned the name of the grandmother of his children as Mme. Livaudais. In another letter, dated July 1, 1808, at Tchoupitoulas, twelve or fourteen miles above New Orleans, he mentions the names of his children, and notes the names of their uncles as being Fleuriau, Livaudais, and Dugué, and their aunts, Trudeau and Dugué. He asks his children not to forget their brother, St. Pé, and their cousins, François Livaudais, and Marigny.

And so, with these parting admonitions of affection and remembrance, the Chevalier Joseph Dubreuil de Villars not long afterwards passed to his enternal rest. His early and most of his subsequent years of manhood had been spent far from the place of his nativity where, under the skies of the tropics, the graceful palm and broad-leaved banana casting their shadows on the white sands bordering southern seas, he had spent many years. His last days were passed in the shade of the spreading live oaks, on the bank of the great river that flowed by the land of the Tchoupitoulas.

Claude Joseph Dubreuil de Villars, called the Sieur Dubreuil, married Marie Payen de Noyan, and from this marriage were born two sons, Claude Joseph de Villars and Louis Dubreuil de Villars. Claude, the elder son, married Catherine Laboulaye. Like his father, he was also a captain in the militia of the colony, and was thus designated in the marriage contract of his daughter, Félicité, dated March 5, 1768, with Jean Trudeau, called in his day the "Chesterfield of Louisiana," and who was the son of the first Trudeau in the colony. The other children of Claude de Villars and Marie Payen de Noyan, were: Joseph de Villars, born in 1744, who married Madame Saint Pé, Louis Dubreuil de Villars, married to Mlle. de la Chaise and Jeanne Dubreuil de Villars, who became the wife of Jean Baptiste Fleuriau. Their elder son, Joseph Dubreuil de Villars became eventually artillery officer in Guadaloupe and San Domingo, and Chevalier de Saint Louis. Louis Dubreuil de Villars, their second son, married Félicité de la Chaise and their six children were: (a) Louis de Villars, married Marie Louise Vallée; (b) Jacques, who did not marry; (c) Rose, who married the Sieur Desalles; (d) Félicité, who married Hypolite Amelot; (e) Raymond, and (f) Joseph Dubreuil de Villars. Members of the branch of Louis de Villars went to St. Louis, Missouri, and many of their descendants populated Missouri and Indiana. There is on record in the year 1770 a Louis Dubreuil de Villars, of St. Louis who was a lieutenant of the Louisiana Batallion stationed there.

The foregoing gives a list of the members of the first and second generations of the Villars family in Louisiana. The frequency of the use of the name Dubreuil by the Villars appears to be cleared in the following memoire written by a member of the Dubreuil family.

"The first of my ancestors on the subject of whom I have information was, Abel Dubreuil, *écuyer*, Sieur des Granges, who married Demoiselle Silvine de Mareuil. The contract of marriage was passed before Gilles Casault, *Notaire tabellion* at Viesur-Naon; the second, Francois Dubreuil, son of the proceeding, écuyer, Sieur de Granges, who married Demoiselle Anne Arrobert, by contract of marriage before Garnier, notary at Montechaume. Louis Dubreuil, son of the foregoing, *écuyer*, Sieur des Augis, who married Demoiselle Claude de Laurens. This contract of marriage was passed August 12, 1624, before Martin Souchet, notary of Gracay. Fourthly, Jacques Dubreuil, son of the foregoing, *écuyer* Sieur de Marchais, parish of Poulaines, election of Romorentin, bailliwick of Berry, Gentleman, who married Francois de Marigny, the marriage contract having been passed May 12, 1653, before Gigot, notary at Gracay.

"This Jacques Dubreuil, by authentic act of September 3, 1668, election of Romorentin, parish of Poulaines, *generalité* of Orléans, is authorized to be inscribed and included in the catalogue of nobles which was to be made and prepared according to, and in conformity with, the decree of the Council of March 22, 1666. The arms authorized by this decree are as follows: *Azure*, two swords, forming a chevron, accompanied with three *fleur-de-lys or*, each one surmounted with a five-pointed star *or*, placed two and one, the whole surmounted with a helmet ornamented with a plume.

"Fifthly, Claude Dubreuil Villars. I do not know exactly the relationship between him and the preceeding. He died in 1756. He married Marie Payen. It is in the person of this Claude Dubreuil Villars that the name of Villars appears for the first time in the papers that I have in my possession. The traditions of my family represent that there is relationship between the Dubreuil and the Villars of the family of the celebrated *Maréchal of France* Louis Claude Hector, duke and Marquis de Villars.

"From the time of Claude Joseph Dubreuil Villars the name Villars always has been retained in the family down to our day. Without prejudice, however, to the name of Dubreuil, this Claude Joseph Dubreuil Villars is the first of the family who appears in Louisiana. It is to be remarked here that I possess several papers, in which my ancestors are named sometimes Dubreuils Villars and sometimes Villars Dubreuil."

According to Dimitry, the connection between the names of Dubreuil and Villars as the family name of the Louisiana Villars, is presumed to have resulted from the latter name becoming attached to the former by the acquisition of an estate called Villars by matrimonial alliance between a Dubreuil and a lady named Villars, and this was a family tradition in New Orleans in 1892 when Dimitry recorded the genealogy of the Villars then living in New Orleans. In the male line they were: J. C. Villars and his brother C. A. Villars, and Paul E. Villars and Gaston Villars, also brothers.

The parents of J. C. and C. A. Villars were Adolphe Dubreuil Villars and Eveline de Léry. Their paternal grandparents, who also bore the same relationship to Gaston and Paul E. Villars, were Bernard Dubreuil Villars and Aurore Trudeau. The parents of Gaston and Paul Villars, were Didier Dubreuil Villars and Cécile Dugué de Livaudais. The children of Bernard Dubreuil Villars and Aurore Trudeau were: (a) Théophile Villars, who married Evéline de Léry; (b) Gaston Villars, whose wife was Adéle Fortier; (c) Aurore de Villars, who married Henry Bouvier Favrot, of the Baton Rouge family of that name; (d) Adolphe Villars, and (e) Didier Villars. Of these children, Théophile Villars by his marriage with Evéline de Lery, became the father of Louis Alcide Villars, Aginé Villars, and Eulalie Villars. Louisé Alcide Villars married Célia Le Breton and their surviving children were: (a) Théophile Villars, who married a Mlle. St. Amand, and had two daughters, Marie and Louise Villars; (b) Alcide Villars, who married Eliza Logan, whose children were: Louise, Edna, and Elize; (c) Cidalise Villars, who married a Mr. Vienne; (d) Octavie, (e) George, (f) Didier, (g) Séphise, (h) Nathalie, Septime, Emma, and Edouard Villars. Aglaé Villars, the second child of Théophile Villars and Evéline de Léry, became a *réligieuse* in the convent of the Good Shepard, St Louis, and Eulalie Villars, the third child, married Jules Sougeron.

Gaston Villars, second son of Bernard Villars, married Adéle Fortier. His eldest daughter became Mrs. Edouard Drouet, and the second daughter, Cidalise, married Théophile Villars, a brother of J. Claude and Albert C. Villars.

Aurore Villars, only daughter of Bernard Villars, by her marriage to Henry Bouvier Favrot, became the mother of Aurore, Joséphine, Octavie, Octavie, Eveline, daughters, and Charles Didier Favrot, who married Miss Kent; Joseph Claude Favrot, who married Miss Williamson, and St Claire Joseph Favrot killed in the Civil War. (q. v. Favrot)

Adolphe Villars, father of Claude and Albert Villars, married Evéline de Léry, who at the time of this marriage was the widow of his brother Théophile. They were the parents of Théophile who married Victoria Curell, whose children were: Fernand, Stella, Ada, Chalmette, who married Miss Tudury, of Bay St Louis, Miss.; Aurore, who married John E. Livaudais, and left nine surviving children, viz, Anais, Gustave, Arthur, Walter, John, and Emilie and Noemie, who became *réligieuses* in the convent of the Good Shepard in New Orleans; Adolphe, who married Fanny Huff; Eliza, who was the first wife of Jules Sougeron, and whose children were, Eveline, George, Marie, Jeanne, Philomene, Nisida, and Louise Sougeron. Eveline married Dr. Thomas Layton and had four children, to wit: Thomas, Eveline, Robert and Buxton Layton. George Sougeron married Georgie Taney, and had two children, Louilda and Lucille. Marie Sougeron married Peter Hyde. Jules Sougeron's second wife was his sister-in-law, Eulalie Villars.

Joseph Claude Villars, by his marriage with Inez Coulon de Jumonville, had nine children, namely: Inez, Aurore, Chevalier, Nathalie, Florence, Dubreuil, Claude, Thomas and Georgie. Adolphe Villars married Ezilda Sougeron, and had four children,—Theodore, Victoria, Berthe, and Eliza.

Claude Albert Villars, younger brother of Joseph Claude Villars, married Adéle Leverich, daughter of William Henry Leverich and granddaughter of René Trudeau, sugar planter of Jefferson parish, and who, through her Leverich kinship, was related to Mrs. W. E. Leverich, Abe Leverich, Mrs. Frank Eshleman, of New Orleans, a niece of Mrs. Samuel Cox of Garden City, and Eliza Jane Leverich. Claude Albert Villars and Adele Leverich had nine children, viz, René, Alice, Henry, Adèle, Albert, Marie, Jeanne, Régina, and Adolphe.

Gaston and Paul E. Villars were sons of Didier Villars and Cecilie Dugué Livaudais. Gaston Villars married Victoria Sougeron. Two children were born of this marriage, Gaston and Evelina, while Paul E. Villars married Caroline Trudeau, and was the father of Carmen, Odessa, and Trudeau Villars.

During the Civil War J. C., Gaston, and C. A. Villars served in the Confederate army.

The Dimitry genealogical sketches of the de Villars family are to be found in the New Orleans **Times-Democrat**, September 25, October 2, 1892. The present record has been considerably revised by the Editors.

FORSTALL Family

O N the escutcheons of families to which, because of their ancient lineage, or on account of services rendered by their founders, armorial bearings have been given, it often occurs that in the arms thus granted a glimpse may be had by one conversant with heraldry, of the origin, the service rendered, or the early conditions of families possessing such suggestive or significant arms. The armorial bearings dating from a remote past of the Forstalls of Louisiana, a family of distinguished personality and which, through many generations of residence in Louisiana has borne itself with loyalty, courage, and honor, suggest an interesting historical beginning.

The Forstall coat-of-arms tells the story of the silver lining to the cloud of one of the gloomiest tragedies in English history—a tragedy wherein a king of England was slain in the forest, shot through the heart with an arrow.

It is with the significant three pheons, or broad-arrows, which constitute the device on the shield of the Forstall coat-of-arms in association with the motto: *In corda inimicorum regis,* "Into the hearts of the King's enemies," that one is introduced to the story of the de Forestier, or le Forestier, family of the twelfth century in England, ancestors of the Louisiana Forstalls, and that are disclosed the dramatic circumstances which preceeded the granting to that family of three arrowheads as their armorial design, together with the loyal motto that accompanies them. The incident referred to is the killing of William, surnamed Rufus, King of England, successor of William the Conqueror, by an enemy while that monarch was hunting in the forest. The agency of death was an arrow, and the king's heart received the shaft, and it seems clear that, because, perhaps, of some personal association in defense of the king on that occasion by a member of the de

Forestier family, or simply as an evidence of the loyalty of that family to the house of Normandy, the tell-tale three arrowheads and the eloquent motto, "Into the heart of the King's enemies," became blended in the de Forestier, now Forstall, coat-of-arms, which in the language of heraldry is described as a field *sable*, with three pheons (arrowheads) *argent*.

The record of the Forstall family from the year 1066 to the time of its arrival in Louisiana presents not less than five removals from one country to another. They changed their skies and climes but not those aspirations in the direction of honor and integrity of purpose which have ever distinguished those who have borne that name.

Among the great Anglo-Norman families which became established in Ireland in the reign of Henry II of England, as far back as the twelfth century, was that of le Forestier, or Forstall, which became possessed of, and long enjoyed, extensive territorial estates in the county of Kilkenny. The first ancestor of the Forstalls in England was William le Forestier, a Norman knight, who crossed the channel with William the Conqueror, A. D. 1066. The first of the name who settled in Ireland was Laurence Le Forestier who was one of the companions in arms of Richard de Clare, surnamed "Strongbow," Earl of Penbroke, in the invasion of that country in the year 1169. Families such as the Forstalls, although bearing no title, had all the attributes of the purest nobility, ancient lineage, distinguished alliance, territorial possessions, the hereditary right to armorial bearings and the highest local station.

According to the register in the office of the Ulster king-of-arms, Dublin Castle, in Ireland, the Forstalls of Louisiana are of descent from Peter Forstall, Esquire, one of the descendants of the Laurence Le Forestier, mentioned above, who are entitled to the armorial devices, the three broad-arrows shown in his coat-of-arms. Peter Forstall, whose will was probated in 1683, married Mary, daughter of Nicholas Aylward, Esquire, of Shankhill, and had several children. His oldest son was Edmond Forstall, of Rinn, Kilkenny, who married Eleanor Butler of Dangan, a descendant of the noble house of Ormonde. They had several sons, all of whom were knights of Jerusalem.

A son, named Edmond, entered the military service of France, holding the rank of captain of dragoons in the army of Louis XIV. In the year 1694 Edmond Forstall married Elizabeth, daughter of Henry Meade, Esquire, of Ballyheale, Kilkenny. From this alliance were born a number of children. Nicholas Forstall, one of the sons, began life in the castle of Gurteen, in 1700. Having attained manhood he became a resident, first, of Nantes, in France, and afterwards of Pierre on the island of Martinique, where he married, in 1725, Jane, daughter of Jean du Barry, *Conseiller du Roi*, in the island of St. Kitts.

The surviving issue of this marriage was a son, Nicholas Michel Edmond Forstall, the first of the name in Louisiana, who removed from Martinique to New Orleans. He was born September 21, 1727, and died in 1808. After assuming residence in New Orleans, he was made commandant of the Opelousas country, and married about 1762 Pélagie de la Chaise, daughter of Jacques de la Chaise, *Garde des Magasins du Roi*, and Marguerite d'Arensbourg, she was also the granddaughter of Jacques de la Chaise, who arrived in the colony of Louisiana in 1722, and the Chevalier Charles Frederic d'Arensbourg.

By this marriage Nicholas Forstall had seven children.

1.—Edouard Pierre Charles Forstall, born August 14, 1768, who married Céleste de la Villebeuvre and left six children.

2.—Elizabeth Louise Forstall, married to J. B. Poeyfarré, after whom Poeyfarre street in New Orleans was named. She left no descendants.

3.—Edmond Forstall, born July 16, 1776, who died January 18, 1802. He married Marguerite Adélaide Joséphine Mélanie de Morant, born June 6, 1786, died February 1831. They left four children.

4.—Felix Martin Forstall, born November 24, 1780, married Marie Céleste Fabre d'Aunoy and left four children.

5.—Louis Edouard Forstall, born November 28, 1802, not married.

6.—Emérante Forstall, who married Jacques Montplaisir Chauvin de Léry and left four children.

7.—Mélanie Forstall, unmarried.

Nicholas Michel Edmond Forstall was a man of importance and influence in the colonial affairs of Louisiana. When the control of that colony passed from the hands of France to those of Spain and Count O'Reilly took possession of the province as governor, the *Cabildo* replaced the Superior Council of the French colony, and was composed of two *regidors*, six *alcaldes*, an attorney general and a clerk, over whose deliberations the governor presided. The two *regidors* were choosen annually on the first day of the year and were, individually and by virtue of their office judges within the city in civil and criminal cases. Nicholas Forstall was chosen *alcalde* for the years 1771, 1774, 1801 and 1803.

The first branch of the Forstall family is represented in the posterity of Edouard Pierre Charles Forstall, who married Céleste de la Villebeuvre, daughter of Jean Louis Fidel Farault de la Villebeuvre, Chevalier de Garrois, and Jeanne d'Arby. The family of la Villebeuvre is among the most honorable and justly esteemed families of Louisiana. Six children were born of this union: (a) Edmond John Forstall, born November 7, 1794, who married Clara Durel; (b) Francis Placide Forstall, born September 30, 1796, who married Delphine Lopez; (c) Felix Jean Forstall, born November 24, 1800, who married Héloise De Jan; (d) Louis Edouard Forstall, born November 25, 1802, who married Mathilde Plauché; (e) Eliza Forstall, who became the wife of Delphin Villeré, and (f) Belzire Forstall, who was the wife of Z. Ben Canonge.

Edmond John Forstall, the oldest of these children, by his marriage to Clara Durel, became the father of four sons and five daughters: (a) Eugene Forstall, who married Lise Cantrelle; (b) Victor Forstall, who married a Mlle. de la Villebeuvre; (c) Henry Forstall, who married Mildred Plauché; (d) Ernest Forstall, who took for his wife Mathilde Taney; (e) Oscar Forstall, who married Mlle. St. Maurice

Bérault; (f) Désirée Forstall, who became the wife of Charles Roman; (g) Eugénie Forstall, who married Valérien Chopin; (h) Héléna Forstall, who married Adolphe Schreiber; (i) Leda Forstall, who married Charles Olivier, and (j) Anna Forstall, who became the wife of Arthur Polk.

François Placide Forstall, the second son of Edouard Forstall and Céleste de La Villebeuvre, married Marie Francisca de Borgia Delphine Lopez y Angullo de la Candelaria, a daughter of Don Ramon Lopez y Angullo le la Candelaria, a high ranking Spanish officer, and Delphine de Macarty, of the distinguished Louisiana family of that name. Placide Forstall's wife, best known by one of her given names, Delphine, became the mother of nine children. She was also nicknamed *Borquita* due to the fact she was born on shipboard when her mother was returning to Louisiana from Spain where she had gone to successfully plead with the king to save her husband from military punishment. The nine children of Placide Forstall and *Borquita* Lopez y Angullo were: (a) Anatole J. Forstall, who married Pauline Gelpi; (b) Oscar Forstall, who married his cousin Louise Forstall; (c) Céleste Forstall, oldest of the beautiful and accomplished Forstall girls, who married Henry Alaston Rathbone; (d) Emma Forstall, who married Emile de Buys; (e) Pauline Forstall, who became the wife of Eugene Peychaud; (f) Laure Forstall, who was the wife of Felix Ducros; (g) Julia Forstall, who married Robert J. Tanney, a grandnephew of a chief justice of the United States Supreme Court; (h) Adéle Forstall, who married Jules Lemore, and (i) Delphine Forstall, who never married.

Céleste Forstall, by her marriage to Henry Alaston Rathbone became allied with a distinguished New England family. Her husband was the son of Samuel Rathbone of Stonington, Connecticut, a descendant of Samuel Rathbone. Henry A. Rathbone came to New Orleans sometime after the Battle of New Orleans, and by his marriage with a daughter of the Forstalls became an integral part of the exclusive Créole social circle of that day. The Rathbone home in Esplanade avenue, presided over by the charming and brilliant Céleste Forstall Rathbone, became the center of many social activities. The children of this marriage were five daughters: (a)

Emma Rathbone, who became the wife of John B. de Lallande de Ferrières; (b) Pauline Rathbone, who married Peter Labouisse; (c) Stella Rathbone, who became the wife of James Gaspard de Buys; their sons were Rathbone de Buys, James Gaspar de Buys, Walter de Buys and Dr. Lawrence R. de Buys, well known in New Orleans; (d) Alice Rathbone, who married William Phelps Eno of New York, and (e) Rita Rathbone, the youngest of the five lovely Rathbone sisters, who married Edgar de Poincy.

Louis Edouard Forstall, born of the Forstall-Lavillebeuvre union, by his marriage with Mathilde Plauché, daughter of the distinguished commander of the *Batallion d'Orléans*, General J. B. Plauché, was the father of Emilie Forstall, who married Charles D. de Lassus; Amanda Forstall, who did not marry, and George Forstall who married a Miss Maurin.

From the union of Jean Felix Forstall, a fourth son of the Forstall-Lavillebeuvre marriage, and Heloise De Jan, issued six children: Arthur Forstall, Paul Forstall, William Forstall, Suzanne Forstall who married Mr. Duplantier; Angèle Forstall, who married Emile Duplantier, and a third daughter married to Octave Forstall.

Belzire Forstall, daughter of Edouard Forstall and Céleste Lavillebeuvre, who married Z. Ben Canonge, was the mother of Rosa Canonge, who became the wife of George Binder, and Cora Canonge, not married, who lived and died in Paris.

Eliza Forstall, a sister, married to Delphine Villeré, was the mother of two sons: Edouard Forstall Villeré, whose wife was Marie Bouligny, and Placide Forstall Villeré, who married Miss Cantrelle.

From Felix Edmond Forstall, born July 16, 1776, died January 18, 1846, the second son of Nicholas Michel Edmond Forstall, the first in Louisiana, and Pélagie de la Chaise, is derived the second branch of the Forstall family. He was at one time connected with the United States Mint in New Orleans, and married, June 11, 1805, Marie Marguerite Adélaide Joséphine de Morant, born June 6, 1786, died February 1831, the daughter of Charles de Morant and Catherine Amelot. Their children were: (a) Coralie Forstall, who married Gustave Durel; (b) Elmina Forstall, who married Anatole Villeré, and became the mother of

Alcée J. Villeré, Alfred L. Villeré, and Henriette Villeré;
(c) Ophélia Forstall, who married Theodore Penneguy, and
was the mother of Marie Penneguy, who married Mr. de
Livaudais; William Penneguy and Alfred Penneguy; (d)
Alfred Forstall, their only son, married Célestine Fletcher,
a granddaughter of Joseph Roy de Villeré, and became the
father of Théobald Forstall and Numa Forstall, the former
leaving several children who resided in Chicago.

The third branch of the Forstall family is of descent from
Felix Martin Forstall, third son of Nicholas and Pélagie de
la Chaise, who was born in New Orleans March 10, 1781.
He married, November 25, 1806, Marie Celeste Favre
d'Aunoy, daughter of Charles Favre d'Aunoy and Catherine
de Macarty. Their children were: (a) Charles Edouard
Forstall, born August 24, 1810, died August, 1892, who
married Marguerite Elizabeth de Poincy, daughter of Paul
Rossignol Desdunes de Poincy, whose mother was a daughter
of the Comte d'Aquin by his wife Louise Allemand of
Charleston. They had an only son, Charles Oscar Eugéne
Forstall, born November 28, 1831, who later in life resided
in Paris. Their second child was a daughter, Célestine For-
stal, who married Adolphe Durel, and whose descendants
were Céleste Durel, second wife of Paul de Poincy and
Marie Durel, Paul de Poincy's first wife. The third child
was a daughter, Rosa Forstall, who married Edouard Le
Beau, by whom she had three children: Edgar Le Beau,
who lived in New Orleans, and two daughters who lived
abroad, one becoming the wife of Count de Seminiatelli of
Italy. The fourth child of Felix Forstall and Marie d'Aunoy
was Estelle Forstall who married Edouard Tricou, and
whose only child, a daughter, married Dr. Henry d'Aquin,
and at her death left a daughter, Mrs. Allain, who resided
with her husband in Paris.

The fourth branch of the posterity of Nicholas Edmond
Forstall and Pélagie de la Chaise is found in the descendants
of Emérante Forstall, their daughter, who was married, November 2, 1804, to Jacques Monplaisir Chauvin de Léry,
and who left seven children: (a) Eugéne M. de Léry, who
married Emma Toutant de Beauregard; (b) Mlle. de Léry,
wife of Belleviel d'Oriocourt; (c) Irma M. de Léry, who

married J. B. Avequin; (d) Auguste de Léry, who died at eighteen; (e) Lucien de Léry, who died at twenty-one; (f) Athalide M. de Léry, who became the wife of Thomas Jeff. Spear; and (g) Placide de Léry, who died at seven.

Eugéne de Léry, by his marriage to Emma Beauregard had four sons and three daughters; Oscar, Henri, John, and Fillmore de Léry, and Joséphine de Léry, who married Emile Dupré; Anna de Léry, who married A. Luminais, and Louise de Léry, who became the wife of Edgar Bouligny.

Irma de Léry Avequin left no descendants, while Athalide de Léry Spear left a son, Placide J. Spear, and two daughters, Cécile Spear, who married William Surgi, while her sister Lise Spear married Paul Surgi.

The original Dimitry article on the Forstall family appeared in the New Orleans Times-Democrat, October 30, and November 6, pps. 17 and 16. The foregoing account has been considerably amplified by the Editors with the assistance of members of the family.

The Forstall coat-of-arms

ROUQUETTE

NEAR Bordeaux, in France, resided the Rouquettes, a family of distinction, out of which came to Louisiana about the year 1800 Dominique Rouquette to establish in the then Catholic Spanish colony a family which, like its parent stock in distant France, was to enjoy great esteem, consideration and reputation. As among the Rouquettes of Bordeaux, there lived a poet of celebrity who bore the family name, so also have those of Louisiana produced another maker of beautiful verses, Adrien Rouquette, *Chahta-Ima*, poet, priest, and missionary.

Dominique Rouquette, born near Bordeaux, came to New Orleans from France, and engaged in the occupation of wholesale merchant and importer of Bordeaux and other French wines. He married Louise Cousin, daughter of François Cousin, a member of a French family which had been established for some time in Canada previous to the coming to New Orleans of François Cousin, who was the founder of this well-known Louisiana family, and twice married. His first, from which issued the mother of Abbé Adrien Rouquette, and his bother Dominique Rouquette, was with Mme. Carrière, who, at the time of her marriage, was a widow and the mother of two sons, Terrance Carrière, owner of a large brickyard at Bonfouca, and another son, who married and left a large family of sons and daughters, of whom only one bearing the family name of Carrière resided in New Orleans. The children of François Cousin and the widow Carrière were François Cousin, Louise Cousin, who became the wife of Dominique Rouquette, and Céleste Cousin, who married Etienne Reine, of St. Charles parish. In second nuptials, François Cousin married Mlle. Ducré of Bayou Lacombe, St. Tammany parish, from which marriage were born three sons and two daughters, the sons being Anatole Cousin, Terence Cousin, and Adolphe Cousin, all three polished scholars of their day. Anatole Cousin was not only a proficient Greek, Latin, English, and French scholar, but he was also a writer of prose and a poet. Many of the descendants of these three gentlemen live in New Orleans and St. Tammany parish, all of cultured minds. Anatole Cousin studied law in Philadelphia under William Rawle, a celebrated constitutional lawyer of that city. Of the two daughters of François Cousin and Mlle Ducré, one, Eliza Cousin, married M. Levasseur, a Frenchman of distinction.

From the marriage of Dominique Rouquette and Louise Cousin were born four sons and one daughter, Dominique Rouquette, Adrien Rouquette, Adéle Rouquette, who married Louis Donnet; Felix Rouquette, and Terence Rouquette. Dominique Rouquette, the father, died about the year 1818, and his residence, built by himself, was in Royal street, three doors from the Louisiana Bank building. It bore in the iron work of the balcony-railings the initials of the builder "D.R." Louis Donnet, who married Adéle Rouquette, was born in Nantes, France, and went to New Orleans from that city, about 1818. His father, Jean Donnet, served in the army of the first Napoleon, and his mother was a descendant of the family of Rabutin, of France, to which belonged the witty accomplished letter writer of the days of Louis XIV, Mme. de Sévigné. One of his sisters was a wife of M. Duvergé of Nantes. From the marriage of Louis Donnet and Adèle Rouquette were born one son and four daughters. The son was O. L. Donnet, of *l'Abeille de la Nouvelle Orléans.* One of his sisters married Numa Dufour associated with his brother-in-law in *The Bee.*

Dominique Rouquette, Jr., was educated at the College Royal of Nantes, France, where he was noted for his brilliant scholarship and his intellectual powers. About the year 1840, while in Paris, he gave to the world his only book, a volume of poems entitled *Les Meschacébéennes,* and then returned to Louisiana. Until his death in 1890, he lived with relatives at Bonfouca, in St. Tammany parish. He married a daughter of Edouard Verret, and niece of Durcy Verret, whose home was below Algiers. By his marriage he had two sons, one of whom, James, sailed around the world with Admiral Farragut.

Adrien Rouquette, second son of Dominique Rouquette and Louise Cousin, was born in New Orleans, February 26, 1813. He was variously called Abbé Rouquette, and, lastly, by that appelation which he seemed most to cherish, *Chahta-Ima*, meaning "Like a Choctaw." This name being conferred on him by his Choctaw Indian pupils of Bayou Lacombe when he was elected to fellowship by the remnant of that once powerful tribe which, in the unrecorded past of Louisiana, were the lords of the soil.

When he was about ten years old, while his mother was residing on the Bayou Road, at a time when, like a phantom of a forgotten day, the lithe form of the Choctaw, with brass-mounted rifle on his arm and hunting bag slung across his shoulder, might have been seen gazing gloomily into the slowly rising and ebbing tide of the Bayou St John—recalling, perhaps, that hour of colonial Louisiana's *Noche Triste* when his ancestors had marched with their war-chief Alibamon-Mingo to the Natchez country to help the French settlers in their wars against the Natchez Indians, in those years of his early youth, Adrien was the playmate and the friend of the Indian boys of the vicinity. Then, doubtless, was born in his heart that sympathy which led him in after years to devote himself to that work of Christianizing the remnant of the Choctaw tribe in Louisiana, which proved to be the mission of his life. If this work had been decreed in the solemn profundities of a day that was not of this world, therefore, was *Chahta-Ima* called to accomplish it.

Adrien's truant disposition rendering his mother, his surviving parent, as his father had died when he was about five years old, apprenhensive and anxious, he was sent to Transylvania University, in Kentucky, in 1824, when he was just a little more than ten, and later received lessons in a private school near Philadelphia, at a place called Mantua. It was at these places of learning that he obtained his knowledge of English that made him such a renowned and fluent conversationalist in that tongue, and which enabled him in after years to write in that language the poems contained in his *Wild Flowers*. It was 1829 that he went to Paris to round out his education and he studied at the College Royal of Paris and The College Royal of Nantes, until 1833 when he returned from the gay and brilliant associations of France, going first to New Orleans and then seeking the seclusion of the green forests of St. Tammany and the quietude and natural beauty of Bayou Lacombe. He, so he described himself, became "a half savage, and dressed as did the young *Chactas*." He had read with intense interest the *Atala* of Chateaubriand. His heart throbbed with strange feelings at the perusal of the pitiful story of the exiled Natchez, the people of the Eight Villages on the Mississippi. So, in the restful quiet glades lying between Bayou Lacombe and Mandeville he dreamed of a new *Atala*.

Although Adrien Rouquette returned to New Orleans it was not the solitudes of the Bayou Lacombe woods that sent him again to mingle with civilized man, for there are deeper solitudes in towns than those of forest and desert—the human heart, too, has its lonelinesses. His sweetheart, the daughter of a Choctaw chief, was named *Oushola*, meaning "Bird-Singer," died and, from her shell-decorated grave on the shores of that little inland sea called Lake Pontchartrain, Adrien returned to the city of his birth.

Then he went back to Paris, where he made a futile attempt to interest himself in the study of law. As he himself said of it, he found the law "only a weary pell-mell of contradictions and chicaneries." Abandoning law altogether, he once more returned to New Orleans. But again he was restive, and once more crossed the ocean to Paris in 1842, and there in the gay capital of France published his prose poem *Les Savannes*. It met with a generous welcome; Lamartine, Chateaubriand, Saint-Beuve, Thomas Moore, the Irish poet, and other distinguished writers, praised it. Then followed his *Wild Flowers*, in English, *La Thébaïde* and *L'Antonaïde* poems in French. All these productions of his fervid poetic fancy received their just meed of recognition, the press of the United States uniting to acknowledge the merits of *Wild Flowers*. The other important work of the poet, *La Nouvelle Atala*, appeared in 1879.

In these writings the religious tendencies of his heart and his love of nature were revealed. It was probably enough for him that he should give expression in these books to the emotions of his soul; Adrien Rouquette cared nothing for a merely worldly success. His gaze was more lofty, his aspirations were higher.

While living in Paris, Adrien's mind was resolving itself upon the future of his life. When he went back to New Orleans he felt that the church claimed it. He determined to enter the priesthood and devote himself, as far as might be practicable, to the Christianizing of his old friends, the Choctaws of Bayou Lacombe and the Tchefuncte. He passed his probation at Bayou Lacombe, and in the seminary of Assumption parish he studied theology and the rules of the Catholic Church. Ordained as a sub-deacon in 1844, the year 1845 saw him a priest, having before his mind the long-entertained thought of establishing a mission at the Choctaw village located at the headwaters of Bayou Lacombe. These people he had known and loved from childhood, as he has written; he would take the wild orange tree and he would transform it by grafting, into the sweet orange; these were the thoughts which illumined his heart, as of crystal, with a pious zeal, and although for fourteen years after becoming a priest he served in the St. Louis Cathedral, at New Orleans, as preacher from the pulpit, delivering strong and masterly sermons, he never lost sight of his purpose, which, eventually, although meeting with much opposition from his friends, he carried out in 1859. Monseigneur Odin, vicar apostolic of Texas, cheered and encouraged him when he said to him: "Continue to devote yourself to your Indians; God will bless you and your work."

The Indian community in which Abbé devotedly labored during the remaining years of his life counted only about one hundred souls, a pitiable remnant of the once powerful Choctaw (or *Chata*, as they pronounced their tribal name) Nation, which at one period occupied nearly the whole of the territory of Mississippi and of Louisiana east of the Mississippi river, who could place in the field in time of war as many as twenty thousand warriors. Abbé Rouquette's missions were altogether among the Indians of St. Tammany parish, in Louisiana. He built and dedicated to worship five cabin-chapels, so situated as to provide religious services for the scattered Indian camps or villages. The first constructed was at *Buchuwa*, which was destroyed in 1861; one mile

east of Mandeville was another, called *Chuka-Chaha*, or the
"night-cabin;" the third was two miles west of Mandeville,
on the Covington road, to which was given the name of
Kildara, "the cabin of the oak;" at the Ravine-aux-Cannes,
between Mandeville and Bayou Lacombe, was situated the
fourth, while the last, called "The Nook," by Father Rouquette, and of which chapel he was especially fond, was situated on the banks of the quiet, sloe-black bayou he loved
so well.

Abbé Rouquette was devoted in all things to his Choctaw
friends and pupils—in spiritual as well as in worldly matters.
During the Civil War, when his Indian charges were dying
of swamp fever, the good priest sought out Admiral Farragut, then in the river opposite New Orleans with his fleet,
and appealed to him to be allowed to take back with him to
Bayou Lacombe quinine to save his flock from death. The
noble-hearted seaman gave him a pass and an order which
permitted Abbé Rouquette to cross Lake Pontchartrain with
any quantity of quinine that he desired to take. When the
captain of the Federal gunboat stationed on the lake read
this order he declined to inspect the Abbé's luggage. "With
this order reverend father," he said, "you can cross with a
hogshead of quinine. I do not believe Admiral Farragut
would have given such a pass to any other man." It is not
strange that the officer should have been surprised, for at that
time quinine was of almost fabulous value, as it was a supreme necessity, within the limits of the Southern Confederacy, and it was the policy of the United States in those days
of war to avoid bloodshed by a systematic embargo on
quinine, which might furnish victims to the hospital in preference to the battle field from among the soldiers of the South.

The years of Abbé Rouquette's life, as mission priest of
the Choctaws, may be summed up in a few words. It was a
life of self-denial, of incessant toil. Almost a hermit in the
forests of St. Tammany, in his occasional sojourns in New
Orleans he was a hermit indeed. His home was a small, dark,
meagerly and poorly furnished cell-like room in which books
piled like pyramids on the bare floor broke the monotony
of the dismal scene.

On his journeys to Bayou Lacombe from Mandeville

Chahta-Ima would pause in his walk to sleep under the floor of one of his little chapels, built on piles. Rolled up in his blanket, "like a Choctaw," he reposed on the hard planks; a brick enveloped in moss was his pillow. Unlike that voluptuary of old, who, sleeping on a bed of roses, fretted because a crumpled rose leaf disturbed his slumber, *Chahta-Ima* did not murmur because it pleased God he should thus sleep.

Abbé Rouquette's prose style was powerful, poetic, and graphic, and touched with pathos, like, humanly speaking, that of the prophets. His poetry, spiritual and delicate, breathed the modesty and beauty of one of the wild flowers that spangled the land he loved. In the annals of Louisiana he will be remembered and honored from generation to generation. He died in *Hotel Dieu*, New Orleans, July 15, 1887, having been ministered to in his last sickness by the gentle Sisters of Charity.

"I do not know how deeply and permanently into the hearts of *Chahta-Ima's* pupils have sunk the teachings of his missionary work among them, wrote Charles Patton Dimitry, in 1892, "but I do know that his was a noble voice which cried in the wilderness of St Tammany that a path should be made straight to the Lord—that in the humble chapels and the Indian dwellings of the parish frequent mention is made of the Name of the Most High and His Just One, and that, whereas less than fifty years ago this people, like Israel by the waters of Babylon, sat lamenting their sorrows by the waters of Bayou Lacombe, they sing now a song of joy, like the song of harvesters returning from the fields in the evening, bearing with them their abundant sheaves."

L'Abbé Adrien Rouquette's family is today represented in New Orleans by his great grandnephews Col. William C. Dufour and Don Dufour and by the children of his grandniece, the late Louise Dufour wife of Joseph Bayle. Colonel Dufour, his sister, Mrs. Bayle, his brother Don, and his brothers Elmore and H. Generes Dufour, are the great grandchildren of Adéle Rouquette, sisters of the Abbé, who married Louis Donnet, and whose daughter married Numa Dufour.

Dimitry's sketch of the Rouquette family appeared in the New Orleans **Times-Democrat**, November 20, 1892 and has been condensed in the present record.

DUCATEL

AT or near Auxerre, in the province of Burgundy, France, resided when the French Revolution of '93 began, a family of gentile birth and ancient lineage named Du Catel de Chemilly. The head of this family was, titularly, Seigneur de Chemilly, and the family was one of high consideration in Auxerre.

Edmé Du Catel was the head of the family in Auxerre in that day. His wife, previous to her marriage, had been Edmée Lésseré. From their marriage issued Germain Ducatel, the founder of the Ducatel family in Louisiana, who was born in Auxerre in the year 1775. At the outbreak of the French Revolution he was a student at the Medical School of Paris. Like all others of military age in France he was compelled, when the French Republic declared war against Holland, to enter the military service, which he did as army surgeon. History falsifies facts when it alleges that the military and naval service of Frenchmen under the Republic was voluntary and optional. Such service was obligatory, and thus Doctor Ducatel, though a young man of Royalist and, therefore, Bourbon, tendencies, was obliged to serve with the republicans. This service on the medical staff of the army, however, he performed faithfully as long as the government of the people prevailed in France, but when Napoleon Bonaparte, then first Consul, treacherously proclaimed himself Emperor of France, Doctor Ducatel, refusing to follow the fortunes of the bold and ambitious Corsican, resigned his post as surgeon, retired from the army, and removed to Baltimore, Maryland, where his brother, Edmé Ducatel, who was a refugee from San Domingo, resided. Doctor Ducatel's services had been with the corps of General Pichegru, one of the foremost Republican army commanders in France. While in Baltimore, Dr. Germain Ducatel married Clémence de La Mulonière, of a family of that name from Nantes, in

Brittany. When the Haytien outbreak occured as a consequence of the French Revolution of 1793, a branch of the de la Mulonière family was residing on the island, and like many French families exposed to the perils of the uprising, they fled San Domingo and found refuge in Baltimore.

Doctor Ducatel's wife was a cousin of Eugene de la Muloniére, a native of France at one time well-known through his writings in the New Orleans press, particularly on *The Bee*, and a learned pedagogue of that city.

Although he did not abandon his practice entirely, Doctor Ducatel, while residing in Baltimore, did not care to assume the responsibilities of a practicing physician, and eventually moved to New Orleans. Two of his children, Amédée Ducatel, and a daughter, Amélia, who married Gaston Bertus, New Orleans, were born in Baltimore, the others were born in New Orleans. They were: Henry Ducatel, who married Marie Polymnie Pilié; Clémentine Ducatel, who married Stephen Legardeur; Odalie Ducatel, who married Henry Pilié; and Emma Ducatel, who left no posterity.

During the campaign of 1814-15 Doctor Ducatel was the colleague of Doctor Sanchez. Serving as surgeon and physician for the New Orleans volunteers and the troops under General J. B. Plauché on the field of Chalmette, he gave prompt and efficient service to the few American and the hundreds of British wounded, in a hospital established on the river front of the plantation of Bosque, not far from the celebrated Marigny plantation home. As neither Doctor Ducatel nor Doctor Sanchez could speak nor understand English, the duty of interpreter fell on the youthful shoulders of Amédée, the doctor's son, who was born in 1807 in Baltimore, and learned the English language. The eight-year-old boy's appearance in the hospital in the morning was the signal for calls to him from every quarter to come to the bedsides of the sufferers so that he could inform his father, Doctor Sanchez or the French-speaking nurses of the needs of the sick.

The little boy gained another honor during the strenuous days of this conflict. During the operations preceeding the historic and conclusive battle of January Eighth, General Andrew Jackson's wife, Rachel, remained in New Orleans while her gruff "Old Hickory" was afield with his fighting forces facing the veteran redcoats of Pakenham, determined that they should not reach their goal. So that she could communicate with her husband on the firing line it was necessary that Mrs. Jackson have a messenger, and this made Amédée, who was selected as her Mercury, the most envied eight-year-old-boy in New Orleans. Every Saturday an army wagon was sent from the city to General Jackson's headquarters at the Macarti plantation. This wagon was kept in a yard at St. Louis and Chartres streets, a square from Mrs. Jackson's residence and near the rendezvous of the Veterans' Corps, a body of elderly and substantial citizens of New Orleans, many of whom had seen service with the French and Spanish colonial troops, under the command of Captain Gaspard De-Buys. Therefore, every Saturday Amédée Ducatel received from Rachel Jackson any message she might wish to have delivered to her husband. This good lady was partial to rye bread, and on each occasion of his visit to the Royal street home the eight-year-old messenger received from the General's wife's hands several hot rolls of rye bread, buttered and sweetened with sugar, to sustain him on his trip. Thus equipped with his *bonne-bouche* of rye for a luncheon, and a bundle of letters for the grim-faced commander of the American forces, together with other letters for members of Plauché's sturdy battalion of French-speaking fighters, Amédée climbed on the army wagon and was driven to Chalmette, often its only passenger. How the other boys of old New Orleans envied him!

One can imagine how on those Saturdays the eagle-eyed and iron-faced man predestined f o r t h e achievement of great things, were turned to the distant city, looking up the level levee-road, perchance, to catch the first glimpse of that plain wagon which bore, if not Caesar and his fortunes, at least the loving words of a cherished wife—for it was not the least of the heroic attributes of this man of will and brains that he loved his wife Rachel with a tender and knightly love. Thus when passing down Royal street on hoseback on that day big with his own fortunes and the destinies of New Orleans—not of the United States, for the battle of New Orleans was fought, unfortunately, some three months after

the signing of the treaty of peace between the United States
and the Kingdom of Great Britain at Ghent, which crowned
the American cause with victory—, it is to be presumed that
when Jackson rode down Royal street on December 23,
1814, to meet the first advance of Pakenham, he had before
his eyes the face of his wife when he paused for a moment
to speak a word of encouragement to Mrs. J. B. Labatut,
wife of the general in command of the New Orleans militia.
"Madam, I say to you and the ladies of New Orleans, not
to be too much troubled or solicitous, for, indeed, except it
be over my dead body, the English soldiers shall not enter
this city as victors."

In after years when General Jackson was a candidate for
the Presidency of the United States and was visiting New
Orleans as a guest at the residence of his friend Martin Gordon, in Royal street, between St. Louis and Conti,—a house
afterwards the residence of Judge Alonzo Morphy, and
where the celebrated chess champion Paul Morphy, met his
death, now known as the *Patio Royal*—Amédée Ducatel
again met and shook hands with the hero of Chalmette and
was delighted to learn that the grim-faced warrior remembered the eight-year-old boy who had carried his wife's letters
to him.

In after years, when the members of Captain de Buys'
command paid their annual visit to the fields of Chalmette's
plantation where they had hurled back the veterans and
flower of England's best troops, Amédée Ducatel, with a
red woolen pompom on his cap, marched with the gray and
white-haired veterans, for he had been made an honorary
member of that command and thus won the distinction of
being the youngest veteran of that memorable engagement.

Doctor Germain Ducatel, father of Amédée following the
close of the war, gave up his practice and devoted his time
to a drug store, but in 1816 he abandoned this occupation,
and after a visit to France, where he purchased a large stock,
opened a large dry goods store and operated it until the day
of his death in 1849, which occured at his residence at Royal
and Toulouse streets.

Amédée Ducatel, oldest son of Germain Ducatel and
Clémence de La Moulonière, received his primary education

at the famous classical academy of the Reverand Dr. Hull, the first clergyman of the Episcopal Church domiciled in New Orleans. In that college, the stepping-stone to collegiate days of those who attended, were entered at various decades of the nineteenth century, many sons of New Orleans whose names have become famous in the history and the social life of the community. Among his classmates were the Kenners, the Cenas boys, Ursin de Lavillebeuvre, the Sterrets, John L. Lewis, Alexander Dimitry and his brother Michael Dracos Dimitry, and many others. In 1818 Amédée Ducatel attended the *College d'Orléans* and two of his fellow students were Charles Gayarré and Victor Labatut. In 1820 he went to France and entered the College Royal of Nantes, graduating five years later. In 1830, after his return to his native city, he was appointed a notary, and formed a partnership first with Felix De Armas, and later with a brother, Octave De Armas.

The marriage of Amédée Ducatel with Aline Bertus, took place in 1813, and from it sprang a numerous posterity. His first child was Ernest Ducatel who married Coralie Ducatel their children being: Coralie who married Henry O'Connell and became the mother of Emilie, Marguerite and Walter O'Connell; the second child was Corinne Ducatel, who did not marry; the third was Lefebvre Germain Ducatel, who did not marry; fourth, Aline Ducatel who married Edgard Bozonnier, and became the mother of Ernest and Lisette Bozonnier; the fifth child was Jeanne Ducatel, not married; the sixth, Paul Ducatel, who married Armide Van Dycke, and became the father of four children to wit: Marie Ducatel, who became the wife of Alfred Oemichen; André Ducatel, Paul Ducatel, and Van Dycke Ducatel; the seventh, Amédée Ducatel, who married Virginia Van Dycke, but left no children; the eighth, Aline Ducatel, who became the wife of Aristide Delvaille, and the mother of Amelia Delvaille, who married Baldo Marquez, whose children were: Jeanne, Paul, Corinne, and Lelia Marquez; Jules Delvaille, who married Anette Grévemberg, and had five children: Aline, George, Louise, Nina and Edna Delvaille; Emile Delvaille, who married Abby McCullogh and had two children, Anita and Soline Delvaille; Lizette Delvaille, who married Emile Allgayer and became the mother of Robert and Louise Allgayer; Aline Delvaille, who did not marry; Marie Delvaille, who married Alfred Théard and became the mother of Delvaille Théard, Albert Théard and Marie Théard, and lastly, Corinne Delvaille, who became the wife of Auguste Dufilho and the mother of Marie and Auguste Dufilho. It will be seen from this list of posterity of Amédée Ducatel that he left a numerous progeny. His three sons, Ernest, Amédée Jr., and Paul, served in the Confederacy and died in New Orleans after the close of the war. The wives of Amédée Ducatel Jr., and Paul Ducatel, were the daughters of Captain Van Dycke and Miss Rémy of New Orleans.

Henry Ducatel, brother of Amédée and son of Dr. Germain Ducatel and Clémence de La Mulonière, was keeper of the register of births and marriages for many years at the St. Louis Cathedral and he, too, left a numerous posterity through his marriage with Marie Polymnie Pilié. They were: first, George Ducatel; second, Marie Céline Ducatel, who married George Ferry and became mother of eight children: George Ferry Jr., Henry Ferry, Albert Ferry, Charles Ferry, James Ferry, Marie Ferry, and Sidney and Lisette Ferry, (twins); third, Nathalie Ducatel, who married Edouard Hernandez and became the mother of Edouard Hernandez Jr., Corinne Hernandez, who married Dr. Albert Rocquet and had one daughter, Olga Rocquet; and Paul Emile Hernandez; fourth, Louise Ducatel, who married Robert Kerr and became the mother of Louise Kerr, Marguerite Kerr, Lorely Kerr, John Kerr, and Blanche Kerr; fifth, Heléna Ducatel, who did not marry; sixth, James Ducatel, not married; seventh, Edouard Ducatel, not married; eighth, Arthur Ducatel, who died in Havana, unmarried, May 7, 1892, at the age of thirty-two; ninth, Aline Ducatel, and tenth, Lucie Ducatel, both unmarried.

Clémentine, a daughter of Dr. Germain Ducatel and Clemence de La Mulonière married Stephen Le Gardeur de Tilly.

The Dimitry sketch of the Ducatel family was printed in the New Orleans Times-Democrat, November 27, December 4, 1892.

DORIOCOURT

AN old and interesting French parchment document long in the possession of the family, testifies to the ancient and honorable lineage of the Doriocourts. It is a legal document and its title, translated into English, reads: "D'Oriocourt Genealogy, in Champagne, originally of Lorraine, produced before me, Mgr. De Caumartin, Intendent in Champaign, in the month of April, 1669." It is partly printed in the old style and partly manuscript, with the genealogical data printed from type, and it furnishes the abstracts of various *pieces justificatives* concerning grants, marriage and other contracts, together with a brief record of the genealogical record of the Doriocourt family for a period of 244 years, or from 1425, the year of the first abstract given, down to the year, 1669, when the genealogy was presented to M. de Caumartin for his signature.

The facts imparted by the earliest of these *pieces justificatives* indicate that the Doriocourts of Noemy, in Lorraine (Alsace-Lorraine), were of knightly origin. The first mentioned, Androwin d'Oriocourt, is styled *écuyer* and the appelation is given to his successors until a little more than a hundred years later when record is made of the addition of the title *seigneur* to the family name in the shape of a memorandum of a division of property made December 14, 1533, at Pons à Mousson, between Claude and Henry d'Oriocourt, brothers, by their father, "*honoré* Seigneur Georges d'Oriocourt, *éscuyer*, Seigneur d'Aulony, and Captain and Chastelain of Noemy."

The first mention on record of the Doriocourt family in the parchment is contained in a statement of provisions made for the charge of Chatelain of the City of Noemy given by Conrad, Bishop of Mets, to his "*ami* and *feal*," Androwin d'Oriocourt, *écuyer*, the last of February, 1425, signed by Marsallo. The second record is that of an annual bond in perpetuity, of June 29, 1425, signed by Royers, notary of Metz, made to Guillaume de Texerant, residing in Noémy, by Jean d'Abocourt and Androwin d'Oriocourt, *écuyers*, and by Demoiselles Isabelle and Hellowis, their wives, daughters of Huttin de Serrieres, *écuyer*. The third record contains a transfer dated July 15, 1425, involving a dowry in gold and silver, amounting to 2,000 livres, of Marie de Bettocourt, wife of Guillaume de Vaishinmont, and referring to an agreement entered into between them and Androwin d'Oriocourt, by the consent of Mgr. Jean, Comte de Salme, upon the subject of the differences existing between them on account of that dowry.

Other records of various kinds are dated in the years 1477, 1481, 1564, and 1584, in which the names of successive generations of the house of d'Oriocourt, called in one of the records *la forte maison d'Oriocourt*, appear.

The d'Oriocourt genealogy printed in this parchment accounting for twelve generations of the family in France down to the year 1669, embraces a period altogether of nearly, if not quite, 400 years, and thus traces the line to the days when the Crusades were being carried on in Europe—days when the Kings of France cowered in the muddy precincts along the Seine in the *Quartier Latin* of Paris, fearing lest some of the powerful barons of that day, whose strength in the field was often greater than that of Kings, might conceive the thought of declaring war against them and of marching upon "the gay capital" under some such threatening device as that borne by one of the *seigneurs* of that transition period the thirteenth and fourteenth centuries, in the history of France, which read:

"*Je suis ni roy ni prince aussi; je suis le Seigneur de Coucy.*"

"I am not King nor prince also; I am the Seigneur de Coucy."

The authority of the feudal system in Europe was sufficiently recognized in 1425 to enable Conrad, Bishop of Mets (Metz) to confer on Androwin d'Oriocourt, in that year, as is recorded in the Doriocourt parchment, the title of *Chatelain* of the City of Noémy, in Lorraine, an office which meant, probably, the governorship of the citadel or castle of

Noémy, and, therefore, included the military governorship of the town. In the provisions of the charge thus given to him, Androwin d'Oriocourt is styled Conrad's *ami et féal*—his friend and vasal, or, it may have been, his friend and faithful one in Church matters. Conrad was perhaps a man of secular as well as ecclesiastical authority.

In the official register of the officers of the colonial troops in Louisiana in the eighteenth century, shortly after the advent of the Spanish rule in the colony, appears the name of Doriocourt, an officer holding the rank of lieutenant. This officer appears, from all information at hand, to have been the founder of the Doriocourt family in Louisiana. While Louisiana was still in the possession of Spain, two sons, François and Antoine Chevalier Doriocourt, were born to this gentleman. The name Chevalier as a family name among the Doriocourts was derived from a title which once had been borne by a member of the family.

François d'Oriocourt married Mlle. Simars de Bellisle, the daughter of Simars de Bellisle, a former commander of the *Côte des Allesmands* and the hero of a most remarkable adventure when he was captured by the Atakapas Indians and forced to remain with them for three years before he was released by Juchereau de Saint Denys.

The children of François Doriocourt were three in number, viz: Azémia Doriocourt, who married Jules Dupuy; Adélaide Doriocourt, who married Joseph Soniat Du Fossat, and Bellisle Doriocourt, a son.

Antoine Chevalier Doriocourt was married twice. By his first marriage with Elizabeth Soniat Du Fossat, he had a daughter, Adéline, who married Beaumont Esnould de Livaudais. By his second marriage with Marie Louise Herrary, he had three children, André Dotremont Doriocourt, Antoine *fils*, and Adéle Doriocourt, who married B. A. Marantes.

André Dotremont Doriocourt married Marie Lombard, and from this marriage were born: Antoine Doriocourt Jr., Francois Doriocourt, Joseph Doriocourt, André Doriocourt Jr., and Marie Doriocourt, who married P. V. Boulmay.

Antoine Doriocourt, youngest son of Antoine Chevalier and his second wife Mlle. Herrary, married, October 30, 1852, Léonide Charbonnet, of the highly esteemed Louisiana family of that name, the daughter of Francois Léo Charbonnet and Adathée Morin, whose father, Antoine Morin, was the first sugar-maker on the plantation of Etienne de Boré, where he made the first thoroughly granulated sugar manufactured in Louisiana.

From the marriage Antoine Doriocourt and Léonide Charbonnet, were born eleven children, viz: Léo Doriocourt, Adathée, who did not marry; Louise, who also remained unmarried; Léonide, who became the wife of William Ganucheau; Adèle, who married G. L. Castanedo; Martin Edward Doriocourt, who married Althée Morel, Dec. 26, 1892; Ines Doriocourt; Antoine Doriocourt, and Marie Antoinette Doriocourt, two of the children, Antoine Chevalier and Henry died in infancy.

André Dotremont Doriocourt, who died in New Orleans May 22, 1881, was a New Orleans notary, deputy registrar of wills in the Court of Probate, and was a member of the state legislature in 1857. His son, Antoine Doriocourt Jr., left a daughter, Antoinette Doriocourt, at his death.

Antoine Doriocourt, youngest son of Antoine Chevalier Doriocourt, was appointed a notary public for the parish of Orleans by Governor Isaac Johnson in 1847, serving as such until May of 1863, when the Federal troops took possession of the city. Then he with his brother André Dotremont Doriocourt left New Orleans as "Registered Enemies," and in Alabama joined the fifteenth Confederate calvary, together with his nephew Joseph Doriocourt, his cousin Joseph Numa Charbonnet, and his brother-in-law, James Alfred Charbonnet, and when the city of Mobile was taken by the Federal forces, he was paroled as a prisoner of war May 5, 1865, and returned to New Orleans, again becoming a notary.

The Dimitry genealogical sketch of the Doriocourt family, appearing in the New Orleans Times-Democrat, December 18, 1892, and January 1, 1893.

CANONGE Family

AMONG conspicuous Louisiana families to which belong the meed of high character and reputation, and with whose names are blended associations for three generations in the state of unusual intellectual endowments, must be placed the name Canonge, familiar as it is to all Louisianians belonging to the ancient French population whose mother tongue was the Gallic language.

On the paternal side the Canonge family was originally from Marseilles in Provence, France, and, intermediately from the island of San Domingo, the ancestors of those who settled in Louisiana having been compelled to leave that island as the result of the revolution there in 1795. On the maternal side they were Louisianians, thus constituting them doubly Creoles, from the parent stock of San Domingo and Louisiana.

The parental head of the Canonges, bearing the family name, was the Marquis de Jussan, a French nobleman of high standing, who served with merit in the armies of Louis XV, according to a commission dated 1747, signed by the monarch and countersigned by Marc Pierre de Voyer, Comte d'Argenson, Minister of War, which appointed the Marquis to a lieutenancy in a company of huzzars.

At a later period the Marquis de Jussan, becoming enthusiastic over the wonderful things told of San Domingo—the delights of its climate, its fertility, and its great resources, emigrated to this West Indian paradise, married there and there founded a branch of his family. Mme. de Jussan was gifted with a nature of highest distinction and was the heiress of a large fortune and of one of the finest domains at Jérémie. The Jussan family also possessed plantations in various parts of the island, homes renowned for the sumptuous hospitality with which guests were entertained, and the kind treatment by the owners of their slaves being equally proverbial. When the emigration of 1804 occured, in consequence of the uprising of the negroes, twelve or fifteen of their slaves followed the family to Cuba, where the Jussans first found refuge. They subsequently came to the United States.

Prior to this event, the Marquis de Jussan had died. There are many family traditions of those days relating to the devotion and heroism of the family servants in those years of danger; how, at the peril of their own lives, they hid the members of the family in the woods for weeks, going out to forage for them and bringing them bananas and ignames for food, and by their watchful attention preserving their lives from the "bandits", as the slaughtering and predatory bands that went about the island were termed. One of these faithful slaves, Antoine by name, and among the most devoted of the number, died in New Orleans after the settlement of the family there.

The Marquis de Jussan had one daughter, Renée de Jussan, who married in San Domingo, Jean Benjamin Canonge, a very rich resident of the island, where he exercised an influence which was due to a high order of intelligence, determined will, extreme liberality and benevolence, and the possession of a large fortune. He died before the flight of the family to Cuba. From the marriage of J. B. Canonge and Renée de Jussan, were born: Auguste Canonge, J. F. Canonge, Benjamin Canonge, Z. B. Canonge, Aurore Canonge, and Elizabeth Aimée Canonge.

Auguste Canonge died in Philadelphia, to which city the whole family repaired after leaving Cuba. Benjamin Canonge died in New York. Both of these brothers devoted themselves to commercial pursuits, in which they occupied conspicuous positions, in an endeavor to recoup their lost fortunes. The other children died in New Orleans, as did their mother, who lived to be nearly 100 years, passing away July 5, 1856. J. F. Canonge, early naturalized as an American citizen, and studied law in Philadelphia under a celebrated attorney named Duponceau, a Frenchman by birth, who served with Washington during the War of Independence. J. F. Canonge was born in Jérémie, San Domingo, in 1785, and died in New Orleans January 19, 1848. After being admitted to the bar he decided on New Orleans as a place of future residence, as the French element was largely represented in the posterity of the early settlers of the Louisiana colony. At the time of his arrival the French and English languages were both used on the floors of the State senate and the House of representatives, and, as a consequence, the clerks of these bodies were called upon to report the French speeches in English and the English speeches in French. Mr. Canonge filled the position of clerk of the lower house for several sessions. Later he became associated with a celebrated lawyer of his day, John R. Grymes, and when Governor A. B. Roman occupied the gubernatorial chair he was appointed to the bench of the Criminal district court, at that time a court unique in its character, in that there was no appeal from its decision.

Judge J. F. Canonge married a young widow, a Mme. Amelung, née Amélie Mercier, daughter of Jean Mercier and Maria Garcia de Fontenelle, noted in her day as a perfect type of the Créole beauty who combined with her exquisite features a fine intelligence, artistic tastes, and who shone in the smart world of Paris with the same brilliancy that she dazzled the social set of New Orleans. She died in Paris, November 10, 1830, at the age of thirty-eight, the mother of six children. They were: Alphonse Canonge, Hippolyte Canonge, Laure Canonge, J. Placide Canonge, Emma Canonge, and Ernest Canonge, All of those children, with the exception of Laure, who died in infancy, were educated at the College Louis-le-Grand, Paris. Ernest Canonge, who became a member of the state's house of representative, completed his studies at Jefferson College, St. James parish.

Alphonse Canonge, the oldest son of Judge J. F. Canonge, who became an eminent New Orleans attorney and was also superintendent of education of that city's schools, died November 13, 1883. Hippolyte Canonge, who like his brother was a brilliant scholar, died at the beginning of his career, January 29, 1855. Ernest Canonge died November 4, 1876.

L. Placide Canonge, third son of Judge Canonge, who became an eminent journalist *feuilletonist* and author, was born in New Orleans June 29, 1822. He returned to the city of his birth after his schooling at the College Louis-le-Grand in Paris, imbued with the French romantic school of literature. He turned his talents to writing and his first effort was a successful vaudeville, *Le Maudit Passeport*, which was performed in 1839 at the old Orleans Theatre. A number of other plays followed: *Gaston de St. Elmo*, a tragedy in five acts; brought out in 1840; *L'Ambassadeur d'Autriche*, a five-act drama; *Un Grand d'Espagne*, *Histoire Sous Charles Quint*, *France et Espagne*, *Comte de Monte Christo*, *Comte de Carmagnola*, all dramas in five acts. He also wrote a comedy of merit, *Qui Perd Gagne;* a series of essays on the principles of American government, published in *La Presse* in Paris. In addition to his other efforts he wrote the words for Mrs. Alonzo Morphy's opera *Louise de Lorraine*. He also wrote and published an amended translation into French of Helper's *Nojoque*, a work on slavery, which in view of the war between the states that followed, proved, indeed, to be *"no joke,"* as Charles Patton Dimitry observed.

Placide Canonge married Héloise Halphen, daughter of Dr. Michel Halphen and Thérése Beult, and his two sons were Placide Canonge Jr., and Henri Canonge, who married sisters, Placide Jr. becoming the husband of Louise Fuselier de la Claire, while Henri married Marie Fuselier de la Claire, daughters of a family from the Attakapas country of Louisiana. The children of Henri Canonge were: René, Henri, Héloise, Yvonne, and Gilberte Canonge.

The Canonge genealogical sketches by Dimitry were published in the Times-Democrat, January 8, 15 and 22, 1893.

Part Two

CLAIBORNE Family

ESTABLISHED in America three hundred and ten years ago, the Claiborne family, a branch of which still exists in New Orleans and counts among its members many prominent men and women of that city, has left an historical record in the annals of Virginia, Maryland and Louisiana unsurpassed by any other family in the United States.

The founder of this distinguished house in the English colonies of America was William Clayborne (or Cleborne), of Westmoreland County, England, son of Edmund Cleborne, lord of the manors of "Cliburn Hall" and Killerby, and Grace Bellingham, daughter of Sir Edward Bellingham of Helsington and Levens. This William Clayborne, whose family was a distinguished one in England, was appointed, by the London Company, surveyor of the Virginia Plantations, and landed, with Governor Wyatt, in Jamestown during the month of November 1621.

He was a fearless and aggressive man and through his energy he attained, on March 24, 1625, the rank of Secretary of State for the Virginia Colony. Locating at first in James City, he acquired, before long, an estate of forty-five thousand acres.

The London Company being desirous of extending its territory southward and of increasing its Indian trade, selected William Clayborne to carry out these plans. Forthwith he bought an estate on Kent Island, in Maryland, where he erected a trading post and established, in 1731, a small settlement, the first in Maryland, over which he ruled like a petty king. In so doing he had not anticipated that a year later Cecile Calvert, second lord Baltimore, would obtain from Charles I a grant to the stretching empire he was to call Maryland, and that Calvert would arrive in 1734, with his brother Leonard and two hundred colonists to found a little village not far from Kent Island, where the powerful William Clayborne exercised his sway.

Clashes were bound to follow as Calvert claimed control over Kent Island and its settlers. This Clayborne fiercely opposed. Resorting to arms, he made frequent sallies on his unwelcome neighbors. His indictment by the outraged legislature of Maryland for murder, piracy and sedition, did not dampen his rebellious feelings. Using the Indians in 1645, and also the Puritans settled near Providence (now Annapolis) to destroy Calvert's forces, he opposed Lord Baltimore's possession of Maryland for many years and during that time was even forced to sail for England to answer serious charges that had been lodged against him.

Smarting under the partiality shown by the British king to Calvert, his enemy, William Clayborne aligned himself with Cromwell, who had defied Charles I, and on September 26, 1651, was appointed by the Parliamentarians a commissioner to secure the Virginia Plantations for the Roundheads. He clashed swords with the Cavaliers, drove them out of office and became Cromwellian secretary of the commonwealth. He died, after an exciting and hectic career, in Virginia about the year 1676.

William Clayborne had married Elizabeth Butler and from her had, among other children, a son, Lieutenant Colonel Thomas Claiborne (born 1647—died 1732) who married Sarah Fenn Dandridge and whose, son, Captain Thomas Claiborne (born 1680—died 1732) married Ann Fox, daughter of Henry Fox and Ann West, a great-grand-niece of the third Lord Baltimore, a traditional enemy of the first Clayborne.

The Claibornes of Virginia, during the American Revolution, sided with the revolted colonists and fought bravely and well, as officers, in the Continental Army. They had the honor of giving to Louisiana William Charles Cole Claiborne, her first American governor, born in Sussex County, Virginia, in 1775. This William C. C. Claiborne (a lineal descendant of William Clayborne of Virginia and Maryland fame), was the son of Colonel William Claiborne and Mary Leigh.

[144]

Colonel William Claiborne, his father, had been a Revolutionary soldier and after the bloody struggle was over it is recorded that the old gentleman often gathered his four sons about him, among whom were William Charles Cole, the second born, and Nathaniel, and would dwell on the hardships of the past conflict, the horrors of the English prison ships and the brutality of the British soldiery in Virginia. Such tales were not calculated to instill in the minds of his children any great love for the red-coats. William C. C. Claiborne, at the age of eight years, showed his intense love for liberty, when he amazed his tutors at Richmond Academy by writing in his Latin grammer: *Cara patris, carior libertas; ubi est libertas ibi est mea patria.* "Dear is my country, dearer is liberty; where liberty abides, there is my country found."

This precocious child was for a while a student at William and Mary College, but returning to Richmond Academy, he graduated, as valedictorian, at the age of fifteen. His father being a poor man, William decided to shift for himself and relieve his parent of some of his burdens. So, he started for New York, practically penniless, where he obtained employment from John Beckley, clerk to the United States Congress, and followed his employer, when Congress moved to Philadelphia. Among the noted legislators and statesmen gathered in that city, he won the friendship of Vice-President Adams, of Thomas Jefferson,, then Secretary of State, and of the celebrated patriot, John Sevier, from Tennessee, who represented that state as a Congressional delegate, and who later on became governor of this commonwealth. At the suggestion of Sevier, young Claiborne moved to Sullivan County, Tennessee, became a lawyer, practised with great success for two years, was elected a member from Sullivan County to the Tennessee Convention, convened to draft a constitution for that territory that had just applied for admission, as a state, in the American Union.

John Sevier, his friend, becoming first governor of Tennessee, young William Claiborne, not yet twenty-two, received from him the appointment of Judge of the Supreme Court of law and equity of Tennessee. Less than two years later, the youthful judge had been elected to Congress by an immense majority. Reelected for a second term, he participated in the fierce balloting that took place in the House of Representatives to decide the tie for the presidency between Thomas Jefferson and Aaron Burr. Thirty six ballots were taken without avail. Claiborne voted steadfastly for Jefferson, though great inducements were offered him by the Burr adherents to change his vote, a vote that would have decided the contest in favor of Burr. Claiborne indignantly repulsed such overtures. The outcome of it was that Jefferson became president and never forgot the young Virginian's loyalty.

In 1801, when the people of the Mississippi Territory, dissatisfied of their governor, petitioned Congress for another chief-executive, President Jefferson appointed William C. C. Claiborne to that office. Reaching Natchez November 23, 1801, Claiborne ruled wisely over Mississippi for two years and became governor-general and intendent of the Province of Louisiana, which he received from France for the United States December 20, 1803.

Governor Claiborne found Louisiana in a state bordering anarchy. Corruption was rampant, and judges were known to sell their verdicts. He faced a mighty task. To make things harder for him, his first wife, Eliza W. Lewis, a beautiful young woman from Nashville, Tennessee, and their infant daughter, died of yellow fever in New Orleans, September 20, 1806, on the same day that Micajah Lewis, his young brother-in-law who had followed him to Louisiana, perished as a result of a duel. Governor Claiborne came near dying at the same time from that terrible scourge then epidemical in the city.

He governed Louisiana wisely and well though he had to contend with intrigues and with unprincipled men who tried to blacken his name and reputation. He was so violently calumniated by Daniel Clark, the wealthy New Orleans merchant, that he was compelled to meet him on the field of honor where Claiborne received a very severe wound.

Governor Claiborne served as provisional governor and intendent of Louisiana until October 2, 1804 when he was appointed regular governor and served as such until 1812 when Louisiana became a full-fledged state in the Union.

Reelected governor in 1816, he had the final honor of being elevated by the suffrage of the people of the state to the United States Senate January 13, 1817, but died of a liver complaint, November 3, 1817. By special dispensation of the Roman Catholic managers of the old St. Louis Cemetery No. 1, on Basin street, his body was interred in a corner of this burial ground reserved exclusively for Romanists, though it was stipulated that the plot where his tomb stood should be surrounded by an iron fence. Later the governor's remains were transferred to his family's new tomb in Metairie Cemetery.

By his first wife, Eliza W. Lewis, Governor Claiborne had a daughter who died, with her mother, from yellow fever. His second wife was Clarisse Duralde, whom he married in 1806. She was the daughter of Martin Milony Duralde, born in Biscaya, Spain, and Marie Josephe Perrault, a native of Quebec. Her paternal grandparents were Pierre Duralde and Marie de Elizaga. Martin Milony Duralde, her father, was a Spanish officer who served at the Attakapas Post. He moved to Saint Louis, Missouri, then in the Illinois country, May 20, 1770 with Don Pedro Piernas, who had been appointed, by Governor O'Reilly, the first Spanish lieutenant governor of Upper Louisiana. Duralde was a highly-educated man of good family. In Saint Louis he married, in 1776, Marie Josephe Perrault, born in Quebec, daughter of Louis Perrault, a merchant of Quebec, and Josephe Bobé. Duralde remained in Saint Louis a few years and returned to New Orleans where his wife's family resided. From his marriage with Marie Josephe Perrault were born four daughters, one of whom married John Clay, brother of Henry Clay, the celebrated patriot; another, Louise, marrying Gui Joseph Soniat du Fossat, son of the Chevalier Gui de Saunhac and Françoise Claudine Dreux; the third, whose name was Celeste, contracting matrimony with Valerien Allain, son of Pierre Augustin Allain and Manette du Plessis, and Clarisse, who became the wife of Governor William C. C. Claiborne.

Clarisse Duralde Claiborne died in Saint Martinville in 1808, having had from her union with Governor Claiborne one son, William C. C. Claiborne (II) born in New Orleans in 1808. In 1812 her widowed husband married a third time, his last wife being Sophronia Bosque, a Spanish lady, from whom he had two children, namely: Charles Cole, who died unmarried, and Sophronia, who became the wife of Colonel Antoine Jacques Philippe de Mandeville de Marigny, son of Bernard de Marigny and Mathilde Morales. She left three children that died without issue.

William Charles Cole Claiborne (II), son of Governor Claiborne and Clarisse Duralde, his second wife, spent his boyhood in Lexington, Kentucky, in the home of Henry Clay Ashland. While sojourning in France in 1832, he met, wooed and married in Paris, Louise de Balathier, of a noble French family. From her he had ten children who were:

(a)—Clarisse Claiborne, who died unmarried; (b)— William C. C. Claiborne (III), who married Jeanne Robelet and had three children: William C. C. Claiborne IV, unmarried; Marie Louise Claiborne married Herbert Cole Claiborne, and Walter H. Claiborne married to Louise Simpson; (c)—Henry de Balathier Claiborne, a midshipman in the United States Navy; (d)—George Washington Claiborne, who died at the battle of Mansfield, Louisiana while serving as a Confederate soldier; (e)—Arthur Claiborne; (f)—Marie Claiborne, who did not marry; (g)— Lucie Claiborne, who died unmarried; (h)—John Randolph Claiborne; (i)—Charles Ferdinand Claiborne, judge of the Louisiana Court of Appeals who married Amelie Soniat du Fossat, daughter of Meloncy Soniat du Fossat and half-sister of the late Col. Hugues Jules de la Vergne, and (j)— Ferdinand Claiborne who married Lolotte Villeré.

The children of Judge Charles Ferdinand Claiborne and Miss Soniat were: (a) Marie Louise Claiborne, who married Dr. Louis Perrilliat; (b) Charles de B. Claiborne, whose wife is Virginia Couturie; (c) Amelie Claiborne, married to Martin Levering Matthews; (d) Lucy Claiborne, wife of Samuel C. Coleman; (e) Martin Duralde Claiborne whose wife is Yvonne Holly Ross.

Ferdinand Claiborne, brother of Judge Charles F. Claiborne, married Lolotte Villeré, daughter of Alcée Villeré and Delphine Fleitas. Two children were born of this union: Clarisse Claiborne and Lieutenant Omer Claiborne, U. S. A.

JUCHEREAU DE SAINT DENYS Family

THE Juchereau family, that gave to Louisiana one of its most heroic pioneers, if not its greatest pathfinder, fighter, and colonizer, Louis Juchereau de Saint Denys (a name usually printed Saint Denis), had its origin in the French province of la Perche. Its founders had held important judicial positions and were numerously represented in the city of Mortagne, where many of them had attained eminence as jurists.

The new land of America appealed strongly to two brothers of that ancient family, who decided to migrate thereto and settle in *Nouvelle France*, as Canada was first called, where many of their countrymen had set up their rustic castles along the placid flow of the St Lawrence and lived like petty feudal lords.

Noël Juchereau, Sieur des Chatelets, and Jean Juchereau, Sieur de Saint Maur, as those two brothers were called, were born in the commune of la Ferté-Vidame, in the diocese of Chartres, where their parents resided. Noël, who had been born at the end of the sixteenth century, arrived in Canada in 1632, and his brother Jean followed him two years later. Noël was already an important man when he set foot on the shores of the new land and the date of his coming had been wisely chosen, as *Nouvelle France*, which since its foundation had been sadly harrassed by want, famine, and Indian massacres, was about to be reborn. The society known as the Company of One Hundred Associates had been organized to rehabilitate the northern province and infuse new blood in its weakened veins. Its success at first had been negligible and in 1632 near bankruptcy, when Samuel de Champlain was selected as governor of *Nouvelle France* and a new policy of management adopted.

So when Noël Juchereau came to Canada he represented

the *Compagnie des Cent Associes* as agent, and, in 1745, was named one of the six directors of the powerful *Compagnie des Habitants*. He became a man of great influence in Canada where he lived for sixteen years before sailing for France where he died, unmarried, in 1648.

His brother, Jean Juchereau, Sieur de Saint Maur, first ancestor of all the Juchereaus in North America, before going to Canada in 1634, had married Marie Langlois, daughter of the Sieur de Langlois, *ecuyer*, Seigneur de la Potherie and de Saint Roch. Less than a year after his arrival he owned a concession or *fief* near Montmagny, in 1647 was the lord of a *seigneurie* near Quebec, and contributed largely in including colonists from the province of La Perche to settle in Canada where they became, in time, the hardest working and most successful and useful agriculturists in the land. Though of an ancient and honorable family his forebears had not been enobled, but in the year 1687, M. de Tracy, lieutenant governor of *Nouvelle France*, recommended the Sieur de Saint Maur to Louis XIV and requested a patent of nobility for him as a reward for his faithful services. Jean Juchereau died before the honor could be conferred. His death occured at Beauport, on the concession of his son, Nicholas Juchereau de Saint Denys, February 7, 1672, at the age of eighty-eight. His wife had died before him, January 14, 1661.

The four children of Jean Juchereau, Sieur de Saint Maur and Marie Langlois were: (a) Jean Juchereau, Sieur de la Ferté, born in France, who became a member of the sovereign council of *Nouvelle France* in 1663. As eldest son he inherited his father's chateau of Saint Maur. He married in Quebec, November 21, 1645, Marie Giffard, daughter of Robert Giffard, Seigneur de Beauport, and Marie Renouard, and had eight children. Jean died November 16, 1685. (b) Nicholas Juchereau, Sieur de Saint Maur, born in France, came to Canada with his parents in 1634. He died at sea unmarried. (c) Genevieve Juchereau de Saint Maur, born in France in 1633, died in Quebec November 10, 1687. She married, October 1, 1648, Charles Le Gardeur de Tilly, a member of the soverign council, and was the mother of fifteen children. (d) Nicholas Juchereau, Sieur de Saint Denys.

This third son of Jean Juchereau and Marie Langlois, was also born in France. In Canada, when grown, he became a member of the sovereign council, fought as a captain of militia, under de Courcelle, against the Agniers, as well as the Iroquois, and exhibited conspicuous bravery in all the Indian campaigns. In 1690, when Quebec was about to be beseiged by Phipps and his English fleet, Nicholas Juchereau de Saint Denys rose to heroic heights. At Beauport, where his manor house stood, he fought at the head of his 300 militia-men for three days, in spite of his seventy years, and repulsed an English landing party with frightful losses while only about a dozen of his men were wounded. In consideration of his heroism on that occasion, Louis XIV granted him and his legitimate descendants a patent of nobility in February, 1692. He died in Quebec, honored and revered, October 4, 1692. His wife, whom he married September 22, 1649, was Marie Thérese, a sister of Jean's wife. She died in Quebec, June 12, 1714, leaving as issue 12 children:

1.—Marie Anne Juchereau de Saint Denys, born in Quebec, August 14, 1653, married François Pollet de la Combe Pocatière, an army captain, while her second husband was François Madeleine Fortune Ruette d'Auteuil, Procureur General of the soverign council of *Nouvelle France.*

2.—Charles Juchereau de Saint Denys, born in Quebec December 6, 1655. He was an army lieutenant in 1691, and judge of the royal jurisdiction of Quebec in 1694. He was wealthy and enterprising. He conceived the idea of establishing tanneries in the Louisiana province and along the Mississippi, but before realizing the benefits of his fur trade he died at the Wabash post in 1703. By his wife, Denise Therese de Bransac, daughter of Jean Baptiste Mignon de Bransac, lieutenant general of Montreal, and Catherine Gauchet de Belleville, he had five children.

3.—Ignace Juchereau du Chesnay de Saint Denys, born at Beauport, August 3, 1658. He married, February 24, 1688, Marie Catherine Peuvret, daughter of Jean

Baptiste Peuvret, and Marie Catherine Nau. By her
he had seventeen children who married in the best families of France and Canada, occupied high positions in
the French kingdom, and left innumerable descendants.
He died April 7, 1715.

4.—Charlotte Françoise Juchereau de Saint Denys, born
in Quebec, February 1, 1660. She married at Beauport, December 17, 1680, François Viennay-Pachot, a
merchant, of Grenoble, France, and widower of Jeanne
Avamy. At the death of her first husband, by whom
she had sixteen children, Charlotte married Captain
François la Forrest of the Marine corps.

5.—Madeline Louise Juchereau de Saint Denys, born in
Quebec, July 11, 1662. She became the wife of Captain Joseph Alexandre de l'Estrigant, Sieur de Saint
Martin, of the Marine corps. She died in Quebec May
30, 1721, leaving four children.

6.—Marie Therese Juchereau de Saint Denys, born in
Beauport, November 8, 1664. She married, August
16, 1684, Pierre de la Lande-Gayon, a merchant of
Bayonne, and had five children.

7.—Nicholas Juchereau de Saint Denys, born August 31,
1666 died in childhood.

8.—Catherine Juchereau de Saint Denys, born in Quebec
October 16, 1668, who married, December 19, 1699,
Pierre Aubert, ecuyer, Sieur de Gaspé, and left no
issue when she died in 1703.

9.—François Juchereau de Volezar, born in Beauport,
September 16, 1679. He became a *Garde Marine* in
1693, served with distinction in the French Navy, and
commanded several vessels. In 1714 he became Captain General in Normandy. He left no issue from his
marriage with Marguerite Gagneur, whom he married
at La Rochelle, June 23, 1705, nor from his second,
who was Françoise Le Trotteur (widow Duromp)
whom he married at Cap François, Saint Domingue,
where he died in 1741.

10.—Louis Juchereau des Aulnaies, born at Beauport, January 8, 1673, who died unmarried in Quebec November 11, 1691.

11.—Jacqueline Catherine Juchereau de Saint Denys, born
at Beauport, September 4, 1679. She became a nun
and died April 21, 1722.

12.—Louis Juchereau de Saint Denys, born in Quebec, September 17, 1676, who went to Louisiana when a mere
boy, eventually becoming one of its outstanding pioneers.

This Louis Juchereau de Saint Denys is said to have first
reached Louisiana in his early youth. His second trip to that
province was as a companion of Pierre le Moyne d'Iberville
and Jean Baptiste de Bienville in 1699 when he was twenty-
three. Saint Denys sailed from Canada aboard the *Renommée*
as *officier bleu* or temporary commander. He witnessed the
erection of the first rough French fort built on Mobile Bay
the year he arrived. Instead of leading a lazy life at the settlements his love for adventure and the trackless wilds, led
him into the Louisiana wilderness, and he became a pathfinder and fearless invader of those dangerous primeval solitudes. From the beginning he showed rare diplomacy and
tact in dealing with the Indians who eventually grew to worship him as much as the white men honored and respected
him.

When Lamothe-Cadillac, governor of Louisiana, decided
to stimulate trading relations between Louisiana and the
Spaniards in Mexico, Saint Denys was selected as his ambassador of good will. Leaving the post on Mobile Bay,
August 23, 1714, the daring young Canadian proceeded
overland toward the territory of the Natchitoches Indians,
who had adopted him as a member of the tribe in 1701.
There on the Red River, he built a rude fort, which he
designated Fort St. Jean Baptiste, around which eventually
grew the present city of Natchitoches, the oldest in Louisiana.
Leaving it defended by a small garrison, he proceeded to the
land of the *Tejas* (Texas) accompanied by only twelve
men.

On this hazardous journey he traversed almost the whole
breadth of the present state of Texas until he arrived at
Presidio del Norte where he took up the details of his mission, which was to establish trade relations, with the commandant Don Diego de Sanchez Ramon.

[153]

Here he met the Spanish commander's attractive grand-daughter, Doña Manuela de Sanchez Ramon. The meeting proved to be a case of love at first sight for both of them. Lovemaking, however, was brought to an abrupt termination for Saint Denis was arrested by order of the governor of *Caouis* (Coahuila) and was later sent on to Mexico City where he was thrown into prison. According to one tradition, the motive for the arrest and incarceration was due to the fact that the Spanish governor was jealous of the handsome young French officer who had won the heart of the fair *señorita* the governor himself desired to wed.

He lingered three months in jail. Then, through the intercession of a former French officer, who had served with Saint Denys, he was liberated and presented to the Spanish Viceroy, the Duke de Linares, who offered him a high position if he would enter the Spanish service. It was refused with the simple statement: "I am a Frenchman. I will remain a Frenchman." Whereupon Linares, appreciating his fidelity, treated him with proper respect. Mounted on a splendid horse, which the viceroy gave him, with his saddlebags well lined with Spanish gold, Louis Juchereau returned to the *señorita* at *Presidio del Norte* where the marriage was solemized. After a honeymoon of six months, the bridegroom returned to Mobile October 10, 1716, leaving his bride to await his return.

Later he planned a trading invasion of Spanish territory with Sieurs de Graveline, Derbanne, and the Chauvin brothers, but the expedition met with disaster, his goods were seized by the Spanish authorities, and he returned to Mobile March 24, 1719. At various times he was commander of many posts in the wilderness. In 1720 it was that of the *Riviere aux Cannes*. Then in 1721 it was in the territory of the Nassonites. He did not become commandant of Natchitoches until December 2, 1721. The post that he had named *le fort de Saint-Jean-Baptiste de Naquitoche*, had been built by another French officer named du Tissenet under Bienville's orders, and the village was called *Naquitoches* after a tribe of Caddoan Indians that inhabited the vicinity.

Here he established himself and his family and remained the commander of the post until the day of his death, June

11, 1744, twenty-two years later. Up to the time he was appointed commandant of Natchitoches he had served as a volunteer without regular pay or rank. He was then made a captain. Praised by every early Louisiana historian his death was universally deplored. Le Page du Pratz expressed the opinion that Louis Juchereau de Saint Denys would have made an ideal governor for Louisiana. He was worshipped by many Indian tribes, who mingled their lamitations with those of the white colonists who gathered about his grave in the little cemetery of St. Francois, where Father Barnabé, the Capuchin missionary, laid him to rest.

Louis Juchereau de Saint Denys, who by his valor had won the military cross of Saint Louis, a decoration that carried knighthood with it, left as issue of his marriage with Doña Manuela de Sanchez Ramon, seven children:

1.—Marie Rose Juchereau de Saint Denys, born in the parish of St. Jean Baptiste, in the district of the *Presidio del Norte.* She married in Natchitoches July 6, 1733, Jacques de la Chaise, keeper of the king's stores, son of the famous Jacques de la Chaise, *Commissaire Ordonnateur* in Louisiana, and Marguerite Cailly. She died in Natchitoches April 28, 1737, leaving a son and two daughters. The daughters were Marie Louise, born May 21, 1734, and Anne Marie, born January 27, 1736. The son, Louis Antoine de la Chaise, born, as were his sisters at Natchitoches, March 8, 1737, afterward became the first *alcalde* in New Orleans under the Spanish domination. His father, after Marie Rose's death, later married Marguerite d'Arensbourg, daughter of the Chevalier Charles Frederick d'Arensbourg. (q.v.)

2.—Louis Charles Juchereau de Saint Denys, born in the *Presidio del Norte.* He died in Natchitoches on February 7, 1778. Following his distinguished father's footsteps, he became a soldier and in 1765 was already a lieutenant. Under the Spanish regime he sat, in 1770, as an Ordinary Alcalde in the New Orleans Cabildo. He married Marie Barbier but left no issue.

3.—Marie des Douleurs (or Dolores) Juchereau de Saint Denys, born in the *Presidio del Norte.* She married in Natchitoches, June 9, 1750, Cesaire de Blanc de Neuveville (widower of Elizabeth Gugol), knight of St. Louis and second commander of the Natchitoches Post, a native of the parish of Acoules, in Marseille, France. Two children were born of this union, (a) Louis Charles de Blanc, who married in New Orleans, in 1772, Elizabeth Pouponne d'Erneville; (b) Jacques Maurice de Blanc, born in Natchitoches October 22, 1756, commandant at both Natchitoches and *Poste de Atakapas* (now St. Martinville), no date of his marriage, and issue, or death are procurable.

4.—Louise Marguerite Juchereau de Saint Denys, born in the Presidio del Norte, who died before April 3, 1741, apparently unmarried.

5.—Marie Pétronille Feliciana Juchereau de Saint Denys, born in Natchitoches. She married, April 18, 1746, the Chevalier Athanase de Mezières, a native of the parish of St. Sulpice, in Paris, and died before him. Their union was blessed by only one daughter, Félicité de Mezières, about whom no record exists. The widowed Chevalier de Mezières then remarried Pélagie Fazende, by whom he had six children. He became commandant of the Natchitoches Post during the early days of the Spanish domination and died November 2, 1779 in San Antonio, Texas.

6.—Marie des Neiges Juchereau de Saint Denys, born in Natchitoches August 5, 1734. She became the wife, on June 2, 1754, in Natchitoches, of Don Manuel de Soto Bermudez. She was still living in 1781. Several children were born of the Bermudez-Saint Denys union but their names and records are not available.

7.—Pierre Antoine Juchereau de Saint Denys, born in Natchitoches June 20, 1770. On account of his distinguished military services, he was made a knight of St. Louis. He died, unmarried, in Natchitoches on September 29, 1782.

The coat of arms of the Juchereau de Saint Denys family is "On a field *gules* the head of St. Denys *argent*."

KENNER Family

WILLIAM KENNER the founder of the Louisiana branch of the Kenner family, was a Virginian by birth, and was just one month old when the American patriots put their hands and seals to the Declaration of Independence. Of his childhood little is known but as his parents were in comparative affluence, he did not, like many successful men, struggle with early poverty and privation. Yet this did not restrain his adventurous disposition, for arriving at manhood he left the home of his fathers and sought fame and fortune in the territory then known as Louisiana, and before the close of the eighteenth century we find him established in New Orleans in partnership with a Mr. Oldham and a Mr. Clargue, under the name of Kenner & Co. The firm carried on a general mercantile and commission business, and to show their enterprise and progressive character, it is said that among the cargo of the first steamboat that paddled down the Mississippi river, the *New Orleans*, was a consignment to this firm.

In addition to his mercantile business, William Kenner turned his attention to the culture of sugar, then in its earliest infancy. So successful was he that his plantation rivalled the average sugar estate of the early '90's in equipment and production.

About the year 1820 reverses came to the hitherto wealthy merchant, and his prosperity began to decline. His partner, Oldham, in whom he reposed the greatest confidence, absconded with a large part of the partnership's assets, and obligations falling due that could not be met, bankruptcy was the consequence. A few years later death claimed the energetic man of business and he was gathered to his fathers. His portrait shows a stout, florid gentleman, with mild blue eyes beaming benevolently from behind a pair of large spectacles, with his shirt collar up to his ears. He died in 1823, hardly reaching the meridian of life, being only forty-seven years of age.

In 1801, at the age of twenty-four, William Kenner married Mary Minor, daughter of Major Stephen Minor, an officer in command of the Spanish forces in the northern part of Louisiana, with headquarters at Natchez. This lady was only fourteen years of age at the time of her marriage, being born in 1787. Her portrait, yet extant and in the possession of the family, painted in 1802, shows us a delicate, girlish figure and pretty childish features, intensified by the low-necked, sleeveless dress of muslin, with the waist under the armpits. She died in 1814, at the age of twenty-seven, having been the mother of seven children, six of whom lived to reach middle life.

Four sons and two daughters survived William Kenner and Mary Minor. Through the able exertions of Etienne Mazureau the famous New Orleans lawyer, sufficient was saved from the wreck of their father's fortune to give each a competence. This the sons invested in sugar plantations. Sugar at that time was worth from ten to fifteen cents a pound; planting was extremely profitable and they rapidly accumulated fortunes for themselves.

Minor Kenner, the eldest son, born in 1808, married Eliza Davis, a half sister of Dr. D. C. Holliday, of New Orleans, and cultivated *Belle Grove* plantation in Jefferson parish. When the railroad now known as the Illinois Central was built, it passed through the place and Minor Kenner became imbued with the idea that a boom was about to take place in real estate along the line of the railroad. He therefore cut up his plantation into building lots and laid off streets and avenues of a future city. But the venture was a failure, although the town of Kenner still exists, with a charter, mayor, council—everything complete for a thriving city with the exception of inhabitants. Minor Kenner died in 1862, and left a widow, a son, named Minor, and a daughter, Minnie, who married a Mr. Bradford of Mobile, Ala.

William Butler Kenner, the second son of William Kenner and Mary Minor, was born in 1810. He owned and cultivated *Oakland* plantation in Jefferson parish. On this plantation was erected a vaccum pan for the manufacture of sugar, one of the first used in the state. When the Citizens' Bank was organized in New Orleans, William Butler Kenner became a large stockholder, and in accordance with the charter of the bank he heavily mortgaged his plantation. The bank failing to pay the dividends expected, the interest due the bondholders had to come out of the pockets of the mortgagees, and the drain was more than the Kenner plantation could stand. This, coupled with the Civil War, reduced the once magnificent estate to a wilderness of weeds. In 1873, during a yellow fever scourge, William B. Kenner, with members of his family, passed away in his forty-third year.

W. B. Kenner, in 1832, had married Ruhamah Riske, of Cincinnati, grand-daughter of Benjamin Chambers, a pioneer settler of Pennsylvania, and founder of the town of Chambersburg, of that state. She was also related to the Ludlow family of Cincinnati. Of seven children, five survived: Philip Minor Kenner, who became a sugar and rice planter of St Charles parish; Frederic Butler Kenner, who removed to Minnesota and engaged in farming, banking and real estate business in that state; Charlotte Kenner who married George Harding, a patent attorney of Philadelphia, and left a large family; Josephine, who married Charles M. Shepard, and whose children resided in Montana and New York; Mary Minor Kenner, who first married Horace Binny, son of a celebrated jurist of that name, and on being left a widow, re-married W. G. Milliken, of the Cohansey Glass Works of Philadelphia; the third son, George R. Kenner, born in 1812, was in partnership with his brother, Duncan F. Kenner, and cultivated with him *Ashland* plantation in Ascension parish, but, having married a Mrs. Charlotte Jones, of Cincinnati, George sold out his interest in the plantation to his brother, and purchased a part of an estate of his wife's half-brother, Israel Ludlow, in Kentucky, just opposite Cincinnati. When Texas was admitted into the Union, George Kenner purchased a tract of land in Matagorda county and attempted sugar cane culture, but did not live to see the success of his venture, dying in 1853 and leaving no descendants.

Duncan F. Kenner, youngest son of William Butler Kenner, was born in 1813. Arriving at his majority, he followed

his father and brothers into the sugar planting business, was
first half-owner and then sole owner of *Ashland* plantation.
When the war broke out between the states he did not hesi-
tate to cast his lot with the South and was elected to the
Confederate Congress. In 1863 he was sent to France as
special commissioner and minister plenipotentiary to induce
that country to recognize the Confederate States. Before
sailing on that mission he had an interview with Jefferson
Davis, in which the advisability of emancipating the slaves as
a measure likely to influence the European governments in
favor of the seceding states was discussed. Although a large
slave-owner—probably the largest in the South—Duncan
Kenner urged in the strongest manner that Jefferson Davis
issue the proclamation. The head of the Confederacy did not
issue the proclamation.

Duncan F. Kenner married Nanine Bringier, in 1839, and
only three of a number of children reached maturity. Rosella,
the eldest daughter married General Joseph L. Brent and
resided in Baltimore and their daughter Nannie Brent married Thomas Sloo. The other daughter of Duncan Kenner
married Samuel Simpson, a New Orleans cotton merchant.
The son, George Kenner, died during the life time of his
father, leaving one son who resided in Nashville, Tennessee.
Duncan F. Kenner died in 1887, at the age of seventy-four.

Of the two daughters of William Kenner, and Mary
Minor, the eldest, Martha Kenner, born in 1804, married
John B. Humphreys, nephew of John Brown, Louisiana's
first United States senator, and lived on *Roseland* plantation
in St. Charles parish. After the death of Mr. Humphreys,
Martha married a Mr. Bruce, who also left her a widow.
Her third husband was Charles Oxley, of Liverpool, England, also a cotton broker of New Orleans. Mrs. Oxley died
in 1873, and left eight children.

The second daughter of William Kenner and Mary
Minor, Frances Ann Kenner, born in 1806, married when
quite young a Mr. Dick. Being left a widow, she married a
second time George Currie Duncan. She died in 1875 leaving no descendants.

Abridged from an article by Hiddleston Kenner, New Orleans **Times-
Democrat**, October 23, 1892.

DONNAUD—DE DUCHÉ—ALEXANDER

NO better example of the commingling of the blood of the various root-stock families of French and English foundations can be cited than the marriages that united the Donnauds, the de Duchés, and the Alexanders in one well-known Louisiana family whose descendants are now prominent in the state.

Abel Donnaud, born in Port-au-Prince, on the island of San Domingo, May 6, 1791, was of French parentage, his mother and father having left France during the disturbance attendant on the outbreak of the dread French Revolution in 1789, when all the nobility who did not join with the Republicans were forced to flee the land of their birth. M. and Mme. Donnaud made their way to San Domingo where they remained until the outbreak of the blacks in 1803 forced a number of white families from the island. Many of the white planters and slave-owners were killed and the uprising of the slaves resulted in the independence of Haiti and the formation of the so-called "Black Republic." After leaving San Domingo, the members of the Donnaud family settled in Norfolk, Virginia, where they remained until about 1808, when they moved to Philadelphia.

Comte René Roch de Duché, a French nobleman, was also expelled from France at the time of the Revolution, and with his family settled in San Domingo. Along with other French and Spanish families, the de Duchés were forced from the famous West Indian island to escape death at the hands of lust-maddened slaves, and arrived in the United States at the same time the Donnauds settled at Norfolk. The friendship formed on the island continued in Philadelphia and when Abel Donnaud arrived at man's estate he married Eugénie de Duché, daughter of Count Réné Roch de Duché. After a short stay in Philadelphia the young couple decided to live out their lives in Louisiana, and they settled at Thibodeaux, in Lafourche parish, in 1831, where they resided for years, beloved and respected citizens. Abel Donnaud died there in 1853, in his sixty-second year.

From the marriage of Abel Donnaud and Eugénie de Duché, two sons and three daughters were born: Adolph Donnaud, the eldest son, who married and settled in Thibodeaux; Alfred Donnaud, who removed to New Orleans with his mother and sisters, studied medicine and became a physician of note in that city; Rosina Donnaud, who Married F. W. Moore, of Pattersonville; Julia Donnaud, whose husband was Captain Henry Carr, prominent steamboat man; and Pauline Donnaud, who married Thomas Lawson, a Jefferson parish planter.

Dr. Alfred Donnaud, born August 25, 1822, and died April 22, 1862, was a prominent physician of New Orleans. At the time of his death he was surgeon of Company A., Continental Guards, holding the rank of lieutenant, and his funeral, April 23, 1862, was the last Confederate military funeral held in New Orleans, as on the following day the warships of Farragut's squadron fought their way past the river forts and took possession of the Crescent City. Dr. Donnaud had married Laura Lucretia Beale, April 24, 1846. She was born November 25, 1831, at Alexandria, Virginia, and died in New Orleans February 27, 1915, at the age of eighty-four.

Laura Beale Donnaud was the daughter of John Hancock Beale and Almira E. Alexander. Her mother was the daughter of a very interesting Virginia family, the city of Alexandria, across the Potomac river from Washington, D. C., being named after Almira's paternal ancestor. In 1660, Captain Robert Hawson brought 120 colonists to Virginia and was repaid by a grant of land containing 600 acres. Captain Hawson sold all this land to John Alexander, the father of Amos Mark Alexander, in 1667 for 6,600 pounds of tobacco. In 1730 a tobacco warehouse was erected at a point where the city of Alexandria now stands. A small settlement grew up about the warehouse, which was first called Belle Haven. In 1748 the general assembly of Virginia passed an act constituting Lord Fairfax, Gerald Alexander, and Philip Alexander, among others, trustees to design buildings and maintain the town of Alexandria, which was decided upon as a fitting new name for the town that was to succeed Belle Haven. George Washington, then seventeen, assisted in making the surveys.

John Alexander was the father of Amos Mark Alexander, who married Elizabeth Wroe, a daughter of Absolom Wroe and Anna Clark Daniels, a widow whom he married in 1805. The Wroe children were: Elizabeth, who became the wife of Amos Mark Alexander, and three sons, Richard, Samuel, and Everett Wroe. (Rohanna, a sister of Anna Clark, married William Rhodes of Alexandria, 1787).

The children of Amos Mark Alexander and Elizabeth Wroe were: Almira E. Alexander, who married John Hancock Beale; Maria Alexander, who married a Mr. Carlisle; and seven sons, Walter W., Amos, Charles R., Albert, Oscar, Robert, and Samuel Alexander. John Hancock Beale, who married Almira Alexander, was related to Major John Harper of Revolutionary fame. With his wife and sisters Beale settled in Texas, where he died at Columbia. His sister, Anna Beale, married F. M. Gibson of Richmond, Fort Bend county; Mary Beale married a Mr. Harris of Austin, Texas, while Julia Beale married a Mr. Smith of Richmond, Texas.

After the death of John Hancock Beale, Almira Alexander Beale, with her daughter, Laura Lucretia Beale, came to New Orleans. Her second husband was William R. Hall and, when on October 4, 1867, she was left a widow a second time, she married Mark Frederick Bigney, a native of Cumberland, Nova Scotia, who became a prominent New Orleans newspaper editor. He died April 20, 1886, at the age of of sixty-nine. His wife, Almira, died August 30, 1884, at the age of sixty-six. The daughter of Almira Alexander by her first marriage, was named Laura Lucretia Beale. At the age of fifteen she married Dr. Alfred Donnaud as already noted. Five children were the result of the union. After the death of Doctor Donnaud, Laura Beale Donnaud married, on January 13, 1868, William Davidson, a native of Leith, Scotland, his death occuring

June 10, 1871. There was no issue from this second marriage. She died February 27, 1915, at the age of eighty-four.

The children of Dr. Alfred Donnaud and Laura Lucretia Beale were:

1.—Eugénia Donnaud, born in Thibodeaux, Louisiana, September 19, 1848, and died in New Orleans, November 14, 1920. She married Captain Richard J. Lowden, a shipmaster, and had seven children, viz: (a) Thomas Lowden, (b) Laurence Lowden, (c) Laura Lowden (who married Thomas J. Tulley), (d) Richard Lowden, (e) Eugénia Lowden, (f) Ella Lowden, and (g) Bessie Lowden (who became the second wife of T. J. Tulley). The only descendants are the son of Laura Lowden, Thomas J. Tulley, Jr., and the children of Bessie Lowden Tulley.

2.—Alfred John Beale Donnaud, born in New Orleans January 1, 1849, died January 27, 1850.

3.—Albert Louis Henry Donnaud, born in New Orleans December 10, 1851, and died June 24, 1929, married Siddie Dawkins, daughter of George Dawkins and Delzora Shute, of Union parish, Louisiana. Their three children were (a) Alfred Donnaud, who married Marie Fluker, and after her death married Gladys Shelburne, (b) Delzora Donnaud, who married Clyde Paine, and (c) Siddie Donnaud, who married Eugene Brierre.

4.—Charles Oscar Donnaud, born in New Orleans December 8, 1853, married Amélie Renaud, daughter of Aristide Renaud of France, and Eliza Bossier of St. Martin parish, Louisiana. Their children were (a) Charles Oscar Donnaud Jr., who married Lila Rose Harvey; (b) Albert Henry Donnaud, who married Viola Temple Hutchinson; (c) Laura Amélie Donnaud, who did not reach maturity; (d) Eliza Bossier Donnaud, died young; (e) Sidney Ira Donnaud, who married Helen Shea; (f) Laurence Donnaud, died in infancy; (g) Delia Irene Donnaud, and (h) William John Beale Donnaud who married Annette Mahoney.

5.—Ella Albertine Donnaud born in New Orleans February 13, 1856, and died in Donaldsonville, Louisiana, March 18, 1900, became the first wife of Linden E. Bentley, editor of the Donaldsonville *Chief*, and later Special Deputy Collector of United States Customs at New Orleans. Their two surviving children were: Ella Bentley, who married Stanley Clisby Arthur, March 20, 1908, and Granville Donnaud Bentley, who married Héloise Sims December 5, 1906.

Alfred and Charles Donnaud, sons of Doctor Donnaud, were well-known newspapermen of New Orleans, and Charles Donnaud was for many years secretary-treasurer of the board of commissioners of the police department of that city. Ella Donnaud Bentley, first wife of L. E. Bentley, was the first vice-president of the Louisiana Press Association, and a writer of prose and poetry that earned her a state and national reputation, a literary ability inherited by her daughter.

Coat of arms of the Dubreuil de Villars Family, page 109

JOHNSON

ABOUT the year 1776 a party of six young men left Liverpool, England, in a stout sailing vessel bound for distant America. All were of good families and each was animated with the splendid purpose of establishing himself in a section of the New World then under the domination of England, a beautiful land skirting the Gulf of Mexico and having for its western boundry the bluff lands on the banks of the Mississippi river, a land called West Florida, and not far north of the gay French-Spanish city of New Orleans. Five of the sextette were un-married—the sixth brought his young bride with him.

The party consisted of Isaac Johnson, a young Englishman, son of a Liverpool divine, sent to the wilderness of America by a Liverpool mercantile firm. He became the honored progenitor of a prominent Louisiana family. Another fresh-faced young Englishman was Richard Devall, who became the ancestor of the Devall family of West Baton Rouge parish. The third Englishman was James Mather, a merchant of Bochin Lane, he who had his bride with him and who became the ancestor of the Conrad family of East Baton Rouge. There was, of course, an Irishman in this party and his name was Philip Hickey, a name he wrote in large and shining letters in the early history of the country he adopted for his own. Two Scots there were, one was named Nicholson, and the other bore the name of Dunbar. The six adventurers, after crossing the Atlantic, made their way down the Ohio and Mississippi rivers by the cumbersome methods of transportation then in vogue, the flatboats, and settled on the bluff lands of British West Florida.

Isaac Johnson's father was the Reverand John Johnson, an Episcopal minister and writer of Liverpool and his mother was Margaret Hunter. Isaac was given the benefit of a splendid education, which stood him in good stead and quickly brought him influence and power in the section of Louisiana he had chosen for his new home. Through the fortunes of war and Galvez's brilliant coup in taking Baton Rouge, Natchez, and Pensacola, this section of the country passed from Britain's domination to that of Spain by 1781 and Isaac Johnson became a friend and intimate of the several Spanish commandants and governors.

Soon after his arrival he married Mary Routh, who with her brothers, Job and Jeremiah, of Virginia, had floated all their possessions down the Mississippi on a flatboat a few years before Isaac and his five companions left England. The Rouths first settled at Walnut Hills, now Vicksburg, and later went further south to the Natchez country.

Isaac Johnson was one of the first *alcaldes*, or judges, appointed by Don Carlos de Grand Pré, the Spanish governor of the Natchez district of West Florida, and was continued in the same office under Governor Manuel Gayoso de Lemos. In recognition of these honors Isaac named two of his sons, Charles Grandpré Johnson and William Gayoso Johnson. In connection with his other activities Isaac Johnson erected a sawmill at *Second Creek*, a short distance from Natchez, which proved most profitable until a spring freshet swept away the mill. He then moved to that section of Louisiana now called West Feliciana (then known as *Distrito de la Feliciana, Florida Occidental*), at the solicitation of his son-in-law, Gilbert Mills, and became a prosperous planter, his home being *Troy Plantation*.

Isaac Johnson and Mary Routh were the parents of twelve children, rearing five sons and five daughters to maturity. They were taught to cultivate fruits and flowers and love nature. They were:

1.—John Hunter Johnson, who was educated by his father and became a man of considerable importance in the Felicianas. He issued the call for the first convention of citizens who formed the Free State of West Florida, and with his brothers, Isaac Jr., Joseph, and Charles, took a prominent part in all the stirring scenes of that historic rebellion against Spanish rule. He was a member of the constitutional convention of Louisiana, and represented his parish in the state legislature during the British invasion in 1815 when Andy Jackson beat back Pakenham's trained army on the field of Chalmette. John Hunter Johnson married Thenia Munson, and lived at *Troy Plantation*, where he died in 1819. His children were: (a) Isaac Johnson, his eldest son, named for his grandfather, born in 1805, at *Troy Plantation*, became the first Democratic chief executive of Louisiana in 1846 and its "war governor" during the hostilities with Mexico. Isaac married Charlotte McDermott, daughter of Bryan McDermott and Nancy Hawkins, by whom he had three children: Ann, Charles and Walter—the daughter married Dr. Percy Sargent, a grandson of Lieutenant Robert Percy, and the sons fell victims to a yellow fever scourge in 1853. Governor Johnson married a second time a Mrs. Johnson of Kentucky (not related) by whom he had one son, Joseph. Governor Johnson died March 15, 1853, at the age of forty-eight. (b) Joseph Johnson, second son of John Hunter Johnson, became president of the Louisiana senate, a position he resigned when stricken with tuberculosis. (c) Charles Lewellen Johnson, the third son, was at one time sheriff of West Feliciana, he married Martha Cureton, by whom he had five sons: William Johnson, John Hunter Johnson, Isaac Cureton Johnson, Charles L. Johnson, and Frank Johnson. Isaac C. Johnson the third son, settled in Avoylles where he became sheriff. (d) Margaret Johnson, the first daughter of J. H. Johnson, married Judge John B. Dawson, who besides his judicial position was elected to Congress and, in 1834, was an unsuccessful candidate against Edward Douglas White (father of the chief justice of the U. S. Supreme Court of the same name). Their daughter, Annie Dawson, married Robert Charles Wickliffe, who became governor of Louisiana in 1858, her daughter, Margaret Wickliffe, marrying Coleman Beckham, a lawyer of Shelbyville, Kentucky, and having two children, Annie, who married Lieutenant Muir of the Navy, and William, who became a lawyer. A son of Judge Dawson and Margaret Johnson, Ruffin Dawson, married Mary Charlotte Smith, and had one daughter, Charlotte Caroline, who died without issue. Another son, John Dawson, married Ann Turner. Their children were: Theodosia, Sallie, Ruffin, and John Dawson. (e) Mary Johnson, the youngest daughter of J. H. Johnson, married Anthony Doherty and had two sons, John Hunter Doherty, and Anthony, who died when a child.

2.—Ann Waugh Johnson, the first daughter of Isaac Johnson and Mary Routh, was celebrated for her beauty and accomplishments. She first married Gilbert Mills and later became the wife of Moses Semple.

3.—Isaac Johnson Jr., named for his father, was a rollicking jolly fellow who was captain of a line of barges that made regular trips between Bayou Sara and New Orleans, and noted far and wide for his dare-devil bravery. He was the Isaac Johnson, who as major of the Bayou Sara calvary, led the cheering patriots who captured the fort at Baton Rouge, September 1810, shot down the Spanish defenders, hauled the royal ensign of Castile and Leon from the pole, and hoisted in its stead a blue banner, with a single gleaming white star—the Lone Star Flag of the short-lived West Florida Republic. Isaac's wife was Melissa Jane Williams and the couple had three daughters who married three brothers named Chaney.

4.—Mary Johnson, second daughter of Isaac Johnson and Mary Routh, noted for her beauty, gentleness, and amiability, married Aaron Gorham from Connecticut in 1809. He was a New Orleans contracting carpenter and as a sugar planter in West Baton Rouge parish he was rapidly making his fortune when he died of yellow fever in 1825, leaving a widow and two sons: (a) John Lyon Gorham, who married Elmire le Blanc and left a son, Daniel Barlow Gorham, who practiced law at Lake Charles, and a daughter, Julia Gorham, who married W. O. Hines of Clinton, Louisiana. (b) Daniel B. Gorham, born May 23, 1813, died March 11, 1855. He became a physician and married Caroline Philips by whom he had a number of children. She was born December 20, 1820, and died January

1, 1888. The children of Doctor Gorham were: Angeline Gorham, who married, first John Barry, and had one daughter and three sons, her second husband being named Thompson; John Gorham, who died at fourteen; William Gorham, born June 26, 1847, died May 6, 1873, not married; Mumford Gorham, who served at the battle of Port Hudson and was never heard of thereafter; Amelia Gorham, who married Theodore Whiteman and had two sons, and Caroline Gorham, who married William Irvine and had four daughters and one son.

5.—Charles Grandpré Johnson, the third son of Isaac Johnson and Mary Routh, became a planter and married, first, October 20, 1815, Anna Ruffin Dawson, the beautiful and gifted sister of John B. Dawson. He was a very tall and finely proportioned man, and captain of the noted Feliciana Dragoons, the troop of mounted men from the West Florida parishes that rendered splendid service to Jackson at the Battle of New Orleans. By his marriage to Anna Dawson he had two daughters: Sarah Ann Johnson, born March 10, 1818, died June 2, 1842, and Margaret Johnson, the elder; Sarah Ann married Albert G. Howell, March 5, 1835, by whom she had two sons. They were: Dr. John B. Dawson Howell, stationed at Vicksburg as surgeon where he died unmarried, and Charles Johnson Howell, born July 12, 1837, died August 31, 1889, who married Jane Percy Dashiell daughter of Christiana Percy (q. v.) and Dr. Addison Dashiell. They had a son and a daughter: Dr. Charles Fisher Howell, born July 17, 1871, who married Mekelabil Catherine Stocking, and Christine Dashiell Howell, who married J. Hereford Percy. The youngest daughter of Charles Grandpré Johnson, Margaret Johnson, married Samuel H. Shipley, a native of the eastern states, and left a daughter, Mary Shipley, who married Garrison Sibley. After the death of his first wife, Anna Dawson, Captain Charles Grandpré Johnson married, on September 1, 1835, Eliza Eddington of Liverpool, England. She died soon after the birth of a son, who became Dr. Charles James Johnson. He studied medicine and married Louise Butler

McCrindall, leaving a daughter and a son: Lise Johnson, who married James Stewart McGehee, and Harry Johnson, who became a practicing physician in St. Louis. Charles Grandpré Johnson died in West Baton Rouge parish, November 1, 1854.

6.—Caroline Matilda Johnson, third daughter of Isaac Johnson and Mary Routh, was born January 19, 1792, died January 3, 1838. She married, March 27, 1811, Benjamin Collins, a Virginian who became sheriff of the Felicianas. Their children were: (a) Mary Collins, who married Ebenezer Cooley, and had one son and six daughters; (b) Charles Bartlet Collins, who first married Miss Jane Harbour, who died at seventeen March 8, 1840. His second wife was a Miss Taylor. Charles B. Collins had five sons, all dying without issue, and one daughter, Mary Charlotte Collins, born in 1863, who married William Taylor and removed to Tallahassee, Florida; (c) John Hunter Collins, born March 24, 1819, died June 11, 1876, who married May Dashiell but left no family; (d) Annie Collins, who first married the Reverand Dean, an Episcopal minister, her second husband being a Mr. Bowie of Pointe Coupée parish. She left two daughters and two sons; (e) Henry Clay Collins, born March 27, 1826, died November 20, 1841, while attending college in Kentucky.

7.—Joseph Eugenius Johnson, fourth son of Isaac Johnson and Mary Routh, was noted for his fondness for literature and writing. During the West Florida Rebellion he was made sheriff of New Feliciana, and in the War of 1812 he was detailed to captain the home guards because the slaves of the Feliciana section became so unruly it required military patrols to keep them in subjection. He served in the battle of New Orleans operations and transported British prisoners to Natchez. His wife was Martha Lane, by whom he had three children, David Lane Johnson, John Hunter Johnson, and Martha Johnson, who married a Mr. Lawrence.

8.—William Gayoso Johnson, fifth son of Isaac Johnson and Mary Routh, on March 18, 1821, married Eliza Collins Johnson, a daughter of William Garrett Johnson, not a relation, and the couple had (a) Richard Johnson, died unmarried; (b) Mary Johnson, who married a Mr. Brady of New Orleans, their children being: Alice Brady, unmarried; William Brady, and Lizzie Brady, who married and left an infant. (c) Isaac Johnson, the second son; (d and e) Judith and Margaret Johnson, twins; (f) Thomas Johnson, who accidently shot himself; (g) Sarah Johnson, and (h) Lizzie Johnson.

9.—Elizabeth Johnson, born in 1794, fourth daughter of Isaac Johnson and Mary Routh, remembered for her perfect blonde beauty, who married March 5, 1817, Thomas Withers Chinn, a sugar planter, born in Vermont, November 20, 1791, well-known financier of his day, prominent in politics, who served as district judge in 1826, moved to West Baton Rouge in 1829, and purchased *Cypress Hall* plantation. Later he went to Washington as member of congress, and under President Taylor was *chargé d'affaires* to Naples. Judge Chinn was a second cousin to Sir Walter Scott, and several of his grandchildren showed marked literary ability. He died at *Cypress Hall*, May 22, 1852, and his widow died there in 1877. The eldest daughter of Elizabeth Johnson and Judge Chinn, named Mary Jane Chinn, married April 16, 1838, William Blount Robertson (son of a father of the same name, who in turn was the son of General James Robertson, the pioneer settler of middle Tennessee). Her daughter, Elizabeth Robertson, named for her grandmother, married John B. Hereford, insurance man of Dallas and New Orleans. Another daughter, Leodicia Erwin Robertson, married, first, Felix Sennette, by whom she had a son and daughter, her second husband being Judge William Harris of Shreveport. Mary Chinn Robertson married Edward Desobry. Three other daughters, Tennessee, Ernestine, and Frances Robertson, did not marry but lived on a plantation opposite Baton Rouge. Katherine Lyle Robertson, who married Charles Lavalle, was noted for her talents in literature and art. Elizabeth Chinn, daughter of Judge Chinn, married William W. Lemmon, and two of their children, W. W. Lemonn Jr., and Mary Jane "Min-

[172]

nie" Lemmon, survived their parents. Bolling Chinn, the only son of Elizabeth Johnson and Judge Chinn, was a veteran of the Mexican War, and served in the Confederate Army as major of the Third Battalion, was wounded at the battle of Baton Rouge and sent to Johnson's Island a prisoner of war. Bolling Chinn married Frances Conrad, and had four daughters, Elizabeth, Frederica, Florence, and Ella, and two sons, Thomas Chinn, and Frederick Conrad Chinn, who moved to California.

10.—Martha Johnson, the fifth daughter and last child of Isaac Johnson and Mary Routh, was born March 1, 1796, at *Troy Plantation*, in the Felicianas, and on February 18, 1823, she married Nathaniel Wells Pope.

Doctor Pope was a young physician, native of Shelbyville, Kentucky, who had settled in the Feliciana country to practice his profession. He was the son of John Pope, who fought in the Revolutionary War; brother of John, Joseph, and Moses Pope, and nephew of Nathaniel Pope of Ste. Genevieve, Missouri. Doctor Pope was born January 23, 1789. When he was studying medicine in Louisville under Doctor Dudley, Nat Pope was employed during his spare time as a clerk by a pair of French storekeepers, "Audubon & Rozier." He later accompanied Audubon and Rozier to Henderson, Kentucky, and soon after went with them to Ste. Genevieve, Missouri. He was the young clerk who would rather hunt in the woods with John James Audubon than tend store with Rozier. Later, when the bird-artist came to the Felicianas to draw portraits of the feathered inhabitants of the magnolia woods, Doctor Pope and his wife frequently entertained the ornithologist and his wife, at their log cabin near St. Francisville.

Doctor Pope had a war record, first serving as private with Captain James S. Whitaker's company, Ninth Regiment (Simrall's) Kentucky Mounted volunteer militia, and being promoted to quartermaster sergeant. He practiced in the Feliciana country until 1836 when he moved to East Baton Rouge parish where he died July 2, 1836, leaving a wife and seven children. Those children were:

1.—Caroline Pope, born October 20, 1823, married Wil-

liam D. Phillips of Baton Rouge. Their children were:
(a) Edward Phillips, who married Belle Lobdell; (b)
Marshall Phillips, who married Camilla Mumford; (c)
Nathaniel Phillips, who married Lula Torras; (d)
Robert Phillips, who married Sally Kent; (e) Mary
Jane Phillips, who married Joseph Hart, and (f) Ger-
trude Phillips, who married William McCausland. The
Phillips family made their home at Lakeland, in the
False River section of Pointe Coupee parish.

2.—Florida Pope, born June 17, 1825, died November 30,
1829.

3.—John Johnson Pope, born July 16, 1826, did not marry.

4.—Nathaniel Wells Pope Jr., born October 30, 1827, married Leodocia Robertson, daughter of James E. Robert-
son, a woman of great beauty and culture. Doctor
Pope's namesake studied law, became a leader in his
profession, was elected judge of his district, and held
the rank of captain in the Confederate Army. Their
children were: (a) Virginia Pope, who married Albert
Barrow; (b) Henry Allen Pope, who married Regina
Schlater; (c) Clarence Johnson Pope, who married
Miss Bennett, and (d) Irene Pope who married Dr.
Oscar Richard, their plantation home being in West
Baton Rouge parish, near Port Allen.

5.—Mary Jane Pope, born September 25, 1829, died October 10, 1902, married Edward White Robertson,
brother of James E. and William B. Robertson. He
was a distinguished member of the bar, and served his
district in Congress. The old Robertson home is a landmark in Baton Rouge. Their children were: (a) Samuel
Mathews Robertson, who married Georgie Blanchard
Sanford; (b) Marshall Pope Robertson, who married
Olive Claire Smith; (c) Caroline Robertson, who married Elijah Robertson, not related; (d) Martha Robertson, who married T. J. Barrow; (e) Frederick Conrad
Robertson, who married twice, Amelia De Lion and,
second, Marie Trist; (f) Lulu Ernestine Robertson,
and (g) Nathaniel Blunt Robertson, who did not marry.

6.—Ann Pope, born September 25, 1832, died in childhood.

7.—Marshall Pope, born November 26, 1833, married Sidney Angela Conrad, member of a distinguished old Louisiana family whose beautiful colonial home is situated on the Mississippi river below Baton Rouge. Marshall Pope studied medicine and became a prominent physician, was chief surgeon of the division of Southern Louisiana and West Mississippi, Fourth Louisiana Regiment in the Civil War. The children of Dr. Marshall Pope and Angela Conrad were: (a) Francis Duncan Pope, died in childhood; (b) Marshall Pope Jr., died unmarried; (c) Maimai Conrad Pope, who married Isaac H. Snyder; (d) Martha Madeline Pope, who married Edward L. Berdon; (e) Podine Conrad Pope, who married George C. Schoenberger; (f) Ripley Conrad Pope, who married Eva Wildes; (g) Sidney Conrad Pope, died in infancy.

8.—William Pope, born August 2, 1836, and died in 1874, married Leonora Holmes, of a wealthy and aristocratic Natchez family. William Pope became a lawyer, was elected judge, served in the Mississippi legislature, and was a captain in the Confederate Army. For many years Judge Pope, his wife and children, lived on the Benjamin Holmes plantation, near Natchez, but after the death of his wife he moved to West Baton Rouge parish. Their five children were: (a) William Pope Jr., the eldest son; (b) Martha Johnson Pope, who married D. M. Raymond; (c) Elizabeth Pope, who married Rollo A. Tichenor of New Orleans; (d) Leonora Pope, the youngest daughter, and (e) John Holmes Pope, died unmarried.

D'ARENSBOURG Family

CÔTE DES ALLEMANDS, "German Coast", Côte d'Or, are the several romantic names given to those rich riparian lands bordering on the Mississippi River in the parishes of St. Charles and St. John the Baptist. The nomenclature is significant; for it was there that the sturdy German colonists who immigrated to Louisiana from 1719 to 1721 settled, and where, for generations, they reaped a rich harvest.

The first German settlement was founded by twenty-one families who came to the colony aboard the ship *Les Deux Fréres* in 1719. It was designated by the French census taker in 1724 as *le premier ancien village allemand*.

On June 4th, 1721, the French sailing ship *Portefaix* arrived in Louisiana with some thirty Swedish officers and three hundred and thirty immigrants, mostly German, destined for John Law's concessions in the Arkansas. Their leader was Charles Frédérick D'Arensbourg. The collapse of Law's financial scheme, news of which was brought to Louisiana by D'Arensbourg, caused the *Compagnie des Indes* to send the newcomers to the German Coast. There D'Arensbourg found the original German village established in 1719. He founded his village nearby but closer to the river. In time it became known as *Karlstein* in honor of D'Arensbourg. D'Arensbourg himself obtained a concession midway between the two villages and was living there but a few months when the disastrous hurricane of September, 1721, practically wiped out the first German village and demolished many of the huts in *Karlstein*. The rehabilitation was rapid, and soon a chapel was built on the river bank, on the site of the present *Le Sassier* or *Trinity* plantation.

Later, when the German colonists, who had previously been sent by John Law to the Arkansas territory, left that section and descended on New Orleans in a body demanding from Governor Bienville a fulfillment of the promises made to them before they left the Old World, the governor sent them to join D'Arensbourg's Germans. They settled above and below his villages and named their upper settlement *Hoffen* and the two lower ones *Mariental* and *Augsburg*. The village of *Hoffen*, which in 1722 had a population of one hundred three persons, was probably named after a town of the same name in Germany; *Augsburg*, with seventy-two men, women and children, was named after a Bavarian town. *Mariental* had a population of eighty-two.

For over fifty years Charles Frédérick D'Arensbourg was the leader, commander, and judge of these composite German settlements. Each village had its head man, *prévôt* or *maire*, as he was called. The Germans found their new life burdensome but happy. Neat, white painted houses were erected along the course of the great river, and the fields were set out with corn, rice, indigo and other vegetables. The dearth of beasts of burden made it necessary for the stalwart German men to harness themselves to their plows for the tilling of the rich, black alluvial soil. The harvests were abundant. The surplus was loaded in boats and rowed down the river to New Orleans. It was a familiar sight on Sunday mornings in the *Place d'Armes*, in front of the Cathedral, to observe the little German boats tied to the river bank, laden with tempting rations. New Orleans relied largely on the German colonists for her food stuffs. She raised practically none herself, and was otherwise dependent on provision ships from San Domingo and even France. When famine virtually threatened the pleasure-loving Orleanians, the produce from the German Coast averted disaster.

The German colony flourished. Its population increased. Gradually the younger generation was assimilated by marriage into the more numerous French population. The process continued until eventually only a few of the original German names were preserved, many of them being Gallicised beyond recognition.

The origin of the celebrated Frédérick D'Arensbourg was for a time the subject of much debate. Prior to the publication (in 1909) of Professor J. Hanno Deiler's interesting and valuable *The Settlement of the German Coast of Louisiana*, accurate genealogical data and notes in the possession of the late Drausin Rosémond Perret (q. v.) and other descendants of the Chevalier had attributed Stockholm to Charles Frédérick D'Arensbourg as his native city. The data and notes in question, together with family tradition, indicated that he was born in 1693, a Swede of noble German ancestors, and that, at the battle of *Pultava*, he had valiently protected the person of the wounded Charles XII of Sweden, and had received from the king on the field of battle, in recognition for his services, His Majesty's own sword, a relic preserved among the Chevalier's descendants.

Such was the genealogy of Charles Frédérick D'Arensbourg until the publication of Professor Deiler's book in 1909. That author, in total disregard of the genealogical data and family tradition above described, and without causing genealogical researches to be made in Stockholm, announced that the Chevalier's name was not D'Arensbourg but Karl Friedrich, that he was born in the village of Arensburg on the Island of Oesel in the Bay of Riga, province of Livonia. According to Professor Deiler, the young man, together with a number of other officers of the Swedish army, preferring exile to Russification, entered into a contract with the *Compagnie des Indes,* just about the time the "Mississippi Bubble" burst, to take German immigrants to distant Louisiana. Professor Deiler suggested that when Karl Friedrich applied for his commission in Paris and was asked whence he came, he wrote his name in French "Charles Frédérick", and, in order to designate his birthplace, added the name "d'Arensbourg." The French officials, mistaking this designation of his birthplace for his last name, issued the commission to Charles Frédérick d'Arensbourg. Professor Deiler concluded that Karl Friedrick then and there adopted the "d'Arensbourg" and added it to his name.

Many of the descendants of the celebrated Chevalier refused to accept Professor Deiler's theory; first, because they felt that the positive data contained in the family genealogical notes was more trustworthy than the author's etymological argument, and, secondly, because they were reluctant to believe that a man with the education known to have been pos-

[178]

sessed by the Chevalier would have rechristened himself so informally.

Thus stood the matter until 1911 when the family genealogical notes and tradition were entirely corroborated. In that year independent genealogical researches were made by a professional genealogist in Stockholm at the instance of Hugues J. de la Vergne, a descendant of the Chevalier. These genealogical notes were published in detail in the *Times-Democrat*, Sunday, December 4th, 1911. They claimed:

Karl Frederik von Arensburg was born in Stockholm in 1693 of noble German ancestry. After a military education, he became a lieutenant in the Sodermanland Battalion of Boarders (naval). On the 25th of May, 1719, he submitted an application for promotion to a captaincy, which he obtained. He had then served His Majesty, Charles XII, eight years, had been made a prisoner of war twice and wounded several times. After the battle of *Pultava*, he obtained leave to go to Germany, but was without the necessary funds. It was then that he obtained service with the West Indies Company. He was the son of Johan Leonard von Arensburg, master of the Royal Mint at Settin. Johan was also a director of minting concerns in Pommerania. He and his brothers were implicated in the political affairs of the Pommeranian Counts Brelcke, as the result of which they were imprisoned for many years. Karl Frederik von Arensburg's mother, Elisabet Eleonora Formandt-Manderstrom, was born July 17th, 1678, and died October 10th, 1710. She was a daughter of Erik Forsmander, chief inspector of customs at Wismar, in the department of Mecklenburg, who was ennobled in 1703 with the name of Manderstrom, now that of a baronial family. Karl Frederik von Arensburg had six brothers and sisters, among whom are mentioned Charlotta Lovisa and Kristian Ludvig, both born in the German parish of Stockholm, the former in 1699 and the latter in 1706.

Charles Frédérick D'Arensbourg was twenty-eight when he came to Louisiana. That he was married in the colony in 1722 to Margaret Metzer, of German birth, is abundantly proved by the records of the census taker for the colony and by Professor Deiler in the volume already referred to. The lady frequently signed her name Metzerine; but this, as

Professor Deiler points out, she did in accordance with an old German custom of adding "in" to a married name. The French officials added the final "e" in order to retain the German pronunciation of the suffix.

Charles Frédérick D'Arensbourg, besides ruling the German Coast for over a half century, participated in wars against the Indians, and was an actor in the Rebellion of the French patriots who protested the taking over of the province by Spain, but fortunately escaped punishment at the hands of O'Reilly. He was made a Chevalier of the French Military Order of Saint Louis on August 31st, 1765. His wife died on December 13th, 1776. His death followed on November 18, 1777. He had lived eigthy-four eventful years.

Chevalier Charles Frédérick D'Arensbourg and Marguerite Metzerine, spelling their names in the present form, had two sons and four daughters. These left numerous descendants who married into the best families of the colony. The sons were:

1.—Pierre Frédérick d'Arensbourg, the eldest son, was married February 20th, in the parish of St. Anne, near the fort of *Nouvelle Chartres*, in the Illinois country, to Elizabeth Duclos de Selle, daughter of Alexandre Duclos de Selle, a retired army officer, and Elizabeth Philippe, in the presence of the following named witnesses: de Villiers, Portneuf, Rochéblave, de Verges, Esnould de Livaudais, and Neyon de Soissy. Six children were the result of this union. Two sons, Pierre and Charles, did not leave descendants. The daughters were: (a) Marguerite d'Arensbourg, who married Joseph Delhommer; (b) Elizabeth d'Arensbourg, who married Etienne de Vaugine; (c) Louise d'Arensbourg, who married Charles Perret (q. v.) of St. Charles parish, and (d) Constance d'Arensbourg, who by her first marriage became Mme. Lallande d'Appremont and, by her second nuptials, Mme. de Neufbourg. Ten other children died young or did not marry and the elder branch became extinct.

2.—Charles Frédérick d'Arensbourg, usually called "Chevalier", the younger son, was married June 18th, 1776, to

Françoise de la Vergne. They became the parents of (a) Charles Frédérick d'Arensbourg III; (b) Zénon d'Arensbourg, who married Céleste Perret; (c) Gustave d'Arensbourg, who married Mlle. Bossier; and (d) Hubert d'Arensbourg who married Pouponne Perret. Two daughters became the wives of Honoré Lagroue de Latournelle, and Casimir Marest de la Tour.

The four daughters of Chevalier d'Arensbourg and Margaret Metzer were: (a) Louise d'Arensbourg, who married Nicholas Joseph Chauvin Boisclair de Léry and died childless; (b) Marguerite Marie d'Arensbourg, who married Jacques de la Chaise, son of a father of the same name who was the king's commissioner sent to Louisiana in 1722 to investigate the conduct of the colony's officials; (c) Pélagie d'Arensbourg, who married Pierre Marest de la Tour, February 3, 1742, and (d) Rosalie d'Arensbourg, who married Eugéne de Macarty. Of these daughters, only Mmes. de la Tour and de la Chaise left children.

The children of Marguerite Marie d'Arensbourg, daughter of the first chevalier, and Jacques de la Chaise were:

1.—Auguste de la Chaise, who served as body-guard to Louis XVI, and later became a member of the Society of French Jacobins established in Philadelphia in 1794. He attempted to foment a Jacobin movement in the young American States through which an expedition would be sent to Louisiana to expel the Spanish. This movement was put down by President George Washington, whereupon young de la Chaise joined the French army, rose to the rank of general, and went to San Domingo with General Leclerc, where he was killed in 1803 during a naval engagement and his body buried with honors in the Gulf of Mexico. He had married a daughter of Pierre Foucher, who was also a granddaughter of Etienne de Boré, but left no descendants in Louisiana.

2.—Marie de la Chaise, who married François Chauvin de Léry, July 23, 1763. She became the mother of twenty-two children but only eight of them left descendants. The sons were: (a) François de Léry, (b) Chauvin de Léry, (c) Boisclair de Léry, and (d) Jacques de Léry, while the daughters were: (e) Charlotte de Léry, who became Mme. Hardy de Boisblanc; (f) Rosa Mélicerte de Léry, who became Mme. O'Brien, and (g) Aimée de Léry, who became Mme. Suzeneau.

3.—Louise Mignone de la Chaise married Joseph Roy Villeré, (q. v.) set down in official papers as *Ecrivain de la Marine en cette ville*, or "Maritime notary", on October 12, 1759. He became a captain of the German militia under his wife's grandfather, the Chevalier d'Arensbourg, and was the Villeré murdered by O'Reilly's Spanish soldiers. Her son, Jacques Philippe Roy de Villeré became the State's first Créole governor.

4—Pélagie Honorine de la Chaise married, in 1763, Michel Edmond Forstall (q. v.).

5—Marguerite de la Chaise married Nicholas Chauvin de la Frénière, (q. v.), another martyr of General O'Reilly's iron rule.

6.—Charles de la Chaise, married Mlle. Chretien.

7.—Philippe de la Chaise married Catherine de Moulion but left no issue.

8.—Charlotte de la Chaise married Charles Lagroue de la Tournelle and died a centenarian.

9.—Mlle. de la Chaise, married Marest de la Tour.

The many female descendants of d'Arensbourg married into families of undoubted French origin such as Villeré, de la Chaise, de Léry, Bosclair, de la Tour, Lagroue, de l'Homme, de la Vergne, de Buys, Perret, St. Martin, Montégut, Lanaux, Beauregard, Bouligny, Durel, Suzeneau, Le Breton, Tricou, Duverjé, de Reggio, to mention only a few.

Honorine Delhommer, one of the daughters of Joseph Delhommer and Marguerite d'Arensbourg, married Charles Boyer of Paris. Their daughter, Clélie Cécile Boyer, married Samuel B. Todd of Lexington, Kentucky, a brother of Mary Todd who became the wife of Abraham Lincoln. During the Civil War, it was at the intercession of Mrs. Todd that the martyred president paroled her cousin, Drausin Rosémond Perret (q. v.), and numerous other Confederate Créoles who were political prisoners at New Orleans.

PERCY

AMONG the old and respected families that settled in that section of Louisiana, later known as "The Florida Parishes," and in the early days of the English domination as "West Florida," and by the Spaniards as "*Neuvo Feliciana*," none is better known than the Percy family, members of which have contributed a sturdy English-Scottish-Irish fibre to the state's present-day population.

Robert Percy, R. N., was born in Kilkenny, Ireland, September 1, 1762. His father was Charles Percy, an English army officer, who came first to America in 1776 and settled in Wilkinson county, not far from the section later designated as Fort Adams, Mississippi. His son, Robert, chose the sea for a career and entered the King's navy as a midshipman at a very early age, obtaining his commission just before coming of age. He began his service on the armed galley *Delaware*, April 26, 1783, and later saw service on the *Resolution, Robust, Africa, Ville-de-Paris, Victory, Powerful, Gorgon,* and *Lord Nelson*. On the latter armed cutter he also served as commander, and while in the Baltic sea conveyed forty-six sailing boats from Elsineur without loss, for which he was commended by the Right Honorable Lords Commissioners of the Admiralty. He served as commander on the *Lord Nelson* until December 8, 1801, and then obtained a leave of absence on half-pay, a leave he enjoyed until he was struck off the rolls September 4, 1804, when he was residing in America.

While he was a lieutenant on H. M. S. *Africa*, Lieutenant Robert Percy was married to Jane Middlemist in St. George's Church, London, September 15, 1796. His wife was a native of Edinburgh, Scotland, born July 16, 1772, being the daughter of Thomas Middlemist and Jean Proudfoot. The first three children of this union, Jane, Edward, and Margaret, were born in London. When Lieutenant Percy's father was accidently drowned in 1794 he left considerable property and the son visited America in 1795 to secure his share of the patrimony. This visit undoubtedly influenced him to emigrate to West Florida, for after his marriage and the birth of his first children, Lieutenant Percy applied for and received his leave of absence from the Royal Navy under date of September 28, 1802, and chartered the ship *Bilboa,* commanded by John Ruggles Soper, for the overseas journey. The two daughters accompanied the parents (the first-born son probably not surviving infancy), as well as Mrs. Percy's nephew, an adopted daughter, and another young lady. Arriving at New Orleans Lieutenant Percy sold the vessel and proceeded to the hill country above Baton Rouge where his father had settled twenty-six years previously.

Charles Percy, a one-time British army officer, who is said to have been a descendant of the Earl of Northumberland, emigrated to the Louisiana colony before his son entered the navy, and when he was accidently drowned in Percy's creek, Wilkinson county, in 1794, possessed considerable wealth as he had taken up extensive properties in that section. When Charles Percy came to the West Florida country it was under the domination of the English, but shortly after his arrival, in 1779, Don Bernardo Galvez, the Spanish governor of Louisiana, conducted his historic campaign against Baton Rouge and Natchez, hauled down the British ensign, supplanting the Union Jack of Merrie England with the red and white castellated banner of Spain. He then became a subject of Spain and was appointed *alcalde* of his district. Charles Percy was a widower when he left England but shortly after his arrival in West Florida married Susannah Collins, by whom he had a number of children, existing records showing only three of them married. They were:

1.—Sarah Percy, who married John Ellis of Adams county, Mississippi, a son of Richard Ellis, on December 31, 1799, and had two children, (a) Thomas George Percy Ellis, and (b) Mary Ellis, who, while attending a

Philadelphia boarding school, married Dr. René de la Roche. After the death of her first husband in 1808, Sara Percy Ellis, married Nathaniel A. Ware of Kentucky, September 1, 1814, and had two daughters, Eleanor Ware and Catherine Ware.

2.—Thomas Percy, who married Maria ——————, of Huntsville, Alabama, and died in 1888. One of his sons, W. A. Percy, of Washington county, Mississippi, opposed secession but when war was declared between the states led his company into battle, and one of his descendants became the late United States Senator Leroy Percy of Mississippi.

3.—Catherine Percy, who was married to Dr. Samuel Brown of Kentucky, September 27, 1808.

Lieutenant Robert Percy took up his residence at *Beech Woods*, a magnificent plantation home near the waters of Little Bayou Sara in the Feliciana country eight years after the death of his father. Here the other children of Robert Percy and Jane Middlemist were born. They were: Robert, Catherine, Thomas, Anna, and Charles.

Robert Percy soon became a personage of importance in *Neuvo Feliciana*, then under the rule of Spain and, like his father, he was appointed an *alcalde*, or local judge, by Governor Don Carlos de Grand Pré. However, in 1810, when the settlers of the Bayou Sara region became restive under the despotism and unfair rule of the Dons during the administration of Governor Carlos de Hault de Lassus, who had replaced Grand Pré, and decided to throw off the Spanish yoke and thus make a bold bid to become independent or, better, a part of the infant United States, Robert Percy performed a brilliant service in the so-called "West Florida Rebellion." After the first, and bloodless, stroke for independence, he with Fulwar Skipwith and Shepherd Brown, became members of the first high judiciary of West Florida. But when the English-speaking residents learned that the Spanish governor was not playing fair with the people of West Florida, and that their necks were in danger, Judge Percy, with other patriots holding responsible positions, ordered General Philemon Thomas to take the fort at Baton Rouge, which was done after a spirited night battle in which several of the Spanish garrison were killed, and the celebrated Lone Star flag of West Florida first unfurled as the royal ensign of Spain disappeared from that part of the United States forever.

Nine years later, November 19, 1819, Robert Percy was laid to rest in the Feliciana country he grew to love so well. His wife outlived him many years, dying March 12, 1831. It was in 1823 that his widow, who carried on the extensive cotton plantations, welcomed to *Beech Woods*, the family plantation home, Lucy Bakewell Audubon, wife of the now-celebrated Franco-American bird artist, John James Audubon. Here, Mrs. Audubon became tutor to the Percy girls as well as daughters of other Feliciana planters, and her school at *Beech Woods* became very celebrated. Audubon, too, lived a part of the time at *Beech Woods* and in the nearby woods hunted birds and drew their portraits, drawings which were afterwards reproduced in his famous plates of the *Birds of America*. It was in the neighboring Sleepy Holly woods that Audubon, with the assistance of Robert Dow Percy, then a youth of twenty, secured the gigantic wild turkey cock that became his most famous of bird drawings.

The children of Lieutenant Robert Percy and Jane Middlemist were:

1.—Jane Letitia Cowan Percy, born in London August 19, 1797, and died in New Orleans, January 5, 1877. She married, February 5, 1814, James C. Williams of Natchez, Mississippi, the step-son of Winthrop Sargent, first governor of the Mississippi Territory. A daughter, Mary Jane Williams, married Seargent S. Prentiss, famous Mississippi statesman, and a grandson of George Kennedy Prentiss of New Orleans.

2.—Edward Powell Percy, born in London, August 19, 1797, died in infancy.

3.—Margaret Jessie Isabella Percy, born in London, July 5, 1799, died in Paris, France, July 10, 1865. She married, December 7, 1824, George Washington Sargent, son of Governor Sargent and half-brother to James C. Williams.

[186]

4.—Robert Dow Percy, born in Louisiana, August 28, 1804, and died November 2, 1863. He married, July 19, 1831, Ellen H. Davis of Wilkinson county, Mississippi, and lived on *Weyanoke* plantation, West Feliciana. Three of his sons, Dr. Robert Percy, Dr. Harry Percy, and Thomas Percy, served in the Confederate army during the Civil War.

5.—Sarah Catherine Percy, born in Louisiana, May 2, 1806, died in Plaquemine, La., October 27, 1831. She married, May 15, 1828, Dr. William Provan of Natchez, Mississippi, and their one son, Mathew, was named for his uncle, Dr. Mathew Provan.

6.—Thomas Butler Percy, born in Louisiana, September 29, and died June 5, 1851. He married, June 4, 1833, Mrs. Elizabeth Leatherbury Randolph, widow of Judge Peter Randolph. Doctor Thomas B. Percy and his wife lived at *Beech Woods* plantation, West Feliciana, and their five sons, Thomas B. Percy Jr., Clarence Percy, Dr. James Rowan Percy, William Chaille Percy, and Robert Sargent Percy, all served in the grey ranks of those who fought to uphold Southern Rights. Thomas B. Percy Jr., fell a victim to typhoid, while Clarence Percy served the entire four years, the first two in the Army of Virginia, and participated in the two battles of Manassas.

7.—Anna Christiana Percy, born in Louisiana, November, 16, 1812, and died October 20, 1877. She married, September 13, 1832, Dr. Addison Dashiell of Maryland.

8.—Charles Evans Percy, born October 20, 1815, and died March 25, 1889. He was married three times. First, on January 5, 1843, to Mary E. Rowan, by whom he had a son; Second, on November 18, 1847, to Mary H. Doherty, of West Feliciana, by whom he had four children; Third, on May 7, 1856, to his second wife's sister, Catherine B. Doherty, by whom he had nine children. His oldest son, Charles E. Percy Jr., by Mary Rowan, was killed in the Battle of Atlanta.

Accompanying Lieutenant Percy and his family to America was Mrs. Percy's nephew, Charles J. H. Middlemist, who married Ann Tuell, a daughter of Samuel Tuell, March 20, 1817. C. J. H. Middlemist died in 1827 and left two children, Jane and John Byron Middlemist; the daughter died as a child. Ann Tuell Middlemist, being left a widow, married Albert F. McCall of Rapides parish. When her son, John Byron Middlemist, came of age in 1848, family records show he received his father's estate from Charles Evans Percy, his tutor.

An adopted daughter of Lieutenant Percy and Jane Middlemist, named Mary Purcell, accompanied the family from England in 1802. On May 20, 1805, she married Judge Elijah Smith of Windsor plantation, near Natchez, and one of her descendants was Harry Percy Veazie of New Orleans. Another young English girl who came to America with the Percys married John R. Chisholm of West Feliciana, and their only child, Virginia Martha Brent Chisholm, first married D. Holl, May 5, 1826, who died a few months after the marriage, and then married a second time, Maximillian Nübling, a nephew of her first husband. She had one daughter by her first marriage, and a son by her second husband. All of their descendants are now dead.

The Lone Star Flag of the West Florida Rebellion. This banner half a century later became the Bonnie Blue Flag of the Confederacy.

[188]

ALSTON-PIRRIE

IN the romantic and spirited history of that section of Louisiana now designated as the "Florida Parishes," a land that has for its western extremity that beautiful section of the state called West Feliciana, and *Feliciana* is Spanish for "happyland," one name stands out in prominence—that of Alston.

John Alston was by birth a Carolinian—a true and loyal British subject. So much so he lived and died an Englishman at heart in spite of the fact he had lived under different flags. He was born in Carolina April 18, 1735, and died in Louisiana in 1802 after living a most adventurous life. Six foot four in his stocking feet, of undoubted courage, set in his convictions, he was descended from a long line distinguished in England. His father was Solomon Alston and his mother Ann (Nancy) Hinton, daughter of Colonel John Hinton of Chowan county, in the Carolina colony. His grandfather was John Alston, the first of the name to come to America from England, who married Mary Clark, daughter of John Clark and Mary Palin.

The John Alston who came to Louisiana married, about 1761, Elizabeth Hynes of Hynes county, and became the father of five children. When the American colonies rebelled against the rule of King George III, John Alston was not in sympathy with the revolution and became a Tory. About 1770 he, his wife and four children, left Carolina and settled in the Natchez section of West Florida where the British flag still flew. John Alston was well-to-do and his children were reared in luxury and educated at home by competent English teachers. He settled on land near Natchez and began operating his plantation, which he named *La Grange*. Here, in 1772, his last child, Lucretia, afterwards called Lucy, was born.

In 1779 the Spanish governor of Louisiana, Don Bernardo Galvez, joined the colonists in their war of independence and John Alston saw his adopted land slip from the grasp of the British Lion when Galvez captured a series of forts from the English, Fort Bute at Manchac, New Richmond, as Baton Rouge was called, and Fort Panmure at Natchez. John Alston, in spite of these changes, remained true to his English patriotism. In 1781, when Galvez and his army were engaged in reducing Pensacola, the last stronghold held by the British, word came to Natchez that the Spaniards had been defeated and that a British fleet was sailing up the Mississippi river to retake Natchez.

The news caused instant excitement among the loyal Britishers at Natchez and a General Lyman at once formed a conspiracy to retake the Natchez fort from the small Spanish garrison guarding it. He formed a force of a hundred men, among whom was John Alston, and on April 22, 1781, began a siege which lasted a week before the Spanish garrison surrendered. The Spanish ensign was hauled down and once more the Union Jack flaunted from the fort's tall flagpole. Then consternation came to the British victors! The rumor of Galvez's defeat at Pensacola was proved unfounded. As a matter of fact it was the English forces in Florida that had been defeated! There was no English fleet coming! The British "victors" at Natchez hauled down the Union Jack and took to the woods!

On July 29, when Don Carlos de Grand Pré, lieutenant colonel of the Spanish forces in Louisiana, appointed as civil and military commandant of the Natchez district, arrived at Natchez he began a series of arrests, seizures, and confiscation of properties of the Englishmen who had retaken the Natchez fort. Having in mind the Spanish cruelty meted out to insurgents in New Orleans ten years before by Governor O'Reilly, many of the Englishmen determined on flight and endeavored to reach the nearest British post on the Savannah river. John Alston started his wife and three younger children, Ann, Solomon, and Lucretia, with a score of negro slaves as protectors, eastward on an overland journey, while he and his two older sons, William and Lewis, remained to face the Spanish music. Mrs. Alston had been gone only two days when her horse fell and she had several of her ribs broken. So, cared for by her children, she returned to *La Grange*, their plantation home, on a litter, where she died a few weeks later from the injuries.

Shortly after the death of his wife, John Alston and his sons attempted to escape from the punishment Spain decided to mete out to the revolting Englishmen. The sons succeeded but John Alston was considered too big a prize, and was betrayed and taken to New Orleans for trial. Found guilty, he was sent to Moro Castle, Havana, sentenced to confinement for life.

Previous to his capture in the Indian Nation, John Alston had asked a Doctor Farrar, who had a plantation on the west bank of the Mississippi river, near False River, to give protection to his three younger children. A faithful slave, known as Mammy Pratt, who had reared Mrs. Alston, remained with the children and in their hour of trial was their faithful protector. There was but one room in the cabin concealed in the swamps where they lived for more than a year. The boy Solomon was only twelve, and on his immature shoulders fell the task of securing a living for his sisters. A small dog of Mammy Pratt's also contributed to their scanty fare for it would hunt small game, such as rabbits, opossums and raccoons. Fish from the nearby river, and other edibles were smuggled to the fugitives by those on nearby plantations.

One man proved to be a real friend to the three Alston children. He was Alexander Stirling, a young Scot who had left his home in Forfar, Angushire, North Britain, a few years before to seek his fortune in the New World. He was plantation manager for Doctor Farrar and became devoted to the three Alstons, especially so to Ann, the elder girl, and on May 26, 1784, they were married. The Stirlings made their home in the Feliciana country, settling at Murdock's Ford on *Rio Feliciana*, (as Thompson's Creek was then called), where Alexander opened a modest mercantile establishment, which proved successful and the Stirlings became independent. Later William and Lewis Alston, in view of their youth, were pardoned and permitted to return to the Spanish country, and they took up lands in the Tunica section and established successful plantations.

Meanwhile, John Alston lanquished in solitary confinement in Moro Castle. In the winter of 1783 the heir to the British throne, then Midshipman William Henry (afterwards King William IV) visited Havana and finding many of his countrymen incarcerated, some of them under sentence of death, interceded for them and as a result John Alston was liberated, under the promise he would never return to Louisiana or any other lands under Spanish domination. Fearful that Alston and other leaders of the Natchez rebellion would again give trouble to His Catholic Majesty's domains, a reward of five thousand dollars was promised anyone who would find John Alston in West Florida or any other part of Louisiana again.

Fearful for his children, and hearing that they were in destitute circumstances, John Alston one day reappeared in New Orleans and presented himself to Governor Galvez. Boldly he declared his name and claimed the reward offered for his head, asking that the reward money be paid to his loved ones. Touched by the father's devotion, the Spanish governor released him, merely demanded of John Alston his word of honor that he would never again bear arms against Spain. Alston remained true to his promise and to the day of his death never raised his hand against the Dons. He found his daughter Lucretia in a convent in New Orleans. She had been sent there by her sister Ann to be educated; returned to the Feliciana country and found Ann married and a mother; he located William and Lewis on Tunica bayou, and opened another plantation nearby on the Lake of the Cross. He was able to claim some of his former slaves and by persevering energy and industry soon again became a wealthy planter in the Feliciana country.

The children of John Alston and Elizabeth Hynes were:

1.—William Alston, who married Mildred Wells of Rapides parish, Louisiana. His descendants lived in Mississippi.

2.—Lewis Alston, whose first wife was Mary Ann Gray, no issue; by his second wife, Rebecca Kimball, he had four children: (a) Isaac Alston, who did not marry; (b) Lewis Alston, who married Lydia Adams, and left one son who lived in Pointe Coupée; (c) Anne Alston, who married Samuel Wimbish, and left four children, Ruffin Wimbish, Mary Ann Wimbish, Charlotte Wimbish, and James Wimbish, all married and with children; (Mary Ann married Abraham Gray, Charlotte married John Baker, James married Sarah Doherty, and Ruffin married Lucy Davis of Baton Rouge); (d) Elizabeth Alston married Arthur Adams but left no children.

3.—Ann Alston, who married Alexander Stirling (q. v.), and had nine children.

4.—Solomon Alston, never married. As a captain in the Spanish troops he captured the Kemper brothers, who had led an ill-advised and unsuccessful revolt against Spanish rule at Tunica Bayou. The Kempers escaped their captors a few hours after their arrest and hounded Solomon to his death, brought about by sleeping night after night in a skiff on the Mississippi river to escape their fury. However, it was not *his* ears Ruben Kemper cut off and kept for years in a bottle as a warning to everyone that it was unhealthy to trifle with anyone named Kemper.

5.—Lucy (Lucretia) Alston, born 1772 in *La Grange,* Hommochito, Mississippi, died May 13, 1833, at the age of 61. Her first husband was Ruffin Gray, of Hommochito, the brother of Lewis Alston's first wife. Her second husband was James Pirrie, of Feliciana, who was an *alcalde* during the Spanish rule, of a fine Scottish family, born in 1769, who died March 7, 1824.

The union of the Alston family with that of James Pirrie brought another line of distinguished ancestry into the Feliciana country. Lucy Alston, by her first marriage with Ruffin Gray had four children. Two, Edmund and Elizabeth, died in infancy. A son, Ruffin, died October 12, 1817, when he was twenty-two. A daughter, Mary Ann, born a few months before her father's death. Ruffin Gray had opened a magnificent plantation in the Feliciana country, which he named *Oakley,* when his health, which had been delicate, failed him and he died in the Hommochito, country. Lucy Alston Gray went to the new home and later married James Pirrie, a friend and fellow countryman of Alexander Stirling.

Oakley, the Pirrie plantation home, has become famous

[193]

in Louisiana as it was the place where John James Audubon, the famous bird artist, had his first introduction to the magnolia woods of Feliciana and where his talents as a bird artist first burst into full bloom. In June of 1821, Mrs. Pirrie, seeking a tutor who could give her daughter Eliza certain accomplishments in the arts, found Audubon in New Orleans penniless and lowspirited, induced the Frenchman to go with her to the plantation and devote half of his time to her daugher's education, giving him the rest of the day to wander through the fragrant woods in search of birds. For several months Audubon lived at *Oakley*, and here drew many of the original bird portraits that afterwards won him fame when they were reproduced in his spirited plates of the *Birds of America*. Audubon called the daughter Eliza: "My beautiful Miss Pirrie of Oakley," in his diary of that period.

By her marriage with James Pirrie, Lucy Alston had three children, two dying in infancy, but Eliza Pirrie, born October 6, 1805, became one of the acknowledged beauties of the Feliciana countryside and was much sought after by the young men of that section. Eliza, although her mother and father wanted her to marry Dr. Ira Smith, in June 1823, eloped with her cousin, Robert H. Barrow, of *Greenwood* plantation. As the two were on their way to Natchez to be married young Barrow had to wade the Hommochito bayou, then running bank full, with his bride-to-be in his arms. On July 18, six weeks after their marriage, the bridegroom died from pneumonia brought on from the wetting.

The children of Lucy Alston Gray Pirrie who reached maturity were: two daughters:

Mary Ann Gray, who married twice. Her first husband was Jedidiah Smith, of Adams county, Mississippi, by whom she had three children, Eliza, who died in infancy; Catherine, and Sarah Pirrie Smith. Her second husband was Dr. Ira Smith of New York, the unsuccessful suitor for her half-sister Eliza's hand. There were no children by this union.

Eliza Pirrie, was three times married. Her first husband was Robert H. Barrow by whom she had a posthumous child, Robert H. Barrow Jr., who married Mary E. Barrow, a daughter of David Barrow of North Carolina. They lived on *Rosale* plantation and had nine children, those who survived infancy being: Charles Barrow, Sarah Barrow, Elipa Barrow, Bennett Barrow, Robert Barrow, Isabelle Barrow, and Samuel Barrow (q. v.).

Eliza Pirrie Barrow's second marriage was with the Reverend William Robert Bowman, of Brownsville, Pennsylvania, born December 7, 1800, died August 30, 1835. The marriage took place in 1828 while Bowman was rector of Grace Episcopal church at St. Francisville, which has the distinction of being the second Protestant church built in Louisiana. By this marriage she had two children: Isabelle Bowman, who married William Wilson Matthews, and had six children: (a) Robert Bowman Matthews, (b) Cora Slocum Matthews, (c) Lucy Pirrie Matthews, (d) Ida G. Matthews, (e) Leonard Finlay Matthews, (f) William Wilson Matthews. The son of Eliza Pirrie's marriage to Rev. Bowman was James Pirrie Bowman, who married Sarah Turnbull. From this union there were ten children, born at *Rosedown*, one of the most noted and beautiful plantation homes in the Feliciana country. They were: (a) Martha Bowman, (b) Eliza Bowman, (c) Sarah Bowman, (d) Anna Bowman, (e) Daniel Bowman, (f) Mayme Bowman, (g) Mina Bowman, (h) James Bowman, (i) Carrie Bowman and (j) Belle Bowman.

Eliza Pirrie Barrow Bowman's third marriage was with Henry E. Lyons of Philadelphia, in 1840, five years after her second husband's death. Mr. Lyons became a '49-er in California. By her marriage she became the mother of Lucy Lyons, who died at 18; (b) Cora Lyons, who married Captain Richard Floyds, and Eliza Lyons, who died when two years old. Eliza Pirrie Barrow Bowman Lyons, died April 20, 1851, and was placed at rest beside her clergyman husband in a grave in the pleasant Feliciana countryside she knew and loved so well.

HUCHET DE KERNION Family

RECORDS in the old Cabildo show that Jean François Huchet, *écuyer*, Sieur de Kernion, arrived in Louisiana in 1720, on the ship *La Loire*, from Lorient. He is mentioned on the ship's rolls as a staff officer destined for the Ste. Reyne Concession located in the Tchoupitoulas district. The vessel that carried him to his new home left Lorient August 11, 1720. He was born in the parish of St. Mathieu, city of Quimper, Brittany, December 28, 1700. His father, Pierre Guillaume Huchet du Rest, and his mother, Thomase Renée Guesdon de Keravel, belonged to ancient Breton families.

Both England and Holland vie with one another for the honor of having been the cradle of the Huchets. To speak first of the English claim, it was in the year 1350 or thereabout, while the forces of the Count de Blois and those of the Count de Montfort were waging a fratricidal struggle to decide the question as to who should exercise supreme power over Brittany, that there landed on the Breton shore Sir Richard Bembrough, an English knight, who pledged his faith to the cause of the Count of Montfort.

After being appointed governor of the city of Ploermel, Bembrough, learning that a companion-at-arms, Sir Dagworth, had been assasinated by an adventurer in the service of Charles de Blois, resolved to avenge his death by bloody reprisals on the Breton followers of that party. Thereupon ensued a reign of terror in the city of Ploërmel, which induced Robert de Beaumanoir, one of the bravest of the Breton knights, to issue a challenge to Bembrough. It provided that the Briton was to select thirty of his most trusty knights and meet Beaumanoir and twenty-nine of his followers, in a mortal combat. This engagement, immortalized by the Armorican bards and known in Breton annals as the

Combat des Trente, took place March 26, 1350. It was fought on the highroad between Ploërmel and Josselin, and though the Breton knights were victorious, the English, none the less, fought like tigers and slew many of their adversaries with their lances, maces, broad swords and battle axes. Among the followers of Bembrough on that glorious day was an English esquire, Hucheton de Clamaban, of Norman origin, who, according to several ancient authors, settled permanently in Brittany and founded the Huchet family.

Some time-stained records in the *Bibliothèque* Nationale of Paris assert, however, that the Huchet family descends from Hugues de Hornes, of a princely Dutch house, who settled in Brittany in 1297 and changed his name for that of Huchet. Though these records enumerate his descendants up to Bertrand Huchet, Sieur de la Huchetaye, who before 1420, was the Secretary of State of John V, duke of Brittany, and is the first well-authenticated founder of the family, this data is more or less traditional. The Huchet de Kernion family of New Orleans belongs to one of the younger branches of a venerable tree whose real origin is lost in the darkness of the ages.

About the year 1640, Jean Huchet, a scion of the oldest branch of la Bédoyere, born in Rennes in 1604, left upper Brittany to settle in Quimper. Being a younger son of a Seigneur de la Bédoyere who had many children, Jean Huchet, as such, under the unjust French feudal laws of inheritance then prevailing, was entitled to no share in the paternal estate. Evidently of an ambitious temperament, he set out alone to carve a worthy career. In Quimper he became known before long as an honorable and prosperous merchant and married Marie le Lièvre de Boisdanet, of an impoverished noble family. He died in the parish of St. Julien, Quimper, May 6, 1661, and was buried in the chapel of the Convent of St. François.

From his marriage were born thirteen children, of whom six were girls. His sons exercised the professions of priest, lawyers and notaries. One of them, Huchet de Kerourin, did not live to see several of his own grandchildren perish under the guillotine. Nor did he live long enough to glory in the achievements of another of his grandsons, the immortal

[197]

physician René Théophile Laënnec de Kerlouarnec, who discovered the stethoscope and to whose memory a statue has been erected in Quimper by the doctors of France and the whole world.

Pierre Guillaume Huchet du Rest, another son of Jean Huchet and Mlle. le Lièvre de Boisdanet, born in Quimper in November 156, married twice. His first wife was Renée Salaun, dame du Rest, daughter of Théophile Salaun du Rest, who served under Vauban and was a lawyer in Parliament, and Catherine Paillar. By this marriage, Pierre Guillaume became uncle of Théophile Malo Corret de la Tour d'Auvergne, national military hero of France, surnamed by Napoleon I *Le Premier Grenadier de la République*, whose venerated ashes now repose in the *Panthéon* in Paris.

From the first marriage of Pierre Guillaume Huchet du Rest to Renée Salaun were born four boys and four girls. Two of his daughters became nuns, and among his sons, one was appointed *Procureur du Roi* in the Parliament of Brittany and another became *Avocat du Roi* in the *Présidial*, or high court of justice, of Quimper. His first wife, Renée Salaun, dying July 23, 1699, Pierre Guillaume Huchet du Rest took as his second spouse, on October 19th of the same year, Thomase Renée Guesdon de Keravel, daughter of François de Keravel and Marie Vase de Mello de la Garenne. This Guesdon family ownd many beautiful feudal chateaux in *Basse Bretagne*, some of which are still occupied by their lineal descendants. From this second marriage was born one child, Jean François Huchet de Kernion, who settled in New Orleans in 1720.

In the Census of July 1, 1727, he is mentioned as living with Charles Petit de Livilliers "on his plantation on the left side going up the river." It was on this plantation that Jean François Huchet de Kernion signed, on October 4, 1736, a marriage contract with a wealthy young widow, Jeanne Antoinette de Mirebaise de Villemont, widow of Antoine Rivard Jr. She was born in 1715 in Poitiers and was the daughter of Henri Martin de Mirebaize, *écuyer*, Sieur de Villemont, and Antoinette Fourrier. She came with her parents and her sister to Louisiana in 1719 on the ship

Deux Frères. Her father, who was a French lieutenant, settled on his concession on the Rivière Noire, one hundred and twenty leagues from New Orleans, and in 1722 distinguished himself by pursuing with a band of Indians twenty soldiers who had revolted at Fort Toulouse and massacred Marchand, their captain. He captured them and killed most of the murderers.

The first husband of Mlle. de Villemont (Madame de Kernion) was Antoine Rivard Jr. Antoine Rivard, his father, from Ile Dauphine, in Canada, came to Louisiana before the foundation of New Orleans. He died in that city February 11, 1739. The elder Rivard resided on his concession, on Bayou St. John as early as 1721. He married twice, his first wife being Marie Briard and his second spouse being Antoinette Fourrier, widow of Henri Martin de Villemont, whose daughter, Jeanne Antoinette, married his son, as has already been stated, and at his death contracted, in 1736, a second mariage with Jean François de Kernion. At the time of her second marriage she had two daughters, one of whom became the wife of the Chevalier Christophe de Glapion. The marriage contract of de Kernion and the young widow Rivard, still piously preserved by the Kernion family, is a very curious document on sheepskin. Among the many signers thereto appear the names of Governor Jean Baptiste le Moyne de Bienville and other notables of the colony.

On March 1, 1748 Jean François Huchet de Kernion received a commission from governor de Vaudreuil as Councillor Assessor in the Superior Council of Louisiana. He had been serving already for quite a while as a militia officer in the colony, participating in all the Indian campaigns. He took a very active part in the quarrel between Rochemore and Kerlerec. He was one of the signers of the *mémoire* drawn up in 1760, certifying to Rochemore's incompetency. In 1762 he received from Louis XV his commission as Titulary Councillor in the Superior Council of the province. Thoroughly French at heart, he protested against the cession of Louisiana to Spain in 1765. So active was his animosity against the Hispanic king, that Father Hilare, a missionary in Louisiana, addressed a letter to France at that time complaining bitterly against his conduct. The cleric said that "the Sieurs de Kernion and de la Frénière, officers of the Superior Council, who had become all powerful in the colony" made certain rebellious proposals to him, which as a minister of God and a servant of his king, he duly spurned.

It was de Kernion and Piot de Launay who on October 29, 1768, after examining as a special committee of the Superior Council the petition presented by the colonists demanding the expulsion of Ulloa, first Spanish governor of Louisiana, made a report that resulted in the Spaniard's banishment from the province. That de Kernion did not share the fate of La Frénière and others for his part in the rebellion of 1768 is explained by the fact that he died on his Bayou St. John plantation June 13, 1769, five weeks before the arrival of O'Reilly, the Avenger.

From his marriage with the widow Rivard, he left only one child, Jean René, born in 1737, who died April 25, 1806. This son became an officer in the French and Spanish colonial troops and received a pension of two hundred livres a year from the French king, from September 16, 1763, when he was retired from active service. He served also as an Alcalde in the Cabildo in 1785. He married twice, the first time June 19, 1767, taking for his wife Louise Constance, daughter of Antoine Chauvin de Léry and Charlotte Faucon du Manoir. From her he had seven children.

1.—Louise Constance Huchet de Kernion, who married in New Orleans, Pierre Pascalis Volant de la Barre, son of Francois Pascalis de la Cestière and Charlotte Volant. From this union were born François de la Barre, who married his first cousin, and Jean Baptiste de la Barre who married Philomise Chauvin de Léry.

2.—Balthazar René Huchet de Kernion, who died in childhood.

3.—Marguerite Modeste Huchet de Kernion who married Laurent Lucien Chalon and left no issue.

4.—Jacques Huchet de Kernion, born September 5, 1778. He married three times. By his first wife, Marguerite Constance de Vergès, he had two sons who died unmarried and two daughters, one of whom, Constance, married Laurent Lucien Chalon, her uncle by marriage.

The second and third wives of Jacques de Kernion were Marguerite Aimé Desdunes de Poincy (widow of Mathurin Guerin) and Adélaïde la Molère d'Orville, by whom he had no issue.

5.—Marguerite Marie Huchet de Kernion, born 1780-81, died April 8, 1861, unmarried.

6.—François Dangeville Huchet de Kernion, born 1787-1788, who died unmarried.

7.—Pierre Huchet de Kernion, born February 6. 1784, who became a sub-lieutenant in the Spanish service and died in New Orleans December 4, 1855. He married September 25, 1800, Marie Genevieve, daughter of Charles Philippe Coulon Jumonville de Villiers and Marie Louise Clara de Acosta. From this marriage issued seven children: (a) Aventin Charles, who married Catherine Landreaux and died without issue; (b) Joseph Gustave, a Jesuit priest; (c) Alfred, who married Henriette Garidel and left three children, namely: Alfred, unmarried, Henriette (Mrs. Michel Gaudet), and Amelie (Mrs. George Gaudet); (d) Emilie, who married Stephen Rousseau and left no issue; (e) Félix, who died a Jesuit scholastic; (f) Adèle, who married Charles la Bédoyere de Kernion, her first cousin and left one son; (g) Emma, who married Adolphe Prieur and died with issue.

At the death of Mlle. Chauvin de Léry des Islets, first wife of Jean René de Kernion, her widowed husband took as his second spouse Marguerite Modeste de Vergès, daughter of Pierre de Vergès, a former *alcalde* and distinguished officer in Louisiana, and Marie Josephe Catherine Poupart. From this union were born three sons:

1.—René Dorestan Huchet de Kernion, who died unmarried.

2.—Pierre Ladislas Guermeur Huchet de Kernion, born September 27, 1800, died April 22, 1832. He marmarried, November 13, 1832, Céleste Roseïde, daughter of Pierre Volant de la Barre and Marie Rosine Chauvin de Léry. By this union he had three daughters: Marie Célestine, first wife of Charles le Breton; Marie Roseïde, second wife of Charles le Breton, ,and Charlotte Emilie, unmarried.

3.—Crispin Charles la Bédoyère Huchet de Kernion, born October 25, 1796, died December 5, 1846, who, as a mere lad of eighteen fought bravely under Andrew Jackson at the Battle of New Orleans. He married, January 28, 1820, Euphémie Aimée Lambert, daughter of Pierre Joseph Lambert and Marie Constance Wiltz. This union was blessed with the following nine children: (a) Charles La Bédoyère, born November 9, 1826, died June 28, 1861, who married his cousin, Adèle de Kernion, and left a son married to Cora Rivard; (b) Louis Dangeville, born August 25, 1834, died March 21, 1879, who married Blanche, daughter of James Dupuy and Azémia d'Oriocourt, from which union were born: (1) Louis Dangeville, married to Anna de Buys, who left three children, Sidney, Dangeville and Blanche Huchet de Kernion, all married and with issue; (2) George La Bédoyère, married first to Léontine Carrière from whom he had three sons, George, Charles and René Huchet de Kernion, all married and with issue. From his second wife, Anna Chaudin, George La Bédoyère Huchet de Kernion had no issue; (3) Ida La Bédoyère, unmarried; (4) Marie La Bédoyère, unmarried; (5) Charles La Bédoyère, married to Anita de la Lastra, of Mexico, without issue; (c) Pierre Octave, who married Heloise Fortier and died without issue; (d) Anatole La Bédoyère, who died in childhood; (e) Aman Arthur, who died young; (f) Rene Arthur, who died in childhood; (g) Marie Emma La Bédoyère, who married Emile Théodule Bernard du Montier and left issue; (h) Idalie Elizabeth La Bédoyère, who married Pierre Oscar Peyroux de la Rochemolive and left issue; (i) Anatole La Bédoyère (second of the name), born December 21, 1838, died June 16, 1909, who married Fanny Evélina Héloïse Campbell (of the Campbell of Argylle family of Scotland), daughter of Françoise Zoé Lambert de St. Omer and James Campbell. From this marriage were born several children, the four surviving being Marie Heloïse La Bédoyère (Mrs. S. R. Buchanan), Eulalie Régina La Bédoyère (Mrs. Raoul Jeanjean, of Marseilles,

France), George Campbell La Bédoyère Huchet de Kernion, whose wife is Aline d'Héreté, and Corinne Euphemie La Bédoyère (Mrs. Etienne Chevalier, of Algiers, Algeria). These four children are still living and have issue.

The coat-of-arms of the Huchet de Kernion is thus described: On a field *argent* three huchets (or hunting horns) *sable*, placed two and one. This escutcheon is quartered with the ancient coat of the de la Bédoyère family, which became extinct at the beginning of the fifteenth century, when Jeanne de la Bédoyère, last heiress of her house, married Bertrand Huchet, Secretary of State of John V of Brittany. The arms of the de la Bédoyères show on a field *azure* three pierced *billettes argent*, placed three, two and one. The family mottoes of the Huchets are: *Honor et Caritas* and *Hostibus et Feris*.

The Huchet family has made its proofs of nobility before such genealogists as d'Hozier, Chérin and others. In the possession of the family today, and in New Orleans, is a wonderful document, dated 1668, which is a proces verbal of the proofs made that year by members of this family before the commissioners of Louis XIV to be maintained as nobles. This voluminous record, which is duly signed and sealed, and which recognizes the ancient lineage of the appearers, meticulously enumerates every generation of this house from 1400 to 1668.

Seal of the Compagnie des Indes

LE PELLETIER DE LA HOUSSAYE

THE founder of the Le Pelletier de la Houssaye family in Louisiana, which family at the present time counts numerous representatives throughout the state, was Messire Paul Augustin Le Pelletier de la Houssaye (also called Pierre Augustin), knight of the Royal and Military Order of St. Louis, who settled at an early date in the colony and married Magdeleine Victoire Petit de Livilliers, of one of the bluest-blooded and most powerful families in the land. His bride was the daughter of Charles Petit, *Seigneur* de Livilliers, and of Louise Etienette de Malbec. Her parents were numbered among the first Louisiana pioneers, her father, Charles, being mentioned in the census of the province, dated July 1, 1727.

His plantation, at that time, was on the west bank of the Mississippi River, not far from New Orleans. In the census of 1727 he is said to be a native of Verteuil (in the present department of the Gironde), an officer of the *Compagnie des Indes* and a brother of Louis Petit de Coulanges, who had come with him to settle in the colony. He became eventually a *Capitaine detaché de la Marine*, and married, as already stated, Louise Etienette de Malbec, daughter of Jean de Malbec, Commissaire de la Marine, and of Anne del Thomas le Clerc.

The Petit de Livilliers family (q. v.) was on both paternal and maternal sides descended from the most distinguished French and Canadian ancestry, having passed through *Nouvelle France*, where it made its mark, before reaching Louisiana. Later on we find Paul Augustin Le Pelletier de la Houssaye holding the important office of *Major de Place* in New Orleans and Mobile during the French domination and becoming, at the beginning of the Spanish regime, in 1769, Commandant of the provincial militia.

By his fortunate nuptials the Chevalier de la Houssaye became a brother-in-law of the Sieur Jean François Gouyon des Rochettes, captain in the Regiment of Ponthieu (infantry) and also of the Marquis Etienne de Vaugine de Nuisement, first and second husbands of Antoinette Pélagie Petit de Livilliers, his wife's sister.

Distinguished as the Le Pelletier de la Houssaye family was, it is more than passing strange that its history has not been written by any of the genealogists that have heretofore labored to unravel the tangled skeins of Louisiana pedigrees. The only way that such apparent neglect or oversight can be explained is that perhaps, by a strange twist of Fate, its annals and records have been less available than those of other families to students and investigators of Louisiana lineages, or again that those records have been lost or mislaid for a long period of time.

Some of them that have recently been brought to light, give us a clear insight of the true character of its Louisiana founder and his sterling worth as a Christian, a parent and a true French *gentilhomme*. Buried in the old musty archives reposing since 1776 in the court house of St. Martinville, Louisiana, was recently found, not only the last will and testament of the Chevalier Paul Augustin Le Pelletier de la Houssaye, who died in St. Martinville before November 23, 1777, but also two series of written instructions, duly signed by him and addressed to his children for their guidance through life.

The will of the Chevalier, as well as a document entitled "Instruction that will be handed to my children at the time of my death," were written and signed by him on November 1, 1776, at the *Poste des Attakapas*. His will begins with the usual preamble of French testaments of that period wherein Heavenly pardon is besought by the testator for his sins and the intercession of the Holy Virgin and all the saints of Paradise is asked by the writer for his soul's repose. The Chevalier, who had known rank and power, shows in his will humility of heart. Though a knight of St. Louis, he requests an unostentatious funeral. Only six candles shall stand around his bier, and not more than eight shall rest in the sconces on the altar. The clapper of the church bell shall strike only five blows for his requiem. His body shall be consigned to Mother Earth in the most retired spot of the little Attakapas churchyard. While he does not seem to fear dissolution, it is apparent by his will that he perhaps dreaded the thought of being buried alive, as others, presumably dead but still really alive, had fared already in the primitive country where he dwelt, at a time when doctors were either hard to secure for post-mortem examinations and burial certificates, or, if found, were often poorly versed in real medical lore.

The first request he makes of the Marquis de Vaugine, his brother-in-law and testamentary executor is that, as soon as he has closed his eyes in eternal sleep, he shall proceed to have the soles of his feet slashed open. It shows his desire to avoid premature entombment.

Even the smallest of his creditors is remembered in his testament. Not only the estate of the mighty Chevalier de Lantagnac, to which he is indebted, must be paid in full but also small sums borrowed by him from three humble soldiers, now dead, must be duly liquidated by his executor, and paid to their estate.

He had known happiness in Louisiana, a colony where, nevertheless want and danger were ever lurking, and not unmindful of this nor of *la belle France*, where in his younger days he had known comfort and elegance, he considers his native land a fitter place of residence for his children in the days to come. His wife had promised to take them back to his country and kin after his death and his will ends by reminding her of this pledge and by soliciting its fulfillment.

Coming from fighting stock, the Chevalier de la Houssaye wanted his sons to follow in the footsteps of their ancestors. They must not only be established as officers in proper military commands, but must ever strive to rise in their martial profession. To attain such end he advises them to be faithful to their duties, respectful to their superior officers and polite toward everyone. They must seek only the worthy as companions, and avoid wine, women and gaming table. Between the lines we read that in his youth the Chevalier had sown his wild oats and repented for it afterward, as he states that he has experienced how dangerous is the feminine sex and wants to warn his sons about such peril. He specially abhors actresses, some of whom evidently had once ensnared him, and he begs his boys to avoid their wiles. In choosing a wife the sons of his flesh should not seek coquettes or be dazzled by the youth, the eyes or other attractions of a pretty woman. Beauty is only skin-deep. True worth and character is what they should endeavor to find in taking a life mate. Above all they should live and die honest men and good Christians, serving faithfully their God and their King at any cost. They should abhor falsehood and love, cherish and respect their worthy mother.

This summarises the advice of an eighteenth century sage who had known Life well and had drunk the bitter dregs from its cup. After appending his name to it, he writes that his signature is watered with the tears that his tenderness had caused to start.

The Chevalier Paul Augustin Le Pelletier de la Houssaye, on reaching Louisiana as an officer in the royal French troops, settled in the Attakapas country, and served at that post for a long time. Five Louisiana parishes, viz St. Martin, St. Mary, Iberia, Lafayette and Vermilion have been carved out today from the vast territory lying between the Mississippi River and the Gulf, that was ruled and protected by the Commandant of the *Poste des Attakapas* in the old days. The Chevalier was amongst the earliest settlers around that Post, which later on became the rallying point of the Acadian exiles from Canada. Of a very noble and ancient family of France, he retired with his bride, Mlle. Petit de Livilliers, to this quiet spot to rear his family. His worth, not only as a military officer, but also as a judge, is shown by the fact that he was selected by the French Crown as one of the five Commissioners who were to examine the facts and evidence in the Rochemore-Kerlerec quarrel and report thereon to the King.

The Chevalier Paul Augustin Le Pelletier de la Houssaye had from his marriage to Mlle. Petit de Livilliers two sons: Alexandre (or Alexandre Etienne) Le Pelletier de la Houssaye, the younger, born in New Orleans in 1765, who married at the Attakapas Post, July 30, 1787, Jeanne Louise Pellerin, daughter of Louis Pellerin, former colonial officer in Louisiana, and Marthe Pellerin. The descendants of this marriage, a least in the female line, still exist in Louisiana. Louis Le Pelletier de la Houssaye, eldest son of the Chevallier Paul Augustin, served as an officer under Bernardo de Galvez, Spanish Governor of Louisiana, and participated with him in his victorious campaigns against the English. At the end of the eighteenth century he had risen to the rank of captain of grenadiers. He married at the Attakapas Post, August 1, 1787, Louise Charlotte Pellerin, a sister of his brother's wife.

From his marriage to Miss Pellerin, Louis Le Pelletier de la Houssaye had a son, François, who married, June 14, 1814, Micael Eulalie Martin de Lino de Chalmette, daughter of Ignace de Lino de Chalmette and Victoire de Vaugine. Their descendants, at least in the female line, still exist in Louisiana. Another son, named Louis, was born of the marriage of Louis Le Pelletier de la Houssaye to Miss Pellerin. This son married Isabelle Marcelite de Blanc, born in Natchitoches, April 14, 1790, daughter of Louis Charles de Blanc, last commandant of the Attakapas Post from 1798 to 1803 (deceased in 1825) and Elizabeth Pouponne d'Erneville. The paternal grandparents of Mlle. de Blanc were César de Blanc, knight of St. Louis, commandant of Fort St. Jean Baptist in Natchitoches, and Marie des Douleurs (or Dolores) Juchereau de Saint Denys, a daughter of the celebrated Louisiana pioneer, the Chevalier Louis Juchereau de Saint Denys. Her maternal grandparents were the Chevalier Pierre Henri d'Erneville and Pélagie Fleuriau.

From the marriage of Louis Le Pelletier de la Houssaye to Isabelle Marcelite de Blanc, were born six children:

1.—Louis Alexandre, born in 1808, who married in St. Martinville, during the year 1833, Sidonie Perrett, famous French literary woman of Louisiana, daughter of Ursin Perrett and of Françoise Pain. From this union issued in turn, six children: (a) Henry Joseph, died without issue; (b) Lilia, unmarried; (c) Charles, died young; (d) Marie Lilla, who became the wife of J. B. Tarleton and left six children: Stella, unmarried; Caroline, wife of Wm. G. Brady; Lawrence, unmarried; Sidonie, unmarried; Emma, wife of Mr.

Stafford; Gabrielle, wife of S. J. Cross, and Charles, unmarried; (e) Louis, born November 22, 1845, who married Lou Kitchen and had five children: Louis Jr., married to Marie A. Cason, from whom issued two children: Nadia, wife of John St. Paul Jr., and Louis Pierre, unmarried; William H., married to Agnes Fi London; Ella, who became Mrs. A. H. Beers; Lelia, unmarried, and Edna Sidonie, wife of Henry W. Rayner; (f) Arthur Alexander, who married Emilie Perrett and had six children: Marie Sidonie born December 3, 1862, who married René Hébert and left issue; Arthur Joseph, born June 8, 1868, who married Martha Foster and has issue; Mary, born May 27, 1870, wife of Placide Sigur, with issue; Joseph Henry (twin), born August 27, 1871, who married Anais Pecot; Louis George (twin), unmarried; and Edward Anthony, born June 13, 1866, who married, in New Orleans, Louise Gourdain, from which union issued seven children: Ray Edward, married to Marguerite Larue; Ethel, unmarried; Edward Anthony, married to Heloise Fay; Arthur Alexander, married to Phoebe Dykers; Joseph Kléber, married to Mamie Drew Daniels; Malcolm Louis, unmarried, and Sidonie, unmarried.

2.—Charles, died 1832-1833 at the age of eighteen.

3.—Barthelemy César, who married in New Orleans in 1836, Marie Claire de Fontenette, daughter of Jacques de Fontenette and of Charlotte Pellerin, from which marriage were born two sons: Octave, who died young, and Octave Gérard.

4.—Louis Charles, who was assasinated for his money.

5.—Francois Livilliers, died in 1832-1833 at the age of sixteen.

6.—Louis Daguesseau, who married and left issue.

The files of old Louisiana newspapers disclose a decided romantic story in the Le Pelletier de la Houssaye that should be preserved. It is recorded that shortly after the cession of Louisiana in 1803, there came to New Orleans an able painter and miniaturist by the name of Mouchette, whose studio stood on the corner of Royal and St. Peter streets.

Among his closest friends and associates was a certain Guy de la Houssaye, also skilled with the brush, who had lost his parents at the age of ten and had been sent to France for his education.

He was very wealthy and had inherited a plantation in Louisiana. Visiting Mouchette's quarters, after his return to New Orleans, he fell madly in love with a woman, whose picture stood on an easel in his friend's studio. Learning that the original of this painting was Céleste de Miramon, a young widow whose husband had lately been killed in a duel and whose plantation was located 40 miles from his own, he resolved to win her at any cost.

Going back at once to his country estate, he began to ride at frequent intervals in his coach, past her plantation to get a glimpse of her. His impatience of possessing her growing greater with every passing hour, de la Houssaye hit upon a desperate plan to hasten things along. Jean, his negro coachman, was called into play. He was told that if he would deliberately drive his master's coach, while he rode in it, against the massive gates of the Miramon estate, so as to break the vehicle into splinters and make it appear that the horses had run away, he would be remembered to the extent of many hundreds of dollars in his master's will. Jean obeyed. The coach was duly wrecked. Guy de la Houssaye, desperately hurt, was carried into the Miramon home and slowly nursed back to life and health by the charming young widow. He had risked his life for the sake of winning her affection but he obtained his reward as the *Courier de la Louisiane*, on January 1, 1809, recorded the fact that Father de Benoiteau, the curate, had united, on Oakland Plantation, the young widow and her impetuous lover in the holy bonds of matrimony.

DE BLANC

NO family in Louisiana deserves more fully to be classed among its foundation families than that of the de Blancs, whose author, the Chevalier Césaire de Blanc de Neuveville was the second commander of the *Fort Saint Jean Baptiste des Natchitoches.* He married on June 9, 1750, in the little church of that post, Marie des Douleurs (or Dolores) Juchereau de Saint Denys, daughter of the Chevalier Louis Juchereau de Saint Denys (q. v.), founder of Natchitoches.

This Césaire de Blanc de Neuveville, by his prowess in the colony, had attained the dignity of knighthood in the order of St. Louis. He was born in the parish of Acoulès, in Marseilles, France. When he married Mlle. de Saint Denys he was a widower, having buried his first wife, Elizabeth Gugol, on June 27, 1749.

His father, Charles de Blanc de Neuveville was a captain in the royal armies of France, and his mother, Marguerite d'Espagnet, belonged to one of the oldest families of Provence. The d'Espagnets, as their family records show, had become famous in Provence long before this province was reunited to the kingdom of France. It had originated, however, in Spain, its first forebears to reach the realm of the Gallic Bourbons having arrived in the train of the Counts of Provence, from the race of Aragon, who, with many noble gentlemen-in-waiting, had left Spain to rule over French Provence.

As early as 1418, the name of Jean d'Espagnet, of this ancient family, appears as a member of the Sovereign Council which Louis III of Anjou, king of Naples and Count of Provence, established in Aix. His descendants, up to the year 1501, when the Parliament of Provence was duly created, were members of this Council. A branch of the d'Espagnet family, residing in Aix, produced in 1586 Raimond d'Espagnet, a councillor in its parliament, who fought so bravely in the wars of the League, that the parliament selected him to command the troops of the whole province. This he did with marked success.

The d'Espagnets escutcheon is described: On a field *azure* three *soucis* branched and leafed *or*, proceeding from a common stem, with a *chef cousu gules*, charged with a sun *or*.

The Chevalier Césaire de Blanc de Neuveville died in Natchitoches on April 8, 1763. From his second wife, Marie Dolores Juchereau de Saint Denys, issued two children: Louis Charles de Blanc and Jacques Maurice de Blanc, the last born in Natchitoches, October 22, 1756, who died unmarried.

His elder brother, Louis Charles de Blanc de Neuveville, born in Natchitoches April 29, 1753, served from 1798 to 1803 as Commandant of Natchitoches and the *Poste des Attakapas*, or St. Martinville. Louis de Blanc was appointed as one of the commissioners to turn over the province to its new owners. He died in 1825 on his estate which stood on land now included in the corporate limits of New Iberia. He is remembered in those parts by the descendants of the Acadian exiles who sought refuge in the Attakapas country, as one of their noblest and most generous friends. He was buried in the old churchyard of St. Martinville.

Louis Charles de Blanc came to New Orleans to find a bride and married in that city, in 1772, Elizabeth Pouponne d'Erneville, daughter of Pierre Henri d'Erneville, knight of St. Louis (of a distinguished family of Normandy), and Pélagie Fleuriau. They left a numerous progeny, twelve children being born in Natchitoches from their marriage. They were:

1.—Joseph Marie Charles de Blanc, born April 14, 1776. He married Madeleine La Cour, from whom issued one child, Marie Josephe Zoé de Blanc, born in Natchitoches November 30, 1795. At the death of his first wife, he married Marie Adèle Olivier de Vezin. They had two daughters, one of whom, Elmina, became the wife of François Des Mazillières Dusuau de la Croix, and the other, Clara, married a cousin, Charles d'Espagnet de Blanc.

2.—Marie Louise Marthe de Blanc, born July 30, 1777, who became the wife of Neuville Brognier de Clouet.

3.—Louis Césaire Marie de Blanc, born September 7, 1779, apparently died unmarried.

4.—Jean Baptiste d'Espagnet de Blanc, born January 20, 1782. He married, in 1806, Adélaïde, daughter of Balthazar Dusuau de La Croix and Marie Dufouchard de Gruy. They had nine children: (a) Marie Estelle, wife of Joseph Dusuau de La Croix; (b) Louis, who married Constance La Branche; (c) Charles, wedded to his cousin, Clara de Blanc; (d) Adèle, married to Jules Germain Olivier de Vezin; (e) Saint Denys, married to Caliste Villeré; (f) Emilie, wife of Dr. William Moore; (g) Césaire, husband of Eliska Villeré; (h) Adolphe, married to Mathilde Fortier; (i) Rosa, wife of Pierre Charles Des Mazillières Dusuau de La Croix.

5.—Célestine Mathilde de Blanc, born June 15, 1783. She married Charles Olivier de Vezin.

6.—Jean Baptiste Thomas de Blanc, born September 8, 1784. His wife was Zoé de La Croix, daughter of Emmanuel Des Mazillières Dusuau de La Croix and Anne Françoise Genevieve Le Breton.

7.—Pierre George Césaire de Blanc, born January 14, 1786.

8.—Marie Aspasie de Blanc, born March 12, 1788, wife of Jean d'Arby.

9.—Isabelle Marcelite de Blanc, born April 14, 1789, wife of Louis Le Pelletier de la Houssaye, son of Louis Le Pelletier de la Houssaye and Louise Charlotte Pellerin.

10.—Marie Josephe Constance de Blanc, born October 26, 1791, married to François Saint-Marc d'Arby.

11.—Marie Medeleine de Blanc, born October 4, 1793.

12.—Maximilien d'Erneville de Blanc, born October 12, 1794, who married in St. Martinville, Aspasie Castille, and had by her a son, Joseph Aristide de Blanc, born in St. Martinville, November 30, 1823, who died in New Orleans, December 8, 1882.

LE GARDEUR DE TILLY

FATHER LE JEUNE, early Canadian chronicler, in his *Relation*, dated 1636, says that Quebec at that time was only a "little corner hidden at the end of the world." In it nothing could be seen except a few houses and a handful of European colonists. Many noble families, however, arrived there as permanent settlers in the days of the Sieur de Montmagny, who was appointed governor of *Nouvelle France*, January 15, 1636, to succeed Samuel de Champlain, who had died December 25th of the preceding year. Among them were the Le Gardeurs from Normandy.

Those desirable colonists, according to this early historian, numbered all forty-five persons. The Le Gardeurs were represented in this welcome contingent by two brothers, of whom Pierre Le Gardeur de Répentigny was the eldest, and Charles le Gardeur de Tilly the youngest. With them came their mother, Catherine de Cordage, second wife of René Le Gardeur de Tilly, as well as the wife of the eldest son, their sisters and several children.

The father of the Sieurs de Répentigny and de Tilly was René Le Gardeur de Tilly, of a noble and ancient family of Normandy. His first wife, whom he married on May 3, 1582, was Marguerite de Coste. Catherine de Cordage became, on June 27, 1599, his second wife. It was from this last marriage that were sprung the two early soldiers of fortune of his name came to *Nouvelle France*.

Their father was in turn the son of Boniface Le Gardeur, Sieur de Tilly and the grandson of Jean Le Gardeur, Sieur des Crozilles, who married in 1510 Jeanne Le Tavernier.

The success of the two Le Gardeur brothers in Canada was very rapid. Pierre, eleven years after his arrival, was already a petty potentate, having been granted the *fief* of Répentigny in the parish of Our Lady of the Assumption, on April 16, 1647, by the *Compagnie de la Nouvelle France.* His estate measured four leagues front by six in depth. In the fall of 1644 he had been sent as a Canadian ambassador to the court of the Bourbon king. On this journey he was accompanied by Jean Paul Godfroy, an adventurous young nobleman, son of a king's councillor in Paris, who, in order to reach Canada quickly some years previous, had enrolled as a common sailor on one of Champlain's vessels during his first voyage.

The Sieurs Godefroy and Le Gardeur de Répentigny were charged to obtain from the monarch additional concessions, in the matter of the fur trade, for the *Compagnie de la Nouvelle France,* which they represented. They pleaded their case skillfully and returned to Quebec with the desired royal privileges.

On October 1, 1675, we find Pierre Le Gardeur de Répentigny signing, as a witness, in Quebec, the marriage contract of Louis Jolliet, of Beauport, the famous Canadian trader and companion of Father Marquette, and Claire Bissot, daughter of François Bissot, a burgher of Quebec, and Marie Couillard. In this contract is noted the interesting fact that the Sieur de Répentigny was a cousin of the bride.

Be that as it may, we meet again this same Sieur Le Gardeur de Répentigny on October 26, 1678, when, with nineteen others of the most ancient and important colonists in the land, he stood in the Assembly Hall of the *Chateau de St. Louis* in Quebec. Governor de Frantenac, acting under orders of Louis XIV, had summoned them to deliberate on the subject of the sale of *eau-de-vie,* or rum, to the red nomads. Pierre Le Gardeur de Répentigny was evidently not a prohibitionist as he was numbered among the fifteen councillors who expressed on this occasion their belief that the sale of rum to the Indians was necessary for the prosperity of the province.

On October 10, 1682, then a very old man Governor Lefebvre de la Barre, shortly after his arrival in Canada, selected him as a member of the Council of War, convoked in the Jesuit College of Quebec, to decide as to whether or not war should be officially declared against the murderous Iroquois.

[215]

Charles Le Gardeur, Sieur de Tilly, who came with his elder brother to Canada in 1636, followed, like him, the rocky road that leads to success, and soon reached the seats of the mighty. Twelve years after his arrival in *Nouvelle France*, he had won the hand of Genevieve Juchereau de Maur, daughter of Jean Juchereau, Sieur de Maur, and Marie Langlois. Her family was one of the most illustrious in the country, and its influence, as well as the Sieur de Tilly's personal worth, contributed in his being appointed, on September 18, 1663, a member of the first Sovereign Council of *Nouvelle France*—a council whose establishment meant the dawn of real civil government in Canada. He occupied this honorable position until 1695, on November the tenth of which year he died in Quebec at the advanced age of eighty-four years, his wife having preceded him to the grave eight years previous, or on November 5, 1687.

Charles Le Gardeur de Tilly enjoyed the friendship of the mighty Governor de Frontenac, who in 1674 served as godfather at the baptism of his daughter Louise. He was also among the early benefactors of the church of *Notre Dame de la Recouvrance* in Quebec. Mixed up, as a member of the Sovereign Council, in their quarrel with Governor de Mézy, he escaped the disgrace that befell several of the rebellious councillors and was even named as a beneficiary, to the extent of five hundred livres, in the will of the said governor. From his marriage with Genevieve Juchereau de Maur, he had fifteen children:

1.—Catherine Le Gardeur de Tilly, born in 1650 and died June 24, 1732, in Saurel, Canada. She married in Quebec, October 10, 1668, Pierre de Saurel, captain in the *Régiment de Carignan*. He was a native of Grenoble and son of Michel de Saurel and Jeanne de Giraud. He served with distinction in many English and Indian campaigns and died in Montreal, November 26, 1682. The present city of Sorel (or Saurel) in Canada is named after him.

2.—Marie Le Gardeur de Tilly, born in Quebec, February 10, 1651. She became the wife of Alexander Berthier, Seigneur de Bellechasse, captain in the Régiment de Carignan. He fought under Frontenac with great brilliancy and died in 1709, leaving two daughters and one son.

3.—Pierre Noël Le Gardeur, Seigneur de Tilly, born December 24, 1652, and died in the parish of St. Antoine de Tilly August 13, 1720. He was an officer in the Marine detachment and became a member of the Sovereign Council of Nouvelle France. His first marriage to Marguerite Volant was solemnized in 1675, from which was born a daughter, Genevieve Françoise, who died, unmarried, July 25, 1699. By his second wife, Marie Madeleine, daughter of Pierre Boucher, Seigneur de Boucherville, governor of Trois Rivieres, and Jeanne Crevier, he had fourteen children, among whom Nicolas, born in Boucherville, December 4, 1688. After serving in the Canadian army, he migrated to Saint Domingo and became commandant of Nippes on that island. From him descend the Louisiana branch of the Le Gardeur family. He married in 1730 Suzanne d'Allemant and had a son, Etienne Simon Le Gardeur de Tilly, of whom we will speak later.

4.—Jean Baptiste Le Gardeur de Saint Michel, born in Quebec June 13, 1655. He died unmarried. He was a captain in the French royal navy.

5.—Marguerite Le Gardeur de Tilly, born in Quebec July 29, 1657, who died February 25, 1742. She became, on January 29, 1694, in Quebec, the wife of Captain Louis Joseph Le Goues de Grais, one of the bravest fighters, under Frontenac, against the Iroquois. She had three children from this marriage.

6.—Charles Le Gardeur de Tilly, born in Quebec August 24, 1659, who died in Montreal November 20, 1702. His wife was Genevieve Margane de la Valtrie.

7.—René Le Gardeur de Beauvais, born in Quebec October 3, 1660, who died in Montreal December 26, 1742. He fought at the head of a party of Christian Iroquois against the Algonquins and Abenakis with great brillancy and served, as an officer, under Governor de Frontenac. He was married three times.

8.—Marie Madeleine Le Gardeur de Tilly, born in Quebec July 20, 1662. She became a nun and died May 6, 1734.

9.—Augustin Le Gardeur de Tilly, born October 15, 1663, who died unmarried.

10.—Genevieve Gertrude Le Gardeur de Tilly, born in Quebec, April 19, 1666, who died in Montreal September 3, 1759. She married, September 25, 1704, Jean Baptiste Céloron, Sieur de Blainville, a lieutenant in the Marine detachment, who distinguished himself, under Bienville, in his Louisiana campaign against the Chicassas.

11.—Marie Louise Le Gardeur de Tilly, born in Quebec October 28, 1667, who married in the same city on September 1, 1689, Augustin Rouer de la Cardonnière, a member of the Sovereign Council, and Catherine Sevestre. From this marriage were born nine children.

12.—Jean Baptiste Le Gardeur de Tilly, born in Quebec June 24, 1669. For distinguished services in the French Navy he was made a knight of St. Louis. He married Elizabeth Girard and left a daughter and a son. One of his grandsons, Armand Le Gardeur de Tilly, served in the French Navy during the American Revolutionary War, became a rear admiral and Fleet Commandant, a knight of St. Louis and a member of the American Order of Cincinnatus.

13.—Charlotte Françoise Le Gardeur de Tilly, born in Quebec October 8, 1670 and died on April 7, 1706. She married in Quebec, on October 11, 1689, René Damours, Sieur de Clignancourt, a Canadian officer, and left, by him, seven children.

14.—Daniel Le Gardeur de Tilly, born in Quebec March 27, 1672. He died while fighting against the Indians in Canada.

15.—Louise Le Gardeur de Tilly, born in Quebec March 24, 1674, who died January 11, 1698. She became the wife of Louis de Gannes de Falaise (widower of Barbe Juchereau de St. Denys), having married him in Montreal on July 12, 1695.

We have seen by the foregoing that Pierre Noël Le Gardeur, Seigneur de Tilly, third child of Charles Le Gardeur de Tilly and Genevieve Juchereau de Maur, had married twice and had had by his second wife, Marie Madeleine

Boucher de Boucherville, fourteen children. Among them was a son, Nicolas Le Gardeur de Tilly.

This son, after serving as a military officer, settled on the island of San Domingo, where he became commandant of Nippes. He married Suzanne d'Allemant and had from her a son, Etienne Simon Le Gardeur de Tilly, who married, in 1766, Rose Agnès de Lominé Marmé. From this last union were born, in turn, four children: (a) Mademoiselle Le Gardeur de Tilly, who became the wife of the Count Ridouet de Sancé; (b) Joseph Louis Simon Le Gardeur de Tilly, born in Jérémie, island of St. Domingo, who married on that island, in 1803, Eugénie Perrault, widow of the Sieur Cartier, and daughter of Jean Perrault and Jeanne Catherine Monnier; (c) Jean Baptiste Le Gardeur de Tilly, designated in all official acts as the Count de Tilly, born in San Domingo July 25, 1775. He participated, as a French officer, in several brilliant naval campaigns, from 1791 to 1795, in American waters, as well as off the Newfoundland and St. Domingan coasts. Known in Europe as a brilliant officer, he took part in many engagements in Germany and Holland and was given a naval captaincy by Louis XVIII in 1814. The next year he became adjutant of the royal castle of the Louvre, was granted other honors by the king and made an honorary gentleman-in-waiting of the king's bedchamber, in 1830. He was decorated with the cross of St. Louis and the Legion of Honor. From his marriage to Miss Waters, he left no children and he died in Saumur October 27, 1861; (d) Nicolas Charles Le Gardeur de Tilly, who married, about 1800, Madeleine de Vilmé.

Louis Joseph Simon le Gardeur de Tilly and Nicolas Charles de Tilly, sons of Etienne Le Gardeur de Tilly, came to New Orleans in the early days of the nineteenth century and founded families therein that are still numerously and honorably represented in New Orleans.

Nicolas Charles Le Gardeur de Tilly had a son, Charles Antoine, who married in New Orleans, in 1835, Clémentine Ducatel, from which marriage was born Charles Eugene Le Gardeur de Tilly. The last-mentioned, from his union with Althée Nicaud, of New Orleans, left a son, Maurice Le Gardeur, whose children still live in this city.

Louis Joseph Simon Le Gardeur de Tilly, brother of Nicolas Charles, from his wife, Eugénie Perrault, had a son, Antoine Gustave Le Gardeur de Tilly, who married in 1828 Solidelle de Neurisse. From this marriage issued a son, Michel Gustave Le Gardeur de Tilly, born in 1831, well and favorably known as a lawyer and notary. He married Adélaïde Pitot de la Beaujardière, of New Orleans, and their sons, René, Jacques and Philip Le Gardeur de Tilly are numbered today among the most highly respected citizens of New Orleans.

The coat-of-arms of the Le Gardeur de Tilly family shows on a field *gules* a lion *argent*, tongued *or* and holding in his two front paws a patriarchal Latin cross recrossed *or*. This family is mentioned in the *Nobiliare de Normandie*, by de Magny.

The white banner of France with its three golden fleur-de-lys, the second flag to float over Louisiana

COULON DE JUMONVILLE AND DE VILLIERS
Family

WHEN the dashing and unconquerable Coulons, Sieurs de Jumonville and of de Villiers, flashed on many occasions, like flaming meteors, across the darkened skies of French colonial Canada and Louisiana, leaving in their wake trails of imperishable brillancy, history was written. Their escutcheon, on a field *azure* a chevron *or* accompanied in chief by two stars and in point by a stag, all *or*, was never tarnished or dishonored by any that bore their respected family name, but all of them, by their lives and their accomplishments, added additional lustre to its glory and fame.

Originating in Normandy, the house of Coulon became one of the most illustrious in the French colonial possessions in North America. Its founder, in *Nouvelle France*, was Nicolas Antoine Coulon, *écuyer*, Seigneur de Villiers, born about 1682 in Nantes, Brittany. He was the son of a certain Sieur Coulon de Villiers, a commandant in the French royal army. As the first of his race in America, he set a high example for his descendants to follow. Neither the biting winds of the Northern forests nor the treacherous red enemy that was perhaps hiding behind many of the ice-clad trees, when in the depths of winter he trudged through the piling snow drifts to uphold the glory of the lilies of France and extend the dominion of his king, daunted him. A fighter by instinct, he courted danger and seemed able to meet it when confronted by it.

He was in Canada in 1700, and though then only eighteen years of age, had already won his spurs and was en ènsign in the military branch of the government. His activities as a soldier did not blind him, however, to the attractions of the fair sex. On December 7, 1705, in the Seigneurie of Verchères, that faced the St. Lawrence and stood between Sorel

[221]

and Montreal, he was married to Angélique Jarret de Verchères, one of the young *chatelaines* of that manor.

She was the daughter of François Jarret de Verchères and Madeleine Perrot. Her father had come to *Nouvelle France* before 1672 as an officer in the blue-blooded *Régiment de Carigan*, and though in France he had known a certain degree of ease and affluence, his father being a lawyer in Parliament, in Canada he won, at the point of his sword, a *fief* and selected for his concession an isolated spot, facing the howling wilderness on three sides and subject to the fury of the merciless Iroquois.

Nouvelle France never forgot the heroism of Mlle. Marie Magdeleine Jarret de Verchères on an eventful twenty-second day of October, 1692, when her father and mother having left their manor for a visit to a near-by town, entrusted its safety and that of their two young sons, as well as many female domestics, to her keeping. She was only eighteen years of age and in case of attack she could count on no other assistance than that afforded by a white-haired man servant of eighty, and two soldiers.

Having gone, of a morning, to the banks of the river, she was startled by a rifle shot and by Indian war whoops. Presently she beheld forty Iroquois, in war paint and feathers, rushing toward her. Leaden missiles of death were flying all about her. Calmly she retreated toward her father's stockade, but not before a red warrior had succeeded in snatching her scarf from her shoulders. Fastening the ponderous doors securely, she prepared for a siege. Like a seasoned general, she harangued her insignificant forces. "Let us fight unto death for our country and our faith. Let us not forget the lessons that our fathers have taught us. Gentlemen are born for naught but to shed their blood in the service of their God and their King!"

The siege lasted nine days, during which a puny girl of eighteen baffled every attempt of a maddened horde to capture the fort or set it afire. Though it meant sleepless nights and superlative courage and strength, she proved equal to the test. At last armed help arrived from Montreal. The chateau was safe and Marie Magdeleine Jarret de Vercères had won immortality.

It was in such a family that Nicolas Antoine Coulon de Villiers had gone to choose a life mate and bride. His subsequent actions never brought the blush of shame to her cheek. By his bravery afield he won, in 1715, a lieutenancy and commanded an important post in 1725. On April 1, 1733, his valor in attacking the Outagamis was rewarded with a captain's commission, but on September 13, of the same year, he made the supreme sacrifice and fell under the fire of the Sakis.

His thirteen children, several of whom were left to mourn his loss and to glory in his fame, were:

1.—Marie Coulon de Villiers, born in 1706 and died before 1740. She married in Montreal, on August 7, 1720, Alexandre Dagneau-Douville.

2.—Magdeleine Coulon de Villiers, twin sister of Marie, who became the wife, first, of François Lefebvre du Plessis Faber, Seigneur de l'Isle Ronde, a distinguished officer who perished during an Indian campaign; second, of Claude Marin de la Perrière, an officer in the Canadian army; and, third, of Joseph Damours, Sieur des Plaines.

3.—Nicolas Antoine Coulon de Villiers, born June 25, 1708, in Verchères, parish of Contrecoeur. He began his fighting career in 1725 and commanded at the *Poste des Puants* in 1733. He became a lieutenant in 1734 and married, October 7, 1732, Marie Anne Tarieu de la Pérade (widow of the Sieur Tétu de la Richardière), daughter of the Sieur Tarieu de la Pérade and Marie Magdeleine Jarret de Verchères, the Canadian heroine. In 1746, Nicholas Antoine Coulon de Villiers was a captain and as such commanded on June 5, 1746, the French troops at Grand Pré, where he defeated the British fighting under Col. Noble. A serious wound he received in the arm during that engagement and which necessitated eventually its amputation in 1750, compelled him to retire temporarily from the military service. Granted a furlough in 1747, he lingered with his wife for two years at Bareges, in France, seeking health in vain. When he returned to Canada, the cross of St. Louis was pinned on his breast and a commission of major of *Trois Rivières* reposed in his portfolio. In the spring of 1750 he died in Quebec from the result of a surgical operation he had undergone, and left no issue. His widow married, March 12, 1752, Jean François Gaultier, councillor and King's Physician in Nouvelle France.

4.—Louis Coulon de Villiers, born in Verchères August 10, 1710. In his early youth he became a fighting man and served in 1729 under his father as a cadet. Rapidly promoted for his daring against the Iroquois, he commanded at the Miami Post from 1750 to 1753, when he was made a captain. On December 23rd of that year he married Amable Prud'homme and had no male issue from her. His life is filled with a record of brave deeds. Leaving Lake Chutaqua, in what is now New York state, on June 16, 1764, he proceeded in birch bark canoes, with a force of Algonquins and Nipissings, toward Fort Duquesne. Arriving there eight days later, its commandant, Pécaudy de Contrecoeur, sent him, at the head of five hundred French troops and some Indian auxiliaries to attack the English at Fort Necessity. They had just killed his younger brother, Coulon de Jumonville, while he advanced to parley with them under a flag of truce. Fort Necessity was commanded by George Washington, then an English officer, and James MacKay. Louis Coulon de Villiers attacked it valiantly on July 3, 1754, and forced it to capitulate the next day. Not satisfied with the renown he had won by this exploit throughout *Nouvelle France* and the Province of Louisiana, he met the English again in June 1755 at Fort Niagara and tenaciously opposed their plans to seize Canada until 1757, when he once more reaped additional laurels at the capture of Fort William Henry and won the cross of St. Louis. He died of small pox on November 2, 1757, without issue.

5.—Coulon de Villiers (first name unknown), who served as a young cadet under his father's orders and was killed on September 16, 1733, while fighting the Sakis at the *Baie des Puants*.

6.—Pierre Coulon de Villiers (also known as Lespiney de

Villiers), born in Verchères May 4, 1720. He served in March 1742 at the St. Joseph River Post in the Illinois country, was a *cadet a l'aiguillette* in 1744, fought against the English in Acadia in 1746, and died during that campaign at Beaubassin, in Acadia January 2, 1747.

7.—Joseph Coulon de Villiers, known in the annals of Louisiana and Canada as the Sieur de Jumonville, born in Verchères September 8, 1718. At the age of fifteen he was serving at his father's post on the *Baie des Puants*. In 1739 he was warring against the Chicassas. When de Ramezay campaigned in Acadia against the British in 1745, Joseph Coulon de Villiers served with *éclat* under him. He was almost constantly on some battlefield or other. In 1747 he led the French forces at *Rivière-aux-Sables* Post and again crossed swords with the Britons under Corler. The next year he was still campaigning against them. When the British invaded the Valley of the *Belle Rivière*, or Ohio, claimed by the French as their own, the ensign Joseph Coulon de Villiers was sent by de Contrecoeur, commandant of Fort Duquesne, to request their peaceful withdrawal from this contested territory. On the night of May 27-28, 1754, at *Grandes Prairies* (or Great Meadows), he advanced toward the English fort under a flag of truce, to read his general's request for its evacuation. His little army consisted of only thirty-four French soldiers. George Washington, then a young English officer, was in charge of the block house. Whether due to a misunderstanding of the French ensign's intentions, or otherwise, the Britons opened fire upon him and killed him in his tracks. His death created profound indignation throughout Canada and Louisiana, and his slayers were accused of having foully murdered him and of having disregarded one of the fundamental rules of civilized warfare by firing upon a white flag. The unfortunate young ensign de Villiers had married in Montreal, October 11, 1745, Marie Anne Marguerite Soumande, daughter of Pascal Soumande and Ursule le Verrier. He left no children from her. She was the granddaughter by marriage of the Marquis Pierre Rigaud de Vaudreuil, who had chosen her grandmother, Charlotte Fleury d'Eschambault as his second wife. The widow of Joseph Coulon de Villiers married, after his death, the Chevalier Pierre Bachoie de la Barrante, senior captain in the Regiment of Béarn.

8.—Marguerite Coulon de Villiers, who became the wife of Pierre de Gannes Falaise.

9.—Marie Anne Coulon de Villiers, born in 1722, who became the wife of Ignace Aubert de Gaspé and died March 18, 1789.

10.—Madeleine Angélique Coulon de Villiers, born January 20, 1726, who married at *Trois Rivières* on October 23, 1749, Charles Thomas de Gannes Falaise.

11.—Thérese Coulon de Villiers.

12.—Charles François Coulon de Villers, born June 14, 1721, who died in childhood.

13.—François Coulon de Villiers, born in Verchères in 1712, founder of the Coulon de Villiers and de Jumonville family in Louisiana.

This François Coulon de Villiers died in New Orleans, on May 22, 1794, at the advanced age of ninety-one. His record is as remarkable as that of any of his brave brothers. He first appears as a *cadet a l'aiguillette* on September 19, 1739, when he received his baptism of fire and was wounded in the arm by a Saki bullet. Then he became a second ensign and on November 4, 1740, was an *enseigne-en-pied* after his campaign against the Chicassas.

Commanding the post on the St. Joseph River, in the Illinois district, in 1745, he served during the next year under de Muys, being in charge of the Indian auxilliaries. He came to Louisiana about the year 1752, when he is designated as a lieutenant. The next year he was a full-fledged captain, and on July 13, 1756, he left Fort Duquesne to avenge the death of his brother, Joseph, known as Jumonville, killed by the English at *Grandes Prairies.*

His destination was the British fort known as George de Craon. Taking the wrong trail, he found himself instead, on July 26 of the same year, before the British Fort Grandville in Pennsylvania. After a stubborn fight, he captured this important block house, spiked every cannon, reduced its buildings to ashes and took its entire garrison as prisoners of war. His eagerness to fight the English never relented. After serving in 1757 as Aide-Major at Fort Chartres, he proceeded in April of the following year, under orders of Maccarthey MacTaig (or Macarty), toward Virginia, where he proved himself a disturbing factor to the Britons.

At the attack of Fort Duquesne in 1758, serving under Aubry, he added laurels to his fame. In 1759 he had left the soil of Virginia and on July 6th of that year, as he was hastening with Aubry and others along the Gorge of the Niagara River, to reinforce Pouchot, commander of the nearby French citadel then beseiged by the British General Prideaux, he and his companions fell into a trap at a spot now known as Devil's Hole, where a terrible massacre took place.

By a sheer miracle, François Coulon de Villiers escaped with his life but, with Aubry and a few others, was made prisoner and sent to New York. Eventually exchanged, he returned to Louisiana, visited France in 1761 and returned to New Orleans in 1762 to enjoy at last a well-earned and permanent rest. He had previously received in New Orleans, from the hands of Governor Louis Billoart de Kerlerec, and in the name of Louis XV, the cross of St. Louis as a badge of his heroism.

The Chevalier François Coulon de Villiers married three times, having issue by each marriage. His first wife was Elizabeth Groston de Saint Ange de Bellerive, sister of the last French commander of the Illinois country. This first union was contracted before 1740 and from it issued four children; (a) Isabelle, born in 1740, who became the wife of François de Volsay, captain in the Illinois district; (b) Joachime, born in 1746, who married Captain François Picoté de Belestre; (c) Joseph, born in 1747, who died without issue; (d) Louis, born in 1751, who married in the Attakapas section Marie Fontenelle, and left many descendants still living in Louisiana.

The second wife of the Chevalier François Coulon de Villiers was Madeleine Marin, daughter of Captain Paul Marin, serving at the *Fort de-la-Rivière-aux-Boeufs*. From this second marriage was born only one son, François Coulon de Villiers, who died in Havana. This son married in New Orleans, August 1, 1784, Joséphine Catherine Griffon d'Anneville, daughter of Antoine Simon Griffon d'Anneville and Marie Joseph Catherine Poupart, by whom he had ten children, as follow: (1) Marie Victoire, born October 19, 1785, married to Jean Innerarity, with issue in Louisiana and in Pensacola, Florida; (2) Jean François, born August 9, 1786, who settled in Havana; (3) Marie Joseph Hugues, married to Arnould Guillemard, without issue; (4) Charles Marie Hucher, born February 20, 1795, who settled in Havana; (5) Marie Suzanne, born October 28, 1792, who married September 30, 1814, Joseph Ignace Cruzat (q. v.), and died November 18, 1860, leaving issue; (6) Marie Jean, born March 30, 1796, who settled in Havana; (7) Firmin, born September 26, 1797, with issue; (8) Louis, born August 17, 1799, who settled in Havana; (9) Manuel, born August 13, 1801, who married in Spain; (10) Felix, born March 15, 1804, who settled in Havana.

From the third marriage of the Chevalier François Coulon de Villiers, contracted in New Orleans June 28, 1762, issued only one son, Charles Phillippe Coulon de Villiers, who married twice. From his first wife, Marie Louise Clara de Acosta, daughter of a Spanish officer who came to Louisiana with General Alessandro O'Reilly in 1769, were born three children: (a) François Coulon de Jumonville de Villiers; (b) Marie Genevieve Claire Coulon de Jumonville de Villiers, who became the wife of Pierre Huchet de Kernion and left numerous descendants; (c) Amable Coulon de Jumonville de Villiers who married R. Ducros.

From Marie Françoise Aimée Esnould Beaumont de Livaudais, the second wife of Charles Philippe Coulon de Villiers, issued six children: (1) Gustave, who married Stéphanie Guérin, with issue; (2) Louis, known as chevalier Jumonville, who married, first, a Miss Buisson and later a Miss Commagère. He left issue known now as Jumonville; (3) Alexander, who married Miss Véla. His issue is also now known under the name of Jumonville; (4) Aimée, who married (a) Mr. Canon, and (b) Mr. Dupuy, with issue;

(5) Célestine, who became Mrs. Fleitas, with issue; (6) Odile, married to Mr. Guerin, with issue.

The Chevalier François Coulon de Villiers, father of six children by his three marriages, after a long life spent mostly on battlefields, died in New Orleans May 22, 1794, at the extraordinary age of 91 years. In the old St. Louis Cemetery on Claiborne street, his grave, still faithfully preserved in perfect condition by his grateful descendants, attracts, by its epitaph, the eye of the casual passer-by. Pausing before it for a while, one reads on the marble slab the following chiselled inscription:

> Here lies François Jumonville Coulon de Villiers
>   Relic of an illustrious race
> Who unceasingly opposed his great heart to the
>   attacks of Fate
> And in the narrow path of Honor always followed
>   the trace of his ancestors.

CAVELIER DE LA SALLE

WILTZ

THE progenitors of the Wiltz family in Louisiana belonged to that class of sturdy German and Saxon agriculturists who embarked in the early days of the eighteenth century for Louisiana, with buoyant hearts and with souls filled with grim determination. Though thousands of their countrymen had already sailed from the Fatherland to establish themselves in America and a large number had perished on the way, the more vigorous among them survived and, in Louisiana, where they came in droves as early as 1717, to till the rich alluvial soil of the Mississippi Valley with their primitive hoes and ploughs, they proved themselves the founders of the worthiest families in the land that, becoming gradually Gallicized, eventually married representatives of the noblest French houses established in the Province.

If we may believe the statement made by one who inquired into the history of the Wiltz family in Saxony, the first of the name to come to the French colony on the Mississippi River belonged to a Thuringian house that had once possessed a barony and had borne the title worthily. While this is not an authenticated fact, written evidence exists that proves that the first colonists of that name to come to Louisiana were highly esteemed settlers, of unblemished character and solid worth, who enjoyed the friendship of the highest-born and most powerful in the country.

A certificate to that effect, dated February 7, 1776, signed and sworn to by the Sieurs Nicolas Forstall, François Marie de Reggio and the Chevalier Charles Frédérick d'Arensbourg, still exists in the French Colonial Archives in the Cabildo at New Orleans. Those blue-blooded witnesses assert that Johan Ludwig Wilsz, one of the original settlers of that name in Louisiana, as well as his father and mother and their antecedents were "old Christians, pure of all bad races of Moors, Jews, Mulattoes and Indians," and that they were not recent converts, but had been ever devoted to the Roman Catholic Church.

It was during the first half of the eighteenth century that two brothers named Wilsz bid adieu to the farms of their ancestors in Thuringia and started on a long pilgrimage across the sea. One of them established himself around the Mobile Post and the other, Johan Ludwig Wilsz, born in Eisenach, Thuringia, Saxony, in 1711, settled in or near New Orleans. They were the sons of John Theodore Wilsz and of Christine Francken, natives of Eisenach.

Of the two Wilsz brothers who first came to Louisiana, the one that established himself near the Mobile Post left issue, which formed the Mobile branch of the family. The other, Johan Ludwig Wilsz, who had married in Saxony, in 1731, a Miss Ziriac, came with his wife to New Orleans and eventually became the owner of a farm at the *Côte des Allemands* on the Mississippi River. His wife was the daughter of Wilhelm Ziriac, a native of Ilmenstadt, near Mayence (a former employee of King Stanislas of Poland), who also migrated to Louisiana and established himself as a farmer at the German Coast.

Miss Ziriac, first wife of Johan Ludwig Wilsz, having died, her widowed husband married in Louisiana, Marie Dohl (or Dolc), a native of Frankendell, in Saxony, daughter of Andres Dohl and of Anna Barba Fetiguenin, natives of the same place and early settlers in Louisiana. From this time on the surname undergoes a slight change, "t" taking the place of "s", making the spelling Wiltz.

From this second marriage of Johan Ludwig Wilsz were born two children; Margarethe Wiltz, who married twice: (a) Joseph Milhet, the richest French merchant at that time in New Orleans, who was implicated in the colonial insurrection of 1767-1769 against Spain; (b) Jacinto Panis, Spanish captain and sergeant-major in New Orleans, son of Jacinto Panis and of Maria Antonia Tadda y Sana, both natives of Callea, Spain. This second marriage was solemnized in New Orleans in 1777. The other child was Joseph Wiltz, who married in 1759, in New Orleans Susanna

Zweig, or Labranche (q. v.), daughter of Johan Zweig from Bamberg, in Bavaria, and of Suzanne Marchand, native of the parish of St. Marcelin, bishopric of Grenoble, in Dauphine, France. From the marriage of Joseph Wiltz to Susanna Zweig were born: (a) Jean Louis Laurent Wiltz, captain of militia in New Orleans, who served under Galvez against the English during the American Revolutionary War, and who married Marianne Colomb, daughter of Jean Colomb. He signed as a witness at the wedding of the chevalier Pierre Denis de la Ronde and Eulalie Guerbois, in New Orleans, on January 31, 1788; (b) Hortense Wiltz, who married in 1789, Jean Leonard Arnould and had three children: (1) Julien Arnould, who married in 1829, Manuela Amasilie Fabre d'Aunoy; (2) Jeanne Aimee Arnould, who became the wife of François Trépagnier; (3) Louise Mathilde Arnould, who married Jean de Dieu Garcia.

Jean Louis Laurent Wiltz and his wife, Marianne Colomb, had a son, Jean Baptiste Wiltz, born in Mobile, who married, in New Orleans, Suzanne Langliche by contract dated April 5, 1770. She was the daughter of Jacques Langliche and Elizabeth Pujol, and died in New Orleans before May 24, 1786. At her death her husband remarried, May 24, 1786, Marie Joseph Bahy, daughter of Joseph Bahy and of Marie Durocher. From this second marriage issued Félicité Wiltz, who married on August 6, 1810 or 1811, Sevère de St. Amand, residing at the German Coast. He was the son of Antoine de St. Amand and of Eulalie Zéringue.

From the first marriage of Jean Baptiste Wiltz to Suzanne Langliche, issued, among others, a daughter, Marie Constance Wiltz, born in New Orleans about 1771, and died there July 5, 1831. She married, February 7, 1786, Pierre Joseph Lambert, born at the Arkansas Post about 1756, son of Pierre Lambert and of Catherine Landrony. His sister, Marie Joseph Lambert, married in New Orleans, October 24, 1785, André Joseph Fernandez. Pierre Joseph Lambert died in New Orleans on July 9, 1836.

From the union of Pierre Joseph Lambert to Marie Constance Wiltz were born three children: (1) Marie Joseph, who married in New Orleans on July 6, 1810, Jean François Ballon des Ravines, native of Plaisance, department of Horte, in St. Domingo, son of Francois Ballon, Chevalier des Ravines, and Isabella de l'Herve, established in St. Domingo; (b) Joseph Desravines Lambert, who married Natalie Volant de la Barre, and at her death, married her sister, Léocadie, both of whom were daughters of Jean Baptiste Volant de la Barre of Philomise Chauvin de Léry; (c) Euphémie Aimee Lambert, who married in New Orleans on January 28, 1822, Crispin Charles Le Bédoyère Huchet de Kernion and left issue.

This Lambert family had lived in New Orleans since its earliest days and was highly esteemed in the colony. Its members had married into the most prominent families of the land. It was evidently of German origin for the reason that Pierre Lambert was established in the Arkansas district, where his son, Pierre Joseph, was born before 1756. History tells us that John Law, the financier, had obtained at the beginning of the XVIII century from the French king certain land grants in the Arkansas country for 1,300 settlers, composed of Germans, Provencals and others, who were to settle therein. After the fall of Law, many of his German colonists in the Arkansas district migrated south and established themselves at the Côte des Allemands near New Orleans. We believe that the Lambert family, which had settled in the Arkansas country before 1758 was part of Law's original German colonists.

In the Cabildo Museum, New Orleans, hangs today an ancient oil picture of Jean Baptiste Wiltz, who married Suzanne Langliche. He is represented in his hunting costume, aiming his muzzle-loading musket at a flock of ducks flying over the marsh in which he is standing. It is part of a family tradition that this picture was posed for by him on the site where now stands the St. Charles Hotel, which location was at the time beyond the fortifications of the *Vieux Carre*, and was part of the wilderness. In the Cabildo Museum is also to be seen the picture of his daughter, Marie Constance Wiltz, as well as that of her husband, Pierre Joseph Lambert.

PETIT DE LIVILLIERS DE COULANGES Families

IN the reign of Louis XI, there lived in the realm of this Bourbon king, Charles Petit, a most powerful nobleman. He had risen by his worth to the exalted position of *Grand Audiencier de France.* His wife, Charlotte, was the daughter of Pierre de Brissonet, Seigneur de Praville and de Carmes, Treasurer General of Languedoc in 1492, and of Anne de Compaign. Among his children was Charles Petit, also a court favorite when Charles VIII sat on the throne, and an officer in the *Gardes de Corps,* or King's Bodyguard.

So highly esteemed was he by his royal master that when this monarch decided to visit Italy, Charles Petit was commanded to accompany him as gentleman-in-waiting. In memory of this trip and as a reward for his faithful services during this voyage, Charles VIII authorized him to add a golden *fleur-de-lys* to his escutcheon.

The son of Charles Petit, also named Charles, is designated in the ancient records as *homme d'armes des Ordonnances du Roi,* or military officer in the King's service. He married Marguerite du Pas de Champaigne. Of the five children born of this marriage, Jean became Canon of the Cathedral of Bourges, and another, Louis Petit, who had married Philippe de la Sonnerie, of a knightly house in Poitou, and continues the line, had fourteen children. Among them was Jérome, canon of the Church of Nevers and prior of Fontaine, in Autun; a daughter who became the wife of Pierre Prevot, lord of Livilliers; and Guillaume Petit, who succeeded his father as head of the Petit family.

This Guillaume Petit is the first to be designated as Seigneur de Livilliers. He obtained that *fief,* or land, by donation from Pierre Prévot, his brother-in-law, who was its lord and owner. The chateau de Livilliers stood near Pontoise. Guillaume Petit, its new master, eventually wedded Antoinette, daughter of Claude de Coulanges, Seigneur de Bustance, in Auvergne, and of Madeleine d'Aguesseau, who was the daughter of Christophe d'Aguesseau, Seigneur de la Collaterie, a famous lawyer in the Parliament of Paris, and of Antoinette de Stemple. Among the descendants of this Christophe d'Aguesseau may be mentioned his son, Antoine, who was president of the Parliament of Bordeaux, Councillor of State and Director of Finances. He died in 1645 and from his third wife, Anne Gives de Bouilly, he had a son, Henri d'Aguesseau, president of the Grand Council and member of the State Financial Council during the minority of Louis XIV, the French king. This last son, in turn, became the father of Henri François d'Aguesseau, a celebrated Chancellor of France in 1717.

We now return to Guillaume Petit de Livilliers and his wife, Antoinette de Coulanges. From their union issued a son, Robert Petit, Seigneur de Livilliers, wedded to Elizabeth de Berruyer. Among their offspring appears Claude Charles Petit de Livilliers, who sailed for North America and settled in Canada. He married in *Nouvelle France*, Madeleine, daughter of René Gaultier de la Véranderie, governor of *Rrois Rivières*, and of Marie Boucher de Boucherville. René Gaultier had settled in Canada prior to 1667 and died there in June 1689. His daughter, Madeleine, by her marriage to Claude Petit de Livilliers, became the mother of six children, of whom five were boys. Among them were Louis Petit de Coulanges and Charles Petit de Livilliers, both distinguished military men in the French service, who came to Louisiana before July 11, 1727.

Louis Petit de Coulanges, the first-named, married in New Orleans, Mademoiselle Galard de Chamilly. He had by her a son, Louis René Petit de Coulanges, who died while still a child, and a daughter, Marie Louise Petit de Coulanges. This daughter became the wife of Vincent Guillaume de Sénéchal d'Auberville, *Commissaire de la Marine* in Louisiana, by whom she begot two daughters, namely: Elizabeth Céleste, who died young and unmarried, and Marie Louise le Sénéchal d'Auberville, who married, in New Orleans, François de Bouligny, Colonel of the Regiment of Louisiana, and of illustrious Spanish ancestry. From this union were born four children: (a) Marie Louise Josephine Bouligny, wife of the Chevalier de la Roche; (b) Dominique Charles Bouligny; (c) Francois Maxime Bouligny; (d) Louis Bouligny. The descendants of these children are still very numerous in Louisiana and are numbered among members of the Baldwin, Landry de Fréneuse, Bernard, Arnauld d'Andilly, Nott, La Barre, Villeré, Smith and other prominent Louisiana families.

Marie Louise Petit de Coulanges, at the death of her first husband, Vincent Guillaume le Sénéchal d'Auberville, married again, this time Jean Pierre Girard de Villemont, lieutenant-colonel in the Spanish troops of the colony. From her second marriage issued two sons: Louis Joseph de Villemont, *Gendarme de la Reine*, or Queen's Bodyguard, stationed in Lunerville, and Charles Melchior de Villemont, captain in the Battalion of Louisiana.

Having given the descendants of Louis Petit de Coulanges, one of the two Petit brothers, who founded the family in Louisiana, we must now speak of Charles Petit de Livilliers, the other. This Charles Petit was established in Louisiana before 1727 as his name appears in the census of July 1st of that year. He resided then on his plantation, or *concession*, on the west bank of the Mississippi River, near New Orleans. This census reports him as being born in Verteuil, perhaps on a trip that his father and mother, who had married and settled in Canada, had taken to France. When Charles Petit de Livilliers first reached Louisiana, he was an officer of the *Compagnie des Indes* that then owned the trade monopoly of the province. He served later in Louisiana as captain in the Regiment de la Marine. In New Orleans he married Etiennette Louise de Malbec, daughter of Jean de Malbec (or Malbeque), *Commissaire de la Marine*, and of Anne Thomase le Clerc, and sister of Mlle. de Malbec, who married M. de Verteuil.

From this marriage of Charles de Livilliers to Mademoiselle de Malbec issued the following five children:
1.—Charles César Petit de Livilliers, officer in the French royal navy, who settled in Port-au-Prince, Hayti, and

died before 1770. He married in that city Marie Louise Gauthier, and did not leave issue.

2.—Charles Etienne Petit de Livilliers, who apparently died unmarried.

3.—Magdeleine Victoire Petit de Livilliers, who became the wife of the Chevalier Paul Augustin Le Pelletier de la Houssaye, *Major de Place* in New Orleans and Mobile, from which marriage were born two sons, Louis and Alexandre Le Pelletier de la Houssaye (q. v.), the first of whom has left numerous descendants still living in Louisiana.

4.—Antoinette Pélagie Petit de Livilliers, who married twice. Her first husband was the Sieur Jean François Gouyon des Rochettes, captain in the infantry regiment of Ponthieu. At his death she married the Marquis Etienne de Vaugine de Nuisement, captain in the French royal army. By her first marriage she had a daughter, Etienette Stéphanie Gouyon des Rochettes, who became the wife of Jean Baptiste Garic, early and well-known notary in French Louisiana (q. v.). From the second marriage of Antoinette Pélagie Petit de Livilliers to the Marquis de Nuisement issued five children (a) Françoise Pélagie de Vaugine; (b) Madeline Victoire de Vaugine, who became the wife of Ignace Martin de Lino de Chalmette (q. v.); (c) Etienne de Vaugine; (d) Mathurin de Vaugine, and (e) Françoise de Vaugine.

The coat-of-arms of the ancient and illustrious family of Petit de Coulanges and de Livilliers is described: On a field *azure* three pals *argent* and a chevron *or*, on the point of which appears a *fleur-de-lys or, brochant* on the middle pal.

CHAUVIN—DE LERY—LA FRENIERE Family

WHEN one interested in the history of Louisiana colonial days opens her golden book, the treasured volume that lists the strenuous deeds and the identity of her beautiful courageous women and brave adopted sons, he finds written in bold characters the names of four strong men, and their two sisters, who came to the infant colony with the intrepid Le Moyne brothers. They were the Chauvins who, like their leaders, Iberville and Bienville, attached to their patronymic or family surname, certain additional designations.

In this fashion the descendants of Joseph Chauvin de Léry are known by the name of de Léry (or Delery, as it is spelled today). The children of Nicholas Chauvin de la Frénière, became known as la Frénière, and one made it imperishable in the blood-stained pages of Louisiana's history. The descendants of Louis Chauvin de Beaulieu, and there were many of them, called themselves simply Beaulieu. The oldest of the four brothers, Jacques Chauvin de Charleville, who died in Biloxi in 1729, and his son, Jacques, who settled in the Illinois country, were the only ones to retain Chauvin as a surname.

Pierre Chauvin, born in Anjou, was the son of René Chauvin and Catherine Avard de Solesne. He died in *Nouvelle France* August 4, 1699. On March 3, 1653, he was established in the parish of Ville Marie, on the Isle of Montreal, and received a grant of land in Canada in 1654. His wife was Marthe Autreuil, daughter of René Autreuil and Françoise Lachaunerlin, from which union were born eight children, six sons and two daughters, six of whom became splendid pioneers in French colonial Louisiana. They were Jacques Chauvin de Charleville, Joseph Chauvin de Léry, Nicolas Chauvin de la Frénière, Louis Chauvin de

Beaulieu, Barbe Chauvin, wife of Ignace Hubert de Bellair, and Michelle Chauvin, who married Jacques Nepveu.

The six brothers and sisters, leaving the comfort and security of their Canadian homes, arrived in the Louisiana colony at Biloxi in 1706 or earlier. They made the long sea-trip from Canada to the Gulf of Mexico as passengers aboard one of those French vessels that brought at rare intervals from France or the Northern Province, settlers for the little colony on the Gulf, that had come to life in 1699.

While some of the less daring amongst the colonists that clustered around *Fort Louis de la Mobile*, were preparing their little garden patches for future necessary harvests, three among the newly-arrived Chauvins, Joseph de Léry, Nicolas de la Frénière and Louis de Beaulieu heard the call of the virgin forest and heeded its voice. Bienville, the governor, was then endeavoring to enter into amicable trading relations with the Spaniards of Mexico. The Chauvins, sensing their opportunity, obtained permission from him to start out for the *Presidio del Norte*, on the Rio Grande.

Leaving Biloxi on October 10, 1716, and taking with them necessary trading merchandise, worth 43,200 livres, they entered the state now called Texas, by way of Natchitoches, where St. Denys had established a little block house, known as *Fort Saint Jean Baptiste*. At this point, they were met by the daring Louis Juchereau de Saint Denys (q. v.), its commandant, and by Graveline and Darbanne, associates in their commercial enterprise.

The country traversed by them was occupied by the Cenis Indians. Near a fork of the Trinity River were lead mines worked by the Spaniards and not far away stood a small mission, called *Tejas*, guarded by a few Hispanic soldiers. The Chauvin brothers traversed the whole width of the present state of Texas and reached the Presidio in April, 1717, where the jealous and suspicious Spaniards rejected Bienville's well-intended plan for reciprocal trading rights, and seized the merchandise of his commercial envoys. The Chauvins and Saint Denys returned to Biloxi in 1718 empty-handed, but the path blazed out by them and Saint Denys from Natchitoches across the then nameless region of Texas, was for many a day the only known road from the Louisiana borderland to the Presidio on the Rio Grande.

The archives of French colonial Louisiana disclose that in March 1719, Joseph Chauvin de Léry, one of the six original pioneers, filed with the Superior Council an application for a concession of six *arpents* front on the Mississippi, in the *Tchoupitoulas* district. At the same time three of his brothers, as well as one of his nephews, requested from the Council a similar concession in the same place. Being desirable settlers, their request was promptly granted and the four Chauvin brothers and their nephew became landed proprietors in Louisiana in 1719, a short while after the foundation of New Orleans.

Joseph de Léry was the first to establish himself in the *Tchoupitoulas* section. Later on Nicolas de la Frénière and his nephew began to clear their land, and not long thereafter, as a result of their arduous labor, an impenetrable forest gave way to a smiling, sun-lit and productive plain.

The plantations of the Chauvin brothers stood next to the lands belonging to Governor Bienville. In 1720 their immediate neighbors were Dulude, manager of the Sainte Reyne concession, and Claude Joseph Dubreuil de Villars, eventually known as the Louisiana Creosus, his wife and two children. At that time the total population of the *Tchoupitoulas* district amounted to twenty-one white masters, twenty-one white servants, three hundred and sixty-five negro slaves and eleven Indian vassals. There were also three hundred and thirteen heads of horned cattle, forty-five horses and eight hundred parcels of land under cultivation. Among the settlers in that primitive Arcady, Joseph de Léry and his three children, Louis de Beaulieu, his wife and three children, and Nicolas de la Frénière, his wife and three children, shared in its increasing affluence.

Jacques Chauvin de Charleville, one of the original six Louisiana pioneers of the name of Chauvin, died in old Biloxi in 1729. His son, Jacques Chauvin de Charleville, eventually migrated to St. Louis in the Illinois country, where he died in 1785. He had married in Kashaskia, about 1740, Genevieve Bonacceuil, and left six children, all born and settled in and around St. Louis. His eldest son, Jacques

Chauvin III, born in the Illinois district in 1743, died there May 8, 1826, at the ripe old age of eighty-three years, on a concession he had obtained in 1799, opposite the village of St. Charles, Missouri, from Don Carlos de Hault de Lassus, the last Spanish lieutenant-governor of Upper Louisiana. He married a daughter of Joseph Michel-Tayon, one of the founders of St. Louis. In his younger days, Jacques Chauvin III was a well educated young officer in the French colonial service, stationed at Fort Chartres in the Illinois. He retired from the army when Louisiana became a Spanish province, and at his death left six sons and four daughters, whose descendants are still to be found in the present state of Missouri.

His father, Jacques Chauvin de Charleville II, had, beside him, at least four other sons and two daughters: Jean Baptiste Chauvin, who married Françoise Brazeau, of Kaskaskia; Louis Chauvin, whose wife was Thérese Lemoine des Pins; Charles Chauvin, who married Marie Louise Lemoine des Pins; François Chauvin, apparently unmarried; a daughter who became the wife of Daniel Blouin, a prominent merchant of Kaskaskia, and another who married Jean Baptiste St. Geme-Beauvais, of Saint Genèvieve.

Nicolas Chauvin de la Frénière, one of the six first Chauvins to come to Louisiana, married Marguerite Le Sueur, whose father had come from Canada to Louisiana with Iberville and Bienville. In 1699-1700, Le Sueur, with Louis Juchereau de Saint Denys, Father Pinet and other daring spirits, explored the unknown country of the Natchez, the Illinois, the Arkansas and the Minnesota. During the reign of Louis XIV, de l'Isle, the celebrated French geographer, drafted a remarkably accurate map of the Mississippi River from information furnished him by this Sieur Le Sueur, who died in Louisiana after a trip to France in 1702.

Nicolas Chauvin de la Frénière, from his marriage with Marguerite Le Sueur, had, among other children, Nicolas Chauvin de la Frénière *fils*, born in New Orleans, *Procureur Général du Roi* in Louisiana, who became, at the time of the cession of the province by France to Spain, a most heroic figure. He was tried by a drum head court martial for rebellion against Spain and shot on October 25, 1769, by order of Governor Alessandro O'Reilly, in the barracks facing the *rue du Quai*, behind the old Ursuline convent in Condé street. He will remain forever immortal in the annals of Louisiana, not only as the leader of the Martyrs of 1769, but as one of the most brillant and remarkable men of his time. In certain records still preserved in the colonial archives of New Orleans, he is given the title of count. He was of imposing appearance, with a noble face and his bravery was unquestioned. It is said that he bore a striking resemblance to Louis XIV and that he had been educated in France, which accounted for his learning and polish. Gifted with a golden tongue, he held his hearers spell-bound with his eloquence. He was by far the best-beloved man in old New Orleans. After his cruel death, Louis XV, who had not raised a finger to save him from the fury of Spain, made late amends by granting his widow the sum of 10,000 livres as a paltry indemnity for his ungrateful attitude toward one of French Louisiana's most valuable sons.

The unfortunate Chauvin de la Frénière had married twice. His first wife was Mademoiselle Hubert de Bellair, his cousin, and daughter of Jacques Hubert de Bellair and Catherine Nepveu. From this first marriage was born a daughter, Mademoiselle de la Frénière, who became the wife of the dashing Jean Baptiste Payen, Sieur de Noyan, captain of cavalry, knight of St. Louis and nephew of the revered Jean Baptiste le Moyne de Bienville, founder of New Orleans. In spite of his influential family connections, the Chevalier de Noyan shared the fate of his illustrious father-in-law and died in 1769, before a Spanish firing squad.

His second wife was Marie de la Chaise, daughter of Jacques de la Chaise, former Comptroller General of Louisiana, and Marguerite d'Arensbourg, and granddaughter of Jacques de la Chaise, the incorruptible *Commissaire Ordonnateur*, and Marguerite Cailly. She was also a sister of Louise de la Chaise, who became, October 2, 1759, the wife of Joseph Roy de Villeré, *Ecrivain de la Marine* and commandant of the German Coast section in 1767. Villeré was also numbered among O'Reilly's victims and died as bravely as la Frénière, Payen de Noyan, Marquis, Caresse, and Milhet, who were all immolated in 1769.

Louis Chauvin de Beaulieu, one of the original six Chauvin brothers and sisters, married Charlotte Orbanne Duval. At his death his widow became the wife of François de Mouy. His posterity is not known outside of the descendants of a granddaughter, Françoise Chauvin Beaulieu de Monplasir, born in New Orleans, May, 1755, who married Michel Dragon (q. v.), and whose daughter in turn married Andrea Dimitry (q. v.). A son was François Chauvin Beaulieu de Monplasir, born at Biloxi, who married Mariannne la Lande d'Apremont born at Fort Condé.

Barbe Chauvin, eldest girl of the Chauvin sextette, married Ignace Hubert Bellair, a native of Canada, who belonged to a family of *voyageurs* engaged in the northern fur trade. Barbe and her husband left Louisiana and returned to *Nouvelle France*, living in Montreal, where they both died before April 13, 1737. Their daughter, Catherine Bellair, married in Louisiana, Jacques Nepveu, her first cousin, son of Jacques Nepveu and Michelle Chauvin.

Michelle Chauvin, the younger Chauvin pioneer, had also married in Canada. Her husband was Jacques Nepveu. They returned to Montreal, where they settled, but on April 16, 1737, while enroute for the Illinois Post, Michelle and her husband were murdered by Indians. It was their son who married his cousin, Catherine Bellair.

The Nepveus in Canada were a prosperous family. The archives of *Nouvelle France* show that a certain Jean Baptiste Nepveu, a merchant of Montreal, acquired from Jacques Bourdon d'Autray, November 28, 1716, the ancient *seigneurie d'Autray*, established in 1637, on Isle Dupas, in the St. Lawrence river, and in 1731 became owner of the *fief* of La Morraye in the same place. He was, therefore, included among the petty Canadian lords during the French regime.

Joseph Chauvin de Léry, another of the six original Chauvin pioneers, was a militia captain in the colony and a Choctaw Indian trader. His first wife was Hypolite Mercier, who died at la Rochelle. Thereupon, in May 1726, he married Françoise Laurence (or Lorance) Le Blanc, daughter of Henri Le Blanc and Servanne Lemarié. She was a native of Saint Laurant, in the diocese of St. Malo, Brittany, and was well connected in Louisiana, the Councillor Bruslé being her brother-in-law, and the *Procureur Général* Fleuriau as well as the Councillor Fazende being, by marriage, her second cousins. Madame de Morières was likewise her aunt. When Joseph Chauvin de Léry Sr. was killed by the Indians in 1729 at the Natchez Post, he left, from his second wife, three children: Françoise, Marguerite, and Laurence Chauvin de Léry.

Marguerite Chauvin de Léry, his daughter, married twice. Her first husband was the Marquis Dominique de Verbois. At his death she became the wife, on August 14, 1759, of Bernard de Verges, an ensign in the colonial troops, son of Chevalier Bernard de Verges (q. v.), chief royal engineer in Louisiana, and Marie Thérese Pinau.

François Chauvin de Léry, eldest child of Joseph and Françoise Laurence Chauvin de Léry, married, July 26, 1763, Marie de la Chaise, daughter of Jacques de la Chaise and Marguerite d'Arensbourg. She was a niece of Père de la Chaise, confessor of Louis XIV. From her union with François Chauvin de Léry issued ten children: (a) François, born August 6, 1764, who married Constance Le Sassier and left five children, (1) Charles Chauvin de Léry, married to Amice du Tillet; (2) Felix Chauvin de Léry, married to Fénélie d'Auterive; (3) Céleste Chauvin de Léry, who became Mrs. Guigue; (4) Victoire Chauvin de Léry, who married a cousin, the Sieur de Léry, and (5) Josephine Chauvin de Léry, who married Jubel Reynoy; (b) Louis Boisclair Chauvin de Léry, born August 19, 1794, who married Marie "Tonton" Corbin Bachemin and had eight children: (1) Chauvin de Léry, who married his cousin, Victoire de Léry; (2) Dr. Charles Chauvin de Léry, a prominent New Orleans physician and distinguished writer, who married Odile Chauvin de Léry; (3) Boisclair Chauvin de Léry, whose wife was a Miss Tricou; (4) Edouard Chauvin de Léry, married to a Miss Boutté; (5) Victoire Céphise Chauvin de Léry, whose first husband was Homer Fortier and second, J. P. Dubreuil de Villars; (6) Eveline Chauvin de Léry, who also married twice, first, Théophile Dubreuil de Villars, and second, his brother, Adolphe Dubreuil de Villars, father of J. Claude and Claude Albert de Villars, and (7) Eliza Chauvin de Léry, who became the wife of Prosper de Trouard; (c) Jacques Monplaisir Chauvin de Léry, born November 2, 1805, first married Emérente Forstall and, secondly, Adèle de Trouard, among whose grandchildren by his first wife were Lucien de Léry, married to Miss Flotte; John C. de Léry, husband of Miss Fernandez, and Lucille de Léry, who became the wife of Edgar Bouligny; (d) Marie Aimé Chauvin de Léry, who married Mr. Seuzeneau, and (e) Marienne Constance Chauvin de Léry, who became the wife of Hardy de Boisblanc.

By his first wife, Hypolite Mercier, Joseph Chauvin de Léry, *pére*, who was killed at the Natchez Post in 1729, had three children :

1.—Antoine Chauvin de Léry des Ilets (or Islets), who married Charlotte Faucon du Manoir, daughter of Jean Baptiste Faucon du Manoir and Charlotte le Jaloux. From this marriage issued six children: (a) Jean Baptiste de Léry, who married Marthe Bienvenu; (b) Marguerite Françoise de Léry who married, first, Jean Baptiste Esnould de Livaudais, and, second, the Chevalier Vincent de Morant; (c) Charlotte de Léry, who married, in New Orleans, March 10, 1763, Jacques Esnould de Livaudais; (d) Jeanne de Léry, who became the wife of François Beaumont de Livaudais; (e) Judith de Léry, who married the Count de MacNamara; (f) Louise Constance de Léry, who became, June 19, 1767, the first wife of Jean René Huchet de Kernion (q. v.).

2.—Joseph Chauvin de Léry, *fils*, who married, December 13, 1738, in New Orleans, Marie Faucon Manoir, whose sister Charlotte had become the wife of his brother Antoine. Joseph de Léry met the same fate as his father, being killed by the Indians, before February 31, 1736. The widow Chauvin de Léry, *fils*, married, March 14, 1739, Pierre Benoit Payen de Noyan, Seigneur de Chavoy, who was king's adjutant at the Fort Condé de la Mobile, and son of Pierre Jacques Payen de Noyan, Seigneur de Chavoy, a naval lieutenant.

The estate of Joseph Chauvin de Léry Sr., killed by the Indians in 1729, was settled in 1734, his *Tchoupitoulas* plantation being sold, October 28, to Augustin Payen de Noyan for 1000 livres. His widow, Françoise Laurence Le

Blanc, deserves special mention for her many and varied matrimonial ventures. She married a second time in New Orleans, June 25, 1734, Louis René François de Manne, a noble *écuyer*, born in the parish of Saint Jean, in Bonichard, Touraine, a son of René de Manne and Charlotte de Blanchy.

However, this second marriage was declared null and void, August 20, 1737, by the Vicar General of New Orleans, as de Manne was conclusively shown to be a bigamist, the first to earn such an unenviable title in Louisiana. Not disgusted by this disastrous matrimonial fiasco, Françoise, after the annulment of her marriage with the bigamist de Manne, chose for her third spouse the very noble and distinguished Chevalier de Saint Aignet.

But this was not the last of her many nuptials. The Chevalier de Saint Aignet, breathing his last at *Fort de l'Assomption*, while serving under Bienville in his Chickasaw campaign, Françoise stood for the fourth time before the altar, November 22, 1744, with Messire Henry Aymé Elizabeth de Montaut, Chevalier de Montbéraut, a native of Polaminy, in the Comté de Foix, bishopric of Rieux, son of the Marquis de Montbéraut and Marguerite de Blondel. That Françoise was still a popular woman in the colony is shown by the fact that the *grand marquis*, Pierre Rigaud de Vaudreuil, among other notables, signed, as a witness, her marriage contract.

To cap the climax of her matrimonial adventures, Françoise Laurence Le Blanc de Léry de Manne de Saint Aignet de Montaut, burying her fourth husband, married for the fifth time the Marquis de Verbois.

LABRANCHE Family

FOUR ships were ploughing their way through the stormy Atlantic sailing toward the West. They were freighted with six hundred and forty-one souls, exclusive of the officers and crews, and among their passengers were eight hundred and seventy-five German colonists and sixty-six Swiss. *Les Deux Frères, La Saonne, La Charente* and *La Garonne*, as those sailing vessels were called, had left the port of Lorient, in Brittany, on June 24, 1721, bound for Louisiana.

Their human cargo, hard-working, worthy but impecunious men and women, had been lured by John Law's enticing and deceiving pamphlets, from the farms of their ancestors to the so-called *El Dorado* of the West. They came from the German Palatinate and the country along the Rhine. They had left a land where want and famine ruled—a land that had been almost destroyed by the Thirty Years' War and the havoc wrought by the armies of Louis XIV.

Many of their countrymen, before them, had wended their way in droves to various ports of France, on their way to America, believing that they were following the road that led to fortune, only to find out later that they were trudging the path that ended at Golgotha.

They were herded like cattle, but with far less consideration, by the agents of John Law. In many a French port, Death's angel had begun to visit them before they had even embarked. But in their intoxication, they would not retrace their steps homeward. Though many of them already reposed in the churchyards of Lorient, la Rochelle and Brest, victims of disease and privation, the survivors determined to carry on. Only the strongest would survive the rigors and dangers of the long ocean voyage. Pestilence was to carry off many others when they reached the shores of that alien Promised Land!

How many of them started for Louisiana from the Fatherland will never be positively known. Estimates vary. Six to ten thousand of them sailed for the French province between 1717 and 1721. Only one-third of that number reached their destination! What with the tempests and gales their ships encountered many of the vessels on which they sailed fell into the hands of pirate or corsair, and were looted and sunk. Others never reached port and their disappearance remained unsolved mysteries and riddles of the sea. Lurking in the rigging of their ships, pestilence and sickness, like carrion vultures were ever watching for their prey. When the shores of Biloxi were reached, decimated in numbers, the survivors landed on a sandy beach where new trials awaited them. It was a fearful toll that Death had taken of them on the high seas. The annals of the world had never seen anything to equal it.

Of the four ships mentioned at the beginning of this chapter, only three reached Mobile on March 1, 1721. *La Garonne* had disappeared, but *Les Deux Frères*, *La Saonne* and *La Charente*, survived the storms and the grappling hooks of the buccaneers. Those still alive among the passengers had a tale of horror to relate that congealed the blood and caused an icy sweat to start on the brows of their hearers. A merciless sickle had mowed down many of those strong German agriculturists on the Atlantic. Like blades of grass they had fallen before the onslaughts of the Grim Reaper. On one vessel alone—*Les Deux Frères*—one hundred and seventy-three out of two hundred and thirteen Teutonic colonists had perished.

Aboard this ill-fated vessel were two brothers, John Adam Zweig and John Zweig (or Zink, as the name appears on some of the old records), who were natives of Bavaria. The first-mentioned had married, in the Fatherland, Anna Kuhn. She was the daughter of Simon Kuhn, of Weissenberg, Ausbach, Bavaria, who followed John Adam to Louisiana with their daughter, Anna Margarethe Zweig, born in Bollweller, Alsace, and her father who also settled in the Louisiana colony, Simon Kuhn obtaining a concession at the *Côte des Allemands*. Johan Adam Zweig became an agriculturist in the section around *Fort Condé de la Mobile*, where his daughter, Anna Margarethe, married Pierre Bridel, a soldier from Brittany. Johan Adam Zweig, who was a Roman Catholic, died in Biloxi without male issue.

Johan Zweig, his brother, was also married, having taken for his wife in Bamberg, Bavaria, Catherine Corius, who shared with him the trials of that terrible voyage across the Atlantic. When they arrived in the colony, they had three children with them Andrew (or André) Zweig, who at the time of the Louisiana census of 1724 was twelve years of age; Margarethe Zweig, and Johan Zweig. John Zweig and his wife probably died before 1724, as they are not mentioned in the census of that year. They had settled at the *Côte des Allemands*, and it is probable that Johan, their youngest son, lived for a while with his paternal uncle, Johan Adam Zweig in Biloxi, after his parents' death.

André Zweig, the eldest son of this couple, born in Bamberg, married at the German Coast, April 23, 1743, Christine Greber (or Grabert), native of that section and daughter of Christian Greber, a German colonist in Louisiana, and Anne Marie Hirters. This marriage was celebrated by Father Pierre de Luxembourg, apostolic missionary, and the witnesses to these early nuptials included Johan Zweig, brother of the groom, and his wife, Suzanne Marchand; Joseph Verret, husband of Margarethe Zweig, sister of the groom, and Joseph Wiltz, who later on became the husband of Suzanna Zweig, a niece of the groom. There is no record extant of the issue, if any, of André Zweig and Christine Greber.

Margarethe Zweig, a sister of André, married Joseph Verret in 1724. Her husband was one of the earliest settlers at the *Côte des Allemands*, and acquired later a plantation, known as *La Providence*, on the Mississippi, opposite the little town now known as Waggaman. Margarethe Zweig Verret left issue and her descendants are now found in the Villeré, Cassard and other prominent Louisiana families.

Johan Zweig, the third child, born in Bamberg, bishopric of Metz, lived, before his marriage, at *Cannes des Brulés*. He was a hard-working farmer, like his forefathers had been, and earned his daily bread by the sweat of his brow. On November 6, 1737, he signed his marriage contract with Suzanne Marchand, a young French girl of New Orleans which was drawn up by *Maitre* Henry, one of the earliest royal notaries of the capital.

His bride, an orphan at the time and under the tutelage of the worthy Ursuline nuns, resided with them in their wonderful new convent in the *rue Condé* in New Orleans. On the day he took Suzanne for wife, Johan found himself suddenly Gallicized, for *Maitre* Henry gave him a new family name! Henceforth he was to be known as the Sieur Labranche for "Zweig" translated into French meant "a branch." The French notary, unable to tussle with the orthography of a German name containing the letter W, which does not exist in the French alphabet, without further ado dubbed the groom "Labranche," and drew up his marriage contract accordingly. Even the Germanic "Johan" became a French "Jean."

The bride of the young German, so suddenly dignified with a Gallic name (which all of his descendants adopted as their own), was born in Saint-Marcelin, bishopric of Grenoble, in Dauphiné. Suzanne's parents, early settlers in New Orleans, were Jean Baptiste Marchand and Suzanne Mathis. The signing of her marriage contract was honored by the presence of Monsieur Gatien de Salmon, *Commissaire Ordonnateur* and ranking judge of the Superior Council of the province, as well as of his aristocratic wife, who are stated, in the contract, to be "the special protectors" of the orphaned bride.

"Jean Labranche" had saved enough from his earnings to dower his young wife with the sum of three hundred livres. The young couple prospered. In 1737 Jean and Suzanne acquired an estate on the right bank of the Mississippi, opposite the plantation of Joseph Verret, their brother-in-law. There they lived happily, while enjoying the respect and friendship of the best families in the land. They made their joint last will on October 21, 1780, and died before 1785, having brought forth six children to perpetuate their worth and the name the notary gave them. They were:

1.—Michel Labranche, who married Louise Fortier and left seven children. He died in 1787 and his descent in the female line is represented today by no less than twenty of the outstanding families of Louisiana: the Le Blancs,

Pothiers, Sarpys, Fortiers, Soniat du Fossats, Augustins, Beugnots, Wogans, Duprés, Villerés, Larendons, de la Barres, Godberrys, Seconds, de Lesseps, Browns, Oxnards, Sanchez and Chastants.

2.—Alexandre Labranche, born in 1756, who became a planter and a distinguished citizen of Louisiana. He joined the service of Spain as a volunteer in the Hispanic troops, on January 1, 1770, and was for more than nine years an officer of militia at the German Coast. For twelve more years he served with the Carbineers and finally commanded the Mixed Regiment of Louisiana. Under Galvez, he served as a second lieutenant at the attack on Fort Bute and the siege of Baton Rouge in 1779 and was also at the siege of Mobile in 1780. Not satisfied with such a record, he was also a colonel under General Andrew Jackson at the Battle of New Orleans in 1815. When the first constitution of the state was drafted in 1812, he was numbered among its signers. From his marriage to Marie Jeanne Piseros, of distinguished Spanish ancestry, were born five children, among whom Alcée Labranche, born in St. Charles Parish in 1806, who attained prominence in his native state. He was a member of the Louisiana house of representatives from 1831 to 1833 and on January 7th of the latter year, he was made its speaker. Chosen as United States *Chargé d'Affaires*, or Ambassador, to the Republic of Texas on March 7, 1837, he served as such, with great ability, until April 2, 1840, when he resigned this office. He was then elected, as a Democrat, to the Twenty-Eighth Congress of the United States on March 4, 1843, holding this position until March 3, 1845. When war was declared against Mexico, Alcée Labranche took an active part in the organization of volunteers from Louisiana and Texas to serve in that bitter struggle. He was a well-educated and brillant man, having graduated from the University of Sorreze, in France. Very punctillious in matters of honor, he fought a famous duel with James Hueston, a gentleman of Northern birth, on account of an objectionable article that was published by the latter about him in the Baton

Rouge *Gazette* during August 1845. They fought with shot guns and Hueston was killed. Alcée Labranche died August 17, 1861. His last domicile was *Glendale*, a plantation, in St. John the Baptist parish, which belonged to him and Jean Baptiste Sarpy, and operated under the name of A. Labranche and Company. He had married Aimée Sarpy, daughter of Pierre Lestang Sarpy, and left two daughters, Victorine and Pauline, and a son, Alcée. To mention all of his descendants would require more space than a genealogical book of the size of this present one will allow. The female descendants of Alexandre Labranche, father of Alcée, married into the Tricou, de la Barre, Soniat du Fossat, Chalard, Dupuy, Metéyé, Michel, Sarpy, Haydel, Fortier, Ganucheau, Aime, Piseros, Villeré, Augustin, Schreiber, Toby, Frédéric, Brou, Le Blanc, Grevemberg, Bérault, Lallande, Blois, Wood, Jumonville, Bouligny, Albert Baldwin and Dr. Smythe families.

3.—Jean Baptiste Branche, who died unmarried.

4.—Suzanne Labranche, who married in 1759, Joseph Wiltz, son of Johan Ludwig Wilsz (q. v.), and Miss Ziriac. From this union issued two children: Hortense Wiltz, who became in 1789 the wife of Jean Leonard Arnould, and Jean Louis Wiltz, captain of colonial militia, who married Marianne Colomb.

5.—Genevieve Labranche, who married Alexandre Bauré and left issue.

6.—Marie Louise Labranche, who married François Trépagnier and left issue.

While the Labranche (or Zweig or Zink) family did not boast of titles or the heraldic trappings of nobility, they were of that industrious, patient and industrious class of American colonists, that, ignoring the cruel tricks of Fate, proved itself equal to every emergency, overcame, with dogged tenacity, almost insurmountable obstacles, and laid the foundation for the future expansion and prosperity of the American Republic.

DE VERGES Family

THE ancient *Seigneurie* de Vergès, belonging to the French Colonial family of the same name, established in Louisiana since 1720, was located in the parish of Sazos, in the valley of Bareges. It was subject to the ancient Counts of Bigorre. Those who owned it and the strong feudal castle that defended it since the twelfth century, were also the founders and patrons of the church and parish of St. Julien de Sazos. In the ancient Latin charts and titles their name appears as *de Viridariis* and *de Viridario*. In the French records it is variously spelt de Vergès, de Vergez and du Verger. The first known author of this distinguished Béarnais house was Garsie Arnaud de Vergès, *Damoiseau*, who was lord of Vergès and patron of Sazos in 1253. The arms of this family are described: "On a field *argent*, a *sinople* tree, with a band *gules* surcharged *en coeur* with a rose *argent*."

There lived in Béarn between the years 1560 and 1580, six doughty and renowned captains—Guillaume, Jean, Charles, Roger, Raimond and Joseph de Vergès. They were brothers and at this early date began to form separate and distinct branches of a venerable race. It was from one of those offshoots that the Chevalier Bernard de Vergès, who settled in Louisiana in the early days, descended.

This worthy colonist, who made a most remarkable record in his adopted country, was born on January 10, 1693, in the parish of Eurt, *Terre de La Boure*, Bayonne, in Béarn. He was about 27 years of age when he arrived in Louisiana in 1720. His father, François Artus de Vergès, was an officer in the *Régiment des Bandes Gramontoises*, in Béarn, who had married twice in France, one of his wives being Marie Lagrenade, mother of the Chevalier Bernard de Vergés. By these two marriages, Françoise Artus had six children, two daughters and four sons, all born in Béarn. The sons were: Armand Xavier de Vergès, Pierre de Vergès, Dominique de Vergès, and Bernard de Vergès, born in 1693, who founded the Louisiana branch of the family.

Bernard de Vergès went to Louisiana in 1720 on the vessel *Le Dromadaire* of the *Compagnie d'Occident*, commanded by Captain Saint Mar. Aboard this ship were sixty passengers, including Le Blond de la Tour, chief royal engineer in the colony, and de Boispinel, a future chief royal engineer in Louisiana. When de Vergès landed in the province he was a *dessinateur*, or draftsman. Seven years later, July 31, 1727, when the Ursuline nuns arrived at the jetties on the ship *La Gironde*, Bernard de Vergès, then commandant of the *Fort de la Balize*, was the first to greet the ardently expected women who had left Lorient early in February to educate the young women of the colony. In their annals, the Ursulines have preserved a record of the charming hospitality they enjoyed in the home of the gallant young Béarnais commandant, after their trying sea trip.

This first de Vergès led a very active life in Louisiana. In 1737 Governor de Bienville sent him, then a king's lieutenant, out in the wilderness to survey the Chicasaw territory, which he intended to invade, and to map the country. Two years later, he followed the governor on his ill-fated expedition against the warring Chickasaws, and in 1740 he was again at the Balize, serving as royal engineer. When the government buildings at that place were blown down by the fearful hurricanes that prevailed from September 11th to 18th, 1741, it was de Vergès who drew the plans for the new structures that arose on the ruins.

In 1743 the young royal engineer acquired, in partnership with Adrien de la Place, one of his relatives, a plantation of 17 arpents front on the Mississippi River, which estate he owned until the day of his death. It was exactly opposite New Orleans and he christened it *Trianon*. It was a large plantation home, some fifty feet in length and had eleven rooms, with glazed windows, doors and windows provided with locks and keys, shingled roof, brick chimneys and fireplaces and a large attic. Here the engineer came to relax with his wife and children whenever his official duties allowed him a breathing spell.

It was Bernard de Vergès, who in 1746, drew the plans for the strong fort at English Turn on the Mississippi, five leagues distant from New Orleans, and superintended its construction. Although ever busy with his surveys or in blazing out new trails in the wilderness under incredible hardships, de Vergès incurred the il-will of Governor Bienville. He complained of this in a letter he addressed to the French Minister as early as 1739, and, without specially mentioning the governor, said that he was the victim of jealousy and of conflict of power, to which he attributed in a great measure, the ill-success of Bienville's Chickasaw campaign during that same year.

For many years the young engineer Bernard de Vergès had nourished a dream. He wanted to be appointed *ingenieur-en-chef*, or chief royal engineer in Louisiana. Bienville fought his attempts to get this coveted prize, favoring the reward for Saucier, another able colonial engineer. In spite of Bienville's opposition, the worth of de Vergès was recognized by his royal master and in 1754, at the time he made a perilous trip to the Illinois country to lay out the plans of the mighty *Fort de l'Ascension* (or Massac) at the confluence of the *Rivière des Cherokees* and the Ohio River, which he had drawn and on which France contemplated spending 200,000 to 270,000 livres, he was styled as Chief Royal Engineer of the colony.

It was de Vergès who, in December 1759, at the time that war was about to break out between France and England, was charged with preparing the defenses of New Orleans against English invasion. He presented, on January 2, 1760, to the Council of War sitting in the capital, complete plans for the city's protection, which were unanimously adopted. It was thus, at his suggestion, that old New Orleans was completely surrounded by a palissade and moat. The carrying out of the Vergès' defensive measures, which were completed on December 21, 1760, cost France not less than 459,725 livres.

De Vergès, like every other prominent man in Louisiana, was involved in the mighty quarrel between the *Ordonnateur*

Rochemore and Governor de Kerlerec and was numbered among the Governor's warm adherents. In 1763, Louis XV, as a reward for 43 years of faithful and indefatigable services in the colony, conferred upon Chief-Engineer de Vergès, the cross of the Royal and Military Order of St. Louis, the greatest honor that could be bestowed upon a French military man.

De Vergès led a busy and useful life and had reached his seventy-third year, when on January 17, 1766, he calmly breathed his last in his city home on Bienville street near Chartres, surrounded by his bereaved wife and children. He had served under the first five colonial governors of Louisiana. The Chevalier de Vergès married in New Orleans, December 9, 1733, Marie Thérese Pinau, born on April 3, 1714, in the parish of St. Sauveur, in la Rochelle, France. She was the daughter of Pierre Pinau, contractor of the king in Louisiana, and of Susanne Meunier. From the de Vergès-Pinau marriage were born seven children:

1.—Bernard de Vergès II, infantry officer in Louisiana, who married in New Orleans, August 14, 1759, Marguerite Chauvin de Léry, widow of the Chevalier Dominique de Verbois, former officer in the colony, and daughter of Joseph Chauvin de Léry, captain of militia in Louisiana, and of Françoise Laurence Le Blanc. Their children died young.

2.—Pierre de Vergès, celebrated military man in Louisiana, who married in New Orleans, May 4, 1769, Marie Joseph Catherine Poupart, widow of Antoine Simon Grifon d'Anneville, King's storekeeper in the colony, and of whom we shall specially write further on.

3.—François Xavier Dagobert de Vergès, Sieur de St. Sauveur, who married in New Orleans, December 24, 1777, Madeleine Victoire Josephine Héloïse Martin de Lino de Chalmette, daughter of the Lieutenant Louis Xavier Martin de Lino de Chalmette (q. v.), and of Magdeleine Broutin. His posterity will follow in the course of this article.

4.—Louis Joseph Augustin de Vergès, Sieur de St. Luc, who does not appear to have married.

5.—Marguerite de Vergès, who married in New Orleans, April 26, 1753, Henri le Grand d'Orgon, knight of St. Louis, captain of infantry and former commandant of the Natchez Post, with a distinguished colonial record. This Chevalier d'Orgon was born in Paris about 1695 and came to Louisiana in 1737. He was reputed to belong, by the bend sinister, to a princely European house. From his marriage to Mlle. de Vergès in 1753 at the Natchez Post, was born a daughter, Henriette Marie le Grand d'Orgon, who became on May 2, 1772, the wife of Jean Arnould Valentine Bobé des Closseaux (or Cloziaux), *Controleur de la Marine* and Intendent pro-tem in 1769, widower of Françoise Elizabeth Bernoudy. He, his wife and mother-in-law, in 1773, left for France aboard an English frigate which was lost at sea, with all of its passengers.

6.—Marguerite Françoise de Vergès, who married in New Orleans, Jean Baptiste Chauvin de Léry des Islets, son of Antoine Chauvin de Léry des Islets, militia officer in the colony, and of Charlotte Faucon du Manoir.

7.—Charlotte de Vergès, who married Gabriel Fazende, Colonial Secretary in Louisiana, Commissaire under Rochemore in 1762 and an important civil officer in the colony until 1776. He was the son of Jean Baptiste Gabriel Fazende and of Charlotte Dreux.

We must now return to Pierre de Vergès, second son of the old Chevalier Bernard de Vergès, who continued the elder branch of the family in New Orleans. His wife, Marie Joseph Catherine Poupart, was born in *Fort Condé de la Mobile* and was the daughter of the Sieur Joseph Poupart (who died at Fort Toulouse de la Mobile in 1740) and of Marie Roy. Mrs. Pierre de Vergés died in New Orleans in 1779. The de Vergès-Poupart marriage contract, passed in New Orleans, May 4, 1761, is signed by Governor Aubry and other notables of the colony. When it was signed, the bride, who was the widow of Antoine Simon Grifon de'Anneville, had four surviving children from her first marriage: Charles Antoine, Daniel, Catherine, and

Victoria Marie Josephine Grifon D'Anneville. The last-named became the wife of Jean Marc Coulon Jumonville de Villiers.

Pierre de Vergès was a native of New Orleans. On September 14, 1758, he distinguished himself in the attack upon Fort Duquesne, under Aubry, when the immortal George Washington, then an English officer, and his garrison were forced to capitulate to the French. The ensign Pierre de Vergès, singled-handed, killed two of three Englishmen who were pressing him closely and captured the third. When English reinforcements arrived, under General Forbes, to recapture Fort Duquesne, Aubry, the French commander, with ensign de Vergès and the balance of his troops, set the fortress afire, spiked the guns and destroyed the ammunition, and on flat boats, with flags proudly waving above them, floated down the Mississippi to New Orleans, where they were received with fitting honors.

Pierre de Vergès was *alcalde* in the Cabildo from 1779 to 1780, under Governor de Galvez. From his marriage to the widow Grifon d'Anneville were born three daughters but no son. They were: (a) Marie Joseph Modeste de Vergès, born in New Orleans, who became the second wife of Jean René Huchet de Kernion, Spanish *alcalde* and Colonial officer. She died on her Gentilly plantation on June, 7, 1815; (b) Marguerite Constance de Vergès, who married in New Orleans, Jacques Huchet de Kernion, son of Jean René and his first wife, Miss de Léry des Islets, and (c) Marie Prudence de Vergès, who died unmarried.

François Xavier Dagobert de Verges, Sieur de St. Sauveur, younger son of the chevalier Bernard de Verges and Mlle. Pinau, was an officer in the colonial troops. He married, as has already been shown, Madeleine Victoire Josephine Martin de Lino de Chalmette (q. v.). From this union was born, among other children, a son, Pierre, who married Heloise Martin de Lino de Chalmette, born in 1788, who died January 15, 1856. She was the daughter of Martin Ignace de Lino de Chalmette and Madeleine Victoire de Vaugine. This Pierre and his wife, Mlle. de Chalmette, had three sons:

1.—Paul de Vergès, baptized July 26, 1812, who married on January 19, 1836, Marie Stéphanie Lanusse, and died on May 27, 1870. He left seven children: (a) Pierre, born March 24, 1837, died March 23, 1904; (b) Charles Ernest, born December 21, 1838, died January 7, 1920, who married Edvige Fortier and left issue; (c) Jean Baptiste, born February 14, 1843, died July 9, 1915; (d) Pierre Paul, born July 21, 1840, died April 2, 1919, who married February 16, 1870, Mathilde Cruzat and left issue; (e) Louis Edmond, born November 17, 1844, died September 29, 1906; (f) Marie Alice, born November 6, 1847, and (g) Corinne, born December 17, 1854, died May 12, 1855.

2.—Pierre François de Vergès, born September 1, 1807, died February 19, 1865, married to Victoire Coralie Lanusse, daughter of Paul Lanusse and of Marie Celeste de Macarty (or Maccarthey-Mactigue). No son was born of this marriage.

3.—Malvina de Vergès, who married Manuel Cruzat and left two daughters.

The de Vergès family is still numerously represented in Louisiana by some of its outstanding citizens and their patronymic enjoys to the fullest extent the respect and consideration which the achievements of their worthy forebears have made illustrious.

Cross of the Royal and Military Order of Saint Louis
given Chevalier de Verges by Louis XV

SONIAT DU FOSSAT Family

NOT the least conspicuous among the young French noblemen that filled the barracks and attended the *levées* in the drawing room of Governor Pierre Rigaud de Vaudreuil, *le grand marquis*, in early New Orleans, was a dashing stripling from Gascony. Known as the Chevalier Gui de Saunhac du Fossat, he had won his spurs at the siege of Maestricht, where, as an officer, he received his first wound on a battlefield. Born in an ancient citadel, built by his chivalric race along the course of the dreamy Lot River, Gui, when still a boy, forsook a peaceful valley, nestling, like a child asleep, under its venerable trees.

He had his fortune to make. His race was a virile one that admitted of no weaklings and he had to follow the path his forebears had blazed for him. Thus he came to New Orleans in 1751 with an important contingent of troops, but brave warrior that he was, he had to chronicle before long his first capitulation. He had surrendered unconditionally to the charms of one of Louisiana's fair daughters. In the once fabulous region of Louisiana he had found a treasure that surpassed all others. She was Françoise Claudine Dreux, daughter of Mathurin Dreux, Sieur de Gentilly, whose fertile acres lay along the banks of the *Ruisseau de Saint Jean*, and in her veins flowed the blood of the Dreuxs, once sovereign *ducs de Bretagne*.

The Saunhacs (or Soniats, as the name is now spelled) had their origin in the remotest times. Since 1538 the chateau de Fossat in Gascony, had belonged to them being acquired during that year by François de Saunhac, Seigneur de Belcastel, direct ancestor of the Chevalier Gui. It was in this old manor, built to resist the battering rams of feudal barons, that the chevalier was born in 1726. In his twentieth year he was already a soldier and in 1748 had won a lieutenancy in the *Régiment de Monaco.*

The Chevalier Gui Soniat du Fossat was not only a fighting man. He possessed also a deep knowledge of engineering and thus was called upon to contribute his talents in the building and strengthening of fortresses in Louisiana. He also wielded a facile pen and wrote a very interesting monograph on Louisiana and her resources (which was published long after his death by Charles T. Soniat, one of his many descendants), and was rewarded for his splendid achievements with the coveted Cross of Saint Louis which he amply deserved.

The Spaniards, who appreciated his worth, offered him a commission in their military service when the flag of Spain succeeded the golden *fleur-de-lys* of France. Gui accepted their offer and under Governor O'Reilly, became captain of the Battalion of Louisiana in 1769. Eventually he discarded his military uniform for a judicial toga, sitting in 1772 in the Hispanic Cabildo of New Orleans as a solemn *alcalde.*

Tired both of military and judicial life, he resolved to become a planter and spend his remaining years in his fields of indigo, corn, sugar cane and other staples. Thus in 1778 he acquired a country estate, below New Orleans, from the Ursuline nuns. Disposing of it to Bernard de Marigny, he located on a high stretch of ground above New Orleans, where he erected a roomy and picturesque plantation home that is still standing today on the Jefferson Highway and is now called the Colonial Country Club.

In Louisiana, however, in the early days, a worthy and able man like the Chevalier Gui was not allowed to retire from public service prematurely, or, for that matter, at any time before death had settled upon him. On this account he found himself in 1786 an *alcalde* again, under Governor Miro. He was reaching the end of his useful career and breathed his last in 1794 in his sixty-eighth year.

By his wife, Françoise Claudine Dreux, he had nine children. They were: (a) Françoise; (b) Agathe, wife of Jean Enould Beaumont de Livaudais; (c) François Gui, whose wife was Cécile, daughter of Jacques de Lassudrie and Marguerite de Toucheboeuf; (d) Lucy; (e) Jeanne Elizabeth, married to Antoine d'Oriocourt; (f) Gui Joseph, whose first wife was Marie Anne Arnoult and the second one was Louise Duralde, a sister of Clarisse, wife of Governor William C. C. Claiborne, first American chief executive of Louisiana; (g) Marie Emilie, who became Madame Jean Baptiste Bermudez; (h) Catalina; and (i) Jean Baptiste, unmarried.

The Soniats were a prolific race, for while the founder of the family in Louisiana left nine children, Gui Joseph, one of his sons, by his two wives, left no less than fourteen and Charles Théodore, his grandson, who married Amélie Labranche, could boast of five sons and five daughters.

Among the children of the Chevalier Gui and Melle. Dreux, his eldest son, François Gui, who had married Cécile de Lassudrie, was an officer under Governor Galvez in his expedition against the English, became a knight of Saint Louis, also a lieutenant in the Louisiana troops in 1780, and shortly thereafter left Louisiana to settle in France in the old castle du Fossat, where he took the title of baron he had just inherited from a paternal uncle.

His brother, Gui Joseph Soniat du Fossat, by his first wife, Marie Anne Arnoult, left five sons, namely: (a) Gui Joseph, who died in the land of his ancestors; (b) Joseph; (c) Pierre Antoine; (d) François Gui, and (e) Jean Ursin, who married Célestine Allain. By his second wife, Louise Duralde, Gui Joseph had four daughters and five sons. They were: (a) Edmond; (b) Charlotte Adine; (c) Martin Valmont; (d) Charles Méloncy; (e) Valérie; (f) Gustave; (g) Célestine; (h) Joseph Théophile; (i) Charles Théodore, who married Aménaide Labranche, daughter of Lucien Labranche and Mathilde Fortier.

From this last-mentioned Soniat-Labranche marriage were born: (a) Lucien; (b) Charles Théodore, eminent notary of New Orleans, who did not marry; (c) Louise, who became the wife of Amedée Fortier; (d) Gustave Valérien, whose wife was Louise Marie Sarpy; and (e) Meloncy Charles, well-known notary and leader at the New Orleans bar, who married Louise Anne Exilée Fortier.

STIRLING Family

ALEXANDER STIRLING, a native of Fofar, Angushire, North Britain, came to the West Florida section of Louisiana prior to 1779, for we find him a second lieutenant in the first company, third battalion of the First Regiment of Grenadiers (also known as the Royal Legion Mixed Militia of the Mississippi), under the command of Don Enrique White, that saw service under Don Bernardo de Galvez when the doughly Spanish governor of Louisiana defeated the British under Colonel Dickson at Baton Rouge, and removed the Union Jack from this section of Louisiana forever.

At the termination of this campaign, Alexander Stirling turned to peaceful pursuits and in 1781 he was managing the plantation of Doctor Farrar in Pointe Coupée, and while there he took care of the fugitive children of John Alston (q. v.), and thereby won the affections of the oldest, Ann Alston. They were married in Baton Rouge, May 26, 1784. The young bridegroom and his bride took up a primitive outpost home at Murdock's Ford of the *Rio Feliciana*, as Thompson's Creek was known in those days, and opened a small store. The mercantile venture proved successful and later they moved to a spot on a creek and acquired a plantation they called *Egypt*, and which later became known as *Rosale*. They became quite wealthy and the creek that flowed through his plantation is known today as Alexander's Creek.

Alexander Stirling acquired a great deal of land through Spanish grants and by purchase, copies of some of these grants being still in the possession of the family. He was made an *alcalde*, or local judge, of his section during the Spanish domination, and was a man of considerable importance in the Feliciana country when he died in 1808 at the age of fifty-five years, leaving practically a principality to be divided among his seven surviving children. They were:

1.—Henry Stirling, born June 5, 1785, died September 1, 1827, who married, August 2, 1810, Mary Bowman of Brownsville, Pennsylvania. They had six children: (a) James A. Stirling, who died without issue; (b) Harriet Stirling, who married Thomas McCrindle, from whom was descended the late Dr. Harry McCrindle Johnson, of San Antonio, Texas, one of the pioneers in this country in urology, whose distinguished service gained him national recognition; (c) Isabella Stirling, who married Col. Micajah Courtney; (d) Louise Stirling, who married Pierce Butler (q. v.), member of a distinguished Louisiana family; (e) William H. Stirling, who married first Mary McCausland, and second, Sallie Miller of Mississippi; his daughter by the second marriage, Georgia Stirling being widely known as a temperance lecturer and reformer; (f) J. Bowman Stirling, who married Penelope J. Stewart,, daughter of a Mississippi cotton and sugar planter, their children being: (1) Julia Ann Stirling, who married William R. Stirling; (2) Bowman Stirling, who married a Miss Carter, and is president of the First National Bank of Jackson, Miss.; (3) Louisa Butler Stirling, who married Dr. Theoderic C. Linthicum, of Helena, Ark., and (4) Mary Stirling, who married John H. Thompson.

2.—Lewis Stirling, born November 9, 1786, died April 3, 1858. He married, July 14, 1807, Sarah Turnbull, who died December 21, 1875. Lewis Stirling was an outstanding actor in the stirring scenes attendant on the West Florida Rebellion, and was later made quartermaster of the tenth militia regiment of the state of Louisiana, holding his commission from Governor William Charles Cole Claiborne under date of January 8, 1814. He established *Wakefield* plantation, in 1833, nearly a century ago and built the old home, a part of which still stands. At the death of Mrs. Stirling the heirs divided the estate, what were then the upper stories of the house were taken down and utilized in the building of two other homes on the divided property. *Wakefield* is now owned by the Allain family, descendants of a daughter of Lewis Stirling who married John L. Lobdell of New York, and is occupied by Miss Hélène Allain. The children of Lewis Stirling and Sarah Turnbull were: (a) Catherine Mary Stirling, born June 7, 1809, who married, December 18, 1828, Dr. John B. Hereford of Virginia (q. v.); (b) Ann Mathilda Stirling, born January 2, 1811, who was married at a double wedding to John L. Lobdell of New York, when her sister, Catherine, married Doctor Hereford; (c) James L. Stirling, born December 25, 1812, died April 7, 1860. He married, April 26, 1838, Sarah Pirrie Smith, granddaughter of Lucy Alston Pirrie (q. v.). James L. Stirling became a member of the state legislature, and a senator in the upper house, and was elected to the bench. He left no descendants; (d) Lewis Stirling, born March 5, 1819, died May 10, 1901, who earned the title of Colonel Stirling in the Civil War; (e) Daniel Turnbull Stirling, born February 18, 1821, died June 28, 1863. During the Civil War both Lewis and Daniel Stirling were taken prisoners by the Federals and placed on a gunboat to be sent to prison. Daniel, an expert swimmer, had sworn he would never go to a Yankee prison, and leaped from the boat hoping to escape by swimming. He was never heard from again although his mother continued to wait and watch for him up to the day of her death, in December 1875; (f) Ruffin Gray Stirling, born August 11, 1827, died September 9, 1881, married, April 28, 1859, Catherine Leake, member of a prominent West Feliciana family. He became prominent in the medical profession. Doctor Stirling's children were: (1) Sarah Turnbull Stirling, died February 1929, prominent in Baton Rouge literary and historical circles; (2) Dr. Louis Gray Stirling, retired physician and surgeon, dean of medicine in Baton Rouge; (3) William Leake Stirling, West Feliciana parish planter and member of legislature; (4) Robert Hereford Stirling, planter of West Feliciana parish; (5) Mary S. Stirling, who married Sidney H. Lemon of Cleveland; (6) Daniel Turnbull Stirling, who served in the Spanish-American war, and (7) Margaret Stirling, who married Mr. Seymour of Baton 'Rouge, and served for many years in the office of the Secretary of State.

3.—Alexander Stirling, born June 23, 1791, died November 3, 1819. Married Alice Lackie of Woodville, Mississippi. He was a major in the state militia during 1814-15.

4.—William Stirling, born August 17, 1792, died 1842. Married Eppie Hall of Attakapas, Louisiana. Nine children were born to this union, and among their decendants are the Parkersons and Palfreys of New Orleans, the Careys of Atlanta, Georgia, and the Smiths and Stirlings of Franklin and New Orleans.

5.—Ruffin Gray Stirling, born April 5, 1795, died July 17, 1854. Married Mary C. Cobb of West Feliciana. They built *The Myrtles*, a beautiful plantation home just north of St. Francisville. Their children were: (a) Lewis Gray Stirling, born April 30, 1831, died October, 1854; (b) Sarah M. Stirling, born July 4, 1833, died April, 1878, married W. D. Winter, of St. Louis, and their son, Brigadier General Francis A. Winter, retired army surgeon, died January 11, 1931; (c) Clarence Stirling; (d) Ruffin Gray Stirling Jr.; (e) Ruffin Gray Stirling 3d; (f) Mary Stirling, died in infancy; (g) Stephen C. Stirling, born December 20, 1847, died 1927, married Amanda P. Smith, niece of Jefferson Davis, of the Confederacy, their children being (1) Nannie D. Stirling; (2) Mary Maul, who married her cousin, William Richards Percy; (3) John Bryson Stirling; (4) Francis W. Stirling, and (5) Jefferson Davis Stirling; (h) William R. Stirling, born April 27, 1850, died August 1886. Married Julia Ann Stirling, daughter of his cousin, J. Bowman Stirling; and (i) Henry Stirling, born February 14, 1853, married Zell Polk, daughter of Thomas Polk of Tennessee, their daughter, Mary Ruffin Stirling, being born February 10, 1878.

6.—Ann Stirling, born November 27, 1797, died March 3, 1888, married, first, Doctor Haynie of Maryland; second, Andrew Skillman of New Jersey, by whom she had (a) Ann Elizabeth Skillman, who married Calvin C. Routh, grandson of Jacob Routh (see Johnson family), one of the earliest American settlers at Natchez, and their daughter, Anne Mathilda Routh, married Captain Allen Thomas Bowie, a descendant of the distinguished Maryland family of that name; (b) Judge J. J. Skillman; (c) Frank Skillman; (d) Sarah Skillman, and (e) Louise Isabella Skillman, who married a Mr. Lea, their daughter, Fannie Lea, marrying Colonel Henry G. Hester, the celebrated figure on the New Orleans C o t t o n Exchange; Harrison Parker Lea, their son, went down on the ill-fated *Arga*. Their other children were: Annie Lea Salisbury, Eunice Lea Stafford, Isabel Lea Sbodgrass, Richard Henry Lea, and James Lea.

7.—John Stirling, born September 19, 1799, died August 27, 1829, married Edith Lilly of East Baton Rouge parish. Their children were: (a) Eunice Stirling, who married, first, a Mr. Forester, and second, Isaac Hudson Boatner. Their son, Dr. Elias Stirling Boatner, married Olivia Berwick, daughter of the Berwick for whom Berwick's Bay in St. Mary parish was named, and had five children: Olivia Boatner, who married Francis Mayo, and Eunice Boatner, Hudson Boatner, Burton Boatner, and Sadie Boatner; (b) Sarah Edith Stirling, who married Mark Boatner, and their three children were: (1) Edith Lilly Boatner, who married Christopher V. Haile, of New Orleans, one of the pioneer promoters of the electric street car system, and left two children, Clarisse Haile and Hudson B. Haile; (2) Charles J. Boatner, who married Fannie Mayo, daughter of Judge O. Mayo, a prominent Louisiana jurist. Their four children were: Judge Mark M. Boatner of New Orleans, Stirling S. Boatner, Orin Mayo Boatner, and Charles J. Boatner Jr.; (c) John Stirling, who married, first, Deborah J. Mayo, daughter of Judge Mayo, and whose three children were (1) John Stirling; (2) Charles Mayo Stirling; (3) Daborah S. Boatner. By his second marriage with Martha Dulant, his children were (4) Dunbar Stirling, (5) Shirley Alston Stirling, and (6) Sarah Stirling.

ROMAN Family

ON September 27, 1689, the twelfth century church of Saint Laurent in Grenoble, the most important city in Dauphiné, was witnessing another marriage ceremony. That day, the contracting parties were Balthazar Roman, a merchant glover of that industrial centre, and Marguerite Reynaud. The groom was a son of Noël Roman (born about 1645), an esteemed *bourgeois* of Grenoble, whose wife was Antoinette Reynaud.

The early Romans belonged to that social class known as the *haute bourgeoisie*, which though possessing no titles nor coats-of-arms, were none the less looked upon with favor by the *noblesse* of France and virtually considered by them as their equals. When Balthazar Roman married Marguerite Reynaud, some of the witnesses that signed the church register were men of a certain importance in official circles. One of them, the Sieur Claude Fayolle, was *premier huissier et concierge du Roi en la Chambre des Comptes*, or first usher and door-keeper for the king in the Chamber of Accounts. Another, the Sieur Aubert, was a *procureur*, or attorney, in Parliament.

Marguerite Reynaud, the bride of Balthazar Roman, was a daughter of Etienne Reynaud, a burgher of Colombe, and Dominique Paris. Her mother, Mlle. Paris, belonged to a family that had begun to accumulate great wealth. She was the sister or aunt of Joseph Paris du Vernay, who was to become one of the largest *concessionaires*, or land owners, in French colonial Louisiana.

This Joseph Paris du Vernay had three brothers, Antoine Paris, Paris de la Montagne, and Jean Paris de Marmontel, who were granted patents of nobility by Louis XV and acquired one of the largest fortunes of their times. A son of Balthazar Roman and Marguerite Reynaud, was Jacques

Roman, baptized in Grenoble December 15, 1697. His god-father was the Sieur Jacques Pasquier, a merchant glover of the town, and Marthe Reynaud, a maternal relative, was his god-mother.

Jacques Roman saw a chance of establishing himself in the colony of Louisiana, across the sea, where so many other sons of France had already obtained plantations and farms and were steadily improving their fortunes. His maternal kinsman, Joseph Paris du Vernay, the important *concessionaire* in that distant French province, had even suggested his going there under his special patronage. It was an invitation which no young man in Grenoble, or, for that matter, anywhere else in France, would have turned down in the early days of the eighteenth century.

Thus Jacques Roman sailed across the Atlantic and established himself at the *Côte des Allemands*, near New Orleans, where, on October 24, 1741, he was married by Friar Prosper, to Marie Josephe Daigle, a native of the place. Her parents were Joseph Daigle (also known as Malbrouck) and Suzanne d'Esperon. The Chevalier Charles Frédérick d'Arensbourg, commandant of the German Coast section, graced her nuptials with his presence, as he did on all such occasions when worthy colonists in his district were the contracting parties.

Jacques Roman and Josephe Daigle had several children, all born at the *Côte des Allemands*, among whom was a son, Joseph; Marie Josephe Roman, baptized December 16, 1742, who married Louis Alexandre Harang; Jeanne Roman, who married Gabriel Fuselier de la Claire, commander of the Opelousas post, and had one son, Agricole Fuselier de la Claire (Gabriel again married, February 24, 1770, Anne Marguerite Harang, sister of Louis Alexandre Harang) ; Elizabeth Roman, whose godmother was Eléonore d'Arensbourg, when she was baptized December 13, 1744, and Jacques Etienne Roman, baptized October 27, 1748.

This Jacques Etienne Roman, in turn, took for wife Marie Louise Patin, born October 20, 1762, and baptized on November 10th of the succeeding year, in the parish of Saint François, Pointe Coupée, Louisiana. She was a daughter of Jacques Patin and Louise Barré, both of Opelousas. Jacques Etienne Roman settled with his wife in Opelousas, where he eventually became known as a cattle king, owning the largest herds in Louisiana. He also possessed a sugar estate in the *paroisse Saint Jacques*. Six sons and one daughter were born to him and his wife. Their daughter, Joséphine Roman, became the wife of Valcour Aime, princely planter of the colony, whose sugar plantation in Saint James parish was dubbed, on account of its magnificence, *Le Petit Versailles de la Louisiana*.

The oldest son of Jacques Etienne Romand and Mlle. Patin was André Bienvenu Roman, while the youngest was Jacques Télesphore Roman. Both of them became leading sugar planters in this state, their plantations being on the west side of the Mississippi river.

André Bienvenu Roman, the eldest, is justly considered as one of Louisiana's most distinguished Créoles in antebellum days. Born in Opelousas March 5, 1795, his childhood was spent on his father's plantation in Saint James parish. Leaving this pleasant spot for scholastic halls, he matriculated at Saint Mary's College, near Baltimore, and graduated in July 1815. His after years were one continuous series of successes.

Becoming a sugar planter on his own account, in St. James parish, he was honored in 1818 by being elected to the house of representatives of Louisiana, serving as a legislator for several terms, during four of which he occupied the speaker's chair. This was just the beginning of his political triumphs. Serving for a while as parish judge, he became governor of Louisiana on January 31, 1831, for a four-year term.

His public duties did not prevent him, however, from devoting some of his time to the pursuits of literary and educational matters. He is remembered today as one of the founders of Jefferson College, in Saint James parish. But this was only one of his many achievements. During his incumbency, the state penitentiary was constructed in Baton Rouge, New Orleans was not forgotten, as through his untiring efforts, a company was organized to drain the swamp lands around that city and to protect it from destructive floods. It was he who purchased the first edition of the

Elephant Folio plates of John James Audubon's famous *Birds of America* for the State of Louisiana.

Had all the wise suggestions of Governor Roman been faithfully carried out, the state, which he so properly and honestly governed, would have prospered even more than it did during his term of office. Realizing that agriculture is the greatest asset of a commonwealth, he urged the organization of a state agricultural society and the establishment of a model state farm. His zeal, nevertheless, could not rouse the apthy of the easy-going Créole planters of Louisiana, and his project fell short of realization.

After serving from 1831 to 1835, as chief executive, Governor Roman felt that he was entitled to a well-earned rest. But his constituents, who had grown to value his talents, called him once more to the governor's chair in 1839 for a second four-year term, which proved as successful as his first. He had become so essential to the welfare of his native state, that he was compelled, again and again, to accept new responsibilities.

In 1845 he sat as a member of the constitutional convention. Three years later he was in Europe, discussing important financial matters as agent of banking institutions of New Orleans. In 1852, he was a member of the constitutional convention of that year, and when the Civil War between North and South broke out, Governor Roman was heard in the secession convention of 1861. A believer in the preservation of the Union, he cast aside his private opinion and embraced the Southern cause with sincere enthusiasm. One of the three commissioners sent by the Confederate Congress to Washington, D. C., in order to attempt to secure the peaceful secession of the southern states from the Union, he handled this delicate, though unsuccessful, mission in a proper and diplomatic manner.

Having cast his lot with his revolted people, Governor Roman refused to take the oath of allegiance to the United States, even though such a course might mean the loss of everything he possessed on earth. Surviving the trials and sufferings of a bloody struggle, he died suddenly in his seventieth year, on January 26, 1866, while walking down the *rue Dumaine* in New Orleans' *Vieux Carré*.

Governor André Bienvenu Roman married Miss Parent, and from this union was born, among others, a daughter, Jeanne Roman, who became the wife of Eli Victor Farrault de la Villebeuvre, son of Jean Ursin de la Villebeuvre and Chariclé Jourdain. The issue of this de la Villebeuvre-Roman marriage was: (a) Anna de la Villebeuvre, who became the wife of Thomas McCabe Hyman, son of a former Judge of the Supreme Court of Louisiana, who left several married daughters; (b) Judge Charles Farrault de la Villebeuvre, who married his cousin, Marie Buchanan, daughter of Philip Buchanan and Octavie Roman, and died without children; (c) Ida de la Villebeuvre, wife of Lezin Becnel, without issue.

Charles Roman, son of Governor Roman and Miss Parent, is represented today by his granddaughters, the Misses Desirée, Amélie and Marguerite Roman.

Judge Alfred Roman, another son of Governor Roman and Miss Parent, was a man of high literary attainments. He served on the staff of General P. G. T. de Beauregard during the Civil War, and married twice, his second wife being Sally de Saussure Rhett, of Charleston, South Carolina, a member of one of the most distinguished families of that city. From this marriage were born several sons and the Misses. Jeanne, Madge and Sally Roman, and Elise Roman, the eldest, married to Albert Dufour, a brother of Judge Horace Dufour.

Jacques Télesphore Roman, brother of Governor Roman and youngest son of Jacques Etienne Roman and Mlle. Patin, was born in Opelousas, May 22, 1800. His godfather was Agricole Fuselier de la Claire and his godmother Genevieve Barré. His wife, Marie Thérese Célina Joséphine Pilié, born in New Orleans June 6, 1816, was a daughter of Gilbert Joseph Pilié, a native of the parish of Mirvalais, in San Domingo, and Thérèze Anne Deynaut, born in the parish of Saint Martin de Dandan on the same island. Her paternal grandparents were Louis Pilié and Marguerite Marie Isabelle Deschamps, her maternal ones being Louis Christophe Deynaut and Marie Thérese Valladé.

From the Roman-Pilié union were born three children, Henri, Octavie, and Louise Roman. Henri Roman married

Thérèse de Bouligny, and their children were: Harry Roman, who married Laura Stout and has one son; René Roman, husband of Mabel Howard, without issue; Corinne Roman, wife of Arthur Scott (brother of Dr. Joseph T. Scott of New Orleans), without issue; and Aimée Roman, unmarried.

Octavie Roman, daughter of Jacques Télesphore Roman and Mlle. Pilié married Philip Buchanan, son of Alexander Mackenzie Buchanan, judge of the Supreme Court of Louisiana. They had three children: James, Marie and Sydney Roman Buchanan. James Buchanan married twice, his first wife being a Miss Grevemberg and his second one a Miss Belly. By his first wife he had a daughter, Effie Buchanan, married to Homer Pecot. By his second marriage issued three daughters, Gabrielle, Amélie and Louise Buchanan, the last of whom married Norman Blitch, from South Carolina. Amélie married John E. Ryan.

Marie Buchanan, daughter of Octavie Roman and Philip Buchanan, became the wife of Judge Charles Farrault de la Villebeuvre, her cousin. No children were born from this marriage.

Sydney Roman Buchanan, youngest son of Octavie Roman and Philip Buchanan, married, December 6, 1898, Marie Héloïse La Bédoyère Huchet de Kernion, daughter of Anatole La Bédoyère Huchet de Kernion and Fanny Evélina Héloïse Campbell. Their issue consists of three daughters, Gladys, Hilda and Héloïse, all unmarried.

Mademoiselle Louise Roman, last child of Jacques Télesphore Roman and Mlle. Pilié, became a Carmelite nun and later was made Mother Superior of the order in New Orleans.

LA VILLÉBEUVRE—PETERS—TOLÉDANO
Families

AN old Breten name that commands the utmost respect is that of the de la Villebeuvres, who came to French province of Louisiana during the last half of the eighteenth century. The first to establish himself in the colony was Jean Louis Fidel Farault, *ecuyer*, Sieur de La Villebeuvre. He was born in the parish of Toussaint, bishopric of Vannes, Brittany, and was the son of Louis François de La Villebeuvre and Jeanne de Beaucour.

A short time after reaching New Orleans, he married in that city, Jeanne d'Arby, daughter of Jonathan (or Jonathas) d'Arby, a militia officer and church warden, and Marie Corbin Bachemin. Jonathan d'Arby had settled in Louisiana before 1725, being at that time a director of the Cantillion concession. This Jonathan d'Arby was the son of another Jonathan d'Arby, an English gentleman, doctor of the University of Oxford, and Anne Segre. The junior d'Arby had married, in New Orleans, February 18, 1737, Marie Corbin Bachemin, daughter of Jean Corbin (also known as Bachemin) and Judith le Hardy, a native of Saint Malo.

When Jean Louis Fidel Farault de La Villebeuvre arrived in New Orleans it was under the protection of his uncle, the Baron de Carondelet, then governor of Louisiana. He served as a colonial officer in the province, distinguished himself as a captain and Indian Commissioner, and was recommended by Governor Miro for a commission of lieutenant-colonel, the governor asserting that this promotion was due him for penetrating one hundred and twenty-eight leagues into the wilderness on an important expedition that was fraught with grave peril. History relates that in 1788 Captain Don Juan de La Villebeuvre (as he was known to the

Spaniards) accomplished his purpose admirably, as at an assembly of the Choctaw tribe, he secured from them their promise that they would no longer receive the Americans in their territory but would ever remain faithful subjects of Spain.

His son, Jean Ursin de La Villebeuvre, married, in New Orleans, Eulalie Trépagnier, daughter of Pierre Trépagnier, a wealthy planter of St. Charles parish, and Isabelle Renaud. This Jean Ursin was also an officer in the Spanish troops, and in 1815 participated in the Battle of New Orleans as an American officer. From his marriage with Mlle. Trépagnier he had three sons and one daughter: (a) Placide de La Villebeuvre, who married Mademoiselle Arnoult, whose son, John de La Villebeuvre, took for wife a Miss Gamotis; (b) Emma de La Villebeuvre, who married, in New Orleans, May 22, 1823, Pierre Théodore Rion, from Bordeaux, son of Jean P. Rion and Madeleine Labat, and (c) Jean Ursin de La Villebeuvre II, who married Mlle. Jourdain.

This last-mentioned Jean Ursin became one of the most prominent citizens of New Orleans in ante-bellum days. His wife was Isabelle Chariclé Jourdain, whom he married in New Orleans April 4, 1825. She was the daughter of Etienne Victor Jourdain and Aspasie Peytavin. For many years Jean Ursin and his wife were known as the social leaders of New Orleans. On their plantation, above that city, they entertained such distinguished visitors as the Marquis de Lafayette, General Zachary Taylor and others. They had eight children: (a) Eulalie Aspasie, born June 7, 1826, who married Samuel Jarvis Peters Jr., son of Samuel J. Peters Sr. and Myrthé de Silly. One daughter was born of this marriage, and died in childhood; (b) Elizabeth Marie Adine, born December 22, 1827, who did not marry; (c) Eli Victor Farault, born October 29, 1829, who married Jeanne Roman, daughter of Governor André B. Roman; (d) Edouard, born October 7, 1830; (e) Josephine Stéphanie, born February 20, 1832, who married Victor Forstall and became the mother of Eugenie Forstall, wife of Fernand Chopin; (f) Suzanne Eugénie, born March 21, 1834, who first married Benjamin Toledano and, secondly,

Oscar Dupierre, leaving issue by her first husband only; (g) Victor Jourdain, born September 8, 1835, who died unmarried, and (h) Marie Adine, born November 17, 1836, also unmarried.

Eulalie Aspasie de La Villebeuvre, eldest child of Jean Ursin and Isabelle Chariclé Jourdain, married Samuel Jarvis Peters Jr. Their only child dying young, they adopted as their own the children of Eulalie Aspasie's cousin, Francoise Zoé Lambert de Saint Omer, who had married James Campbell, among whom was Fanny Evelina Héloïse Campbell who married Anatole La Bédoyère Huchet de Kernion.

Samuel Jarvis Peters Jr. was the son of S. J. Peters Sr. from Stamford, Connecticut, and Myrthé de Silly, from St. Domingo. The elder Mr. Peters is remembered as one of New Orleans' foremost business men and a well known banker in that city during the first half of the nineteenth century. He was born in Canada, July 30, 1801, where his father, William Birdseye Peters (born in Hebron, Connecticut in 1774), and his mother, Pattie Marvin Jarvis (from Stamford, Connecticut), resided. The Peters, being Royalists, had moved from Connecticut to Canada during the American Revolution.

William Birdseye Peters came from old and distinguished English stock. He was a lineal descendant of Hugh Peters, born in Fowey, Cornwall, who came to America on the Mayflower and returned to England to paticipate, as a general, in the Cromwellian Rebellion. This Hugh was one of those who signed the death warrant of Charles I. For this offense he was executed with barbaric cruelty by the royalists on October 14, 1660, being first hanged in Charing Cross, then quartered, and his head severed and stuck on a pole on London Bridge. In spite of this, Hugh Peters had led a godly life, being a minister of the Gospel from 1623 to 1641, first in London, then in Rotterdam and finally in Salem, Massachusetts.

His family was of Norman origin, the first known forebear being Sir William Petres (or Peters) who crossed the Channel in 1056, as an aide-de-camp, in the train of William the Conqueror. His escutcheon shows a field *gules*, with a bar *or*, surcharged with a duckling accosted by two cinquefoils and accompanied by two shells. The Peters' family motto is: *Sans Dieu Rien.*

Samuel Jarvis Peters Sr., who came to New Orleans in 1822, enjoys the honor of being the founder of the New Orleans public school system, as well as one of the organizers of the Pontchartrain Railroad, the first railroad constructed in the South. He held several important federal and state offices, and was at one time mentioned as a member of a presidential cabinet. He died in New Orleans August 11, 1855. He left from his union with Myrthé de Silly several children, among whom was a daughter who married Jules Blanc, son of Louis Antoine Blanc and Louise Gauvain, and became the mother of Delphine Blanc, wife of Judge James McConnell. His other children were: Samuel Jarvis Peters Jr., husband of Eulalie Aspasie de La Villebeuvre, and Benjamin Frank Peters, whose wife was Myrthé Le Monnier, a sister of the well known Dr. Y. R. Le Monnier. The issue of the Peters-Le Monnier union was: Myrthé Peters, unmarried; Wm. F. Peters, married and with children; Jarvis Peters, married; B. Frank Peters, married, and Amire Peters, wife of J. Edwin Lastrapes, with children.

Eli Victor Farault de La Villebeuvre, third child of Jean Ursin de La Villebeuvre and Isabelle Chariclé Jourdain, married Jeanne Roman, daughter of Governor André Roman (q. v.). From her he had three children: (a) Charles Farrault de La Villebeuvre, who married his cousin, Marie Buchanan, and left no issue; (b) Anna de La Villebeuvre, who became the wife of Thomas McCabe Hyman and has four daughters, Jeanne, Aimée, Louise, and Marie Hyman, all married to United States army officers; (c) Ida de La Villebeuvre, who married Lezin Becnel without issue.

Suzanne Eugénie de La Villebeuvre, sixth child of Jean Ursin de La Villebeuvre and Mlle. Jourdain, married, first, Benjamin Tolédano, son of Christoval Tolédano, a veteran of the War of 1812-1815, and Mlle. Barbay, and grandson of Don Manuel Tolédano, of a distinguished Spanish family. Her second husband was Oscar Dupierre by whom she had no children. From her first marriage to Benjamin Tolédano were born seven children: (a) Corinne Tolédano, who died unmarried; (b) Emma Tolédano, who also died unmarried;

(c) Edgar Tolédano, who married Célina Vinet, daughter of Gen. Léonidas Vinet, and left three daughters, Corinne, Anita, and Stella, all married; (d) Edward Tolédano, whose wife was Bertha Hall, from whom he had three sons, Francis Edward, Frederick Albert, and John Hall Tolédano, the first two married, and the last unmarried; (e) Alfred Tolédano, who married the widow Moses and left no issue; (f) George Tolédano, whose wife was Anna d'Aquin, and by whom he had several children; and (g) John Tolédano, married with issue.

The coat-of-arms of the de La Villebeuvre, from which family descend the Tolédanos, is described: On a field *gules* a three-towered castle, *argent*, doored and crenallated *sable* in the centre, with a star *argent* in the left hand upper corner of the escutcheon.

Old Spanish Fort at mouth of Bayou St. John and Lake Pontchartrain

GAYOSO DE LEMOS Family

IT was a source of great regret to the settlers in the Natchez country and especially to those of English origin, who had become attached to him, to be informed by dispatches arriving from Spain in April, 1796, of the appointment of Don Manuel Luis Gayoso de Lemos, commandant of that post, to the governorship of Spanish Louisiana to succeed Don Louis Hector, Baron de Carondelet, who had been promoted to the presidency of the Royal Audience of Peru, where he was soon to become a puissant viceroy.

The new governor had long dwelt in that popular section of the province which harbored among its best citizens many families from the English colonies of North America. Gayoso had won their hearts completely as he was a polished man, possessed of a winning personality, and highly educated. He spoke four or five languages fluently and his English was faultless. Many years of his life had been spent in England where he attended college, and his *penchant* toward the English-speaking portion of the Louisiana population had become proverbial. So resentful were the Natchez settlers over his leaving that they refused to receive his successor, Don Carlos de Hault de Lassus.

A lieutenant-colonel in the Hispanic colonial forces at the time of his arrival, Gayoso de Lemos had become a brigadier-general and had been named by his king military governor of the Spanish post of Natchez. There he had built himself a palatial home, which he christened *Concord* in recognition of the peace that abided around it. This semi-regal residence was almost always filled with a convivial company of *bon-vivants* and *gourmets*, who came to sip the affable host's mellow wine or to revel on the luscious food that his able chefs knew so well how to prepare. Gayoso de Lemos was immensely popular, and while Natchez mourned at

[279]

losing him as its commandant, New Orleans rejoiced that he and his young wife were to occupy the governor's mansion in the capital city for many a day to come.

The new ruler of Louisiana belonged to a family, one of whose remote ancestors had been a knight of the Holy Roman Empire, in the days of Charlemagne. His escutcheon, displayed on the breast of a spread eagle, bore by this very fact evidence that an early Gayoso (or Gaiosso, as the family name was originally spelt) had been one of those many dauntless warriors who fought with might and main on many a gory field to recover, for the Roman Empire, its lost provinces and possessions.

To quote from the family records of Governor Gayoso de Lemos, still possessed by his New Orleans descendants, his shield was quartered after the fashion used on the Continent to declare the several families to which the bearer was heir. The original and proper arms of the Gayosos, as shown in the dexter principal (or right hand upper corner of the escutcheon) is divided *per fess* (or horizontally) one third from the top. The upper field is *sable*, carrying no charge or emblem. The lower field is *or*, showing a stag passant, *argent*, attacked by a falcon *argent*, which has swooped upon his back. The sinister principal of the quarterly (or left hand upper corner) shows a field *gules* charged with five Saracens' heads *argent*, cropped or cut off. The dexter base quarter (or right hand lower corner) shows a field argent, charged with thirteen bundles, or hurts, *azure*, pierced in the centre. The sinister base quarter (or left hand lower corner) consists of a field *argent*, charged cheque, or carrying three banks of checker board squares alternate *argent* and gules. The quartered coat-of-arms has at its centre an escutcheon of pretense, or a small shield, on which is displayed the arms of the bearer's wife. This shield's field is *argent*, charged with three fishes proper (or in their natural colors), naiant (or swimming) between fesses *sable*. The Gayosos' heraldic insignia is surmounted by a ducal coronet that crowns the spread eagle upon which the coat-of-arms is displayed.

To one conversant with heraldry, each figure shown in the Gayosos' intricate armorial bearings has a special significance. The stag and falcon express the fact that the bearer was a noble, entitled, as such, to hunt in the king's forests. The cropped Saracens' heads denote that the owner of such devices had perfomed some notable feat in the Moorish wars of Spain, if not in the Crusades. The pierced bundles, or hurts, typify wounds received in honorable service. On the other hand the cheques have reference to games of chance in which the gentlemen of the Middle Ages were much engrossed, as gambling was then considered a proper diversion for the well-born. Thus the heraldic shield of the Gayosos epitomizes, not only the achievements of their brave ancestors, but also the noble prerogatives their powerful forebears enjoyed.

Don Manuel Luis Gayoso de Lemos was born in Pontevedra, Spain, May 31, 1751, and died in New Orleans, July 18, 1799. He was the son of Don Manuel Luis Gaiosso y Lemos, born in Santa Maria de Pontevedra, August 30, 1721, and Doña Theresa Angelica Morin y Magallenas. His family tree shows him as belonging to the ninth generation from Don Gregorio Gaiosso, a native of Andeban, and Doña Maria Albanes. The name of Lemos was affixed to his patronymic by his father, also named Manuel Luis, who was the son of Don Andres Manuel Gaiosso and Doña Maria Luisa Rosa de Lemos y Figueroa.

Don Manuel Luis Gayoso de Lemos, seventh Spanish governor of Louisiana, had a brother, Don Francisco, who remained in Spain and became an Hispanic Consul General. Of a more martial disposition, Don Manuel Luis sailed for Louisiana, but accompanied by his wife, Theresa de Hopman, a Portuguese princess, whom he had married in his native land. A son, Manuel, born of this couple before their departure for America, remained in the old country. Don Manuel Luis and his wife Theresa were eventually installed in Natchez where she died.

His second wife was Elizabeth Watts, daughter of Stephen Watts (q. v.), an esteemed English settler in Baton Rouge, to whom he was married in 1792. She died three months later, at the age of nineteen, whereupon Don Manuel Luis, the widower commander of the Natchez Post, married her sister, Margaret Cyrilla Watts, then in her seventeenth year, and she presided over *Concord*, the most hospitable home in the Natchez district, and the governor's mansion in New Orleans where she entertained her husband's numerous guests and friends. Of an ancient and affluent race, her genial mate had perhaps inherited from his forebears his extravagant tastes. He was lavish in the use of his money and spent most of his fortune in sumptuous entertainments.

His administration, as governor, though not a long one, was peaceful and pleasant. Commerce continued to flourish and Louisiana became important enough in the eyes of the young republic of the United States of America to warrant, on the part of that new world power, the appointment of a consul to represent its interests in New Orleans. It was while Don Manuel Luis Gayoso de Lemos occupied the governor's mansion in New Orleans, that three royal princes, the duc d'Orléans, later King Louis Philippe of France, and his brothers, the Dukes of Montpensier and of Beaujolais, honored the capital city of Spanish Louisiana with a visit. They were the guests of the princely Pierre Philippe de Marigny, and lived for a while in his commodious plantation home that stood just beyond the palisade of the *Vieux Carré*, a short distance below the present Esplanade avenue.

Governor Gayoso de Lemos died in New Orleans July 18, 1799, and though most Louisiana historians, including Gayarré, have asserted that his demise resulted from over-indulgence in liquor, records in the possession of his descendants today absolutely disprove this slanderous assertion. The well-beloved governor died, as shown by official reports sent to Spain at the time of his demise, of a malignant fever— probably the yellow one—and was buried under the altar of the St. Louis Cathedral in New Orleans.

By his third wife, Margaret Cyrilla Watts, who remarried after his death, Captain Stelle, was born only one child, Fernando Gayoso de Lemos, born at the Natchez Post July 14, 1797, who died in Natchitoches, January 14, 1837.

Fernando Gayoso de Lemos was twice married. By his first wife, Julia Anne Wikoff, whom he married in Baton Rouge in 1810, he had three children who all died young. From his second wife, Victoria Lodoiski Perez, daughter of Manuel Zirillo Perez (q. v.), and Marie Madeleine Felicité Toutant de Beauregard, whom he married in Baton

Rouge June 17, 1825, issued five children. They were: (a) Caroline, who died young; (b) Marguerite, born May 31, 1828, in Opelousas, died in New Orleans, August 14, 1867, who married May 2, 1845, Merrit Moore Robinson, of Norfolk, Virginia (who died in Pascagoula, Mississippi, May 28, 1850). From this marriage issued Anna Amelia Robinson and Manuel Gayoso Robinson, both unmarried; (c) Aurora Pepita Gayoso, born August 20, 1830, died January 9, 1875, who married Thomas Benton Hart, of Lexington, Kentucky. Her husband died in San Antonio, Texas, January 9, 1875, leaving from his marriage to her, six children. They formed matrimonial alliances with the families of Froneberger, Prescott and West, the last two named being of Waco and Houston, Texas; (d) Fernando Gayoso, born October 9, 1833, in Saint Martinville, Louisiana, died April 9, 1906, in Dallas, Texas, who married, January 18, 1871, in Quitman, Texas, Zilphia Sunedrecker and left by her eight children, that married in the Frazer, Leath, Huber, Hyskell, Kammann and Gowen families; (e) Félicité Toutant Beauregard Gayoso de Lemos, born in Natchitoches, Louisiana, February 1, 1836, died in New Orleans December 31, 1917, who was wedded in Terrebonne Parish, August 28, 1856, to Charles Tennent, born in Seaford, Delaware, March 4, 1822, son of John Tennent and Sarah Polk Hooper. Charles Tennent fought at the battle of New Orleans as a lieutenant in General Coffee's Division. From his union with Félicité Toutant Beauregard Gayoso de Lemos issued Mary Perez Tennent, unmarried, Jennie Lodoiski Tennent, wife of Robert Ruffin Barrow, and Fernando Tennent, unmarried.

Robert Ruffin Barrow, born February 28, 1858, on *Residence* plantation, Houma, Louisiana, died March 24, 1926, on *Roberta Grove* plantation, Houma. From his union with Jennie Lodoiski Tennent were born six children; Volumnia Hunly Barrow and Robert Ruffin Barrow, who died young; Irene Félicié Barrow, unmarried; Zoé Gayoso Tennent Barrow, wife of Dr. Robert S. Topping; Jennie Tennent Barrow, who married Dr. Harris Pickens Dawson, and Hallette Mary Tennent Barrow, who became the wife of Dr. Christian Greenes Cole.

TRÉPAGNIER Family

AN erudite Canadian genealogist says that the primitive name of the Trépagnier family was de Trépagny. For the last century or more, he asserts, it has been written as Trépanier, but by referring to the older Canadian records, one discovers that this family name has seen many transformations. In Louisiana, Claude de Trépagny (or Trepagnier), the founder of the family in that colony, signed his name as Trépanier. His son, François, adopted the form of Trépagnié. Since then the family has used the name of Trépagnier.

The founder of this old, distinguished and very numerous family in the New World, was Romain de Trépagny, born in France in 1627, who migrated to Canada in the earliest times and died in that country, at Chateau-Richer, on March 20, 1702. He had married in Quebec, on April 24, 1656, Genevieve Drouin, born in Canada and baptized in 1643, who died there October 4, 1710.

This Genevieve Drouin was the daughter of Robert Drouin, born in 1606 in the parish of Pin, chatellany of Montaigne, in Perche, France, and of Anne Cloutier, born in Canada and daughter of Zacarie Cloutier and Saincte Dupont. Robert Drouin and Anne Cloutier married in Canada, their marriage contract being signed in the Seigneurie of Beauport, parish of *Notre Dame de la Miséricorde*, on July 27, 1636. This contract, which is still preserved in the archives of the Seminary of Quebec, was the first marriage contract drawn up in *Nouvelle France*, or Canada.

From this marriage of Romain de Trépagny to Genevieve Drouin were born four children: (a) François, baptized at Chateau-Richer on April 7, 1664, who died August 24, 1738, married Anne le François, February 14, 1689; (b) Jacques, baptized at Chateau-Richer July 3, 1685, died

August 11, 1706, married in St. Pierre I. O., Anne Raté, February 20, 1691; (c) Charles de Trépagny, baptized in 1659, married, on January 29, 1686, in Quebec, Marguerite Jacquereau, and died December 2, 1703; and (d) Claude, born in Canada, probably at Chateau-Richer, who came to Louisiana and became the founder of the Trépagnier family in that colony.

Claude Trépagnier and his wife, who was Genevieve Burel (or Burelle), were established at the Mobile Post at the time of its foundation. Their names are often met in the old records from 1708 to 1710 in which they are designated as traders or merchants.

Genevieve Burel Trépagnier had a sister, Jeanne Burel, who was married before 1708 to François Trudeau, a Canadian merchant, doing business at the Mobile Post from 1708 to 1710. The Burel sisters were pious and virtuous Canadians who landed at Fort Louis de la Mobile during the summer of 1704, from the ship Le Pélican. The King's minister wrote to Bienville on January 30, 1704, informing him that His Majesty was sending to Mobile twenty young women to be married to the Canadians and others who had settled around the Mobile Post, so that the colony could be firmly established. All the girls had been brought up piously and virtuously and knew how to work, which made them most useful to the colony, as they were able to teach what they knew to the daughters of the Gulf Coast Indians. In order that none, except those of spotless character, would be sent to Louisiana, the King had requested the Bishop of Quebec to select them from places that had never been suspected of immorality. Governor Bienville was ordered to take proper measures to marry them to men able to provide for their wants with a moderate degree of comfort.

According to the census of the Mobile Post, dated June 28, 1721, Claude Trépagnier lived then, with his wife and seven children, in the village of the Apalaches or St. Louis. He died at the Chatouachas in 1724, leaving an estate which Antoine Bruslé, member of the Superior Council and estimator, valued at 27,104 livres. According to a plan of New Orleans, dated 1728, Genevieve Burel, his widow, owned at that time a house and lot, number 7, at the corner of

Chartres and St. Ann streets, where she lived with her children.

From the marriage of Claude Trépagnier and Genevieve Burel were born seven children:

1.—Genevieve Trépagnier, who married in New Orleans, May 12, 1725, Nicolas Huot, Seigneur de Vaubéry, native of the parish of St. Nicolas-des-Chardonnets, in Canada. He was captain commanding the vessel *Le Dromadaire* of the *Compagnie des Indes*, and was the son of Nicolas Huot, Seigneur de Vaubéry, Captain in the *Régiment de la Vieille Marine*, and of Marie Théreze des Millets.

2.—Françoise Barbe Ignace Trépagnier, who first married in New Orleans, May 7, 1731, François Antoine Damaron, native of St. Germain-en-Laye, in the bishopric of Paris. He was Apothecary of the King in Louisiana and was the son of Antoine Damaron and Jeanne Amour. At his death, Françoise married again. Her second husband was Jean Jacques (or Jean Baptiste) de Maccarthey-Mactaig, a knight of St. Louis, and a son of Barthelmy de Maccarthey-Mactaig, captain in the Irish Regiment of Albermarle.

3.—Marguerite Trépagnier, who married in New Orleans, Joseph Carrière.

4.—Marie Anne Trépagnier, who married in New Orleans, by contract dated March 15, 1735, Bernard Alexandre Viel, correspondant of the *Académie des Sciences de Paris, surgeon-major* of New Orleans.

5.—Ignace Trépagnier, who perhaps did not marry.

6.—François Trépagnier, who married, at the *Côte des Allemands*, near New Orleans, July 18, 1740, Marie Jean Bar, daughter of Jean Bar (known as Lionnois) and of Perrine Davy.

7.—Ursule Trépagnier.

After the death of Claude Trépagnier, his widow, Genevieve Burel, seems to have continued to trade as a merchant in Louisiana. She remarried in New Orleans, July 16, 1726, Joseph de Lassus, a native of Marsilly, in the bishopric of Comminges. He was Surveyor of the *Compagnie des Indes* in Louisiana and was the son of Antoine de Lassus and Jeanne la Forgne.

François Trépagnier, sixth child of Claude Trépagnier and Genevieve Burel, was an officer in the Louisiana colonial militia. From his marriage to Marie Jean Bar were born, among others, the three following children, viz:

1.—Elizabeth Trépagnier, who married, in New Orleans, Louis Alexandre Guerbois. From this marriage issued several children, among whom Eulalie Guerbois, born in 1772, who married in New Orleans, on January 31, 1788, Pierre Denis de la Ronde, born in New Orleans in 1762, son of the Chevalier Pierre Denis de la Ronde, founder of the de la Ronde family in Louisiana (q. v.).

2.—François Trépagnier.

3.—Pierre Trépagnier, militia officer in Louisiana, whe served under Governor Bernardo de Galvez in his campaigns against the English during the American Revolution. He married, in New Orleans, in 1777, Elizabeth (or Isabelle) Renaud.

This Pierre Trépagnier was a wealthy planter in St. Charles Parish. He disappeared one morning in a mysterious manner from his plantation, leaving his family at the breakfast table and driving off with an unknown individual, never to be seen alive again. From his marriage with Elisabeth Renaud were born a numerous progeny, among whom the seven following, namely:

1.—Julie Héloïse Trépagnier, who married, in New Orleans, on July 18, 1803, François Martin Lambert de St. Omer, from Bordeaux, France, son of Etienne Lambert de St. Omer and Marie Reynal de Laval. He had served in all the Napoleonic campaigns and was decorated with the medal of St. Helena. From this Lambert-Trépagnier union were born eight children, all of whom died during childhood with the exception of a daughter, Françoise Zoé Lambert de St. Omer, born September 20, 1806, who married in New Orleans on May 3, 1834, James Campbell, a native of Ballyrobin, County of Antrim, Ireland, son of Josias Campbell and Jane Wilson Moorhead. This Campbell family is a branch of the famous Campbell of Argyle, family of Scotland. One of the daughters of this Campbell-Lambert union, Evélina Fanny Héloïse Campbell, married Anatole La Bédoyère Huchet de Kernion and left four children, Mrs. S. R. Buchanan, Mrs. Raoul Jeanjean, of France, Mrs. Etienne Chevallier, of Algeria, and George C. H. Kernion.

2.—Eulalie Trépagnier, who married in New Orleans, Don Juan de la Villebeuvre, infantry captain in the colonial service of Spain in Louisiana. He was the son of Jean Louis Fidel Farrault de la Villebeuvre, Chevalier de Garrois and of Jeanne d'Arby. Their issue married into the Arnoult, Rion, Jourdain, Roman, Hyman, Becnel and Buchanan families.

3.—Delphine Trépagnier, who married Mr. Barbin de Bellevue, a captain serving in Louisiana. She died in New Orleans on September 20, 1863, aged 69 years.

4.—Hortense Trépagnier, who married a Mr. Perry, a close relative of the famous Commodore Oliver Hazard Perry. Their daughter, Elizabeth Perry, married at the age of eighteen, Oscar Sarpy. She died at twenty-two.

5.—Elizabeth Trépagnier, who married Sylvain de St. Amand, of St. Charles Parish, son of Antoine de St. Amand and Eulalie Zéringue. From this union issued Elizabeth Emilie de St. Amand, a woman remarkable for her beauty and intelligence, who married in New Orleans on October 31, 1822, Antoine Louis Boimare, a native of Paris, France, and son of J. Louis Boimare and Marie Françoise Moret.

6.—Jacques Trépagnier, who married Mlle. Robin de Logny and left three daughters, Héloïse Trépagnier, married to a Mr. Simms; (b) Serafine Trépagnier, wife of a Captain Lambert, from Mexico, and (c) Miss Trépagnier, married to a Mr. Duffy.

7.—Laurent Trépagnier, who married Héloïse Reine.

GARIC

EVERY burgher of Old New Orleans and, for that matter, many living far beyond the palissade of the *Vieux Carré*, knew and esteemed Jean Baptiste, founder of the Garic family in Louisiana, and one of the earliest and most popular royal notaries during the French and Spanish regimes. For forty years, or from 1739 to 1779, his presence was indispensable to the colonists that had settled in the capital city on the banks of the Mississippi. Scrivener, or clerk, of the Superior Council, to him was entrusted the care of keeping the minutes of this august colonial tribunal. When not thus occupied, his services as notary were often requested and it was his quill pen that wrote the very precise and often complicated marriage contracts and testaments of both mighty and humble, drafted the terms and conditions of sales of real and personal property and acted, not only as a scribe but also as a legal advisor of the citizens of the little city.

He soon came to occupy a high position in the social and official circles of the colony and was hailed as a most welcome guest in every home of the town, including the mansion of the royal governor himself. As an *escribano* during the Spanish regime, his popularity grew no less and O'Reilly, as well as Unzaga treated him with the utmost kindness and consideration.

He served as a notary under the administrations of Le Moyne de Bienville, Rigaud de Vaudreuil, Billoart de Kerlérec, d'Abbadie, and Philippe Aubry, the five last French governors of Louisiana, as well as during the terms of office of Ulloa, O'Reilly and Unzaga, the first three Spanish governors of the province. His signature appears on countless colonial documents and scarcely an ancient family of Louisiana there is that does not possess at least a specimen of it on some treasured parchment coming down from an early ancestor.

Jean Baptiste Garic was an upright and able man, as otherwise he would not have continued to enjoy, as he did, for nearly a half century, the confidence of his fellow men in the most important business transactions of their lives. But it does not appear that he was very methodical in the manner of arranging and keeping his notarial acts. He had no system for filing the documents he had drawn up and attested. His own private papers were often mixed with his official ones. He was an indefatigable worker up to the very last day of his life.

This truly remarkable man came from an old family of Languedoc. It is said that he possessed very valuable family records which were destroyed by fire many years ago. Among them, as his descendants assert, was a genealogy that went back hundreds of years and showed the founder of the Garic family to have been quite a romantic individual. He had eloped with the daughter of a powerful nobleman of Alsace-Lorraine, a countess in her own right, and had fled with her to Strasburg or Metz, where they eventually settled. Long after the death of Jean Baptiste Garic, his grandson (who died an octogenerian) expressed the desire that his own grandsons should write to the burgomaster of Metz in order to verify this pretty tale.

Jean Baptiste Garic was born in Chirac, a little town in Languedoc. His father, Jean, born in the same place, April 15, 1671, had, from his wife, Antoinette Proyet, six children, namely: Jean, born November 10, 1709; Benoit, born February 16, 1713; Jean Baptiste (who came to Louisiana), born April 7, 1716; Françoise, born December 22, 1718; Jean Francois, born February 8, 1722, and Marie, born October 1, 1723.

Going one generation further back, we find that the paternal grandparents of our early Louisiana notary were Jean Garic, a merchant and town councillor of Chirac in 1682, and Isabeau Aiguillion. They brought to life a family of four children: Jeanne, who married Marc Blanc, January 5, 1671; Catherine, born September 7, 1667; Jean, born August 8, 1683, and another Jean, who became the father of the Louisiana pioneer. Their third-mentioned child, Jean, appears to have been a priest and to have served in 1720 as chaplain of the ancient church of St. Jean in Chirac, built in the XI century, that is still standing next to the crumbling castle of the feudal baron d'Antraigues. This holy fane was once the rallying point of the devout in Chirac who, on every feast day of St. John, brought their children to be blessed within its sacred precincts.

Jean Baptiste Garic landed in New Orleans about 1738, when he was twenty-two, but not alone. A brother and other relatives had also made the long sea trip and come to share with him his self-imposed exile in Louisiana. His brother did not remain long in the colony. Meeting, it is said, a young Italian woman of wealth and refinement, he married her and resailed across the blue Atlantic with his bride to settle in Genoa, where a Garic family still exists in that Italian city.

Life in Louisiana being dreary without a mate, Jean Baptiste, the young notary, married Marie Antonia Fortuna, evidently of Spanish parentage. This union was apparently a real love affair as his wife was not wealthy and brought nothing to him as a dowry. She died without issue and her widowed husband remained single for a long time. Yet, when he did decide to contract another alliance, in 1769, the woman he selected as his second wife belonged to one of the proudest and most noble families of the colony.

She was Etiennette Stéphanie Gouyon des Rochettes, baptized in New Orleans, February 29, 1748, and thirty-two years younger than her husband. Her parents were Jean François des Rochettes and Antoinette Pélagie Petit de Livilliers. Her mother was of *vieille noblesse* and a daughter of Captain Charles Petit de Livilliers (q. v.), and Louise Etiennette de Malbec, social leaders in the colony. Her father, a captain in the infantry Regiment of Ponthieu, was born July 1, 1726, in Quentin, bishopric of Brime, Brittany. He was a son of Mathurin Gouyon des Rochettes and Marie Abrehamet.

The Gouyon des Rochettes family was among the oldest in Brittany. Its escutcheon is described as being: On a field *argent* a lion *gules*, crowned *or*.

Etiennette Stephanie Gouyon des Rochettes was, if we may believe her aged and learned husband, a remarkable woman, for Jean Baptiste Garic speaks highly in his will of his young wife's character and intellect. He was very happy with her, even though her father defaulted in the payment of the dowry of 4,500 pesos he had stipulated, in the marriage contract, to settle upon his daughter and compromised the matter by handing over to her a single slave named Martha, aged fourteen.

The Sieur Garic and his second wife entertained lavishly during their short married life together. Their home was the Mecca of pleasure-seekers. Wine flowed freely and the inventory of the old notary shows that he was very fastidious in the matter of wearing apparel and yielded nothing in the way of embroidered coats and waistcoats, silk hose, satin breeches and polished swords to the best-dressed men in the town.

His life was at times an exciting one as he participated in the New Orleans rebellion of 1767-1769 that had, as its aftermath, the execution of several French patriots by the Spaniards. But his existence was brightened by the companionship of many devoted and worthy friends, among whom was Don Andres Almonester y Roxas, the famous New Orleans philanthropist and Spanish grandee.

When Garic died in New Orleans on December 10, 1779, he left an estate consisting of a house and lot on Conti street, house furnishings, wearing apparel, guns, slaves, wrought silver, and horses. But his estate was much involved in debt and his widow, in spite of the efforts of Etienne de Vaugine de Nuisement, one of the co-executors, received very little from it. She lived in 1790, in Bourbon street with a daughter and two sons, and died in New Orleans in March or April, 1810.

From her marriage with Jean Baptiste Garic issued four children: (a) Eulalie Garic, born in 1770; (b) François Garic, born in 1772; (c) Céleste Garic, and (d) Etienne des Rochettes Garic, born in 1779. This last-named child was only nine months old when his father, then nearly sixty-four years of age, died.

François Garic married Eugénie de Lavigne, of an affluent family, living in St. Bernard parish, where she was born February 10, 1777, and died in 1833. He became a planter in St. Bernard, his home being near the spot where the present parish court house now stands. He acquired this estate about 1805 and it remained in the possession of his son for many years after his death.

When in the latter part of 1814 the red-coated English phalanxes, led by Sir Edward Pakenham, were advancing over the fields of the Chalmette Plantation on their way to capture New Orleans, François Garic rushed to defend the threatened capital. He participated, as a major under General Andrew Jackson, in the memorable battle of January 8, 1815, when the Britons were routed, but was one of the few Americans captured by the enemy. The rough treatment he received at the hands of the English gave rise to great indignation throughout the parish and is said to have been the cause of his death. He expired a short time after that engagement at the age of forty-three, leaving a son, François, and three daughters, Aglaé, who became Madame de Lemos; Eulalie, who first married a Mr. Chalaire and then became the wife of a Mr. du Muchel, and another who married Cyprien Lefebvre.

François Garic, the son of the veteran of 1815, was born on his father's plantation in St. Bernard, in 1813. His tutor, Santiago Toutant de Beauregard, father of General P. G. Toutant de Beauregard, of Confederate fame, had secured for his ward an appointment to West Point Military Academy. Young Garic was about to start for New York with Pierre Gustave, his tutor's son, the future illustrious general. His trunk was even packed, when at the last moment his mother pleaded not to be separated from her only son and thus cut short his military career.

François Garic inherited a few thousands from the estate of his mother, Eugénie de Lavigne Garic, who died in 1833. He became sheriff of St. Bernard and served for several sessions as a member of the Louisiana Legislature at a time when the state capitol stood in Royal street, New Orleans. He was a man of worth and determination. He numbered among his friends John McDonough, the great philanthropist, who left a fortune to the cities of New Orleans and

Baltimore for the erection and maintenence of public schools.

Regardless of the fact that McDonough had a reputation for parsimony, when François Garic married Armantine Saucier, he sent the young couple, as a wedding gift, the sum of $500 to buy champagne for their nuptials or some useful thing for their residence.

François Garic, grandson of Notary Garic, as already stated, married Armantine Saucier, of an old colonial family of Louisiana, whose founder, in the days of Governor de Bienville, had been a royal surveyor and engineer of Louisiana. Armantine's father, Ducoteau Saucier, owned a plantation at English Turn, on the east bank of the Mississippi, where he lived in comfort with his family. His son, Arthur Saucier, had been brought up at a northern college and later became an honored judge in New Orleans, Armantine Saucier, his daughter, was educated at the aristocratic Ursuline Convent in New Orleans. In spite of all this, Eugenie de Lavigne Garic, mother of François, had higher aspirations for her son. She objected so strenuously to his marriage to Armantine Saucier that it was only consummated after the mother's death in 1833.

François Garic was progressive in spirit. In the forties, he was one of the prime movers in the building of the Mexican Gulf Railroad, later known as the Shell Beach Road, running through St. Bernard parish. The introduction of such an innovation as an iron horse running on steel rails was strongly opposed by a certain element of the ignorant rural population. Too old to serve in the Confederate Army in the days of 1861-1865, François Garic contributed his share to the South's defense by becoming a Home Guard. He sold his St. Bernard plantation in 1845 and settled in New Orleans. At the age of eighty he died, leaving his fifteen children, of whom eight were sons and seven daughters, an untarnished name as part of their legacy. His children married in the Fortier, Thiery, Carrière and other families of Louisiana and their posterity is very large in New Orleans today, some of them being well and favorably known in the business and social circles of that city.

DOUSSAN—FOSSIER Families

THE name of Doussan, though not as ancient in Louisiana as that of other families appearing in this volume, is, on account of its worth no less respected and honored. For more than a century those bearing it have resided in New Orleans and been numbered among its best citizens.

This family had its origin in Grasse, chief city of the ancient French province of Var, now designated as the Maritime Alps, a city long known throughout the civilized world for its extensive gardens and its scientific flower culture. Grasse has ever enjoyed the reputation of being the perfumery manufacturing centre of France—a business which has brought wealth to many of its people.

In that picturesque city, the Doussans had long been established. The Sieur Honoré Doussan, second of the name, born in 1751, was a master surgeon and the son of Honoré François Doussan, first of the name, who is designated in the old records as an *aloyeur*. His mother was Françoise Suquet who died in Grasse September 8, 1770, at the age of 52, and was buried in the church of the *Fréres Mineurs*.

Honoré Doussan, the master surgeon, who died in Grasse January 1, 1809, in his fifty-eighth year, married in that city Magdeleine Marie Levans, daughter of Honoré Levans, also a master surgeon, who died June 25, 1818, at 92 years of age, and Marie Louise Monet, who passed away in her forty-secondth year. The parents of Honoré Levans were Jean Levans and Dorothée Maubert.

Doctor Honoré Doussan, from his union with Mademoiselle Levans (who died on the 5th Fructidor, Year II of the French Republic), had a son christened Honoré, third of the name. He was born in Grasse, February 26, 1784. The life of this child being despaired of at birth, he was privately baptized, or *ondoyé*, by his Christian father, but surviving, was duly carried to the town's church the following day to be properly christened by the curate of the parish.

This boy, Honoré Doussan III, received careful schooling, obtaining on March 29, 1817, from the French Commission of Public Education, the diploma of Bachelor of Arts, having graduated on March 15 of the same year from the Academy of Montpellier at the age of thirty years. His scholastic training was interrupted by the Napoleonic Wars, which fired the brain of young Honoré as strongly as it inflamed the souls of the fighting *jeunesse dorée* of France, for Napoleon's star was on the ascendant.

As these momentous events ran their course, young Honoré Doussan, who was then a medical student, abandoned his books for the army. On November 25, 1805, he was a surgeon and assistant Aide-Major in the *2me. Regiment a Cheval* from Rennes, comprised in the Royal Artillery Corps. As such, he served in many military hospitals. He made, under the imperial eagles, the campaigns of Italy, Dalmatia and the Illyrian provinces.

He was made Surgeon-Major of the Emperor, on the field of battle, on September 23, 1813, a short while before being taken prisoner of war, on December 9th of the same year, at the capitulation of Dresden. He returned to France and on July 27, 1814, the lieutenant-general of the 10th Military Division, by orders received from H. R. H. the duke of Angoulème, Grand Admiral of France, and in the name of the French monarch, conferred upon him the decoration of the *Ordre du Lis*, for his love and devotion to his country and his ruler.

In 1815 Dr. Honoré Doussan was still serving in the French army with the 102nd. Regiment of the Line. The following year he was enrolled with the Legion of the Basses-Alpes. Napoleon having been defeated at Waterloo and sent to die on the desolate rock of St. Helena, Dr. Honoré Doussan asked that he might become one of his attending physicians on his island prison but his request was not granted. Under Louis XVIII he won royal favor again, serving in the King's armies and being created, on October 22, 1817, a knight of the Legion of Honor. His commission as such, still possessed by his New Orleans descendants, is signed by the royal Louis himself.

In 1820, while serving in the mounted artillery Regiment of Rennes, he expressed the desire to migrate to Louisiana. This was due to the fact, as stated by him in one of his letters to France, that former Napoleonic officers were discriminated against by the Bourbons who had returned to power. Obtaining his release on October 10, 1820, he sailed for New Orleans where he took up the practice of medicine and surgery. He was granted a diploma by the Medical Society of Louisiana on February 5, 1821, authorizing him to exercise his profession throughout the state, and in December of the same year was admitted to membership in the Medical Society of New Orleans.

Well established in his new home, he married a young woman of thirty-one, Céleste Stéphanie Ramos de Vilches, widow of Charles Joseph Fossier. Her father, Don Raphael Ramos de Vilches, a native of Grenada, in the kingdom of Andalusia, Spain, was *Contador*, or comptroller, of the Royal Hospital of New Orleans and honorary Commissioner of War in Hispanic Louisiana. Her mother, born in Louisiana, was Françoise Albert, of French-Canadian origin.

The Ramos family enjoyed great social prestige in the province, Madame Ramos, mother-in-law of Dr. Honoré Doussan, forming part of the gay and brilliant petty court of the Baron Louis Hector de Carondelet, while he served as Spanish colonial governor of Louisiana. Don Rafael Ramos, the first of the name in that state, was of an ancient family of Spain, his father being Don Antonio Ramos, native of Illara, in the bishopric of Grenada, and his mother, Dona Paulina de Vilches, having been born in that semi-Moorish part of the Hispanic kingdom.

When Don Raphael Ramos came to Louisiana, in the days of Governor O'Reilly, he married Françoise Albert, daughter of Antoine Albert, a native of Quebec, Canada, and Genevieve Le Rour, born in Louisiana. Among their offspring was Stéphanie Céleste, born in New Orleans on November 20, 1794.

Céleste Stéphanie Ramos de Vilches first married Charles Joseph Fossier, son of Jean Joseph Fossier and Marianne Rixner. Her first husband was born in St. Charles parish, *Côte des Allemands*, in 1771. His grandfather, the first of the name in Louisiana, had arrived on the vessel *l'Union*, commanded by Captain de la Mancelière, which sailed from La Rochelle May 28, 1719. The first Fossier in Louisiana was Joseph, who signed his name "Faussier."

Jean Joseph Fossier, his grandson, who married Marianne Rixner, of a pioneer German family of Louisiana originally known as Richner, had six children, among them being two sons: (a) Alphonse Fossier, baptized in 1774, who married Adélaïde Rixner, daughter of George Rixner and Marguerite Haydel, and had a daughter, Adélaïde Fossier, baptised in 1796, who married Arnould (or Arnaud) Lanaux and became the mother of Antoine Philip Lanaux, baptized in 1816, and of Charles Lanaux, baptized in 1823, from whom descend the numerous family of Lanaux in New Orleans, and (b) Charles Joseph Fossier, baptized in 1771, who married Céleste Stéphanie Ramos de Vilches and had by her several children among whom Emile Fossier, baptized in 1817, who married Lise Ranson, a rich heiress of New Orleans.

This Lise Ranson was a daughter of Zénon Ranson, a wealthy planter on the Mississippi, who had married Adéle Labatut, daughter of General Jean Baptiste Labatut and Marie Félicité St. Martin. Zénon Ranson had another daughter, Clélie, who became the wife of Jules Labatut. The marriages of the two Misses Ranson to Messrs. Emile Fossier and Jules Labatut were celebrated on the same day and were long remembered by the elite of New Orleans. The father of the brides had done things in a princely way. Beside giving each of them, as a *dot*, a sum said to have amounted to not less than $100,000, he had chartered a palatial Mississippi River steamboat, the "White," commanded by Captain John Tobin, for their honeymoon, on which, after the nuptial ceremony, they sailed up the river for their father's plantation with a large number of guests who were royally entertained for ten days at the Ranson family's expense.

From a daughter of this Ranson-Labatut union, who married former Justice O. O. Provosty, of the Louisiana Supreme Court, were born: (a) Olivia Provosty, married to Edward E. Carriere; (b) Adina Provosty, wife of Ulisse Marinoni; (c) Eliska Provosty, wife of John F. Tobin, a son of Captain John Tobin; (d) Andrée Provosty, who became Mrs. Clifton P. Walker, and (e) Michel Provosty, present city attorney of New Orleans.

From the marriage of Lise Ranson to Emile Fossier was born, among other children, Stanislas Fossier, who wedded Albertine d'Hamécourt, granddaughter of a famous French cavalry officer, who after quarreling with his superior officer across the sea, slapped his face and was forced to come to New Orleans, where he became a *maitre d'escrime*, and the best broadswordsman in the city. Stanislas Fossier and Miss d'Hamécourt became the parents of Walter S., d'Hamécourt J. and Dr. Albert Fossier, of New Orleans.

To return to Céleste Stéphanie Ramos de Vilches, about whose first marriage to Charles Joseph Fossier we have just spoken, she became a widow when scarcely thirty and at this time met the young Dr. Honoré Doussan, then about sixteen years her senior. Their marriage was duly solemnized on September 14, 1825, in the St. Louis Cathedral by Bishop Guillaume Valentin du Bourg of New Orleans. Dr. Honoré Doussan died in Mandeville, Louisiana, on March 31, 1865, when he was eighty-one.

Six children were born of his marriage to Mme. Fossier, née Ramos de Vilches. They were: (a) Honorine Doussan, born December 10, 1826; (b) Hypolite Raphael Doussan, born February 12, 1833; (c) Henry Auguste Lazard Doussan, born September 2, 1831; (d) Eugénie Marguerite Doussan, born December 8, 1837; (e) Stéphanie Doussan, wife of Henry James Campbell; (f) Théodore Honoré Doussan, born in 1827, who married Miss Soniat du Fossat and left as issue: (1) Dr. Joseph Edmond Doussan; (2) Joseph Avenel Doussan; (3) Marie Alice Doussan, who became Mrs. Bendernagle; (4) Marie Laure Emilie Doussan; (5) Joseph de Vilches Doussan; (6) Joseph Sidney Doussan; (7) Marie Céleste Doussan, who became Mrs. Bisset; and (8) Laure Emilie Doussan.

PEREZ Family

AN old Spanish name which should not be overlooked in any work treating of worthy and distinguished families that settled in Louisiana during the colonial period is that of Perez, borne by as representative a Hispanic gentleman as ever came out of the ancient kingdom of Leon and Castille. Don Manuel Perez, who introduced it in Louisiana, was born in Zamorra, Spain, in 1735, of a noble family.

Don Manuel came to the Spanish colony on the Mississippi in 1769, with General Alessandro O'Reilly, and formed part of his brillant following, composed of courtly and polished *hidalgos*, among whom the Cruzats, Gayarrés, Almonesters, Alpuentes, Ramos, Navarros, and others as blue-blooded were conspicuously included. It was Spaniards like Don Manuel Perez that, by their affable, congenial and sympathetic natures, contributed very materially in softening the rancor and in healing the deep wounds which O'Reilly's merciless attitude in 1769 toward the most popular sons of old New Orleans, had left in many Gallic hearts.

Governor Unzaga's velvety touch and his commiseration for the friends and relatives of la Frénière, Noyan, Villeré and the other slain patriots, was undoubtedly of some influence in extinguishing the smouldering fires of public resentment against Spanish domination, but the spirit of friendship and good fellowship displayed by Don Manuel Perez and men of his stamp, toward a suspicious and rebellious people who had been forcibly made to accept an alien flag, went far in cementing affections that, at first, refused to be joined to one another.

Could any of the resentful population of the capital city of Louisiana look upon Don Manuel Perez as a Spaniard, and therefore an enemy, when he had shown his affection for them by choosing, in 1776, Jeanne Catherine Dubois, a French matron of New Orleans ,as his lawfully-wedded wife? Her parents, Joseph Gabriel Dubois and Louise Elizabeth Boni, were known to every citizen of the town. Jeanne Catherine, when she married Don Manuel Perez, was a young widow, having buried, some time previous, her first husband, Louis de la Lande de Ferriere (q. v.), of ancient lineage. She was perhaps descended from that venerable and distinguished du Bois family of France, whose earliest known progenitor was Macquaire du Bois, Count of Ronsay, living in the early part of the twelfth century, two of whose lineal descendants, Louis and Jacques du Bois, Hugenot refugees, had sought religious freedom in America and settled at Kingston, New York, during the second half of the seventeenth century.

Don Manuel Perez was a soldier and with his sword he meant to achieve success in Louisiana, his newly-adopted country. The opportunity of so doing soon presented itself. In 1779, Don Bernardo de Galvez had raised the banner of Spain and called to the colors all the manhood of Louisiana, to be led by him against their hated English neighbors. His king had recognized the new American republic, fighting for its life against tremendous odds, and had become the ally of George Washington and his revolted colonists. Captain Perez, who was then in command of the second company of grenadiers, and who, before coming to Louisiana had been garrisoned for six years and eight months in Oran and had participated in the campaign against Portugal in 1762, went at once to the front and did his share in driving out the British from their southern strongholds. We find him among the attacking force at Fort Bute, at the siege of Baton Rouge, at the siege of Mobile, and before Pensacola. His promotion for meritorious service eventually followed.

In 1787, Don Estevan Miro, successor of Governor Galvez, appointed Don Manuel Perez, then a captain in the Mixed Regiment of the colony, lieutenant-governor of Upper Louisiana, a very important and honorable office. Perez assumed his office at St. Louis on November 27th of the same year, succeeding Don Francisco Cruzat. During the four years and eight months that he managed the affairs of the Illinois country, peace abided in Upper Louisiana. His administration was an uneventful one. Perez was well liked by the people he ruled and among his closest friends was August Chouteau, the New Orleans Créole who was one of the founders of St. Louis in 1764. The old records of that city show that the lieutenant-governor and the French merchant and colonizer, had large business transactions together, that undoubtedly proved profitable to both Perez and Chouteau. On July 29, 1792, Don Manuel Perez gave up his lieutenant-governorship to Captain Zénon Trudeau, who had been appointed to this office by Governor Carondelet. But if Miro had recognized Don Manuel's merit in entrusting the safety of Upper Louisiana to his keeping, the Baron de Carondelet, his successor, did as much for Perez when the latter returned to New Orleans in 1792. A commission as Lieutenant-Colonel in His Catholic Majesty's army awaited the former lieutenant-governor as a reward for his achievements. He died in New Orleans in 1814.

From the marriage of Don Manuel Perez to Jeanne Catherine Dubois issued six children. Manuel Cirillo Perez, the eldest, married in New Orleans, June 24, 1801, Madeleine Félicité Toutant de Beauregard. She was born in New Orleans April 8, 1782, where she died June 27, 1817. Her parents were Eli Toutant de Beauregard and Marie Félicité Durel. The nuptials of Manuel Cyrillo Perez to Mademoiselle Toutant de Beauregard brought forth four children: (a) Félicité Amanda Elias Perez, born July 3, 1802; (b) Jeanne Aurore Perez, born in 1805, who became the wife of a Mr. Grey; (c) Victoria Lodoiski Perez, born April 7, 1807, who married Fernando Gayoso de Lemos, son of Governor Manuel Luis Gayoso de Lemos and Margaret Cyrilla Watts, and left issue; and (d) Manuel Florencio Perez, born July 28, 1809.

The remaining children of Don Manuel Perez and Jeanne Catherine Dubois were: Stephen Perez, who died young; Martine Elizabeth Perez, whose husband was Antoine de Saint Maxent; Céleste Perez, who became Mrs. Joseph Hyacinthe Chalon; Marie Rose Perez, who married Jacques Guison, and Eugénie Perez whose wife was the Sieur Favre d'Aunoy.

RIVARD Family

ON the earliest map of New Orleans and its surrounding territory appears the name of Antoine Rivard (also known as la Vigne), who, in 1721, owned a plantation on Bayou Saint John, or the *Ruisseau de Saint-Jean*, as this picturesque watercourse was then designated. This Antoine Rivard had come from Ile Dauphine, in Canada, and at the time of the Louisiana census of 1721, lived on his Bayou Saint John concession with his wife and his six children. He then owned eleven negro slaves, two Indian vassals, four horses and thirty heads of horned cattle.

His family was an ancient one in *Nouvelle France*, where it established itself in the *seigneurie* of Batiscan, parish of *Saint-François-Xavier*. The Rivards were enterprising merchants and fur traders, whose birch bark canoes, manned by daring *voyageurs* and Indian auxiliaries, penetrated the then practically unknown rivers of the North Country and visited such early French posts as Michilimackinac and Detroit at regular intervals.

In the colonial archives of Quebec are found many official permissions granted by the French governors to members of that family, whereby they were authorized to leave Quebec on important trading missions. The first of the Rivard name mentioned in *Nouvelle France* is Nicolas Rivard, Sieur de la Vigne, who, on February 18, 1660, made a certain contract with Jean Gabriel, *dit* Nadaud, before Claude Merlin, royal notary at Cap-de-la-Madeleine.

The Canadian Rivards prospered as a result of their enterprises and in 1721 many of them, close relatives of Antoine Rivard, the first of their name in Louisiana, were included among the notable inhabitants of the Seignory du Batiscan in the parish of Saint-François-Xavier. Among them, at that time, we find Claude Rivard, Sieur de Loranger, captain of militia in the nearby parish of Sainte-Anne; Nicolas, Pierre, Jean, Julien and François Rivard.

The colonial archives of Louisiana give us many interesting details concerning Antoine Rivard, the founder of the Rivard family in Louisiana. He was a very determined character and inclined to be pugnacious when he believed his rights were being encroached upon. Thus on May 24, 1723, or five years after the foundation of New Orleans, we find him instituting legal proceedings against the Sieur de Coustillas, whose two Indian slaves had made many forays during the preceeding five years upon Rivard's herd pasturing in the neighborhood of Bayou Tchoupitoulas, and eaten several of his prized cattle.

At times Antoine Rivard became somewhat dictatorial, which induced the Sieurs Livet and Soubaigné to file, on March 20, 1725, a complaint against him before the Superior Council. As shown in the record, there stood in the Gentilly section near Bayou Saint John, even before the foundation of New Orleans in 1718, a primitive road formerly used by the Indians, but placed in excellent condition by the Dreux brothers, early settlers in those parts, in 1720. Antoine Rivard, without official authority, had not only closed this public road to traffic, but had forbidden any one crossing a little bridge that spanned a small watercourse along this turnpike without his permission. Though this bridge had been built and paid for by the inhabitants of Gentilly, Antoine Rivard wanted them to travel along a new road and cross a little stream that obstructed its course on a bridge consisting of nothing else than the trunk of a cypress tree. The Council came to the rescue of the Gentilly settlers and ordered Antoine Rivard not only to construct a new road in those parts suitable for vehicular traffic, but a new bridge which everyone must be allowed to use freely at all times.

Education in New Orleans was necessarily neglected at the beginning of the eighteenth century on account, not only of a lack of schools and teachers, but also due to the fact that the impoverished early settlers were more concerned in improving the little plantations they had received near the town from the Crown than in giving proper scholastic training to their children. Antoine Rivard, however, was an exception to this rule. Before 1726, he employed the services of François Nicholas de Knepper, one of the first pedagogues of New Orleans, as a teacher for his young family. We find de Knepper, September 11, 1726, suing the Sieur Rivard for some seventy livres due him for tuition fees.

After the death of Antoine Rivard in 1729, his widow and second wife, Antoinette Fourrier, had chosen another teacher, the Sieur Renée Galbée, for their children. He was a respectable man who lived with the Sieur Renaud d'Hauterive. Not being paid for his services, Galbée sued the widow of Antoine Rivard for three hundred and seventy-six livres and obtained a judgment against her for that amount.

Antoine Rivard's first wife was Marie Briard, who came to Louisiana from *Nouvelle France* in 1704, with nineteen other young Canadian matrons, on *Le Pélican*. The twenty of them had been sent to Mobile by Saint Vallier, bishop of Quebec, as wives for the colonists. They came from families well known for their worth and honesty in the North Country. They were the first contingent of young women sent to Louisiana and all of them found husbands before long in Mobile.

From Marie Briard, first wife of Antoine Rivard, were born six children, among whom were the following five:

1.—François Antoine Rivard, born at the Natchez Post, who took for wife on February 30, 1730, Jeanne Antoinette de Mirebaize de Villemont, from Poitiers, daughter of Henry Martin de Villemont, an early settler and officer in Louisiana, and Antoinette Fourrier. At the death of François Antoine, his widow became the wife of Jean François Huchet de Kernion, a colonist and military officer in the province.

2.—Genevieve Monique Rivard, born on Ile Dauphine, in Canada, who married in New Orleans, June 23, 1733, François Boucher, *ecuyer*, Seigneur de Monbrun, a native of the parish of *La Sainte Famille*, in Boucherville, Canada. He was a son of Jean Baptiste Boucher, *Seigneur de Monbrun et de Boucherville*, and of Fran-

[305]

çoise Charest de Lauzon, who belonged to the oldest and most distinguished families of Canada.

3.—Marie Rivard, who became the wife of Joseph Lamy, a native of the parish of Sorel, in Canada, whom she married in New Orleans May 12, 1722.

4.—Françoise Rivard, native of l'Ile Dauphine, in Canada, whose marriage contract with Jean Baptiste Boucher de Monbrun, *ecuyer*, Sieur de Saint Laurent, was signed in New Orleans on February 9, 1736, before *Maitre* Henry, royal notary.

5.—Mademoiselle Rivard who married in New Orleans Jean Baptiste Lafourée.

At the death of Marie Briard, his first wife, Antoine Rivard married again in New Orleans, his second wife being Antoinette Fourrier, widow of Henri Martin de Mirebaize, Sieur de Villemont, by whom he had no issue. Antoine Rivard died on his Bayou Saint John plantation on February 11, 1729. At the time of his death he was a *marguillier*, or church-warden, of the parish of Saint Louis.

His son, François Antoine Rivard, married, Jeanne Antoinette de Mirebaize de Villemont, daughter of the widow Antoinette Fourrier de Villemont, second wife of Antoine Rivard *père*. From this union of François Rivard with Jeanne Antoinette de Villemont, issued three daughters: (a) Jeanne Antoinette Rivard, born in New Orleans February 17, 1732, who died the same year; (b) Jeanne Antoinette Rivard, born in New Orleans in May 1734, who married, June 18, 1757, the Chevalier Christophe de Glapion, son of Charles de Glapion, Seigneur de Mesnilgancoie, in Normandy, and Jeanne Thiboust. Among their children was Jeanne Antoinette de Glapion, who married Edmé Joseph de l'Homme; (c) Marie Françoise Sivard, born 1735-1736, a posthumous child, who does not seem to have married.

François Antoine Rivard died in New Orleans September 27, 1735, leaving his twenty-year old widow, to rear his three daughters. She took as her second husband, Jean François Huchet de Kernion, October 4, 1736, and with him became the founder of the Huchet de Kernion family in Louisiana (q. v.).

WATTS Family

SHORTLY before the American Revolution had started to run its long and bloody course in the thirteen English colonies of North America, the British had become very active in the southern possession, once part of the French province of Louisiana. The benevolent Spaniard, Don Luis Unzaga y Amezaga, then in the gubernatorial chair, exercised his authority over a more restricted Louisiana than that which had once belonged to Louis XIV, the *roi soleil*. Through the fortune of war, part of the southern portion of the North American continent then belonged to Great Britain, and the British, determined to make secure this valuable section, erected many well-garrisoned forts to protect their prized provinces of East and West Florida.

The governors Britain sent there were ambitious and diplomatic and concentrated their thoughts and attention on making this territory more attractive for prospective settlers. Fertile lands were to be found in the Natchez country, around Fort Panmure, formerly known as *Rosalie*, of bloody memory, and it was common knowledge that what was now Fort Charlotte had been, in the days of Bienville and Iberville, *Fort Condé de la Mobile*, a most desirable neighborhood. As Manchac, on the Mississippi river, not far south of Baton Rouge (which the English rechristened New Richmond), had formerly been sought by the subjects of the French kings, and had even been recommended by some of them as a proper site for the future capital of Louisiana, the English pioneers from the thirteen colonies found it no less attractive now that it bore the name of Bute and belonged to their own monarch.

Peter Chester, third British governor of West Florida and probably the shrewdest of all who had ruled over it, was proving successful in popularizing his domains. Settlers were slowly drifting in to establish plantations on rich and fertile soil. Some had deserted their homes on the Roanoke River for stretching fields on the Mississippi, and around British New Richmond. Others had trekked from Georgia, the Carolinas and even Pennsylvania, braving the dangers of the Indian country, to reach the same destination. Tories at heart, they wished to live as far as possible from their seditious countrymen of the thirteen colonies who were about to declare themselves independent from British sovereignty.

The governors who ruled over this southern domain of West Florida to which the dissatisfied had come, had shown great liberality in granting lands to such as arrived to tempt fortune in those parts. Chester's prodigality toward English soldiers and officers who settled there was well known to many living at great distances from this miniature Britain. Not less than one thousand acres were gracefully conceded by him to simple English troopers in the British Floridas and it was not uncommon for a field officer to become quickly a landed baron, as five thousand acres went with his commission.

Such tales spreading far and wide had attracted settlers from the agitated colonies toward Louisiana. Fair as they knew it to be, it had been made more seductive to them by the elegant homes that had arisen in it and by the social caliber of its cultured people. Wealth and happiness had rewarded those planters on English soil so close to New Orleans. Their fields of cotton, rice and corn had brought them a golden harvest. They owned an army of slaves, some of the more prosperous among them boasting of as many as three hundred black menials. And the feminine part of the population was as beautiful and accomplished as could be found anywhere else on earth. New Orleans fed upon the products of West Florida's rich soil, but nothing which the merchants of the Spanish capital of Louisiana had to offer, was considered too costly or luxurious for those fortunate British West Floridans.

Thus it was that Stephen Watts, a British subject, born in Southampton, Pennsylvania, came to West Florida and settled in New Richmond during the year 1775. He was of old English stock, his family name, Watts, being said to have been derived from the Teutonic cognomen of *Walheri*, meaning "powerful warrior." This name became common in England under the British form of Walter, even before the adoption of fixed family names in that country. In time it evolved into the shorter one of Wat, from which Watt and Watts eventually sprung.

Stephen Watts, the first of the name to come to Louisiana, was descended from the oldest branch of the Watts family in America. His first American forebear was John Watts, born in Leeds County, England, on November 3, 1661, who was the only son of Henry Watts, born in the same county in 1616 and who died there May 14, 1679. This Henry Watts had married Elizabeth Duck (or Deek) and was in turn the son of Gregory Watts, who died in 1654 in Leeds Castle, County Kent, England, and the grandson of Sir Thomas Watts, Lord Mayor of London in 1616.

John Watts, the American progenitor of the elder branch of the Watts family in Louisiana, established himself at Pennypack, in Philadelphia County, in 1686. He was then only twenty-one years of age. Joining the Baptist Church, he became later a minister and was placed, as rector, in charge of Pennypack Church, the first Baptist church in Philadelphia country. John Watts had come to a country that was then in the making. It had no room for drones, slackers or dreamers. The newcomer from Leeds county, England, possessed the rugged strength of the pioneer, which he soon displayed as a disciple of the Gospel. On horseback and braving the elements, he calmly ambled along impassable roads, under the torrid summer sum or through the deep snow of arctic-like winters, to bring the word of God to benighted souls dwelling as far as the New Jersey colony. Pastor of the Pennypack Baptist Church, he was likewise looked upon as the guiding spirit of the First Baptist Church in Philadelphia, where his eloquent voice was often heard.

John Watts, the minister, married Sarah Eaton and died in Pennypack in 1702. His issue consisted of seven children, among whom was Stephen Watts, born in Pennypack, Pennsylvania, February 6, 1700, who took a certain Elizabeth (family name unknown) for wife, and died in Southampton, Pennsylvania, in 1785.

This Stephen Watts received, in 1734, a patent from the three brothers Penn for a plantation of one hundred and forty nine acres in Southampton county of Bucks, Pennsylvania. Living thereon as a country gentleman, he discharged during many years the duties of justice of the peace and was also a member of the Pennsylvania assembly. Six children were born to him, of whom no record is available about five, namely Hannah, Arthur, Rachel, Elizabeth and Sarah Watts. His sixth child, Stephen Watts, who came to Louisiana and became a distinguished barrister and jurist, was born in Southampton, Pennsylvania, February 5, 1741. He obtained his scholastic training in the College of Philadelphia, graduating in 1759 with the degree of Bachelor of Arts, and receiving three years later his Master's degree. Adopting law as his profession, he practised for a while as an attorney in Philadelphia. Attracted like many other dissatisfied British citizens in the colonies to English West Florida, he settled in New Richmond during the year 1775. Later on we find him pleading, as a barrister, before the Spanish Court in Pensacola as a qualified Master in Chancery.

Eventually Stephen Watts received the appointment of recorder of deeds for the English on the Mississippi River, became a Justice of the Quorum and King's Attorney for the District of New Richmond. He served as such until British rule in that section of Louisiana was brought to an end by the victories of Galvez and his Spanish army in 1779-1781, when Forts Bute, Manchac, Baton Rouge, Mobile and Pensacola were wrested from the grip of George III.

Stephen Watts had married in Philadelphia, on May 12, 1767, Frances Assheton, who followed him to Louisiana. He died in Opelousas, Louisiana, having had from his wife six children. His eldest son, Stephen Watts, II born August 9, 1768, in Philadelphia, died there during the following year. Assheton Watts, another son, born in Philadelphia, October 20, 1769, left no further record of himself. Susanna Watts, a daughter, born April 4, 1771, married in 1791, William Wikoff, and left nine children. Elizabeth Watts, fourth child of Stephen Watts and Frances Assheton, born May 4, 1773, died in 1792. She married in 1792, in Baton Rouge, Don

Manuel Luis Gayoso de Lemos, (q. v.) seventh Spanish governor of Louisiana, and died three months after her nuptial day. Her sister, Margaret Cyrilla Watts, born on Belmont Plantation facing the Mississippi river, March 23, 1775, thereupon became the second wife of the Spanish governor, the marriage being celebrated in Baton Rouge July 14, 1796.

Governor Gayoso de Lemos died before his second wife, on July 18, 1799, in his capital city of New Orleans, Margaret Cyrilla, his widow, taking for her second husband, Captain James Stelle, by whom she had a daughter named Frances Stelle, who married Joshua Baker; another daughter, Caroline Stelle, became Mrs. John Brownson, and the last, Sarah Stelle married Abner Pride. Three sons, James, Lewis, and Edward Stelle died young or unmarried.

From the first union of Margaret Cyrilla Watts to Don Manuel Luis Gayoso de Lemos, the governor, issued only one child, Fernando Gayoso de Lemos, who married Victoria Lodoiski Perez, daughter of Don Manuel Perez, (q. v.) lieutenant-governor of Spanish Upper Louisiana, and Jeanne Catherine Dubois.

The Watts escutcheon shows a field blazoned with an oak tree, proper. Across the centre of the shield is a bar *azure* charged with a crescent between two mullets. The crest is a forearm forward, grasping an olive branch. The motto reads *Forti non deficit telum*, "The strong man never lacks a sword."

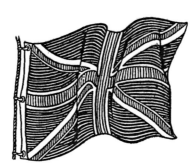

The Union Jack of Old England that floated over the West Florida parishes from 1763 to 1779

[311]

HEREFORD Family

VIRGINIA, THE MOTHER STATE, has contributed many sons to far-off Louisiana and in many instances their blood has mingled with that of the daughters of the Créole and the result has been an upright sturdy race that moves to-day in the most exclusive circles. Such a family having its roots firmly embedded in the soil of Virginia, and flourishing in Louisiana like the proverbial green bay tree, is that bearing the name of Hereford.

The first of the name to come to Louisiana was Dr. John Bronaugh Hereford, who settled in West Feliciana parish and married Catherine Stirling, granddaughter of that stalwart Scottish pioneer, Alexander Stirling, (q. v.). He reared many sons and daughters whose direct descendants are numbered among the prominent citizens of the present generation.

Doctor John B. Hereford, was born June 11, 1794, in London county, his father being Robert Hereford, fifth son of John Hereford and Margaret Ammon. In the parental line he goes back to James Hereford of Westmoreland county, Virginia, a resident of the Old Dominion in 1689. On the maternal side Doctor Hereford also claimed distinguished ascent. His mother was Mary Mason Bronaugh, born in Stafford county, Virginia, and died in Mason county, of the same state, October 2, 1831, who married Robert Hereford December 7, 1790. She was the daughter of Dr. John Bronaugh and Mary Anne Carter, and granddaughter of Jerimiah Bronaugh, who was a vestryman and church warden of Pohick Church, Truro parish, from 1743 to 1749, and Simpha Rosa Ann Field Mason, an aunt of George Mason, the statesman of Gunston Hall.

John B. Hereford was the second of ten children. He studied medicine and when he graduated as a physician, he moved to Louisiana, choosing the beautiful hill country of the

[312]

Felicianas for his future home. I ʒre he became most successful in his practice and acquire l lands and many slaves. Noted alike for his medical skill and his love for the chase, he became a friend of John James Audubon, when that talented but eccentric bird-artist was searching out the birds of the Feliciana countryside as subjects for his talented brush and pencil. Audubon, once when ill, was treated by Doctor Hereford at the physician's home, and spent many hours watching birds and their habits at a beautiful spot in the rear of *Wakefield*, known today as "The Doctor's Spring." The artist records in his famed *Ornithological Biography* how Doctor Hereford assisted him when he was endeavoring to secure a new species of hawk, which was named Harlan's Hawk.

Audubon had secured a female of the species but all his efforts to take the male were set at naught by the bird's shy habits. "I was unable to approach him so long as I had a gun," wrote the artist, "although he frequently allowed me and my wife to pass close to the foot of the tree when we were on horseback and unarmed. I followed it in vain for nearly a fortnight, from one field to another, and from tree to tree, until our physician, Dr. John B. Hereford, knowing my great desire to obtain it, shot it in the wing with a rifle ball, and sent it alive to me."

On December 18, 1828, Doctor Hereford married Catherine Mary Stirling, born at *Wakefield Plantation*, June 7, 1809, daughter of Lewis Stirling and Sarah Turnbull, and granddaughter of Alexander Stirling and Anne Alston, and took his bride to his home *Oak Grove*, where his first four children were born. About 1837 Doctor Hereford moved to West Baton Rouge parish where he continued his practice and also engaged in sugar culture. He was a man of learning, intelligence and culture and a member of the Episcopal Church. He died November 10, 1852 and was buried in the family plot on *Inheritance* plantation.

The children of Dr. John Bronaugh Hereford and Catherine Mary Stirling were:

1.—Robert Francis Hereford, who became a physician, married Julie LeCoq and whose children were: (a) John Bronaugh Hereford, (b) Ruffin S t i r l i n g Hereford, who married Emma Fuselier de la Claire; (c) Catherine Mary Hereford, (d) Joséphine Julia Hereford, (e) Roberta Frances Hereford, (f) Robert Francis Hereford, (g) Louis Victor Hereford, (h) Addie Harris Hereford, (i) William Chamberlin Hereford, (j) Alfred LeCoq Hereford, and (k) Marie Camille Hereford. Ruffin Stirling Hereford, the second son, who married Emma Fuselier, October 9, 1889, in New Orleans, (the daughter of Alexandre Fuselier de la Claire and Corinne Perret of St Mary's parish) was born March 12, 1859, and died October 17, 1925. Their children were: (1) Corinne Fuselier Hereford, born November 1, 1890, died April 28, 1925; (2) Harry Anthony Hereford, born April 5, 1893; (3) Ralph Sidney Hereford, born in New Orleans, March 26, 1898, who married Gladys Verna Keppler, daughter of Charles Lewis Keppler and Ann Reames; (4) Ruffin Francis Hereford, born May 21, 1913 and died July 8, 1913.

2.—Sarah Turnbull Hereford, born 1830, died 1866, did not marry.

3.—Lewis Stirling Hereford married Elizabeth Rowena Percy, their children being: (a) Elizabeth Hereford, (b) Percy Hereford, (c) Sarah Hereford, (d) Robert Hereford, (e) Stirling Hereford, and (f) Randolph Hereford.

4.—Anne Mathilda Hereford, born February 3, 1836, and died July 2, 1898, who married Clarence Percy, born February 1, 1836, died February 22, 1909, their children being: (a) Catherine Sarah Percy, born on *Northbend* plantation Pointe Coupée parish, November 21, 1866; (b) Clarence Percy, born on *Retreat* plantation, West Feliciana parish, February 25, 1868; (c) John Hereford Percy (baptised John Bronaugh Hereford Percy), born on *Stirling* plantation, West Feliciana parish, February 20, 1870; (d) and (e) William Richards Percy and Robert Ryland Percy, twins, born on *Bush Hill* plantation West Feliciana parish, August 8, 1874. Catherine Sarah Percy (a) married, August 28, 1895, Mathew Gilmore of West Feliciana, their children being: Clarence Percy Gilmore, Kathryn Hereford Gilmore, Mathew William Gilmore, Thomas Doherty Gilmore, Grace Lea Gilmore, and Robert Craig Gilmore. Clarence Percy (b) married Mathilde D'Armond of Clinton, East Feliciana parish, December 27, 1906, and had one son, Rhea D'Armond Percy. John Hereford Percy (c) married Christina Dashiell Howell of West Feliciana parish, August 14, 1893, daughter of Charles Johnson Howell and Jane Percy Dashiell, and their children were: (1) Jeannie Howell Percy, who died in infancy; (2) Annie Mathilda Hereford, who married Oscar Menees Thompson; (3) John Hereford Percy Jr., (twin of Annie) who died in infancy; (4) Margaret Lurty Percy, who married William Eugene Bingham; and (5) Louisa Johnson Percy, who married William Heard Wright. William Richards Percy (d) married Mary Maud Stirling, died November 21, 1918 in Minden, La., their children being: Nannie Stirling Percy and John Hereford Percy. Robert Ryland Percy (e) married twice: first to Frances Eugenia McGhee of West Feliciana parish, by whom he had John Edward Percy and Eugenia Corinne Percy; his second wife was Katie Roark of West Feliciana parish, their sons being: Robert Ryland Percy, Jr., and William Connor Percy.

5.—John Bronaugh Hereford Jr., married Elizabeth J. Robertson, and lived in Dallas, Texas, their children being: John, James, Percy, Felix Percy, Mamie Percy, Annie Percy, and Catherine Percy Hereford.

6.—James Stirling Hereford married, three times. First, Adeline Harris, without issue; second, Jennie Chichester, who begot a daughter, Jennie Hereford; third, Mary Brewer, whose daughter was Flavia Hereford.

7.—Catherine Mary Hereford married Anthony Doherty of Baton Rouge, their children being: Anthony Doherty, Jr., Isabelle Doherty, William and Lewis Doherty, twins; Katherine Doherty, Percy Doherty, and Gladys Doherty.

8.—Isabelle Semple Hereford married twice, her first husband being Demaret Hawkins, from whom issued a daughter, Marie Hawkins; her second husband was the Reverend G. R. Upton of the Episcopal church.

PHILIPPE DE MARIGNY Family

NO history concerning the old families of Louisiana would be complete without the genealogy of the Philippe family that added to its patronymic the names of Mandeville and Marigny. The American founder of this celebrated family was François Philippe de Marigny de Mandeville, born in Bayeux, Normandy, who served as an infantry captain in *Nouvelle France* in 1709 and later on migrated to Louisiana, where he became a knight of Saint Louis and a major in the French colonial troops. He is styled an *écuyer* in the old records, a designation that implies that he was of noble birth. Jean Vincent Philippe, his father we believe, had been made a noble in 1654 by the king of France for distinguished service in Canada.

François Philippe de Marigny de Mandeville died in New Orleans November 4, 1724. He had married in that city Magdeleine Lemaire, daughter of Pierre Lemaire and Marguerite Lamothe. At his death his widow remarried in New Orleans, on September 2, 1729, Ignace François Broutin, a royal engineer in Louisiana, who commanded the Natchez Post.

From the union of François to Magdeleine Lemaire issued a son, Antoine Philippe de Marigny de Mandeville who became an officer in the marine detachment in Louisiana. He was born at the *Fort Louis de la Mobile* on February 28, 1722, his godfather being the Sieur le Moyne de Chateaugué, lieutenant of the king and a brother of Iberville and Bienville. This Antoine gave a good account of himself in the colony, became a *Chevalier de Saint Louis*, and added, by his explorations, much additional knowledge concerning the topography and the resources of his native province. He married in New Orleans, January 8, 1748, Françoise de Lisle, and he died there in 1779, being buried, as had been his father, in the parochial church of Saint Louis.

The name of Antoine Philippe de Marigny de Mandeville often appears in the annals of Louisiana as, though he enjoyed the friendship of Governor de Vaudreuil, he incurred the deadly enmity of the Baron de Kerlérec, a later governor, for siding with the *Ordonnateur* Rochemore in his quarrel with Kerlérec. This resulted in his being sent a prisoner to France, where for a while he lingered in its famous Bastille.

Pierre Philippe Enguerrand de Marigny de Mandeville, a son of Antoine Philippe and Françoise de Lisle, was baptized in New Orleans June 15, 1750. He died in New Orleans May 14, 1800. Honored with the cross of Saint Louis, he served as an infantry officer in Louisiana and eventually became, under Spanish rule, commandant of Galveztown. He took for wife, in New Orleans, on July 14, 1772, Jeanne Marie d'Estréhan des Tours, daughter of Jean Baptiste d'Estréhan des Tours, royal treasurer in the colony, and Jeanne Catherine de Gauvry (or Gauvrit). His wife, of distinguished lineage, was a sister of Mme. Etienne de Boré de Mauléon, whose husband was the sugar king of Louisiana. Another sister was Mme. Favre d'Aunoy, while a brother married Mlle. de Saint Maxent, who after his death became the wife of Don Bernardo de Galvez, Spanish governor of Louisiana and later Viceroy of Mexico.

Pierre Philippe Enguerrand de Marigny de Mandeville was undoubtedly the richest man of his day in New Orleans. He entertained in 1798, in a regal manner, the Duc d'Orléans (who became Louis Philippe, king of France) and his two brothers, the Comte de Beaujolais and the Duc de Montpensier, in his New Orleans home. From Pierre's marriage with Jeanne Marie d'Estréhan were born four children: (a) Jean Philippe, who died in New Orleans, unmarried, in his twenty-fifth year; (b) Marie Céleste, born in New Orleans February 2, 1786, who became the wife of Jacques François Enould de Livaudais, captain of militia, later on lieutenant-colonel in the colonial troops, and president of the state senate, during the American régime. He was a son of Jacques Enould de Livaudais and Charlotte Chauvin de Léry des

Islets, and died in New Orleans April 9, 1850; (c) Antoine Marie, also known as *La Perle,* born in New Orleans in 1787, who died without issue; (d) Bernard, the third child mentioned here as fourth for convenience sake.

This Bernard Philippe de Marigny de Mandeville's godparents were Joseph Delfau, baron de Pontalba, and the Comtesse de Galvez, *vice-reine* of Mexico. He was undoubtedly one of the most colorful characters of New Orleans in ante-bellum days, and a worthy representative of the *vieux régime.* He lived during the momentuous period of the Louisiana transfer, and entertained, as a guest, Clément de Laussat, the French Prefect, who received the colony from Spain for France, and turned it over, twenty days later, to the United States government. Bernard' birth occured in 1785 and he died in New Orleans February 4, 1868.

He selected for wife, in 1804, the daughter of Evan Jones, from Pennsylvania, a former American consul in New Orleans, whose wife was Marie Verret, a descendant of early settlers at the German Coast. Mary Ann Jones, as Bernard's wife was called, died in Philadelphia June 4, 1808, in childbirth, leaving, from her union with Bernard two sons. Gustave Adolphe, born June 15, 1808, the youngest, died on the field of honor, like many other hot-headed young Créole duellists had fared, leaving no posterity. Prosper François, the eldest, born March 17, 1807, became the husband of Marie Céleste d'Estréhan, a kinswoman, who married after his death Alexandre Grailhe, a famous New Orleans lawyer. She bore her first husband a son and a daughter. Gustave Philippe de Marigny, the son, took Emma Bienvenu for wife and had, among other children, Zulma de Marigny who married Mr. Dessommes. Marie Odile de Marigny, the daughter, was wedded to Alphonse Miltenberger.

The death of Mary Anne Jones, first wife of Bernard de Marigny, in 1808, did not crush the spirit of this active man. A year or two later, he had chosen a second wife, Anne Mathilde Morales, a daughter of Don Ventura Morales, Royal Contador and Intendent in Spanish Louisiana. Between fighting duels and winning political honors, Bernard de Marigny's time was well occupied. He sat in the legislature of 1810 as well as in the constitutional convention held two years later. At the Battle of New Orleans in 1815, he served with singular dash and bravery as an officer under General Andrew Jackson. So highly thought of was he that on all important state occasions he acted as spokesman in greeting distinguished visitors. Thus we find him in 1825 welcoming the Marquis de Lafayette to New Orleans and two years later doing likewise for General and Mrs. Andrew Jackson, who had come as the city's guests.

A great deal of Bernard de Marigny's time, after his second marriage, was spent on his estate, *Fontainebleau*, near Mandeville, which he purchased in 1820. There he entertained his friends with somewhat of the elegance for which his family was noted. He was a reckless spender and many are the tales related about his prodigality, one of which asserts that, after lighting his cigar with a United States greenback of a high denomination and being reproved for it, he exclaimed: "Bah! What of it? It is only a *bagatelle!*" or trifle. Bagatelle street, in the Third District of New Orleans, is said to have derived its name from that incident.

The large fortune of Bernard rapidly dwindled and he died a very poor man. Louis Philippe, the French king, who had been benefitted by his father's liberality, showed little appreciation for Pierre Enguerrand de Marigny's *largesses* in Bernard's period of declining wealth. It is true that this monarch did not altogether forget the son of his Louisiana benefactor, that he sent him, as a gift, a wonderful silver service, and secured for his son, Mandeville, a place at the French Court and an appointment to the military school of Saint Cyr, but this was scant remuneration for the princely advances made to the royal Louis Philippe by Bernard's father.

Bernard de Marigny, from his second union with Mathilde Morales, had two sons and three daughters. They were:

1.—Antoine Jacques de Marigny de Mandeville, born in New Orleans in 1811, whose wife was Sophronia Claiborne, daughter of William C. C. Claiborne, first American governor of Louisiana. Their three children died without issue.

2.—Rosa de Marigny de Mandeville, born in 1813, married in 1832 Mr. de Sentmanat who was executed in Mexico for conspiring against President Santa Anna. Their three daughters married Nelville Soulé, (a son of Pierre Soulé, American ambassador to Spain), Allain Eustis and Philippe Villeré respectively. After the death of Mr. de Sentmanat, Rosa de Marigny married Adolphe Esnould de Livaudais, a Louisiana state senator but had no children from him.

3.—Angéla de Marigny de Mandeville, born in 1817, married F. Peschier, Swiss consul in New Orleans, and among their children was Claire Peschier, who became the wife of Leon Joubert de Villemarest. The issue of this Peschier-Joubert union was: (a) Leon Joubert, unmarried; (b) Emma Joubert, wife of Major Lutz Wahl, U. S. A.; (c) Claire Joubert, who married first Dr. Paul Emile Archinard and then George Hero; (d) Frederick Joubert, who married Alice Palmer, widow of Lieutenant J. Numa Augustin, U. S. A.; (e) Charles Joubert, unmarried; (f) Louise Joubert, married to Walter H. Cook; (g) Marie Joubert, wife of Gustave Olivier de Vezin.

4.—Armand de Marigny de Mandeville, unmarried.

5.—Mathilde de Marigny de Mandeville, born in 1820, wife of Albin Michel de Grilleau, son of a French consul in New Orleans.

The Marignys left their mark in *Nouvelle France* as well as in Louisiana and will always be remembered in New Orleans as one of its most opulent and aristocratic families.

The coat of arms of Louisiana in Bienville's time.

CHALMETTE Family

THE name Chalmette has been indelibly fixed upon the American mind through the fact that on a plantation owned by a member of that family was fought, on January 8, 1815, the celebrated Battle of New Orleans, giving to the United States the honors of the War of 1812, and undying fame and the presidency of the United States to General Andrew Jackson. Today "Chalmette's Field" has become a national shrine.

Louis Xavier Martin, Sieur de Lino de Chalmette, who was born in Quebec, May 13, 1720, was the first of the name to establish himself in Louisiana. A study of this gentleman's ancestry shows that his family's real name was Martin, and that it originated in France, going to Canada in the first half of the seventeenth century.

Claude Martin, Sieur de Lino, the founder of the family in *Nouvelle France*, and the great-grandfather of Louis Xavier who settled in Louisiana, married Antoinette Chalmette, a native of Saint Nazaire, in the bishopric of Lyons, who died in Quebec December 7, 1721. Their son, Mathurin François Martin de Lino de Chalmette, born in Quebec in 1657, became a member of the *Conseil Souverain* of Canada, and took for wife Catherine Noland, daughter of Pierre Noland, known as *le Chevalier*, and Catherine Houart, widow of Guillaume Le Geay. Their marriage contract was signed by Governor d'Avaugour of Canada, the baron du Menil, and other notables of the province.

The progeny of Mathurin François Martin de Lino de Chalmette was very numerous, no less than seventeen children being born to them—but only three reached maturity. A daughter, Catherine, baptised in Quebec June 15, 1688, married in that city, March 20, 1708, Jean François Hazeur, son of François Hazeur and Antoinette Soumande, and left issue. Another daughter, Genevieve Martin de Lino de Chalmette, baptised May 17, 1699, married, March 7, 1720, the chevalier Gaspar d'Adhémar, Sieur de Lantagnac, son of Antoine d'Adhémar, governor of Manton, in Provence, and Jeanne de Truchi, and had by him ten children.

François Martin de Lino de Chalmette, eldest child and only surviving son of Mathurin and Catherine Noland, was baptised in Quebec April 13, 1686. He became *procureur du roi* and on November 3, 1712, took for wife Angélique Chartier de Lotbinière, born September 2, 1693, daughter of René Louis Chartier de Lotbinière, councillor of the king and later lieutenant general of *Nouvelle France* and Marie Madeleine Lambert.

This François Martin died January 5, 1721, and his widow thereupon married, April 19, 1722, Nicolas Renaud d'Avesne, Sieur des Méloizes and Seigneur de Neuville, a Marine captain. She died December 14, 1772, and was buried near the altar of the *Hospitalières* in Quebec. From her first marriage four children were born in Quebec: (a) Marie Angélique, baptised September 8, 1713, who died two months later; (b) Angélique, baptised November 16, 1715; (c) Ignace François Pierre, baptised May 7, 1718, who married in 1750, Renée de la Vallée, and (d) Louis Xavier Martin de Lino de Chalmette, baptised May 13, 1720, who went to Louisiana.

This youngest child of François Martin and Angélique de Lotbinère was a lieutenant in the troops of the Marine. Just when he came to the Louisiana province is not known but records show he commanded the Arkansas Post in 1751 and, being a close relative of the Marquis Pierre Rigaud de Vaudreuil, governor of Louisiana, became quite important in the colony. He married, in New Orleans, Madeline Marguerite Broutin, daughter of Ignace François Broutin, royal engineer in the colony and commandant of the Natchez Post, and Madeline le Maire. This Mme. Le Maire-Broutin had been the widow of François Philippe de Mandeville, Sieur de Marigny, (q. v.) before she married Ignace Broutin.

Louis Xavier Martin de Lino de Chalmette gave a good account of himself in Louisiana and died in 1755. The following year his widow, Mlle. Broutin, married Pierre Denis de la Ronde (q. v.). One of her daughters, Louise de la Ronde, became the second wife of Don Andres Almonester y Roxas, and a son, Pierre Denis de la Ronde, married Eulalie Guerbois. From her union with Louis Xavier Martin de Lino de Chalmette, Madeline Broutin had three children. They were:

1.—Madeline Joséphine Martin de Lino de Chalmette, born in New Orleans March 6, 1752, died August 26, 1822, who married, December 24, 1777, François de Vergès de St. Sauveur, retired colonial officer, son of the Chevalier Bernard de Vergès (q. v.), chief royal engineer in Louisiana, and Marie Thérese Pinau.

2.—Louis Xavier Martin de Lino de Chalmette, born September 7, 1753, who married, October 30, 1778, Adélaïde Fazende, daughter of Gabriel Fazende and Charlotte de Vergès.

3.—Ignace Martin de Lino de Chalmette, a posthumous child, born August 23, 1755, who married Victoire de Vaugine, daughter of the Marquis Etienne de Vaugine de Nuisement, lieutenant colonel in the Louisiana regiment and knight of St Louis, and Antoinette Pélagie Petit de Livillers. It was on Ignace's plantation that was fought the celebrated Battle of New Orleans.

Ignace Martin de Lino de Chalmette died February 10, a few weeks after the total destruction of his superb plantation home during the fierce struggle of January Eighth. His widow died January 29, 1836. From their marriage were born the following six children:

1.—Victoire Martin de Lino de Chalmette, born August 6, 1777, died February 13, 1868. She became the wife of Antoine Cruzat, treasurer of the parish of Orleans, and the son of Francois Xavier Cruzat (q. v.), lieutenant governor of Upper Louisiana and Knight of Hermengilde, and Nicamora Ramos. They had fifteen children.

2.—Pierre Martin de Lino de Chalmette, who took part in the Battle of New Orleans and married, in the Atakapas country, Adèle de Trouard.

3.—Madeline Victoire Héloïse Martin de Lino de Chalmette, born in 1780, died January 16, 1855, who became the wife of her kinsman Pierre de Vergès de St. Sauveur, son of François de Vergès and Madeline Joséphine Martin de Lino de Chalmette.

4.—Micaëla Eulalie Martin de Lino de Chalmette, born December 12, 1783, died in St. Martinville, July 21, 1823, who married, June 22, 1814, François le Pelletier de la Houssaye, son of Louis le Pelletier de la Houssaye and Charlotte Pellerin (q. v.).

5.—Adzéle Martin de Lino de Chalmette, born July 15, 1781, died October 16, 1853. She never married, her affianced husband, a Sieur de Marigny meeting death by drowning.

6.—François Martin de Lino de Chalmette, who died October 22, 1813, in his twenty-sixth year, unmarried.

A view of Chalmette Field where was fought the
Battle of New Orleans

CRUZAT Family

THE first Cruzat to arrive in Louisiana was Don Francisco Cruzat, born in Taffala, province of Navarre, Spain, March 10, 1739. His father was Balthasar Cruzat, who descended from an ancient Hispanic line, and his mother was Francesca Virto.

Francisco Cruzat was a captain of grenadiers when he came to Louisiana with Allesandro O'Reilly's troops in 1769. "Bloody" O'Reilly being succeeded by Louis de Unzaga y Amezaga as governor of the colony, the latter appointed El Captain Cruzat to the post of lieutenant governor of Upper Louisiana, as the Illinois country was then called, on May 20, 1775, where he served until June 17, 1778. Later, after he had been made a lieutenant colonel in recognition of the services he had rendered under Governor Galvez in the capture of Baton Rouge and Pensacola from the British, he was again appointed lieutenant governor of Upper Louisiana, upon the death of Don Fernando de Leyba, who had succeeded him to that post.

While he was executive of Upper Louisiana and stationed at St. Louis, Don Francisco married a daughter of Spain, named Nicamora Ramos y Tibalde of Carthagena. He remained at this post until November 27, 1787 when he was recalled to New Orleans and promoted to the command of the Louisiana regiment. He died in Pensacola. The children of Don Francisco Cruzat and Mlle. Ramos were:

1.—José Ignacio Cruzat y Ramos, who served as captain in the Louisiana regiment. He married Doña Maria Dolores y Palao y Prast, and died in Havana. Of his four children, a son (a), Joseph Ignace Cruzat married Alix Suzanne Coulon de Villers, daughter of Marc Coulon de Villiers, (q. v.), and Marie Josephine Grifon d'Anneville; (b) Eulalie Cruzat married Pedro Sedano.

Their son, the Count of Casa Sedano, became a councillor of state, deputy in the Cortes, gentleman-in-waiting to the King of Spain, was a Chevalier of the Order of Carlos III, obtained the Grand Cross of Isabella the Catholic, the Grand Cross of Medjidie, and was made a commander of the Legion of Honor of France; (c) Malvina Cruzat, married Nicholas Heredia, a distinguished savant and professor of literature in the University of Havana, and (d) Josephine Olivia Cruzat, married her first cousin, William Cruzat.

2.—Antoine Gerthonde Cruzat y Ramos, second son of Don Francisco, was born in St. Louis and came to New Orleans in 1795, became a cadet in the Spanish Regiment of Louisiana, and remained in its service until Spain relinquished the colony in 1803. By his marriage to Victoire Martin de Lino de Chalmette in 1796, he became the father of fifteen children. When Louisiana passed under the American flag, Antoine Cruzat took out citizenship papers and proved himself a thorough American, his sons fighting the British invaders on their grandfather's historic Chalmette plantation. Antoine Cruzat served New Orleans in 1814 as parish treasurer, and for more than thirty years was warden of the St. Louis Cathedral. He died in 1854. He was noted as an authority on the officials and events of the Spanish Domination.

The children of Antoine Cruzat and Victoire de Lino de Chalmette left numerous descendants by their marriages with members of some of the most distinguished families of Louisiana. Their fifteen children were:

1.—Armand Cruzat, who died in childhood.

2.—Manuel Cruzat, born December 27, 1797, died in 1848, who married Malvina de Vergès, daughter of Pierre de Vergès and Héloïse de Chalmette. Their children were: (a) Malvina Cruzat, who married Denis Villeré, and (b) Odile Cruzat, who married his brother, Edmond Villeré. They were sons of Gabriel Villeré and Eulalie de la Ronde. The two Cruzat girls each became the mother of five children.

3.—Nisida Cruzat, born in 1799, who married, in 1819, Laurent Rousseau, son of Pierre Rousseau, a captain in the United States navy and afterwards a commodore in the Confederate Navy, and Catherine Milhet. She left no issue.

4.—Louisa Cruzat, born December 17, 1801, who married Gustave Laferanderie of San Domingo. They had two daughters: Angélina, who married Robert Upshur, and Evélina, who married Jules Léaumont, and both left descendants in New Orleans.

5.—Ignace Cruzat, died in childhood.

6.—Zoé Cruzat, born October 6, 1803, married Stanislas Nelson Peychaud of Kingston, Jamacia, son of Hyacinthe Mathias Peychaud and Henriette Morel. Stanislas served as a youngster in the Battle of New Orleans. Zoé Cruzat Peychaud was the mother of one child, Eugéne Peychaud, who married Pauline Forstall, and his children were: (a) Eugénie Peychaud, unmarried; (b) Nelson Peychaud, who married, December 17, 1874, Angélina Gelpi, and had two sons, Charles Maurian Peychaud, and Eugéne Peychaud, both batchelors; (c) Jeanne Peychaud, who married, June 2, 1876, George Ferrier of New Orleans. Their children were: (1) Gabrielle Ferrier, died in infancy; (2) George Ferrier Jr., who married Maie Hanson Soria; (3) Louise Madeline Ferrier who married Henry George McCall; (4) Odile Ferrier, who married Joseph Forsythe Simpson Jr., and (5) Auguste Pierre Ferrier, who married Marjorie Clayton.

7.—Laure Cruzat, died in childhood.

8.—Victoire Cruzat, born February 26, 1807, who married James Currell. They had four children: James R., Charles M., Elizabeth Nisida, and Victoria who married Théophile Villars.

9.—Gustave Cruzat, born July 4, 1809, who married Marguerite E. Vienne; they had three children: Henry, Gustave, and Mathilde, wife of Paul de Vergès.

10.—Célestine Cruzat, born March 5, 1811, died July 4, 1854. She married Antoine Amedée Peychaud of San Domingo, a cousin of Zoé Cruzat's husband. Young Peychaud and his sister, named Lasthénie, were separated during the insurrection of the blacks on San

Domingo, and it was not until he reached manhood that he located her in Paris and had her come to New Orleans, where she afterwards married Judge C. A. Maurian. Célestine's only son Charles Amedée Peychaud, after his mother's death, was reared by his Aunt Zoé, and he, in 1862, married Marie Meffre Rouzan, daughter of Julien Meffre Rouzan, a wealthy merchant and *bon vivant* of his day, and Alice Olivier de Vezin.

11.—Mathilde Cruzat, born March 31, 1813, who married Edward B. Harris and lived to be eighty-nine. Her three children were: Edward Harris, married Célestine Prudhomme, James Harris, bachelor and Coralie Harris, who married Edward Durive.

12.—Eulalie Cruzat, youngest of the Cruzat daughters, was born May 18, 1817 and died in 1906. She married Edouard Gardère in 1841. Her husband was the son of François Gardère, the state treasurer of Louisiana, and Elisa Rivière, the daughter of Madame Rivière so prominent among the social favorites that swung around Governor de Carondelet from 1791 to 1797. The children of Eulalie Cruzat and Edouard Gardère were: (a) Louise Gardère, who married George Olivier; (b) Arthur Gardère, (c) Corinne Gardère, (d) Gustave Gardère, who married Emilie Coycault, and (e) Alice Gardère, who, in 1889, married William O'Conor.

13.—Jean Baptiste William Cruzat, who will be noted lower down.

14 & 15.—Charles and Edmond Cruzat, twins, born May 18, 1822, who died young and unmarried.

Jean Baptiste William Cruzat, the thirteenth child, was born September 24, 1819, and died in 1900. He married his cousin, Joséphine Olivia Cruzat, daughter of Joseph Ignace Cruzat, then Spanish consul at Mobile, and Alix Suzanne Coulon de Villers. He became the father of a daughter, who died without issue, and a son, John William Cruzat. The latter, who was born September 3, 1858, left a vivid memory behind him because of his historical researches and his work for the Louisiana Historical Society. He was a veritable mine of information on the subject of the Spanish era of his native state. He married, September 29, 1883, Héloïse Hulse, daughter of Albert Hulse and Mathilde Chauvin de Léry. The union was a most happy one and the two became renowned for their researches into the historical past of Louisiana, both knowing French and Spanish as well as they knew English. Mrs. Héloïse Cruzat, for years after her husband's passing, devoted her life to transcribing the ancient records of the state and translating many of them for publication in the Louisiana Historical Society's bulletins. Their children were Joseph de Villars Cruzat, Marie Joséphine Cruzat, who married James E. Strawbridge; William Cruzat, and Marie Cruzat, who married F. X. de Vergès.

From the marriage of Louise Cruzat, fourth child of Antoine Cruzat and Victoire de Chalmette, to Gustave Laféranderie of San Domingo, were born two daughters: Angélina, who married Robert Upshur, July 1, 1826, and Evéline, who married Jule Léaumont, July 1, 1826. They both left descendants in New Orleans.

The first flag to float over Louisiana. The red and white banner of Spain emblazoned with the arms of Castile and Leon. (1539-1682 and 1769-1785.)

MACARTY Family

WHILE the name Macarty is of undoubted Celtic origin, it is a Créole name of distinction in New Orleans, and the descendants of the two pioneers who brought it to Louisiana are numerous today among the first families of that state, although the name itself is no longer borne by any male descendant.

The Maccarthey-Mactaigs were of ancient Irish stock, one of whom, at least, Bartholomew (or Barthelmy) Maccarthey-Mactaig, a captain in the Irish regiment of Albemarle, fled from his native land to France to escape the political and religious tyranny of the English kings. He settled in the Bourbon realm at the end of the sixteenth century, entered the naval service, was made a knight of Saint Louis, and eventually became major general in charge of the department of Rochefort.

This Barthelmy Maccarthey-Mactaig, (or Macarty, as the name was later on modified), married a lady whose patronymic has not been preserved for posterity, and had by her five children. One of his sons, the Abbé de Macarty, became Vicar of Yoronge, and died in France in 1791. Barthelmy's two daughters, Elénore and Françoise de Macarty, became *chanoinesses*, or canonesses, in Paris, both dying there, the first in 1794 and the other in 1814.

The remaining two sons of Barthelmy, namely Jean Jacques (or Jean Baptiste) and Barthelmy Daniel de Macarty, came together to Louisiana in 1732 as French colonial officers. Jean Jacques, the elder, born in Nimes, Languedoc, in 1698, was thirty-four years of age when he landed in New Orleans as a captain in a company of the marine. His younger brother, Barthelmy, served as a lieutenant in a separate company.

Less than three years after their arrival, or on July 9,

[330]

1735, Jean Jacques de Macarty, who was then a knight of the order of Saint Louis, married in New Orleans Françoise Barbe de Trépagnier, widow of Antoine François Damaron, apothecary of the king in Louisiana, by whom she had three children. The widow Damaron was well-to-do, possessing her home and a number of slaves. Her father was Claude de Trépagnier and her mother Genevieve Burel.

Her marriage to the Chevalier Jean Jacques de Macarty was not a barren one, two sons and three daughters being born to them. The daughters, Catherine Ursule, Elizabeth, and Jeanne de Macarty, died unmarried, two in la Rochelle, and the last-mentioned in New Orleans. Of the two sons, Jean Baptiste de Macarty, the elder, born in New Orleans, went to France and entered the naval service in 1787. He became a major general, won the cross of Saint Louis, commanded a war vessel *l'Achille*, and died unmarried in la Rochelle, December 2, 1798.

His brother, Augustin Guillaume de Macarty, also a *Chevalier de Saint Louis*, was born in New Orleans May 5, 1745. Going also to France, he entered the first company of the King's Musketeers, April 17, 1766. Longing for his native land, he returned and married in New Orleans, Jeanne Chauvin de Léry, from whom he had two sons, Augustin François de Macarty, born in New Orleans January 10, 1774, and the Chevalier Jean Baptiste born in the same city in 1766, who died unmarried in 1797.

After the death of his wife, Augustin Guillaume de Macarty reentered the French navy, served under the Comte d'Estaing in 1751, being a major on board *Le Tendant*, and eventually died in his native New Orleans, December 1793. Augustin François, his eldest son, was elected mayor of New Orleans during the early American days and served as such for several terms. As a descendant of an old and illustrious race, and the personification of the *ancien régime*, he became a noted figure in old New Orleans. During his incumbency as mayor he had the first shipment of natural ice sent into the city dumped into the river as a measure of public protection, asserting that "cold drinks in summer would affect throats and lungs and make the whole population consumptive."

This early New Orleans mayor served with distinction at

the Battle of New Orleans which was fought near his own fields below the city. It was in his plantation home that General Jackson established his field headquarters, and the Macarty estate, as well as that of the de la Rondes, Chalmettes, and Lacostes, was raked by the Congreve rockets fired from the British batteries. Augustin François de Macarty inherited the fortune of his aunt, Mlle. Jeanne de Macarty, and his son, Barthelmy, was appointed secretary of state by Governor W. C. C. Claiborne.

Barthelmy Daniel de Macarty, who came to New Orleans in 1732 with his elder brother, Jean Jacques, there married Françoise Hélène Pellerin. A captain in the French troops he served with credit under Bienville and de Vaudreuil in their Indian campaigns against the Natchez and Chickasaws and, as a reward for his military services, was appointed *Aide Major* of New Orleans. Later he commanded Fort Chartres on the Mississippi river, one of the more important citadels in French colonial Louisiana. By his union with Mlle. Pellerin, he had nine children. They were:

1.—Jean Baptiste de Macarty, born in New Orleans March 7, 1750, died there November 10, 1808. His name appears as a militia officer under both the French and Spanish dominations. His wife, Héloïse Charlotte Fazende, was the daughter of Gabriel Fazende and Charlotte Dreux, and their three children were: (a) Barthelmy de Macarty, unmarried; (b) Edmond (or Edward) de Macarty, whose wife was Marie Eléonore d'Estréhan des Tours, and (c) Marie Céleste de Macarty, who married Paul Lanusse, a native of Orthez, department of Basses Pyrénées, son of Armand Lanusse and Marie Lanret. Paul Lanusse died at Soto la Marino, Mexico, October 19, 1825, in his fifty-seventh year.

2.—Louis Barthelmy, chevalier de Macarty, who married Marie Jeanne Lovable, (widow Lecomte) and had by her five children. Among them was beautiful Marie Delphine de Macarty who married three times. Her first husband was Don Ramon Lopez y Angulo, by whom she had Marie Françoise Borja Lopez y Angulo, the *"Borquita"* who married Placide Forstall (q. v.)

The second husband of Marie Delphine de Macarty was Jean Blanque, prominent New Orleans banker, legislator, and friend and advisor of Jean Lafitte. Her third husband was Nicolas Lalaurie, a native of the parish of Villeneuse-sur-Lot, in the department of Lot et Garonne, and a son of Jean Lalaurie and Francoise Depenne. Marie Delphine de Macarty-Lopez y Angulo-Blanque was married to Lalaurie, June 12, 1825.

3.—Eugène de Macarty, who did not marry.
4.—Théodore de Macarty, who did not marry.
5.—Catherine de Macarty who married Favre de la Jonchère, a famous social leader in Governor Miro's time.
6.—Marie Céleste Elénore de Macarty, who married the Spanish Governor Estevan Miro, became *arbiter elegantiarum* of old New Orleans, and died in France, in the *Chateau Mont l'Evéque*, home of the Pontalbas.
7.—Brigitte de Macarty, another brilliant social butterfly of her time, who became the wife of the Sieur Favre d'Aunoy.
8.—Jeanne Françoise de Macarty, who married Jean Baptiste Césaire le Breton, son of Messire Césaire le Breton, Seigneur of Charmeau, Councillor of the King in the *Cour Souveraine de la Monnaie* in Paris, and Marguerite de la Frénière.

The Macarty plantation home, General Jackson's headquarters at the Battle of New Orleans

GRIMA Family

THE first member of the Grima family came to Louisiana in 1780. He was Albert Xavier Grima of the parish of Ste. Helena, Malta, son of Jean Marie Grima of that Mediterranean island, and Catherine Montaldos. Through his marriage in New Orleans with Marie Anne Filiosa, Albert Xavier Grima became the father of two sons, Bartoloméo Grima, who settled in Mexico, and Félix Grima, born in New Orleans in 1798, and in the old Grima house that stood on the corner of Bourbon and Toulouse streets, a corner that afterwards became historic as the site of the old French Opera House.

Félix Grima graduated from the *Collège d'Orléans*, studied law in the office of Etienne Mazureau, and was admitted to the bar in 1819. When Judge Mazereau became attorney general of the state he appointed young Grima his assistant. In 1829, Governor Henry Johnson placed Félix Grima on the bench of the criminal district court where he served with distinction. Judge Grima was married in 1831 to Adélaïde Montégut. She was the daughter of Joseph Montegut junior and Gabrielle Rose Nicholas de Saint-Céran. Her father, M. de Saint-Céran had been a noted French judge at Port-au-Prince, San Domingo, and her mother was Geneviève de Linois. In 1805, when Joseph Montégut married Gabrielle Rose de Saint-Céran, the bride's first cousin, the beautiful and accomplished Louise Davezac de Castera (widow of M. Moreau de Lassy, a Jamaican trade agent), took for her second husband the celebrated attorney Edward Livingston.

Joseph Montégut's father, Dr. Joseph Montégut, was a native of Rocos Armagnac, France, and the son of Raymond de Montégut, who came to the Louisiana colony in 1760. When Spain dominated Louisiana, Doctor Montégut enjoyed the friendship of Governor Bernardo de Galvez and in 1775 was chief surgeon of the Charity Hospital. During the American domination, Governor Claiborne appointed Doctor Montégut secretary of the treasury. He married Françoise de Lille Dupart, a granddaughter of Pierre de Lille Dupart who owned an extensive plantation on the outskirts of New Orleans. A daughter of Doctor Montégut and Françoise Dupart, became the wife of Mandeville de Marigny. Another was wedded to Barthélmy de MacNamara. Jean Arnoult married the third, and the fourth, named Solidelle Montégut, became the wife of Joseph de Roffignac, the famed mayor of New Orleans in the early American days.

Judge Félix Grima, in addition to his extensive knowledge of the law, was a scholar, a lover of good books, and a linguist of no mean ability. Several of his writings were in the form of contributions to French publications. During the Civil War, especially during the time the Federal troops occupied New Orleans, Judge Grima was forced to leave the city of his birth on twenty-four hours notice. Taking his family with him, he taught school in Augusta, Georgia, and otherwise maintained himself until the close of hostilities, when he returned to New Orleans and again built his fortune through the practice of his profession.

The children of Félix Grima and Adélaïde Montégut were: (a) Félix Grima Jr., died unmarried; (b) Dr. Victor Grima, died unmarried; (c) Alfred Grima, who married Emma Pugh and left as issue: Emma Grima, wife of Bradish Johnson and Walter Grima, died unmarried; (d) Paul Grima, died unmarried; (e) Edgar Grima, unmarried, well known notary of New Orleans, whose pen has contributed many erudite articles for the *Athenée Louisianais*; (f) George Grima, who married Louise Durruty, their children being Marcelle Grima, wife of Joseph Bernard, prominent New Orleans architect, and Victor F. Grima, and Alice Grima, unmarried; (g) Louise Grima, who married Leon Le Gardeur de Tilly; (h) Marie Grima, who died unmarried, and (i) Adélaïde Grima, who also died unmarried.

The descendants of Albert Xavier Grima, the founder of the family in Louisiana, point with pride to the fact that his wife's father Sylvain Filiosa won a unique place in Louisiana's history. He was one of the many intrepid soldiers that France sent to the colony along the Mississippi river. In 1727 he was stationed at Fort Rosalie (Natchez) and participated in the desperate fight that ensued when the Indians made their terrible attack on that post. Filiosa proved himself a hero. He and his company were about to be wiped out by the blood-crazed Natchez, when Filiosa, who was a cavalryman, seized a pair of cymbals and began to beat them furiously. This queer clanging noise so scared the savages that they were deterred from charging on the man and his new, noisesome weapon, consequently Filiosa and his companions escaped the fate of the other soldiers guarding the fort.

In recognition of his valor with the cymbals, or *timbales,* as the French call them, his fellow-soldiers nicknamed him *le Beau Timbalier.*

In after years Sylvian Filiosa married a young French woman, Marie Anne Foucault, who had miraculously survived the slaughter at Fort Rosalie, although she was made an orphan by it. He settled with her on an island in the gulf which was given him by a grant of the King of France in recognition of his famous exploit with the *timbales* and this island, in the southern part of Terrebonne parish, bears his nickname—Timbalier Island.

D'ARTAGUIETTE, D'IRON

LANDRY Family

IF one could by some happy twist of chance gain possession of an intimate history of the pioneer days of old Louisiana plantations, what interesting reading would we have! what romantic tales of the golden past would we know! But such history is not for our eyes—for it has never been written in its entirety and only stray pages from this hardy yet halcyon period come drifting down to us like vagrant petals from a full blown rose.

The strong brave men and beautiful courageous women who, animated by the spirit of pioneering, floated down the mighty rivers in cumbersome flat-boats and paddled up unknown bayous in *bateaux* and *pirogues* to carve a home in the Louisiana wilderness, have left little save tradition regarding their early struggles and their pleasures—some have not left us even their names. A few, a very few, have left, here and there, letters, diaries and journals, from which we must piece together a patch-work picture of that most interesting period.

Through the interest and devotion of a single descendant, two century-old notebooks with faded writing, and several examples of unique wood carvings have been saved from the ravages of time and the waste pile. From the notebooks we learn something of those early days that had been sealed heretofore to our eyes. They were written by Colonel Pierre Joseph Landry, a French *émigré* who came to Louisiana in 1785 and settled in that part of old Pointe Coupée now called Iberville parish, bringing with him from the land of his birth his son who bore his father's name and who, in later years, became a personage of importance.

Pierre Joseph Landry, the elder, was born in France in 1740, at or near Nantes. There are indications in the records he left behind him that he was a personage of distinction and considerable wealth. He undoubtedly held a responsible position in the French army as one of the notebooks he left behind him is a manuscript work on military tactics. The neat handwriting, now faded with age, on the time-yellowed leaves gives directions, couched in ancient words and phrases, for military maneuvers of a bygone day.

What circumstance it was that led this native of old France to seek a home in Louisiana with his fifteen-year-old son no one knows, but as he left France in 1785 one must surmise he was one of the nobility forced to flee the land of his birth by the rising terror of the Revolution.

Pierre Joseph Landry, the second, was twice married and became the father of many children, most of whom lived to maturity and left descendants who by their marriages became allied to many prominent Louisiana families, notably with the Lambremonts, the Comeaux, the Le Blancs, and the Hotards to mention only a few. His descendants are scattered to-day all over Iberville, Pointe Coupée and Ascension parishes and unquestionably there are more than 500 direct descendants now living. And in the direct line the name brought to Louisiana by Colonel Landry has been prominent in the history of the state, giving it a lieutenant governor in the person of Tresimond Landry, a member of the United States congress, and numerous state and parish officials.

Late in his life a misfortune visited Pierre Joseph Landry the second. What he knew as a "white swelling" of the knee-joint proved to be tuberculosis of the bone, and confined him to an invalid's chair. Robbed of an active life and shut off from the outside world he did not sit in his chair to brood over what could not be helped. He must do things and he set about carving from wood little figures. His pocket knifes and the native woods near to hand, usually beech and magnolia, were his tools and working material. One of his most ambitious pieces was the world-old emblem of the wheel of life, encircled with figured designs of the seven ages of man, from the cradle to old age and finally the grave. One is of a mausoleum with the bowed figures of two mourners. Another is a bust of himself, the only likeness of Pierre Joseph Landry in existence, carved from a solid block of wood, hollowed out from below—he knew enough of the nature of wood to be assured if he did not hollow it the block would warp and crack. These examples of wood carving were scattered far and wide among descendants until one of them, L. Valcour Landry, brought them together in one collection and placed the in the safekeeping of the Louisiana State Museum, along with the note books and the military manuel, as lasting mementoes of a distinguished citizen of the long ago.

By his marriages Pierre Joseph Landry, the second, born in St Servant, France January 5, 1770, died in Bayou Goula, Louisiana March 14, 1843, became the father of sixteen children. He first married Scholastique Breaux June 30, 1790, and by this union the following children were born:

1.—Joseph Raphael Landry, born June 6, 1791, died October 22, 1828.

2.—Edoure Leander Landry, born December 7, 1792, who married Emérante Lambremont. Their children were: (a) Sarazine Landry, who married Jack Trosclair; (b) Elizier Landry, (c) Marcelin Landry, (d) Val Landry, who died young; (e) Raphael Landry, (f) Joséphine Landry, and (g) Azéma Landry, who became Mrs. Geautreaux of Bayou Goula.

3.—Marie Prudence Landry, born March 20, 1794, died July 1814, without issue.

4.—Florentine Landry, born February 15, 1796, died April 6, 1830, without issue.

5.—Azaire Landry, born August 4, 1798, married Céline Lambremont, his children being: (a) Eliza Landry, (b) Neville Landry, (c) Gustave Landry, (d) Diogene Landry, (e) Hermogene Landry, (f) Raphael Landry.

6.—Adrianire Landry, born April 7, 1800, who married Philip Comeaux, and became the mother of Philogene Comeaux, who lived in Algiers; (b) Livinsquie Comeaux who died young, and (c) Elizada Comeaux, who married a Mr. Capdeville at Plaquemine.

7.—Pierre Landry, born 1802, died 1827.

The second marriage of Pierre Joseph Landry, second, was with Marguerite Rosalie Capdeville, on January 16, 1804. She was the daughter of Bernard Capdeville and

Anna Clouatre (or Cloatre). Nine children were the issue of this alliance. They were:

8.—Legesseppe Landry, born November 1804, died 1823, no issue.

9.—Marie Caroline Landry, born July 14, 1806. She married, first, J. G. A. Bush, of Grosse Tete, Louisiana, by whom she had (a) Alfred Bush, (b) Winnifred Bush, (c) Emma Bush, who married Mr. Anselam. Her second marriage was with Doville Breau. There was no issue from it.

10.—Lucien Landry, born May 7, 1808, who married Delphine Le Blanc. Their children were: (a) Victorine Landry, (b) Murat Landry, (c) Théophile Landry, (d) Olympe Landry, (e) Armande Landry, (f) Prévost Landry, (g) Florville Landry, (h) Cora Landry, (i) Octave Landry, and (j) Herminie Landry.

11.—Eugene Landry, born 1810, who married Adrienne Hébert. His children were: (a) Eugene Landry, who died without issue; (b) Céasare Landry, (c) Louise Landry, who married Mr. Gimet; (d) Valazie Landry, who married Ermance Lefeaux, and left a son, J. Valcour Landry of New Orleans, and (e) Alice Landry, who married E. Gimet and, later, married Mr. Walker of Mandy, La.

12.—Benjamin Achille Landry, who married Amore Landry. His children were: (a) Allezie Landry, (b) Valérie Landry, (c) Major Joseph Amedée Landry, who married Marie Louise Besson, their children being Alice Landry, Henry Landry, Joseph Peter Landry, Louise Landry, Joseph Amedée Landry, and James Besson Landry; (d) Florian Landry, (e) Nazare Landry, born July 28, 1847, died June 25, 1881; (f) Cécile Landry, (g) Marie Landry, and (h) Volney Landry.

13.—Marie Sophie Landry, married Doctor Rivierre of Plaquemine. Her son named Emile Rivierre, had the following children: Loula Naomie Daniel, Nora, Elphege and Cecile Rivierre.

14.—Jeanne Baptiste Landry who died in infancy.

15.—Onazime Landry, who married Josephine Hotard. His children were: Athos, Louis, Lafalena, Monteleone, who died without issue; Beauregard, Onazime, not married, and Porthos Landry who married Laure Lefeaux and had nine children.

16.—Magloire Landry, who married first, a Miss Lambremont and had Alonzo, Mesiel, Naomi, and Clara Landry. By his second marriage with Elina Breaux his children were: Amalie Landry who married a Mr. Blanchard of New Orleans; Malvina Landry, who married Pierre Caffarel; Sophie, and Aimée Landry.

The marriage of Major Joseph Amedée Landry and Marie Louise Besson united two well known Créole families of French descent. Major Landry was the son of Benjamin Achille Landry, the twelfth child of Pierre Joseph Landry II, and made a record for himself in the Civil War, enlisting as a sergeant and being a major in the Confederate army at the end of the great strife. Mlle. Besson's family tree had its roots in France, the name being brought to Louisiana by Jacques Esprit Besson, born in Marseilles, who settled in St. James parish where he married Françoise Dugas (Dugat). Their children were (a) Joseph Besson, born March 30, 1816; (b) Felix Besson, (c) Félicité Besson, (d) Louise Besson, (e) Irma, and (f) Theresa Besson.

Joseph Besson, the eldest child, married, in 1840, Célestine Richard, daughter of an Acadian family that settled in St. James parish. Their children were: (a) Marie Louise Besson, born August 11, 1841; (b and c) Félicité and Célestine Besson, twins, born June 8, 1843; (d) James Esprit Besson, born May 17, 1846, and (e) Marie Annette Emilie Besson, born August 11, 1852. Marie Louise Besson, the oldest child, married, September 5, 1868, Major Joseph Amedée Landry and their children were: (1) Alice Landry, born July 1869, died July 1880; (2) Henry Landry, born December 1871, died September 1887; (3) Joseph Peter Landry, born September 2, 1872, who married Lizzie Sallis Butler of Rapides parish, daughter of John Samuel Butler; (4) Marie Louise Landry, born January 27, 1876; (5 and 6) Joseph Amedée and James Besson Landry, twins, born March 4, 1879.

DERBIGNY—DE LASSUS Families

THE fifth governor of Louisiana under the American domination, Pierre Auguste Charles Bourguignon d'Herbigny, was born in Laon, near Lille, in the *Départment du Nord*, France, in the year 1767. His father was Augustin Bourguignon d'Herbigny, and Pierre was the oldest of five sons, his four brothers being: (a) Alphonse d'Herbigny, who became aide-de-camp to General Jean Marie Philippe, comte de Serrurier, a *maréchal de France*, and was killed during de Serrurier's brilliant campaign in Italy under Napoleon; (b) Francois Xavier d'Herbigny, general secretary of the *Préfécture du Nord;* (c) Casimir d'Herbigny, an officer of the Marine, and (d) Antoine Valéry d'Herbigny, director of the *enregistrement* at Bordeaux and Arras, man of letters and poet of distinction.

Fleeing the fires of the French Revolution of 1792, Pierre d'Herbigny went to Santo Domingo. Driven from that island by the uprising of the blacks, he moved to Pittsburgh, where he married Félicité Odile de Hault de Lassus de Luzière, only daughter of the Chevalier Pierre Charles de Hault de Lassus de Luzière, founder and commandant of *Nouvelle Bourbon*, a post situated about two miles immediately south of Ste. Geneviève and nearly opposite Kaskaskia on the Mississippi River in Upper Louisiana.

The Chevalier Pierre de Lassus was knight grand-cross of the royal order of Saint Michel. He was descended from an ancient noble family established in the town of Bouchaine, in Hainault, French Flanders. His wife was Domitille Josephe Dumont Danzin de Beaufort. Leaving France with his family at the time of the French Revolution, he went to Spain and later moved to Louisiana. He arrived in New Orleans about 1794, and shortly after was commissioned to take over New Bourbon.

His children were: (a) Charles de Hault de Lassus de Luzière, better known in Louisiana history as Don Carlos de Hault de Lassus; (b) Jacques Marcellin Céran de Hault de Lassus de Saint Vrain, (c) Camille de Hault de Lassus, and (d) Félicité Odile de Hault de Lassus who married Pierre d'Herbigny.

Don Carlos, the oldest son, although a colonel in the Spanish service, was born in Bouchaine, France, about 1764. At Andalusia, in the war between France and Spain, Don Carlos, holding the rank of captain, led a desperate charge of Spanish troops that won the victory for the Dons. After his arrival at the age of thirty, with his father's family in Louisiana, he became commandant of *Nueva Madrid*, in the Illinois District, from 1797 to 1799. Thence he was ordered to St. Louis to succeed Don Zénon Trudeau as last Spanish lieutenant governor of Upper Louisiana, a post he held until March 10, 1804, when he delivered that part of the Louisiana territory to Captain Amos Stoddard of the United States Army.

In the spring of 1807, Don Carlos de Lassus was appointed military commander and governor of West Florida, Spain's remaining possession in Louisiana. He was in command when the Bayou Sara patriots, on horseback, stormed and captured the fort at Baton Rouge, hauled down the banner of Castile and Leon, and set up an independent government under the Lone Star Flag. Don Carlos de Lassus was afterwards tried by a Spanish court-martial and was condemned to death for the loss of West Florida. As he remained in New Orleans at the home of his sister Félicité (Mrs. Pierre Derbigny), the sentence of the drum-head court was never carried out. Don Carlos married Adélaïde Féliciana Mariana di Leonardo, daughter of Gilberto di Leonardo, (or Gilbert Leonard, as he was later called), and sister to Jean or John W. Leonard, father and son being well known figures in the Feliciana country. Don Carlos de Hault de Lassus died in New Orleans May 1, 1842, in his seventy-eighth year, and left one son, Auguste de Hault de Lassus.

Jacques Marcelin Céran de Hault de Lassus de Saint Vrain, the second son of the Chevalier, was born in Bouchaine in 1770 and died at Spanish Point, twelve miles from

St. Louis, June 22, 1818. He served in the French navy before the Revolution. In Louisiana he commanded a Spanish *galliot*, or war vessel, on the Upper Mississippi river. He married, April 30, 1796, Marie Félicité Chauvet Dubreuil, daughter of Louis Chauvet Dubreuil, a native of Rochelle, Aunis, France, who in 1736, had emigrated to St. Louis when he was twenty-nine and there had married Susanne Saintous, September 19, 1772. From the marriage of Jacques and Marie Félicité were born several sons and daughters, among them Charles, Savary, Félix, Céran, and Domitilla.

Camille de Hault de Lassus, youngest son of Chevalier Pierre Charles de Hault de Lassus de Luzière, served as a Spanish officer and English interpreter at New Bourbon without pay, commanded that post in the absence of his father, and also discharged the duties of adjutant. He married and left two sons and a daughter; Léon, Paul, and Odile de Lassus. Each of these sons married in turn and left issue. The daughter became the wife first of Silvestre S. Pratte of St. Louis, and then of Louis Vallé, of Ste. Geneviève, but left no issue.

Pierre d'Herbigny, after marrying Félicité de Hault de Lassus, traveled extensively seeking a climate similar to that of his wife's native France for the benefit of her health. He visited Havana, Florida and finally settled in New Orleans. It was at this time he dropped the apostrophe and the H in his name, writing it Derbigny. His talents and integrity brought him substantial honors in the new territory and subsequent State.

In 1803, he was appointed secretary to Etienne de Boré during the latter's twenty-day term as mayor of New Orleans under the *tricolor*. Later, Governor William C. C. Claiborne appointed Pierre Derbigny interpreter of languages for the new Territory of Orleans. He was, at different times, clerk of the court of Common Pleas, and secretary of the legislative council.

In 1805, he was one of the commissioners who took to Washington a memorial protesting against the admission of Louisiana as a territory, seeking for her the status of a state. Later he became a member of the first state legislature, regent of the schools of New Orleans, and twice secretary of state.

Brilliant lawyer even before he left France Pierre Derbigny's intimate knowledge of the Code Napoleon became valuable when with Moreau Lislet he assisted Edward Livingston with his revision of the Civil Code. Later Derbigny, with George Mathews and Dominick A. Hall, became members of the first state supreme court.

In the third gubernatorial election of 1820, Pierre Derbigny was the choice of the *Créoles*. He was opposed by Thomas Bolling Robertson, champion of the American party. Robertson had received the highest number of popular votes. Derbigny was second, with Abner L. Duncan and J. N. Déstrehan following in the order named. At that time the constitution provided that the legislature should select the governor from the two candidates receiving the most popular votes. Although Derbigny's friends in the legislature were in the majority and certain to select him, Moreau Lislet, on behalf of his friend, declared that Pierre Derbigny had too much respect for the will of the people to wish to secure the governorship in such a manner and requested that the legislative ballot be cast for Robertson who had led Derbigny by some 800 votes.

In 1828, in the fifth gubernatorial election, Pierre Derbigny was again the candidate of the Creole party. He was opposed by Judge Thomas Butler of West Feliciana, Bernard Marigny and General Philemon Thomas. Derbigny although polling the largest number of votes, led Judge Butler by only 400 popular votes. When the supplemental vote was taken in the general assembly, Judge Butler withdrew his name, stating, as had Pierre Derbigny eight years before, that he, too, was adverse to overturning the will of the people.

Less than a year after his inauguration, on September 25, 1829, Governor Derbigny was driving a spirited team of horses when they got beyond his control and in running away overturned the carriage, causing his death five days later.

Pierre Derbigny was the father of four daughters and one son. One of the daughters, Aimée, married Henry Denis, while another became the wife of George Legendre, thus becoming the progenitresses of the later generations of these two well known Louisiana families. Two other daughters married Noël Barthélemy Le Breton (q. v.) only one leaving issue.

Charles Zénon Derbigny, the governor's son, was studying medicine in Paris when his father died. He immediately returned to New Orleans, began the study of law, and entered politics. For several years he was a member of the state legislature and at one time president of the state senate. In 1845 he was a candidate for governor but ran third to Isaac Johnson and William DeBuys. He was also an extensive sugar planter with plantations in Lafourche and Jefferson parishes. He married Joséphine Eulalie LeBreton, by whom he had three daughters: (a) Marie Lucie Derbigny, who married Etienne Dauphin Courmes; (b) Marie Eulalie Derbigny, who married first Edmond LeBreton and, subsequently, Hugh D. Cochrane, and (c) Félicité Odile Derbigny, who became the wife of Pierre Glaitrais LaBarre.

Charles Zénon Derbigny died in 1875 at the age of eighty-one and was the last of the male line, and with his death the name Derbigny became extinct in Louisiana.

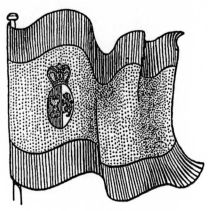

The red and yellow banner of Spain that flew over
Louisiana from 1785 to 1803

BREAZEALE Family

OF the many distinguished old families of Louisiana that of Breazeale stands out in prominence throughout the state and, especially in the vicinity of its oldest town, historic Natchitoches. In the blood of many of the present bearers of the name flows that of another distinguished family, the Prudhommes, known in the annals of the original French colony since the days of the colorful Juchereau de Saint Denys.

The first who brought the name to Louisiana was Drury Wood Brezeale, who settled in Port Gibson, Mississippi, about 1780, where he appears to have been a man of considerable property, with many slaves. He earned an enviable reputation as a lawyer. He was one of three brothers from South Carolina and, as the family were Protestants and members of the Episcopal church, it is presumed that they were of French Huguenot extraction. One of the Breazeale brothers remained in South Carolina, another emigrated to Virginia, and Drury Wood Breazeale undertook the long journey to the distant Southland then under the domination of the Spaniards. He married at Port Gibson and became the father of one son and five daughters. All of the daughters married and left descendants in Mississippi and Louisiana. One became the wife of Senator Foote of Mississippi; Senator Jones of Nevada married another; the third became a Mrs. Haynes, the fourth married Doctor Callendar, and the fifth became Mrs. Robert W. Campbell who removed to Natchitoches and left a large family.

Drury Wood Breazeale settled in Natchitoches in 1800 and purchased a number of parcels of land in northwest Louisiana, especially in Bienville parish. He was buried in a tomb located on a large Indian mound near Port Gibson and died in Natchitoches in 1823. He left a great deal of property in Louisiana and Mississippi, and his will provided that freedom and transportation should be given his one hundred and eighty slaves to Liberia, Africa. This will was promptly contested by his daughter, Mrs. Doctor Callendar, representing, it is presumed, the other children, and the courts declared it null and void, and the slaves remained on the plantations.

Blount Baker Breazeale, his only son, remained in Natchitoches, and in 1826 married Mary Manette Winter, daughter of William Winter and granddaughter of Elisha Winter, a native of England who settled in Philadelphia in 1760 and served in the colonial army during the Revolutionary war. She lived until 1905, dying at the age of ninety-six. The couple had eight children, those that survived infancy being three sons: (a) Winter Wood Breazeale, born in Natchitoches September 5, 1827, who became a colonel in the Second Louisiana Regiment during the Civil War; (b) Walter Overton Breazeale, a lieutenant colonel in the Confederacy, and (c) Blount Baker Breazeale, who served as a private in the gray ranks.

Winter Wood Breazeale spent most of his life in Natchitoches parish where he died March 10, 1896, at the age of sixty-nine. He operated extensive cotton plantations and married, in 1856, Adèline Catherine Prudhomme, born March 6, 1836, died October 27, 1878, daughter of Pierre Phanor Prudhomme (born June 24, 1807, died October 12, 1863), and Suzanne Lise Métoyer (born 1818, died 1825). P. Phanor Prudhomme, who after the death of his first wife, married his sister-in-law Marianne Céphalide Métoyer (born 1817, died 1857), was a son of Emanuel Prudhomme, and a direct descendant of Pierre Emanuel Prudhomme, a surgeon in the French army with the rank of captain who came from France with Bienville in 1699, and located at Natchitoches with Juchereau de Saint Denys.

The children of Winter Wood Breazeale and Adélaide Catherine Prudhomme were:

1.—Hopkins Payne Breazeale, born November 13, 1856, died August 19, 1893, who married Camilla Lachs of Memphis, Tennessee, and was a planter and newspaperman of Natchitoches. His four children were: H.

Payne Breazeale, who married Nita Sims of Donaldsonville; Wynonah Breazeale, who married Sidney K. Johnson of Los Angeles, California; Carmen Breazeale, and Seessel J. Breazeale, who married Marcelle J. Durand, and became professor of French at Peabody and Vanderbilt Institute, Nashville, Tennessee.

2.—Phanor Breazeale, born at Natchitoches, December 29, 1858, married, July 15, 1884, Marie Chopin, daughter of Dr. J. B. Chopin and Julia Benoist, both descendants of notable French families who will be considered later. Phanor Breazeale was educated in Natchitoches, studied law, in 1880, was appointed deputy clerk of the Supreme Court of Louisiana, was admitted to the bar in 1881, and took up the practice of his profession in his home parish. He served the people as district attorney, was sent to Baton Rouge as member of two constitutional conventions, and went to Washington, D. C. to serve his district as a Member of Congress from 1899 to 1905. Since his return to the practice of his profession he has been recognized as one of the foremost citizens of the state and most prominent in politics. In 1920 he was urged from every section of Louisiana to become the Democratic candidate for governor. By his marriage with Marie Chopin, who died September 5, 1826, there issued four daughters: (a) Marie Breazeale, who lives in Natchitoches, and is a member of the state central Democratic committee; (b) Gladys Breazeale, orignator and director of the Natchitoches Art Colony, who in the campaign of 1924 was chosen as one of the Democratic presidential electors, and designated to deliver the Louisiana vote to Congress; (c) Julia Breazeale, who married Arthur C. Waters of New Orleans and has issue, and (d) Katherine Breazeale, who m a r r i e d Shirley Carter Friend, and has issue.

3.—Upshur Breazeale, born October 24, 1860, died February 3, 1927, not married.

4.—Winter Wood Breazeale, born October 24, 1862, died in infancy.

5.—Lise Breazeale, born March 21, 1865, married Thomas P. Chaplin.

6.—Maude M. Breazeale, born July 20, 1868, married Samuel J. Henry.

7.—Mable Breazeale, twin to Malcolm, born September 6, 1872.

8.—Malcolm Breazeale, twin to Mable, died November 14, 1888.

9.—Drury Wood Breazeale, born September 22, 1874, died January 13, 1926, married, February 14, 1900, Mathilde Hyams.

10.—Ross E. Breazeale, born August 1, 1878, died January 27, 1930, not married.

An interesting phase of the political history of the Breazeale family is found in the fact that the two grandfathers of Phanor Breazeale were usually to be found on opposite sides of the political fence. In 1844 Pierre Phanor Prudhomme and Blount Baker Breazeale were both delegates to the constitutional convention of 1844, the first representing the town of Natchitoches and the other the senatorial district. It was noted that whenever B. B. Breazeale voted "yes," Prudhomme would be recorded as voicing a vociferous "nay." And if P. P. Prudhomme voted in the affirmative on any matter, B. B. Breazeale would be found on the negative side. The two foremost families, divided politically, were united by the marriage of Breazeale's son, Winter Wood, to Prudhomme's daughter, Adéline Catherine and the marriage of their second son, Phanor, to Marie Chopin united the Breazeales and Prudhommes to another prominent family of French descent.

Marie Chopin's father was Dr. J. B. Chopin, while her mother was Julie Benoist. The Benoists descended from the celebrated Chevalier Antoine Gabriel Francois Benoist, born in Paris October 6, 1715, the son of Sieur Gabriel Benoist and Francoise de Trévet. Young Benoist went to Canada in 1735, settling in Montreal. He made a startling record as a soldier in the pioneer days of *Nouvelle France* and when he returned to France with his family he wore on his breast the coveted cross of valor—and was addressed as Benoist, *écuyer, Chevalier de L'ordre royal de Saint Louis.* He died in France

January 23, 1776, leaving eight children. Jacques Louis Benoist, oldest son of the Chevalier Benoist, was born in Canada in 1744, married Marie Josephe Soumande, but was drowned a few months after his son, François Marie, was born. This son, François Marie Benoist, born November 2, 1767, went to St. Louis, married Marie Anne Catherine Sanguinette, and had seven children. Charles François, Louis Auguste, Malvina, Josephine Adéline, Sanguinette Hubert Sophie Amanda, and Zoé. The oldest son, Charles François Benoist, was educated in Kentucky but came to Natchitoches in 1820, where he married Suzette Rachal, and had five children; Julie, Charles Clémence, Victor, and Suzette. It was the eldest child, Julie who married Doctor Chopin, and became the mother of five children, Oscar, Eugénie, Victor, Lamy, and Marie. And Marie, the youngest, it was who became the wife of Phanor Breazeale.

Louisiana's "Lone Star" flag adopted at the outbreak of the Civil War. The stripes alternate blue, white, red, white and the single star is yellow on a red ground.

BUTLER Family

WHEN Theobald Fitzwalter accompanied Henry II to Ireland in 1117, he was created Chief Butler of Ireland and in such a fashion came the name of "Butler" which, in the early history of the American Colonies and in the later annals of Louisiana, became one of the most distinguished in American history.

When Theobald, First Butler, died in 1206 he was succeeded by his son, Theobald, Second Butler, who in 1221 assumed the surname of Le Botilier, or Butler. This succession was continued up to 1321 when James, son of the Sixth Butler, was created Earl of Ormonde, in the Peerage of Ireland. This succession was continued until 1515 when Pierce Butler, great grandson of the third Earl of Ormonde assumed the earldom and became the eighth Earl of Ormonde. He had as issue, James the ninth earl, and Richard, first Viscount of Montgarret. James married Joan, the daughter of James Fitzgerald, eleventh earl of Desmond, and had as issue, John, Richard, and Thomas, tenth Earl of Ormonde, who died without issue. Walter, son of John, became the eleventh earl, and was succeeded by James, twelfth earl and first Duke of Ormonde, whose son was killed while in command of the English army at the battle of Senef, 1674, in Flanders.

From Richard Butler, brother of the tenth earl and grand uncle of the Duke of Ormonde, who married and had issue, we can follow the Butler line through the succeeding generations to Richard Butler, eighth Baron Dunboyne, whose third son, Thomas, emigrated to America in 1748 and founded the "Fighting Butlers," famed in every war from the Revolutionary, under Washington, to the World War, under Pershing.

Thomas Butler, founder of the American branch, was

born April 6, 1720, in the parish of Koolkenny, city of Wicklow, Ireland. He married, October, 1741, Eleanor Parker, daughter of Sir Anthony Parker of Carey, county of Wexford. Seven years later the Butlers and their three oldest sons left Ireland for the new lands across the Atlantic and settled in Lancaster county, Pennsylvania, later moving to Mount Pleasant in Cumberland county, where Thomas Butler purchased large tracts of land and erected the first Episcopal church in that section of the country. At Mount Pleasant were reared his family of twelve children, including the five sons who became distinguished during the Revolutionary struggles of the colonies, being conspicuous for their patriotic ardor and their chivalrous contempt for danger. The Marquis de Lafayette set down in an official communication: "When I wish a thing well done, I order a Butler to do it."

Following the close of the struggle for independence it was this extraordinary zeal of the whole family that prompted General George Washington at his own table and surrounded by a large party of officers, to designate them as "Honor's Band," and to give the toast—"The Butlers and their five sons."

Those sons were General Richard Butler, Colonel William Butler, Colonel Thomas Butler Jr., Percival (or Pierce) Butler, Adjutant General of Kentucky, and Adjutant General Edward Butler. Their parents had seven other children, four of them dying in infancy, the survivors being Mary Butler, born in West Lancaster, Pennsylvania, November 5, 1749, who married Jacob Scandrett and died young; Rebecca Butler, also born in West Lancaster, September 19, 1751, who married Captain George McCully, a member of the Order of Cincinnati; and Eleanor Butler, born at Mount Pleasant, Pennsylvania, December 31, 1763, who married James Brown and died at Carrollton, Kentucky.

Richard Butler, the oldest and the most distinguished son of Thomas Butler, was born in the parish of St. Bridgets, Dublin, Ireland, April 1, 1743. He was killed in action November 4, 1791, in the battle of Miami, known as St. Clair's Defeat. He was a major general and one of the most resplendent heroes of the Revolution. Shortly before his death he was made second in command of the American army, and was designated to place the American flag on the British works after the surrender of Lord Cornwallis at Yorktown.

General Butler had married Mary Smith, by whom he had four children: (a) William Butler, who became lieutenant in United States navy and died in War of 1812; (b) Mary Butler, who married Colonel Isaac Meason, and whose descendants married into the Trevor, Sowers, and Henry families of Philadelphia; (c) James who died in infancy, and (d) Captain Richard Butler who married Anna Wilkins, daughter of General John Wilkins. Their children married into the Thompson, Irwin, and Biddle families of Pennsylvania.

William Butler, second son of Thomas Butler, was born in London, January 6, 1745, and died May 16, 1789, in Pittsburg. He entered the Revolutionary army as a captain and was colonel of the Fourth Pennsylvania at its close. He was distinguished for his bravery and was commended on more than one occasion by Washington for his coolness. He married Jane Carmichael of Pittsburgh, who was born in New Orleans in 1751, and died in her native city March 6, 1834. They had four children: (a) Richard Butler, born 1777, died October 5, 1820, at Bay St. Louis. He entered the army and rose to the rank of captain. In 1798, then a lieutenant, he was sent by General James Wilkinson from Pittsburgh to Natchez with important dispatches for Captain Isaac Guion. He made the round trip by barge and *pirogue* from April 11, to June 16, a distance of 3,000 miles. He served at the Battle of New Orleans with the Forty-fourth Regiment. At the close of the war he married Margaret Farar of Adams county, Mississippi, he and his family being swept away by a yellow fever epidemic in 1820. (b) Rebecca Butler, born April 20, 1782, at Carlisle, Pennsylvania and died June 23, 1844. She married Captain Samuel McCutcheon of Philadelphia, and had four children: (1) Jane, who married William Frege Krumbhaar and had four children; (2) Eliza Ann, born January 22, 1811, died November 1842, who married Robert Rhea Montgomery, and had four children; (3) Percival Butler McCutcheon born September 26, 1821, who married Jane Butler Browder, his cousin and had two children, and (4) Zelia Henderson McCutcheon, born April 6, 1828, died July 6, 1864, who married George Carson Lawrason. They had two sons: Judge Samuel McCutcheon Lawrason, of St. Francisville, born July 31, 1852, who married Miss Harriet Mathews, and had nine children, one, Anne Mathews Lawrason, married Edward Butler; George Bradford Lawrason, the second son, born July 26, 1854, married first, Octavie Planc, and second, Daisy Bruns, by whom he had three children. (c) Harriet Butler, born 1787, died July 16, 1830. She married three times, first, Robert Callender, second, Captain Moses Hooke, by whom she had four children, and third, Frederick A. Browder, and her daughter, Jane Butler Browder, married her cousin, Percival Butler McCutcheon. (d) William Butler, fourth child of Colonel William Butler, was a lieutenant in the war of 1812, and died in 1815 without issue.

Thomas Butler, third son of Thomas Butler and Eleanor Parker, was born in Dublin, Ireland, May 28, 1748, and was only a few months old when his parents emigrated to Pennsylvania. He studied law but enlisted as a private when the Revolutionary War broke out. His courage distinguished him and he was in almost every action fought in the Middle States during the course of the war for independence, receiving the thanks of Washington on the battlefield at Brandywine, for his intrepid conduct in rallying retreating troops. He was in command of a battalion at Miami when his brother General Richard Butler was killed and was shot off his horse, his life being saved by his younger brother, Edward Butler. He was a colonel in the regular army at New Orleans in 1805 and died of yellow fever at the age of fifty-seven. He was a member of the Order of Cincinnati, a membership that descended to his son, Judge Thomas Butler.

This Colonel Thomas Butler married Sarah Jane Semple, daughter of Robert Semple and Lydia Steele of Pittsburgh, and their children were:

1.—Thomas Butler III, born April 14, 1785, who received his legal training in the office of his uncle, Steele Semple. Removing to Louisiana he practiced law in the Florida Parishes. In 1811 he purchased *The Cottage*, plantation in West Feliciana parish, and there made his home. *The Cottage* is still owned by the four children of his son, Dr. Ormonde Butler (q. v.). Judge Butler married, August 17, 1813, Ann Madeline Ellis, daughter of Abram Ellis of Adams county, Mississippi, and Marguerite Gaillard whose Huguenot ancestors came to South Carolina after the revocation of the Edict of Nantes. Judge Butler died August 7, 1847. He was the father of twelve children, four dying young. The surviving children were: (a) Percival (or Pierce) Butler, born February 21, 1817, died February 12, 1888. He married Mary Louise Stirling daughter of Henry Stirling and Mary Bowman. Their children were: (1) Thomas Butler, born December 6, 1840, died November 7, 1922, who had a distinguished Civil War record. He married Mary Fort, daughter of William Fort and Sallie Fort and had nine children. (2) James Pierce Butler, born April 26, 1842, died March 15, 1910, who entered the Confederate army at eighteen. He married Mary Louisa Harrison, by whom he had three children. Two of them are: Pierce Butler, dean of Newcomb College, who married Cora Waldo, and James Pierce Butler Jr., who married Laura Finley. (3) Louisa Ann Butler, third child of Pierce Butler and Louisa Stirling, born December 6, 1843, died August 17, 1906. She married, April 28, 1875, Henry Chotard Minor of Terrebonne parish. Of their six children, three are: John Duncan Minor, who married Lucille Gillis, and has two children; Margaret Gustine Minor, who married Charles Conrad Krumbhaar, and has two children, and Mary Louisa Minor, who married David W. Pipes Jr., and has six children.

2.—Richard Ellis Butler, born January 12, 1851, died December 15, 1915, who married Sallie Fort, daughter of William J. Fort, and Sallie Stewart. They had four children. Those living are: Richard Ellis Butler, who married Jessie Simon, and left two children; Sarah Duncan Butler, and Mary Fort Butler.

3.—Margaret Butler, 4.—Anna Eliza, 5.—Sarah Jane

Duncan Butler, 6.—Mary Ellis Butler, four daughters who did not marry.

7.—Robert Ormonde Butler, fourth son of Judge Thomas Butler and Ann Madeline Ellis, was born May 8, 1832, and died April 2, 1874. He studied medicine in Paris, practiced for a time in New York until he removed to New Orleans whence he practiced until his death. Dr. Butler married Marguerite Burthe, daughter of Judge Victor Burthe and Estelle Millaudon. They had four children: (a) Louise Butler, not married; (b) Robert Ormonde Butler, not married; (c) Edward Butler, who married Anne Mathews Lawrason, and has four children: Edward Lawrason Butler, Harriet Mathews Butler, Charles Mathews Butler, and Robert Ormonde Butler; (d) Marguerite Butler, who married Eugene Ellis, son of William Conner Ellis and Eugénie Richardson, has four children: Marguerite Butler Ellis, Eugene Ellis Jr., Amélie de Lesseps Ellis, who married George Ross Murrell, and Eleanor Parker Ellis.

8.—Edward Gaillard Butler, youngest son of Judge Thomas Butler, who was born March 26, 1837, and died August 20, 1887, never married.

Robert Butler, second son of Colonel Thomas Butler (third son of the original Thomas Butler and Sarah Jane Semple), was born, December 25, 1786, and died January 13, 1860. He married Rachel Hayes, daughter of Colonel Robert Hayes and Jane Donelson, niece of Mrs. Andrew Jackson. Their descendants live in Florida. Robert Butler was Andrew Jackson's chief of staff throughout the war of 1812, and at the Battle of New Orleans. He resigned from the army in 1821 and was for years surveyor general of Florida.

Lydia Butler, daughter of Colonel Thomas Butler and Sarah Jane Semple, born March 9, 1788, died 1852. She married Stokely Hays, nephew of Mrs. Andrew Jackson, and had two children, Jane, who married John Rawlins, and Richard Hays, whose descendants live in Tennessee.

William Edward Butler, third son of Colonel Thomas Butler and Sarah Jane Semple, was born January 23, 1790, in Carlisle, Pennsylvania, and died in 1882. He married

Martha Thompson Hays, daughter of Colonel Robert Hays, of Hillsboro, Tennessee, and Jane Donaldson, niece of Mrs. Andrew Jackson. He was surgeon of the Second Tennessee Regiment under Andrew Jackson, and served at the Battle of New Orleans. His descendants were Captain William Ormonde Butler; Mary Ormonde Butler, who married a Mr. Henderson, and lived in Tennessee, and another daughter who became Mrs. Chancellor, and lived in Baltimore.

Percival (or Pierce) Butler, fourth of the "Five Fighting Butlers," was born in Carlisle, Pennsylvania, April 14, 1760, and died September 9, 1821. When only seventeen he enlisted in the Continental Army, and was a first lieutenant in the Third Pennsylvania Regiment, serving under his brothers. He married May 30, 1786, Mildred Hawkins, a direct descendant of Sir John Hawkins, and they had eleven children. The most distinguished of these were:

1.—Thomas Langford Butler, born April 10, 1789, died in Louisville, October, 1881. He was a captain at the Battle of New Orleans and aide to Jackson who brevetted him a major for gallant conduct. He married his cousin, Sarah Hawkins, and their descendants are the Turpins and Southgates of Kentucky. His sons died unmarried.

2.—Richard Parker Butler, fourth child of Percival and Mildred Hawkins, born September 27, 1792, died January 8, 1885, was soldier, lawyer, planter, and politician, and noted as one of the best informed men of Kentucky. His wife was Pauline Bullock.

3.—Percival Butler, born October 4, 1794, married Eliza Sarah Allen, daughter of Colonel John Allen. He moved to Louisville where his descendants live.

4.—Jane Hawkins Butler, born February 4, 1804, died August 8, 1877, married Dr. U. E. Ewing of Louisville and had issue. Her second husband was James Mandeville Carlisle of Washington, D. C.

5.—William Orlando Butler, second son and most distinguished child of Percival Butler and Mildred Hawkins, born April 19, 1791, died in Carrollton, Kentucky, February 6, 1880. He entered Transylvania College, studied law with Robert Wickliffe, enlisted in the army in 1812, was at the massacre of the River Raisin, at the storming of Pensacola, received the brevet rank of major for gallant services at the Battle of New Orleans, where he won high praise of "Old Hickory" for his gallantry under fire. He married Eliza Todd of Carrollton, Kentucky, daughter of General Robert Todd. He was elected to the legislature and then served for two terms in Congress. In 1846 President Polk made him major general of volunteers and ordered him to Mexico, where he participated in all the major engagements until he was desperately wounded at Monterey. Recovering from his wounds, he returned to Mexico, and on January 13, 1848, was made commander-in-chief of the United States forces. In recognition of his services he was voted a sword by Congress and the State of Kentucky presented him with a second one. That same year he was nominated for vice president on the Democratic ticket with General Lewis Cass, against Zachary Taylor and Millard Fillmore, who were elected. He left no descendants.

Edward Butler, the fifth of the "Five Fighting Butlers," was born at Mount Pleasant, Cumberland County, Pennsylvania, December 31, 1763. Like his four older brothers he was a distinguished officer in the Revolutionary War. He enlisted at the age of sixteen, as color bearer in his brother William's regiment; was with "Mad Anthony" Wayne throughout his campaign of 1793-94; was at the seige of Yorktown; was in command of a company at St. Clair's Defeat, where he saved the life of his brother, Colonel Thomas Butler.

Adjutant General Edward Butler, married, July 14, 1787, Isabella Fowler, daughter of Captain George Fowler, who three times led the British "Forlorn hope" against the American patriots at Bunker Hill. Their children were: (a) Anthony Wayne Butler, who died a young man; (b) Caroline Butler, who married Robert Bell of Whitecastle, Louisiana. Their only son died young; (c) Eliza Eleanor Butler, born 1789, who married John Donelson, a nephew of Mrs. Andrew Jackson, their son Edward Donelson, who was in the Mexican War, marrying a Mrs. Watson, who after his death married Bergondy Lapice; (d) Emmeline Butler, born 1790; (e) Richard Butler, who died young, and (f) E. G. W. Butler.

Edward George Washington Butler, born at Lebanon, Tennessee, February 22, 1800, died September 5, 1888, at St Louis. On the death of his father he was consigned to the care of General Andrew Jackson. He graduated from West Point, served in the artillery corps of the regular army; became major general of the Louisiana militia in 1845; reentered the regular army as colonel of the Third U. S. Dragoons, and served in the Mexican War. He was presented with a sword by Congress at the close of the hostilities with Mexico and retired to his plantation in Louisiana, which he named *Dunboyne* after the estates of his ancestors in Ireland. Colonel E. G. W. Butler married, April 4, 1826, Frances Parke Lewis, the oldest daughter of Colonel Lawrence Lewis, a nephew of George Washington, and Eleanor (Nellie) Custis, the granddaughter of Martha Washington. Their children were:

1.—Edward George Washington Butler, Jr., born November 4, 1829, died November 7, 1861. He graduated at the University of Virginia, at Harvard, and the New Orleans Law School. He was secretary of the U. S. Legation at Berlin when the war between the states broke out and returned to Louisiana to enter the Confederate Army as a major. He was killed at the Battle of Belmont. Before expiring he asked General Polk to tell his father he "had died like a Butler, in the discharge of his duty."

2.—Caroline Swanwick Butler, born 1834, died 1876, married William Turnbull of West Feliciana, only brother of Sarah Turnbull, who married James Pirrie Bowman. Their two sons were William and Daniel Turnbull.

3.—Isabel Butler, born 1835, married Colonel George Williamson of Louisiana. He was Minister to Central America. Their five children were: William, Caroline, Isabel, George, and Ann Williamson.

4.—Lawrence Lewis Butler, born March 16, 1837, died at St. Louis, June 3, 1898. He graduated from the University of Virginia and the law schools of New

Orleans and Paris, France. On the outbreak of the Civil War he joined the Confederate forces and served as major on the staffs of Generals Polk and Wright until the end of the strife. He married Mary Susan Gay, daughter of Edward J. Gay of Louisiana. Their children were: (a) Frances Parke Butler, who married Major John Ewens of Vicksburg, and had one child, Frances Parke Butler Ewens; (b) Edward Gay Butler, member of the Order of Cincinnati, as were his father, grandfather, and great grandfather, who married Emily Mansfield of St. Louis, and resides at Briggs, Clarke county, Virginia. (c) Lavinia Hynes Butler, who married Wyatt Shallcross of St. Louis; (d) Anna Gay Butler, who married Richard C. Plater of Nashville, Tennessee, and (e) Mary Susan Butler, who married George A. Whiting of Baltimore, Maryland.

Which brings the record of the "Fighting Butlers" of the United States and Louisiana to a close.

Robert Semple, a brother of Sarah Jane Semple who married Col. Thomas Butler (q. v.), was descended from the Semples of Kirkhouse, Scotland, was born September 10, 1772 and died September 20, 1813. Robert, like his brother, Steele, was a ripe scholar, highly educated and eminently fitted for the profession in which his brother won distinction, but preferring the military life, and while fresh from college, enlisted in 1794 in the Revolutionary Navy. In 1796 he was promoted to a lieutenancy in the first Regiment of the U. S. Infantry. The next year, he was placed in command of troops at Fort Defiance, on the Wabash river. In 1798 he commanded troops for relief of the garrison at Natchez, Mississippi, and later was assigned to duty at Fort Adams a position he held until 1800, when he resigned from the army with rank of captain, and devoted his time to planting.

He married Miss Sarah Percy, daughter of Capt. Chas. Percy, (q. v.). She bore him a daughter, both wife and child died in 1801. In 1804 he married Isabelle Turnbull, daughter of John Turnbull of Scotland, and Katherine Rucker of Culpepper county, Virginia. Isabelle was born in Alabama March 1, 1785, died in Mississippi April 28, 1873.

MINOR Family

THOMAS MINER, second son of Clement Miner, born 1608, came to America in the year 1630 from the *Countie* of Sommersett, England, on the ship *Arabella* and landed at Salem, Massachusetts. He married Grace Palmer in 1634 and settled at New London, Connecticut. In 1653 he removed to Stonington, in the same state, and became one of the founders of that city.

Stephen Minor, his great-great grandson and the eldest child born in that part of Pennsylvania, now Virginia, of the marriage of William Minor (it will be noted the "e" in the surname became "o") and Frances Phillips of Maryland, on February 8, 1760, arrived in New Orleans in the year 1780 and enlisted in the Hispanic forces and later was commissioned a captain in the royal Spanish army.

In 1797, Stephen Minor succeeded Gayoso de Lemos as governor *ad interim* of the Natchez district, when the settlers refused to receive Don Carlos de Hault de Lassus as governor. Stephen Minor died at the age of fifty-six on November 29, 1815, at *Concord*, the historic residence of the early Spanish governors at Natchez, and was buried there. It is narrated in the history of his life that he never lost the confidence of the Spanish authorities and exercised more influence than any foreigner in their employment. Major Minor combined a convivial and social temperament with great dignity of manner and shrewd practical sense. He had remarkable financial abilities, rapidly accumulated property, and was hospitable and liberal. He represented the Spanish government on the boundry commission and continued true to the Spanish interests until the Dons were forced to part with West Florida.

Stephen Minor was married three times. His first wife was a Miss Bingaman, from which union there was no issue. His second wife was Mary Ellis, by whom he had one child, Martha Minor, who married William Kenner (q. v.), and one of her descendants was Nanine Brent who became the wife of Thomas Sloo. Stephen Minor's third wife was Katherine Lintot, daughter of Bernard Lintot of Natchez, formerly a member of the Inner Temple, London.

From the marriage with Miss Lintot there were born four children: (a) Frances Minor, who became the wife of Major Henry Chotard; (b) Katherine Lintot Minor, who married James Wilkins; (c) William J. Minor, who married, in 1829, Rebecca Gustine of Carlisle, Pennsylvania, and (d) Stephen Minor Jr., who married Charlotte Walker, daughter of Charles Walker, territorial governor of Arkansas. All these children were born at *Concord*.

From the marriage of William J. Minor and Rebecca Gustine, nine children were born. Among them were: (a) John Minor, who married Katherine Surget and had issue; (b) Stephen Minor, without issue; (c) William Minor, who married Amenaïde Chaplin, with issue; (d) James Minor, without issue; (e) Duncan Minor, without issue; (f) Henry Chotard Minor, who married Annie Butler, with issue; (g) Frank O. Minor, who married Odile Larue, with issue; and (h) Katherine Lintot Minor, without issue.

John Minor, by his marriage with Katherine Surget, left three children: (a) Katherine Minor, who married Fred Schuchardt, and left issue; (b) Duncan Minor, without issue, and Jeanne Minor, who married Seborne McDowell, but left no children.

William Minor, who married Amenaïde Chaplin, left seven children: (a) Amenaïde Minor, who married Lucien E. Davis, without issue; (b) Rebecca Minor, who married James Colomb and left children; (c) Frances Chotard Minor, who married Alfred Penn Krumbhaar, with issue; (d) Mary Duncan Minor, not married; (e) Katherine Lintot Minor, not married; (f) Mathilde Minor, not married, and (g) Charlotte Minor, who married Andrew H. Payne, and left children.

Henry Chotard Minor, who married Annie Butler, left three children: (a) John Duncan Minor, with issue; (b) Magaret Minor, who married Charles Conrad Krumbhaar, with issue, and (c) Mary Minor, who married David W. Pipes Jr., with issue.

Frank O. Minor, who married Odile Larue, left seven children: (a) Louise Minor, who married J. Martial Lapeyre, with issue; (b) William J. Minor, with issue; (c) Anna Minor, not married; (d) Alphonse Rost Minor, with issue; (e) Marie Amelie Minor, who married Pierre D. Olivier, and has issue (f) George L. Minor, with issue, and (g) Stephen Duncan Minor, with issue.

The escutcheon of the Minor family is described: On a field *gules* a bar *argent* with two besants *argent en chef* and a besant *argent en pointe*. The crest shows a bourrelet *argent* and *gules* with a mailed forearm *argent* issuing therefrom holding a battle-ax *argent*. The family motto is *Spes et Fidelis*.

The Villeré plantation home headquarters of General Pakenham at the Battle of New Orleans.

PERRET Family

JEAN BAPTISTE PERRET, the progenitor of the entire Perret family in Louisiana, was born in le Dauphiné, France. He came to Louisiana from Grenoble in 1723 and established himself in New Orleans as a merchant. Early local church records having been destroyed and family tradition being silent, it is impossible to say whom he married. Accurate family geneological data, however, attributes to him two children: (1) Marie Perret who married Joseph Fossier and left numerous descendants; and (2) Alphonse Perret who married, in 1753, Marie Anne Pugeolle, later spelled "Pujol," who was born 1734 and died 1798.

Alphonse Perret and Marie Anne Pujol were the father and mother of six sons and one daughter. The daughter, Marie Anne Perret, married, first, Louis Pain and, second, Pierre Bauchet St. Martin (q. v.). Her six brothers obtained concessions of contiguous lands in St. Charles Parish. There they erected their homes and developed their plantations. From the birth of the oldest to the death of the youngest a full century elapsed. They were men of culture and learning. Their achievements were noteworthy. Their names are familiar and respected in the private history of early Louisiana. These famous sons of Alphonse Perret and Marie Anne Pujol were:

1.—Jean Baptiste (Noël) Perret, born 1754, who married Françoise Eléonore Pain;

2.—Alphonse Perret, born 1757, died 1818, was an officer in the Galvez expedition against Baton Rouge, who married, first, Mlle. St. Amant and, second, Eléonore Bossier, daughter of Dr. Bossier;

3.—Alexis Perret who married another daughter of Dr. Bossier;

4.—Joseph Perret who also married a Mlle. Bossier.

5.—Pujol Perret, also an officer in the Galvez Expedition, who married, first, Hélène Bossier and, second, Laura de la Tour.

6.—Charles Perret born 1768, died 1849, extensive sugar planter and judge, who, in 1791, married Louise D'Arensbourg, born 1768, died 1840, a daughter of Pierre Frédéric D'Arensbourg (q. v.), and a grand-daughter of the original Chevalier D'Arensbourg.

Fourth Generation Jean Baptiste Perret Line:

The children of Jean Baptiste Perret and Françoise Eléonore Pain were: (1) Eléonore Perret who died in infancy; (2) Célestine Perret who married Pierre Bauchet St. Martin (q. v.); (3) Roséline Perret who married her cousin Norbert Perret; (4) Aimée Perret; (5) Arthémise Perret; (6) Pain Perret; and (7) Jean Baptiste Perret who married Octavie D'Arensbourg.

Fifth Generation Jean Baptiste Perret Line:

The children of Jean Baptiste P e r r e t and Octavie D'Arensbourg were: (1) Léonce Perret who married Louisa LeBlanc; (2) Octavie Perret, maid: (3) Adolphe Perret; (4) Stéphanie Perret; (5) Félicie Perret who married her cousin Leo Perret; (6) Mathilde Perret who married Adolphe Sigur; (7) Blanche Perret, maid; and (8) Alice Perret, maid.

Sixth Generation Jean Baptiste Perret Line:

The children of Léonce Perret and Louisa LeBlanc were: (1) Octave Perret; (2) Charles Perret; (3) Ignace Perret; (4) Laurent Perret; (5) Raphael Perret; (6) Michel Perret; and (7) Louise Perret.

Fourth Generation Alphonse Perret Line:

From the marriage of Alphonse Perret and Mlle. St. Amant three daughters were born who became respectively: (1) Mrs. Benjamin Borne: (2) Mrs. Jean Folse and, in second marriage, Mrs. Antoine Borne;. and (3) Mrs. Maximilien Troxler.

From the second marriage of Alphonse Perret and Eléonore Bossier the following children were born: (1) Eléonore Perret (b. 1791) who married Ursin Jacob; (2) Aimée Perret who married Jean Marie Chiron; (3) Sylvain Perret who died in youth (1816); (4) Alphonse Perret who married Emilie Jacob; (5) Drausin Perret, born 1797, died 1834, who married his cousin Louise Perret, daughter of Charles Perret and Louise D'Arensbourg; and (6) Placide Perret who married Mathilde D'Arensbourg.

Fifth Generation Alphonse Perret Line:

The children of Alphonse Perret and Emilie Jacob were: (1) Emile Perret who married Alice Armelain; (2) Ernest Perret who married Irma Jacob; (3) Alphonse Perret who married Joséphine Haydel; (4) Octavie Perret who married Coline Folse; (5) Adèle Perret, maid; and (6) Emile Perret who married Arthur de la Haussaye, (q. v.).

The children of Drausin Perret and Louise Perret were: (1) Felix Perret, born 1824, who died in youth; (2) Louisa Perret, born 1831, died 1874, who married Louis St. Martin (q. v.); (3) Théophile Perret, born 1834, extensive planter in St. John Parish in partnership with his half brother Pierre Edouard St. Martin, who married Mathilde St. Martin; (4) Drausin Rosémond Perret, born 1822, scholar and expert geneologist of Louisiana families, who, in 1842, married Zoé Brou, born 1821, a great grand-daughter of the original Ambrose Heidel (Haydel) who arrived in Biloxi aboard *La Charante* from Neukirchen in 1721.

From the marriage of Placide Perret and Mathilde D'Arensbourg six daughters and one son were born. Three of the daughters married three brothers and the other three were, at various times, the wives of one man. They were: (1) Livie Perret who married Alfred Pécot; (2) Mathilde Perret who married Ernest Pécot; (3) Eloise Perret who married Octave Pécot; (4) Ermina Perret, (5) Philomene Perret, and (6) Eléonore Perret, all three of whom married Frédéric Sigur; and (7) Placide Perret II, who married his cousin, Fannie Perret.

Sixth Generation Alphonse Perret Line:

The children of Emile Perret and Alice Armelain were:
(1) Marie Régina Perret; (2) Emile Perret, Jr.; (3)
Adolphe Perret; (4) Charles Perret; (5) Fernand Perret;
and (6) Alice Perret.

The children of Ernest Perret and Irma Jacob were: (1)
Marie Lise Perret, and (2) Marie Lélia Perret, both of
whom died in youth; (3) Joseph Octave Perret, no issue;
(4) Louis Dévenay Perret who married Marie Barré; (5)
Stella Perret who died in youth; (6) Pierre Henri Perret
who married, first, Ida Dupas and, second, Julia Morel; (7)
Alphonse Jules Perret, no issue; (8) Joseph Ernest Perret
who married Héléna Belle; (9) Maria Eva Perret who
married Lucin Adam; (10) Lézin François Perret, no
issue; (11) Marie Julia Perret, maid; and (12) George
Joseph Perret who married Emilie Leefe.

The children of Alphonse Perret and Joséphine Haydel
were: (1) Joséphine Perret who maried George Lorio; (2)
Léonie Perret who married Jules Sentille, her brother-in-law;
(3) Alphonse Perret who married Sophie Gaignier; (4)
Noémie Perret who married Wilfred Bethancourt; (5)
Regina Perret who married Louis Sentille; and (6) Lizima
Perret who married Jules Sentille.

The children of Théophile Perret and Mathilde St. Martin were: (1) Mathilde Perret who married George Tassin;
and (2) Léonie Perret, maid.

The children of Drausin Rosémond Perret and Zoé Brou
were: (1) Drausin Perret, born 1845, died 1930, well-
known merchant of New Orleans for over sixty years, who
in 1886 married Marie Lucie Courmes, born 1852, died
1893, grand-daughter of Charles Zénon Derbigny (q. v.),
and great grand-daughter of Governor Charles Pierre Derbigny; (2) Felix Perret born 1846, who married Valérie
Villavaso; (3) Anna Perret, born 1848, who married J.
Octave Fassy; (4) Louise Perret, born 1853, maid; (5)
Charles Henry Perret, born 1855, who married Blanche
Rivet; (6) Emma Perret, born 1858, maid; and (7) Sidney Perret (b. 181) who married Claire Braud.

The children of Placide Perret and Fannie Perret were:
(1) Hélène Perret who married Ernest Pécot; (2) Placide

Perret III, who died in youth; (3) Emma Perret who married Fernand Pécot; (4) Marie Perret who married Noel Barrios; (5) Fannie Perret who married Adolphe Sigur; (6) Corinne Perret, maid; (7) Mathilde Perret, maid; and (8) Ursin Perret, well known physician of Franklin, Louisiana, who married Anna Trépagnier.

Seventh Generation Alphonse Perret Line:

The children of Louis Dévenay Perret and Marie Barré were: (1) L. Dévenay Perret II, who married Daria D'Arensbourg; (2) Irma Perret, maid; (3) Aline Perret, maid; (4) Rita Perret who married Elmore Berthelot; (5) Roger Perret who died in youth; (6) Michel Perret, no issue; (7) Madelaine Perret, maid; (8) William Perret, no issue; and (9) Marie Perret, maid.

From the first marriage of Pierre Henri Perret with Ida Dupas, one child was born: (1) Jeanne Perret who married Ray Starr.

From the second marriage of Pierre Henri Perret with Julia Morel, three children were born: (1) Marguerite Perret who married Thomas McMurry; (2) Lolita Perret who married Winton Waguespack; and (3) Henry Perret, Jr., no issue.

The children of Joseph Ernest Perret and Héléna Belle were: (1) Norman Perret; (2) May Perret; (3) Vivian Perret; (4) Wister Perret; (5) Ernest Perret, III; (6) Ruby Perret; and (7) Warren Perret.

The children of George Joseph Perret and Emilie Leefe were: (1) Louise Perret who married Edward A. Sentille; (2) Adèle Perret who married James Murphy; and (3) George Perret, II, who married Cecile Frances Reinecke.

From the marriage of Edouard Perret and Mathilde Sigur, one child was born: (1) Stella Perret who married Mr. Boudreaux.

The children of Alphonse Perret and Sophie Gaignier were: (1) Evéla Perret who married Oscar Berro; (2) Soline Perret, who married, first, Henri Comes and, second, Lucien Troscler; (3) James Perret; (4) Haydée Perret; (5) Anatole Perret; (6) Icar Perret who married Bertha Fraering, (7) Estelle Perret, maid; (8) Emilie

Perret, nun; and (9) Alphonse Perret, who died in infancy.

The children of Drausin Perret and Marie Lucie Courmes were: (1) Marie Lucie Perret, born 1889, died 1890; and (2) St. John Perret, born 1887, who married, first, Joanna D'Aquin and, second, Mabel Leslie Louderbough.

The children of Felix Perret and Valérie Villavaso were: (1) Joseph Perret who married Marie de Ayala; (2) Léonie Perret who married Achille Guibet; and (3) Celeste Perret who married Emile Plauché.

From the marriage of Sidney Perret and Claire Braud, one child was born: (1) Edmund J. Perret.

The children of Charles Henry Perret and Blanche Rivet were: (1) Marie Perret, maid; (2) Zoé Perret, who died in youth; (3) Jeanne Perret, Mother Saint Henry, acting Provincial for the Northwest Division of the Ursuline Order; (4) Dr. Joseph Maxime Perret who married Inez Shirley Aléman; (5) Edna Perret, maid; (6) Stella Perret who married Wallace Victor Jeanfreau; and (7) Charles Henry Perret, Jr., who married Marie Louise Whitman.

The children of Dr. Ursin Perret and Anna Trépagnier were: (1) Frank Perret; (2) Norbit Perret; (3) Stanley Perret; (4) Roland Perret; (5) May Perret; (6) Sterling Perret; and (7) Anna Fannie Perret.

Eighth Generation Alphonse Perret Line:

From the first marriage of St. John Perret with Joanna D'Aquin the following children were born: (1) Charlotte Adélaïde Perret; and (2) Charles Pierre Perret.

The children of Dr. Joseph Maxime Perret and Inez Shirley Aléman were: (1) J. Maxime Perret, II; (2) Henry Camille Perret; (3) James Thomas Perret; (4) Joseph Paul Perret; and (5) Joseph William Perret.

The children of Charles Henry Perret, Jr., and Marie Louise Whitman were: (1) Charles Henry Perret, II; and (2) Philip Donald Perret.

The children of Joseph Perret and Marie de Ayala were: (1) Marie Perret; (2) Felix Perret; (3) Joseph F. Perret who married Lydia Beiting; (4) Milton Perret; (5) Martine Perret; (6) Carmen Perret; (7) William Perret; (8) Clifford Perret; and (9) John Perret.

Fourth Generation Alexis Perret Line:

The children of Alexis Perret and Miss Bossier were: (1) Ulalie Perret, maid; (2) Justine Perret who married Joseph Perret; (3) Godefroy Perret who married Dorothé Perret; and (4) Justin Perret who married Adéline Perret.

Fifth Generation Alexis Perret Line:

Justin Perret and Adéline Perret were the father and mother of: (1) Gustave Justin Perret who married, first, Marianne Alix St. Martin and, second, Célestine St. Martin.

Sixth Generation Alexis Perret Line:

From the first marriage of Gustave Justin Perret with Marian Alix St. Martin, the following children were born: (1) Pierre Savignien Perret; (2) Evéline Perret, maid; (3) Marie Amazélie Perret, maid; (4) Joséphine Adèle Perret; and (5) Joseph Gustave Perret who married Stéphanie Montz.

From the second marriage of Gustave Justin Perret with Célestine St. Martin, two sons were born: (1) Anatole Perret; and (2) Emilien Perret, both of whom died without issue.

Seventh Generation Alexis Perret Line:

The children of Joseph Gustave Perret and Stéphanie Montz were: (1) Evéline Perret who married Danna Montz; and (2) Justin Perret who married Miss Barrios.

Fourth Generation Joseph Perret Line:

The children of Joseph Perret and Miss Bossier were: (1) Dorothé Perret who married Godefroy Perret; (2) Celéste Perret who married Zénon D'Arensbourg; (3) Joséphine Perret who married Alexandre Macé; (4) Norbert Perret who married Roseline Perret; (5) Adéline Perret who married Justin Perret; (6) Valérie Perret, maid; (7) Victorien Perret, no issue; (8) Evéline Perret, maid; and (9) Lise Perret, maid.

Fourth Generation Pujol Perret Line:

From the first marriage of Pujol Perret with Héléna Bossier the following children were born: (1) Mathilde Perret who married Gustave D'Arensbourg; (2) Amélie

Perret who married Joseph Fabre; (3) Héléna Perret who married a Professor Coudroy, tutor in Pujol Perret's household; (4) Mélanie Perret who married Ludger Perret; (5) Marie Perret who married Daniel Perret; and (6) Ursin Perret, born 1797, who in 1816 married Françoise Pain, born 1802, died 1899.

From the marriage of Pujol Perret with Laura de la Tour, two children were born: (1) Lucien Perret who died a bachelor; and (2) Henriette Perret who married her brother-in-law, widower Coudroy.

Fifth Generation Pujol Perret Line:

From the marriage of Ursin Perret with Françoise Pain the following children were born: (1) Victor Joseph Perret who died at birth; (2) Sidonie Perret, born 1820, a gifted writer, who married Louis Pelletier de la Houssaye (q. v.); (3) Elodie Perret, born 1822, who married Charles Armelain; (4) Valérie Perret, born 1827, who married Sostain de Neufbourg; (5) Corinne Perret, born 1829, who married Alexander Laclair Fuselier; (6) Ursin Perret, born 1832, died 1851, a bachelor; (7) Azoline Perret, born 1831, who married Théodore Fay; (8) Fannie Perret, born 1836, who married Placide Perret; and (9) Léon Perret who married Lévie Freret.

Sixth Generation Pujol Perret Line:

The children of Léon Perret and Lévie Freret were: (1) George Perret who married Elizabeth Kronlage; (2) Léonie Perret who married Daniel Webster; (3) Lévie Perret who married Bentz Braud; and (4) Octavie Perret who married Gustave Louis Klein.

Seventh Generation Pujol Line:

From the marriage of George Perret and Elizabeth Kronlage, one child was born: (1) Elizabeth Perret, maid.

Fourth Generation Charles Perret Line:

The children of Charles Perret and Louise D'Arensbourg were: (1) Charles Perret, Jr., born 1792, died 1836, who in 1812 married Constance de Vaugine, born 1793, died 1871; (2) Evariste Perret, born 1794, died 1817, who in

1815 married Emilie Delhommer; (3) Euphrasie Perret, born 1798, died 1851, who in 1812 married Pierre Dolhonde; (4) Louise Perret, born 1806, died 1865, who in 1822 married, first, her cousin Drausin Perret and, second, Pierre Auguste St. Martin (q. v.); (5) Amélie Perret, born 1796, died 1809; (6) Rosémond Perret, born 1801, died 1809; and (7) Felix Perret, born 1803, died 1809.

Fifth Generation Charles Perret Line:

The children of Charles Perret, Jr. and Constance de Vaugine were: (1) Constance Perret, born 1813, died 1858, who married Joseph Marie Girod, a nephew of Nicholas Girod, the fourth mayor of New Orleans who built the historic house at Chartres and St. Louis Streets, familiarly known as the 'Napoleon House'. Joseph Girod and Constance Perret were the grandparents of Miss Marie Dumestre, student, writer and principal of the French Union School in New Orleans. (2) Charles Perret, III, born 1815, died 1845, no issue; (3) Pierre Perret, born 1818, died 1872, who married Athénaïs Boudousquié; (4) Louis Perret, born 1821, who married Amanda Kerr; (5) Louise Amélie Perret, born 1824, died 1850, who married George Rixner and became the mother of Amélie Rixner who married the count de Sarzana, an Italian nobleman; (6) Evariste Perret, born 1827, who died in youth; (7) Désirée Perret, born 1829, who married Edward Pilsbury; and (8) Héléna Perret who married Dr. Paul Jégou.

From the marriage of Evariste Perret and Emilie Delhommer one child was born: (1) Emilie Perret who married Dr. Alexander Humphreys.

Sixth Generation Charles Perret Lines

The children of Pierre Perret and Athénaïs Boudousquié were: (1) Athénaïs Perret, born 1839, maid; (2) Constance Azéma Perret, born 1840, who married Prosper Trouard; (3) Pierre Perret, Jr., born 1842, died 1864, no issue; (4) Adélaïde Perret, born 1844, died 1887, who married Dr. John Thompson; (5) Alix Perret who married James Johnston; (6) Paul Charles Perret who married Valérie Perret; (7) Aristide Perret who died in youth; (8) Adrian Perret who married Rose de Lisle; (9) Amédée

Perret who died in youth; (10) Gustave Perret, no issue; and (11) Jeanne Anaïs Perret who married Charles Little-page.

The children of Louis Perret and Amanda Kerr were: (1) Eliot Perret, no issue; (2) Valérie Perret who married Paul Charles Perret; (3) Victor Perret; (4) Charles Perret; (5) Louis Perret; (6) Pierre Perret; (7) Amélie Perret who married Joseph Deléry; and (8) Jules Perret.

Seventh Generation Charles Perret Line:

The children of Paul Charles Perret and Valérie Perret were: (1) Paul Joseph Perret; (2) Edwin Watrous Perret, no issue; (3) Norbert Sidney Perret who married Annie Graham; (4) Adrian Elliott Perret who married Inez Le-Blanc Cline; (5) Jane Anaïs Perret who married Felix Richard von Reich; (6) Pierre Charles Perret; (7) Valérie Athénaïs Perret who married Robert van Dolson; and (8) Joseph Deléry Perret who married Cecilia Usner.

The children of Adrian Perret and Rose de Lisle were: (1) Louis Alix Perret; (2) Jane Valérie Perret; and (3) Rose Perret.

Compiled by St John Perret from family documents and archives.

The obverse and reverse of the Cross of the Order of St Louis conferred on the Chevalier Charles Frederich d'Arensbourg, now in the possession of the Perret family.

FAVROT Family

THE conquest and colonization of the great Western world, by the nationalities of Europe brought into prominence many colorful pioneers who were transplanted into strange surroundings to face new dangers and to endure many hardships. Fortitude, indomitable will, and devotion to duty prompted the scions of men of prominence and standing in the Old World to venture into the New as will be found in the following sketch of the Favrot family.

Sieur Joseph Claude de Favrot, engineer of camps and fortifications under Vauban, was the progenitor of a well-known and long-established Louisiana family. In his native country, France, Sieur Joseph Claude de Favrot was a brigadier in the armies of Louis XIV, and one of the constructors of the celebrated Verdun fortress, which gained such prominence in the news of the World War. He was born at Saint-Vigne, five leagues from Besençon, and in 1694 he married Mlle. Françoise de Bouvier. After her husband's death in 1709 she married Joseph de Dondel, Lord of Grand Pré. She died in 1776.

The children of Joseph de Favrot and Françoise de Bouvier were four in number: the first, a daughter, became a *religieuse* and afterwards *abbesse* of a convent in France; the second, another daughter, died *femme seul;* the third, his first son "married below himself," was disinherited, went to Germany, where he attained high rank. One of his sons, returning to France during the French Revolution fell a victim to The Terror. The fourth and last child, was also a son. He was named Claude Joseph de Favrot, (differing from his father's name in that the first and second names are transposed), when he was baptised in the Church of

Notre Dame two days after his birth at Versailles, on September 6, 1701.

He entered the service of France in 1732, qualifying as a lieutenant. He came to Louisiana about a year later with a commission of captain in the French Colonial troops. The trials that beset him and the hardships endured can be best recited in some of the duties assigned to him. In 1734 he was ordered by Bienville to go in a pirogue with six soldiers to the Tunikas and to command there as well as at Pointe Coupée. In 1739 he was ordered to Illinois with four ships, 36 soldiers, 10 savages and 26 negroes to take charge. In 1740 he was ordered to take command at the Balize. In 1742 he was ordered back to Pointe Coupée. In 1747 he was ordered to take command at Natchitoches. In 1751 he was ordered by Kerlérec to take charge of a convoy destined for Illinois after which he was sent to Mobile to command the garrison at that point. In 1754 he was ordered back to the fort of Illinois and there he remained at Fort DuQuesne in charge, with instructions to send a report of the trip indicating rivers and other points of importance.

After distinguished service under the Bourbon Kings for more than thirty years, he was ordered by Louis XV in 1764 to appear and deliver an address before receiving the coveted order—that of Knight of St. Louis.

On October 4, 1736 he was married to Louise Bruslé, daughter of Philip Antoine Bruslé and Marie Faumont; this marriage had been sanctioned by his grandmother Bouvier in France when she wrote him in 1727 "to marry whom he pleased and in whatever country."

It was only after the death of his wife that he was furloughed, went to France to receive the honors above mentioned, and while there he married again the widow Goulet, whom he left one month after the ceremony. In 1777 he fell ill in France and was treated at the Charity Hospital of Senlis where he died.

Of the union of Claude Joseph de Favrot and Louise Bruslé were born two children: a daughter Louise Favrot on September 11, 1737, who married Chevalier de Clouet May 18, 1761. She died in 1814.

The son, Pierre Joseph de Favrot, who, during the Span-

ish domination of Louisiana, was best known as Don Pedro
José Favrot, was born in New Orleans July 16, 1749.
He married Francesca Gérard February 12, 1782 in New
Orleans, and served in the French colonial army as captain
of infantry when the *fleur-de-lys* waved over Louisiana.
When his native land went under the domination of the Dons
in 1763, after serving some years in the French Islands, he
continued his military career and was made *Captain de Gren.
del Regimiente de Infanteria de la Louisiana*, and earned an
honorable and enviable reputation in this service.

Commissioned first lieutenant in 1773 he was immediately
assigned to Fort Rochefort. In 1774 he was ordered on a
boat with a detachment of two hundred men to serve in a
regiment in St. Domingo, also to give detailed accounts of
the voyage and to act as judge in the complaints made by the
soldiers. In 1776 he was assigned to take command of one
hundred eighty soldiers from the ship *Père de Famille* and
take them to the Isle of Martinique.

In 1778 he was granted permission by the French King
to return to Louisiana and with highest recommendation to
the Spanish Crown, he was received by the King of Spain
and given the same honors he held in the French Army. He
was ordered by Don Carlos de Grand Pré to take charge
of the fort at Plaquemine. Later he was designated commandant at Baton Rouge where he served for two years.
He then was sent to Mobile where he remained three years
and at the expiration of his term in 1787 the citizens of Mobile petitioned the governor to order their commander Don
Pedro to remain with them.

When Governor Galvez routed the English troops out of
Baton Rouge in 1779 during the American War of Independence, Don Pedro de Favrot was named commandant
of the fort after its capture. He rose to the rank of lieutenant
colonel in the Spanish army, was made commandant of Fort
St. Philip, below the city of New Orleans, and it was he
who turned over this fortress to the French commissioners
when Spain retroceded Louisiana. He saw the *tricolor* wave
over the colony for the scant space of twenty days, then
watched its red, white and blue drop from the pole to make

way for a new banner of fifteen stripes of red and white and fifteen white stars on a field of blue.

Thereupon he forsook his military career, retired to a plantation he had purchased on the west bank of the Mississippi river nearly opposite Baton Rouge, which was then American soil and prepared to live out the rest of his life in peace and contentment.

Pierre Joseph de Favrot by his marriage to Francesca Gérard, became the father of three sons and three daughters. They were in the order of their birth:

1.—Joséphine Favrot, born October 31, 1785, died April 8, 1836. She was the bethrothed of Louis de Grand Pré, who fell at the taking of the Baton Rouge fort by the West Florida patriots in 1810. She never married, remaining true to her martyred bethrothed. She became a talented artist.

2.—T. Philogene Favrot, born May 4, 1791, died February 11, 1822. He was commissioned by President Madison as ensign in the 24th regular U. S. Infantry on July 23, 1812; participated in the Battle of Orleans; was elected judge in his parish of West Baton Rouge, and was killed in a duel in 1822. He never married.

3.—Louis Favrot, born April 13, 1788, died June 28, 1876, who married Augustine Eulalie Duplantier, and left a son and daughter.

4.—Henry Bouvier Favrot, born April 11, 1799, died December 24, 1881, who married Aurore de Villars, and left three sons and four daughters.

5.—Octavine Favrot, born September 4, 1795, died October 30, 1868, unmarried.

6.—Pulchérie Favrot, born September 13, 1803, died September 7, 1846, unmarried.

Louis Favrot, the second son of Don Pedro Favrot and Francesca Gérard, married Augustine Eulalie Duplantier in 1819. She was of a well known family and was born in 1799. He studied law and succeeded his brother Philogene as parish judge, a position he filled until the outbreak of the Civil War. As best he could he undertook a study of medicine and when not practicing law, for years he administered to the wants of all who sought his services without recompense. In this fashion he lived at the old Favrot homestead until his death in 1876. By his union with Mlle. Duplantier there issued two children: a son, Henri Mortimer Favrot, born November 1, 1826, and a daughter, Augustine Favrot, who married Dr. William Regnaud.

Henry M. Favrot received his early education at Transylvania, Kentucky. Returning to Louisiana he studied law and practiced in his native parish and in Baton Rouge. His life was colorful and he was honored with many positions of public trust. He served one term in the state senate, as a member of the constitutional convention of 1879. He was for many years superintendent of education of West Baton Rouge, and a member of the board of supervisors of the Louisiana State University. While attending a meeting of this board April 1, 1887, he was stricken with apoplexy from which he died fifteen days later.

At the outbreak of the Civil War he organized the Delta Rifles in West Baton Rouge, was made captain, and with this command participated in some of the great battles between the states notably at Shiloh, at the Hornet's Nest, and at Mansfield, in all engagements performing meritorious service.

H. M. Favrot was subsequently raised to the rank of colonel and appointed by Governor Allen of Louisiana to go to Virginia and collect all the records of the Louisiana troops in Virginia. He made the trip to and from Virginia on horseback and guarded his records until the reconstruction days were ended when they were delivered to General Beauregard, adjutant general of the state militia under Governor Nicholls.

Henry Mortimer Favrot married Célestine Dubroca in West Baton Rouge on August 12, 1862, and from this union born were seven children: Henry Louis Favrot, Charles Allen Favrot, Edgar Dubroca Favrot, William Reynaud Favrot, Leo Mortimer Favrot, Louise Favrot, and Corinne Favrot.

Henry Louis Favrot, oldest son of H. M. Favrot, born July 21, 1864, was married to Marie Louise Richmond of Savannah, Georgia, on November 5, 1902. From this marriage were born two children: Henry Richmond Favrot, and Allain DeClouet Favrot.

H. L. Favrot was an ardent student of Louisiana history and accumulated an extensive collection of documents bearing on many phases of the state's history. He studied law and moved to New Orleans where he practiced until his death February 21, 1918. He was active in the militia of the state and volunteered in 1898, receiving a commission as captain and adjutant of the Second Louisiana Regiment during the Spanish-American War. He served in Cuba and after his return to New Orleans continued the practice of his profession. He also served two terms as state senator from his district.

Henry Bouvier Favrot, the third son of Don Pedro Favrot, who married Aurore de Villars of New Orleans, became the father of three sons and four daughters. The sons were: (a) St. Clair Joseph Favrot, who was killed during the Civil War while in the service of the Confederacy; (b) Charles Didier Favrot, who married Ada Kent and whose son became George K. Favrot, former member of Congress from the Baton Rouge district, and (c) Joseph Claude Favrot, who married Miss Williamson and became the father of J. St. Clair Favrot of Baton Rouge. The daughters of Bouvier Favrot and Aurore de Villars were: Aurore, Joséphine, Octavine, and Evéline.

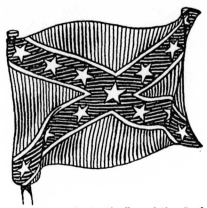

The Stars and Bars, the battle flag of the Confederacy.

THEARD Family

BRITTANY has contributed to Louisiana many estimable families and among those of high intellectual attainments is numbered that of Théard. Rene Théard, its earliest known author, lived near Vitré and married, about the year 1730, Madeleine Lemoine. His life was an uneventful one and he died on his native soil leaving two sons, Jean and René Nicolas Théard. Jean, the eldest, resided until his death in *Bretagne* and left a numerous progeny, represented by many of his name to be found to-day in Algiers, (Algeria) and in Brittany.

René Nicolas Théard, his younger brother, was born April 8, 1758, in the *commune du Tertre*, near Vitré. When the French Revolution broke out, being a fervent Roman Catholic and an ardent Royalist, René Nicolas was forced to flee in order to escape the merciless *guillotine*. He eventually arrived in Santo Domingo and from this island he sailed for New York, where, among other San Domingan exiles who had preceeded him there, he met a certain Sieur Robert, and married his daughter, Marie Rose Robert.

René Nicolas Théard being an architect of exceptional ability and Louisiana offering an inviting field for the exercise of his talents, he went there with his bride and established his home at or near the present site of Paincourtville, in Assumption parish. At this time New Orleans had inaugurated ambitious plans for the construction of new public buildings and the architect Théard was called upon to supervise the erection of many of them. His fame having spread beyond the confines of his adopted state, he was selected by the Federal Government as assistant architect for the construction of the Military Academy at West Point, on the Hudson. In his leisure moments he availed himself of his mechanical skill to devise useful inventions, among which the first working plans for a mill to saw and polish marble are attributed to his genius.

From his marriage to Marie Rose Robert, René Nicolas Théard had three sons and one daughter, all born in Louisiana. They were: (a) René Théard the eldest, whose wife was Agatina Robert and who left as issue two daughters and three sons named William, René and Numa Théard; (b) François Théard, the second son, who married Adélaïde Michel, of Charleston, South Carolina, and left two children, Rodolphe and Amélie Théard; (c) Thomas Théard, the third son, born in Assumption Parish, Louisiana, October 31, 1804, who married, in France, Clémence Delvaille; (d) Marie Constance Théard, whose nuptials to the Count Andre Douat-Deyrem were celebrated in France.

René Nicolas Théard, in spite of his success in America, had not forgotten *la belle France*. When the Bourbons were restored to power, he returned in 1818 to the land of his birth, accompanied by his only daughter, Marie Constance Théard and his youngest son, Thomas Théard. He died in Bordeaux January 11, 1843, at the age of eighty-five, and is buried in the cemetery of *La Chartreuse*. His daughter who became the Comtesse Douat-Deyrem, left two children who died without issue.

Thomas Théard, was educated in the *College de Sainte Foi*, in Bordeaux. He married Clémence Delvaille, adopted a journalistic career, and returned to New Orleans in 1827. From 1849 to 1853 he served as editor-in-chief of *L'Abeille de la Nouvelle Orleans*. He was honored with many public offices, being in turn secretary to the mayor of New Orleans, superintendent of the public schools of the second district, member of the city council, city comptroller and state representative in Baton Rouge. His political career though distinguished was not greater than his record as a writer on historical, philosophical and scientific subjects. His union to Clémence Delvaille was blessed with three sons and one daughter, Paul Emile Théard, Joseph Oscar Théard, James Camille Théard and Claire Antoinette Laure Théard.

Clémence Delvaille, wife of Thomas Théard, preceeded him to the grave and at her demise, he married Clémentine Laroque-Turgeau, daughter of a well-known notary of New

Orleans. From this second union were born three sons, Arthur David Aloysius Théard, Charles Camille Théard, and Septime Lucien Théard. Thomas Théard died in New Orleans September 22, 1873.

Paul Emile Théard, was born in New Orleans December 20, 1828. He became a leader at the bar, served in the Confederate army, and was appointed judge of the Fourth District Court of New Orleans April 3, 1865. As gifted as was his father, Paul Emile contributed remarkable articles to the *Revue Louisianaise*, the Louisiana *Courrier* and other publications, and was ranked among the talented Southern writers. He was also a brilliant orator and received from Pope Leo XIII the decoration of knight of St. Gregory. He married Marguerite Athenaïse Pilié, daughter of Joseph Pilié and Thérese Deynaut. The father of his bride was an architect of extraordinary ability. From the Théard-Pilié marriage issued: (a) George Henry Théard, well-known judge of the Civil District Court in New Orleans for many years, who died unmarried; (b) Charles Joseph Théard, a distinguished lawyer and financier, and present vice-president of the Canal Bank, who married Corinne Baudier and has no children; (c) Alfred Louis Théard, prominent civil engineer, who married Marie Delvaille and had three children, Delvaille H. Théard, New Orleans attorney, Albert L. Théard, architect, and Marie Théard; (d) Sidney Louis Théard, who died in 1910 and was a leader in the medical profession; (e) Marie Thérese Emma Théard, and (f) Marie Joséphine Mathilde Théard, both unmarried.

ST. MARTIN Family

ON the 4th of July, 1632, the Royal French frigate *l'Espérance en Dieu*, escorting two transports, set sail from d'Auray bound for Acadia. The Treaty of Saint-Germain en Laye had just been signed recognizing for the first time Acadia as a French possession, and the Sieur Isaac de Razilly, on instructions from Cardinal Richelieu, was proceeding with three hundred men, recruited from Touraine and Brittany, to take delivery of Port Royal from the English and to establish there a permanent colony.

Among the followers of de Razilly who debarked at *la Hève* on the 8th of September, 1632, were Pierre Martin, his wife, Catherine Vigneau and their young son, also named Pierre, aged six. They were peasants from Brittany. In 1636, Pierre Martin and his wife had moved to Port Royal and in the same year a second son was born to them. He was named Mathieu and was the first child of French parentage born in Acadia. This circumstance earned for Mathieu, in 1680, an enfeoffment of lands near Grand Pré and a noble particule which rechristened him Sieur Mathieu de Saint-Martin.

According to all Acadian censuses, but contrary to the tradition heretofore prevailing, Mathieu de Saint-Martin never married. His title, therefore, descended upon the progeny of his older brother, Pierre Martin.

The profligate and unfortunate expenditure of thirty millions by France in the early part of the eighteenth century for the fortification of Louisbourg on *Ile Royal*, now Cape Breton Isle, attracted numerous Acadians. Thus, it came about that Pierre Bauchet de Saint-Martin, the immediate progenitor of our Louisiana family, and a descendant in the fourth generation of the original Pierre, was born in that fortified port about 1723. Early in life Pierre Bauchet St.

Martin shipped before the mast. He participated in the war of 1744 and witnessed the taking of the citadel at Louisbourg by the Yankees from Boston in June, 1745. In 1750 he was captain of his ship. What caused him to steer his course to Louisiana is not known, nor why it was that he resigned his commission after arriving here.

In 1758, having become a prosperous farmer with an extensive plantation on the present site of Algiers, he took unto himself as wife, Charlotte Thérèse Gallot. After an active and successful life, during which he begot five children, he died, a patriarch, in 1805.

Second Generation:

The children of Pierre Bauchet St. Martin and Charlotte Thérèse Gallot were: (1) Charlotte St. Martin (b. 1759), who died a maid; (2) Pierre Bauchet St. Martin II (b. 1761, d. 1830), who married, first, Genevieve Thérèse de Callongne, widow of Antoine Chouriac and, second, Marianne Perret, widow of Louis Pain; (3) Louis St. Martin (b. 1762), who died in infancy; (4) François Louis Bauchet St. Martin (b. 1766), who married first a Miss St. Amant and second a Miss Roussel, widow Folse; and (5) Marie Felicité St. Martin (b. 1768, d. 1838), wife of the celebrated Jean Baptiste Labatut, who later became a commanding general in the historic battle of New Orleans .

Pierre Bauchet St. Martin II was a distinguished citizen, incorruptable in honor, calm in judgment, judicial in mind, and prudent in counsel. He was, at different times, judge in the parish of St. Charles and speaker of the first state legislature elected by the people which assembled in New Orleans in 1812. His brother François was also a member of the legislature of 1812 and a signer of the first state constitution.

Third Generation Pierre Bauchet Line:

From the marriage of Pierre Bauchet St. Martin II, and Thérèse de Callongne, two children were born; (1) Aimée, who married Doctor Yves Le Monnier, the owner and builder of the three-story residence corner of Royal and St. Charles Streets, immortalized by Cable as the home of "Sieur George", and (2) Pierre Bauchet St. Martin III, a

captain in the war of 1812. He married Célestine Perret
(q. v.). From the second marriage of Pierre Bauchet St.
Martin II and Marianne Perret, there were no descendants.

Fourth Generation Pierre Bauchet Line:

From the marriage of Pierre Bauchet St. Martin III and
Célestine Perret (q. v.), eight children were born: (1) Jean
Alcide St. Martin, who married Adéle Dolhonde; (2)
Pierre Auguste St. Martin (b. 1808, d. 1895), for several
years registrar of the United States Land Office at New
Orleans, who married first, Gustavie D'Arensbourg, and
second, Louise Perret, the widow of Drausin Perret (q. v.);
(3) François Bauchet St. Martin (b. 1810, d. 1893), who
married first, Cécile Perret (q. v.), and second, Calista
Montégut; (4) Célestine St. Martin, and (5) Alix St.
Martin, both of whom married G. Justin Perret (q. v.);
(6) Françoise St. Martin, who died a maid; (7) Delphine
St. Martin, who married Lucien Montégut and left numerous
descendants, and (8) Louis St. Martin (b. 1820, d. 1893),
who married Louisa Perret (q. v.). Louis St. Martin, widely
known as "Colonel" St. Martin, was the first registrar of
voters in New Orleans, being then the only Democrat in the
city hall when the "Know Nothing" party was in power.
He was elected to Congress in 1851, 1866, 1868, and 1884.

Fifth Generation Pierre Bauchet Line:

From the marriage of Jean Alcide St. Martin and Adèle
Dolhonde, four children were born: (1) An unnamed
daughter who died in infancy; (2) Henry St. Martin and
(3) Thomas St. Martin, both of whom died without issue;
and (4) Edmond St. Martin, who married Adèle Perret
(q. v.).

From the marriage of Pierre Auguste St. Martin and
Gustavie D'Arensbourg, three children were born: (1)
Gustavie St. Martin and (2) Aimée St. Martin, both of
whom died maids and (3) Mathilde St. Martin who married Théophile Perret (q. v.).

From the second marriage of Pierre Auguste St. Martin
with Louise Perret, four children were born: (1) J. Alfred
St. Martin; (2) Félix St. Martin; (3) Amélie St. Martin,
all three of whom died without issue, and (4) Pierre Edou-

ard St. Martin (b. 1842, d. 1919), planter, philosopher and writer, who married Isabella Devenport.

From the marriage of François Bauchet St. Martin and Cécile Perret, four children were born, all of whom died without issue; (1) Héloise St. Martin; (2) Delphine St. Martin; (3) John St. Martin and (4) François St. Martin. From the second marriage of François Bauchet St. Martin with Calista Montégut, seven children were born; (1) Charles St. Martin, who married Delphine Montégut; (2) Paul St. Martin, who married Clémentine Lorio; (3) George St. Martin, who married Louise Montégut; (4) Alfred St. Martin, who married Marie Chénet; (5) Caroline St. Martin, who married Alex Chénet; (6) Blanche St. Martin, maid; and (7) Célestine St. Martin, maid.

From the marriage of Louis St. Martin and Louisa Perret, seven children were born. (1) Corinne St. Martin (b. 1848, d. 1928), unmarried; (2) L. Albert St. Martin, (b. 1851), unmarried; (3) Stéphanie St. Martin (b. 1853, d. 1922), unmarried; (4) Aimée St. Martin (b. 1856, d. 1929), unmarried; (5) J. Robert St. Martin (b. 1860, d. 1872); (6) Eusèbe St. Martin, who died in infancy; and (7) Bertha St. Martin (b. 1872), who in 1911 married Armand Edouard St. Martin.

Sixth Generation Pierre Bauchet Line:

From the marriage of Edmond St. Martin and Adèle Perret, one child was born: (1) Louise St. Martin.

From the marriage of Pierre Edouard St. Martin and Isabella Devenport, two sons were born. (1) Armand Edouard St. Martin (b. 1871), who in 1911 married Bertha St. Martin, (no issue); (2) Joseph Preston St. Martin (b. 1878), who married Daisy Patten.

From the marriage of Charles St. Martin and Delphine Montégut, seven children were born: (1) Charles St. Martin who married Denise Ory, (no issue); (2) Pierre Bauchet St. Martin, who married Lizette LaBarre, (many small children); (3) Robert St. Martin, who married Bertha Lyons, (one child); (4) Lionel St. Martin, who married Ada Soileau, (many small children); (5) Amélie St. Martin, maid; (6) Lize St. Martin, maid; (7) Caroline St. Martin, who married Cecil Hooper.

From the marriage of Paul St. Martin and Clémentine Lorio, five children were born: (1) Nelson St. Martin who married Phénolise Catoire, (many small children); (2) John St. Martin who married Martha Andry, (many small children); (3) Denis St. Martin, unmarried; (4) Noélie St. Martin who married Robert Hoeffer and (5) Alice St. Martin who married Lawrence Regan.

From the marriage of George St. Martin and Louise Montégut, six children were born: (1) George St. Martin, unmarried; (2) Lee St. Martin who married Helène Sénac; (3) Norman St. Martin, unmarried; (4) Odile St. Martin who married Alexander Gaudin; (5) Calista St. Martin who married Percy Branninger; (6) Rita St. Martin who married Charles Prados.

From the marriage of Alfred St. Martin and Marie Chénet, two children were born: (1) Mildred St. Martin who married Hampton Percy, and (2) Lucille St. Martin, unmarried.

Seventh Generation Pierre Bauchet Line:

From the marriage of Joseph Preston St. Martin and Daisy Patten, five children were born: (1) Isabel St. Martin who married Sidney Louis Reynaud; (2) Ruth St. Martin who married Wm. Edward Ulmer; (3) Hilda St. Martin, who married William Winthrop Messersmith, Jr.; (4) Joseph Preston St. Martin, Jr., unmarried; and (5) Maurice Edward St. Martin, unmarried.

The progeny of Pierre Bauchet St. Martin II to the present generation having been traced, the progeny of his brother François Louis Bauchet St. Martin follows:

Third Generation François Bauchet Line:

From the marriage of François Louis Bauchet St. Martin and Miss St. Amant, the following children were born: (1) François Bauchet St. Martin II who married Miss Bernoudy; (2) Hermina St. Martin who married Valsin Wiltz; (3) Céleste St. Martin who married Zénon Boudousquié.

Fourth Generation François Bauchet Line:

From the marriage of François Bauchet St. Martin II to Miss Bernoudy, seven children were born: (1) Octavie St. Martin who married Alexander Faurie; (2) Emélina St. Martin who married Pierre Dolhonde; (3) Célicourt St.

Martin who married Miss Aime; (4) Noël St. Martin, distinguished citizen of St. Charles parish, who married another Miss Aime; (5) Septime St. Martin, prominent planter of Jefferson Parish, who married Cidalie Sarpy; and (6), (7), two other daughters, both of whom married Alfred Delery.

Fifth Generation François Bauchet Line:

From the marriage of Cëlicourt St. Martin and Miss Aime, two children were born: (1) John St. Martin and (2) Alicia St. Martin who became a nun.

From the marriage of Noël St. Martin and Miss Aime, six children were born: (1) Valcour St. Martin who died without issue; (2) François St. Martin who died without issue; (3) Noélie St. Martin who married Alphonse Becnel, and left numerous descendants; (4) Nathalie St. Martin who married Albert Becnel and left numerous descendants; (5) Amélie St. Martin who married Alphonse Carrière and left many descendants; and (6) Anaïs St. Martin, maid.

From the marriage of Septime St. Martin and Cidalie Sarpy, five children were born: (1) George St. Martin, (no progeny); (2) Jean Baptiste St. Martin, (no progeny); (3) Septime St. Martin, (no progeny); (4) William St. Martin who married Alice Kilpatrick; and (5) F. Lestang St. Martin who married first, Angèle Mayronne and second, Wilhelmina Cawthon.

Sixth Generation François Bauchet Line:

From the marriage of William St. Martin and Alice Kilpatrick, two daughters were born: (1) Céleste St. Martin who married, first, Dr. William Patton, and, second, Dr. Randolph Lyon; and (2) Cidelle St. Martin who married James L. Rice.

From the marriage of Lestang St. Martin and Angèle Mayronne, one son was born: (1) Sidney St. Martin who married Zoé Vicknair, and has several children. From the second marriage of Lestang St. Martin with Wilhelmina Cawthon, no children were born.

In public life, the St. Martin family, at various times, has attained prominence. In private life, it has always been distinguished for adherence to ideals prompted by a steadfast faith.

Compiled by St. John Perret from family documents and archives.

WILKINSON Family

THE name of Wilkinson occupies a conspicuous niche in Louisiana's Hall of Fame. It was first brought to that colony when it was under the domination of Spain by James Wilkinson, a hero of the Revolutionary War, who became distinguished as the American who opened the Mississippi River to the trade of the interior of the continent and secured for the settlers of Kentucky the right of deposit of their goods at New Orleans.

James Wilkinson was born at Benedict, Calvert county, Maryland, in the year 1757, and died in the City of Mexico December 28, 1825 at the age of sixty-eight. He came of old Welsh stock. The Wilkinsons in Wales married into the Glen Owen family, descendants of Owen Glydwr. The first of the name to emigrate to America was Joseph Wilkinson, who came from England in 1729, and settled on a grant of land in Calvert county, Maryland. He married a Miss Skinner of Maryland, and a son was Joseph Wilkinson Jr., born in 1731, died in 1764, who married Althea Heighe of Maryland. This couple had two sons: the elder being Joseph Wilkinson III, a general in the Revolutionary War, who had two sons: Captain Walter Wilkinson, of the United States army, and Benjamin Wilkinson.

James Wilkinson was the second son of Joseph II, and Miss Heighe. When he was in his twenty-first year, on November 12, 1778, and holding the rank of brigadier general in the Continental army, he married Ann Biddle, daughter of John Biddle of Philadelphia. At the close of the struggle between the colonists and the forces of King George III, James Wilkinson, in 1784, emigrated to Kentucky, founded the town of Frankfort, engaged in mercantile pursuits, and became a leader in politics. He was also a leader among the Kentuckians in their warfare against hostile

Indian tribes and so important did President Washington consider these campaigns that they were the subject of a special message to congress on October 27, 1791. Wilkinson's career in the army during the early struggle for independence had been spectacular. He was studying medicine at eighteen when he abandoned his proposed career and entered the revolutionary army as a private. At twenty he was made a colonel in General Gates' northern army, and from May 1777 to March 1778 he served as adjutant general of the northern department.

Having decided to reenter army life President Washington in December 1791 appointed James Wilkinson a colonel in the regular army where he soon attained the rank of general, and in 1796 was made commander-in-chief of the United States army. In 1803 he was appointed with Governor William C. C. Claiborne one of the two commissioners to receive Louisiana from the French at the time of the Purchase. Claiborne was made governor of the Territory of Orleans and General Wilkinson was made military governor of Upper Louisiana with headquarters at St. Louis. He inspired the exploring expeditions of Long and Pike and took a leading part in resisting the encroachments of Spain in Western Louisiana. He took a prominent part in the War of 1812 in the North, was made a major general and took possession of Mobile. He participated in the campaign against Montreal and then resigned his commission.

After his retirement from the army, General Wilkinson returned to Louisiana and established himself on a plantation 25 miles below New Orleans which he called *Live Oak*. While he was in the City of Mexico in 1825 prosecuting certain claims of New Orleans merchants which would be liquidated by land grants, General Wilkinson was taken ill of fever, and in spite of his strong and rugged constitution died December 28, and was buried in the Baptist Cemetery of the Mexican capital.

General James Wilkinson was twice married. By his first wife, Ann Biddle of Philadelphia, he had three sons: (a) John Wilkinson, born in 1782, died at fourteen in 1796; (b) James Wilkinson Jr., born 1784, died in 1813, and (c) Joseph Biddle Wilkinson, born December 4, 1785, died November 8, 1865, who married Catherine Andrews.

Captain James Wilkinson II, the eldest surviving son of General Wilkinson, was with Z. B. Pike's expedition to the Rocky Mountains in 1806-7 at the age of twenty. He entered the United States army and attained the rank of captain. He was killed in action at Dauphine Island, in Mobile harbor in 1813. He had married a Miss Coleman of Alabama, and had one son, Theophilus Wilkinson, born in 1811, who became an artillery officer in the United States army and died in 1840.

Joseph Biddle Wilkinson, youngest son of General James Wilkinson and Ann Biddle, e n t e r e d the United States navy. He served with Commodore Perry on the Great Lakes, and with Bainbridge in the Mediterranean against the Barbary pirates. He married Catherine Andrews of Williamsburg, Virginia, and became the father of two sons: Robert Andrews Wilkinson, and Joseph Biddle Wilkinson, Jr.

General James Wilkinson's second wife was Célestine Trudeau, a daughter of Charles Laveau Trudeau (q. v.) surveyor general of Louisiana. The marriage was solemized March 5, 1810 in New Orleans. Their issue was twin daughters, born January 23, 1816, named: Marie Isabel, who died in infancy, and Elizabeth Stéphanie Wilkinson who married Professor Toussaint Francois Bigot, September 2, 1833. They had two sons: Charles Arthur Bigot, born May 23, 1834, and Theodore Felix Bigot, born September 21, 1836, both of whom served in the Civil War. The dates of their deaths are unknown and they left no descendants.

Robert Andrews Wilkinson, oldest son of Joseph Biddle Wilkinson and Catherine Andrews, born December 16, 1809, was a lieutenant colonel in the Civil War serving with the Confederacy. He was killed in the Second Battle of Manassas August 30, 1862. He had married Mary F. Stark of Mississippi and they became the parents of six children: Robert A. Wilkinson and Horatio Stark Wilkinson; the daughters were: Katherine, who married Carroll W. Allen; Rose, who married Simeon Toby, and Belle and Mollie Wilkinson.

Dr. J. Biddle Wilkinson, second son of Joseph Biddle Wilkinson and Catherine Andrews, who became a prominent physician and planter of Plaquemines parish, Louisiana, was born April 21, 1817, and died July 22, 1902. He married Josephine Stark and his issue consisted of eight sons and two daughters: (a) J. Biddle Wilkinson, who married Lydia Duval; (b) Theodore S. Wilkinson, who married Pauline Spyker; (c) R. Andrews Wilkinson, who married Lucy White; (e) Horace Wilkinson, who married Julia Merwin; (f) James Wilkinson, who married, first, Mattie Spyker and, second, Cécilia Peters; (g) Ernest Wilkinson, who died at fifteen; (i) Elizabeth Wilkinson, who died at five, and (j) Josephine Wilkinson, who married Thomas Worthington.

Among the numerous descendants of General Wilkinson are: J. Biddle Wilkinson Jr., Philip Wilkinson and Maury Wilkinson, sons of Andrews Wilkinson; Maunsell White Wilkinson and Edward M. Wilkinson, sons of Dr. Clement P. Wilkinson; Leonidas Wilkinson, James Wilkinson, Jr., and Hugh M. Wilkinson, sons of James Wilkinson; Commander Theodore S. Wilkinson, U. S. N., son of Ernest Wilkinson, and Horace Wilkinson, Jr. The sons of Katherine Wilkinson Allen are: Dr. Carroll W. Allen, Robert W. Allen, Henry W. Allen, and Biddle Wilkinson.

The flag of fifteen stars and fifteen stripes that first floated over Louisiana in 1803.

DE LA RONDE Family

WHEN one traces the ancestry of the first de la Ronde who came to Louisiana, the search leads to Canada, and from that province to the ancient town of Tours in Touraine, France. Here it was that one Maturin Denis, Sieur de la Thibaudière, a captain in the Royal Guards, and husband of Mlle. Aubert, died in 1589 and was buried in the church of Saint Simphorien. We read of his son, Jacques Denis de la Thibaudière, who became a military officer of distinction in the armies of Henry III and who married Marie Cosnier de Béseau, daughter of Hugues Cosnier de Béseau and Françoise Jeure.

Now we encounter the son of Jacques Denis and Marie Cosnier in the person of Simon Denis, *écuyer*, surnamed in Canada, Sieur de la Trinité, born in Tours in 1599, who became a captain of the celebrated *régiment de Carignan* and went to Canada during the reign of Louis XIV, and was enrolled in *la Noblesse du* Canada in March of 1668. He became *Receveur Général pour la Compagnie de la Nouvelle France à Quebec*. In his native land, in 1630, he married Jeanne Du Brieul, sister of Sieur Du Brieul, *Procureur du roi au Grénier à Sel de Tours*. They became parents of a son and a daughter. The son, Pierre Denis, *écuyer*, surnamed Sieur de la Ronde, was born in Tours October 8, 1631. He became Grand Master of the Waters and Forests in Canada, and, August 25, 1655, in Quebec, he married Catherine le Neuf de la Poterie, daughter of Jacques le Neuf, Sieur de la Poterie, governor of *Trois Rivières*, and Marguerite le Gardeur de Tilly. Pierre died June 6, 1708, and was buried in the church of the Recollets in Quebec.

This brings us to Louis Pierre Denis, *écuyer*, Sieur de la Ronde, the last child of the just named couple who was born in Quebec August 2, 1765, where he died March 25,

1741. He became a captain in the French colonial troops of the Marine, was made a *Chevalier de l'ordre Royal et Militaire de Saint Louis* in 1724, and earned the distinction of driving the English from Acadia. He was also the royal ambassador sent to England in 1711 from Canada by the governor, Comte de Castabelle. On July 20, 1709, he married Marie Louise Chartier de Lotbinière, daughter of René Louis Chartier de Lotbinière, *Premier Conseiller du Roi*, and member of the supreme council of Quebec, and Marie Lambert. Four sons and three daughters were born of this union, which brings us to the youngest child, named Pierre.

Pierre Denis, *écuyer*, Sieur de la Ronde, born in Quebec November 11, 1726, is of interest in this recital for it was he who established in Louisiana the name he bore, and who died there May 7, 1772. At his baptism, which took place the day after his entry into the world, his *parrain* was Pierre François de Cavagnal, Seigneur de Vaudreuil, father of the Louisiana governor of the same name. Pierre Denis became a lieutenant of the *détachment d'infantrie de la marine* sent to Louisiana in 1750 when he was twenty-four. Seven years after his arrival in the Louisiana colony he married, in New Orleans, Madeline Broutin, daughter of Ignace François Broutin, one of the colony's royal engineers, and commandant at the Natchez post, and Madeline Lemaire. When Madeline Broutin married de la Ronde she was the widow of Louis Xavier de Lino de Chalmette (q. v.) by whom she had two sons and a daughter. She died July 31, 1805.

Pierre Denis de la Ronde and Madeline Broutin had four children. They were:

1.—Louise de la Ronde, born in New Orleans July 25, 1758, who on March 20, 1787, when she was twenty-nine, became the second wife of Don Andres Almonester y Roxas (q. v.). Her one child by this marriage was the celebrated Micaëla Almonester, who became the Baroness Pontalba. Louise de la Ronde, after the death of her seventy-four-year-old husband, married, March 7, 1804, Jean Baptiste Castillion, youthful French consul at New Orleans, the son of Etienne Castillion and Isabelle Lasserre, the ceremony being performed by Fra. Antonio de Sedella.

2.—Marie Thérése de la Ronde, baptised September 4, 1759, died April 20, 1817, who married, April 25, 1778, Juan Prieto, an officer of the Spanish troops, who had accompanied General O'Rielly to Louisiana from Cuba. He was the son of Don Pedro Prieto and Francisca de la Bargos, both natives of Havana.

3.—Marguerite de la Ronde, born June 10, 1761, who married M. de Verges, Sieur de St. Sauveur, a son of the Chevalier de Verges. It is belived that this son was François who became the husband of Madeline de Lino Chalmette (q. v.), and that Marguerite de la Ronde was his first wife.

4.—Pierre Denis de la Ronde II, born in New Orleans April 20, 1762, died December 1, 1824. He married, January 31, 1788, Eulalie Guerbois, daughter of Louis Alexandre Guerbois and Elizabeth Trepagnier.

It was this Pierre Denis de la Ronde II who established the beautiful and historic *Versailles* plantation just below New Orleans and planted the magnificent oak alley, today counted the finest double row of live oak trees in Louisiana. He planted them in 1783, on his twenty-first birthday, which makes them, in 1931, one hundred forty-eight years old. This oak alley connected his pretentious plantation home with the boat landing on the Mississippi River, and is frequently, but erroneously, called today the *"Pakenham Oaks."*

The establishment of *Versailles* brings to mind an almost forgotten real estate scheme of that period. With other landowners of that section, Pierre de la Ronde planned to establish a rival city there which would, so the promoters promised, in a short time completely outdistance New Orleans. The new metropolis was to be called *Versailles* and a sister city, to be established on the shores of Lake Borgne, was to be named *Paris*. A highway, running directly east and west, to be called the *Paris Road*, was to link the two new cities. Today, the remnant of this same highway is frequently miscalled the "Parish Road." The ambitious real estate scheme, however, fell through and all that remains of the enterprise is the picturesque brick ruins of *Versailles* and the time-defying oak alley.

Pierre Denis de la Ronde II was a lieutenant in the second

[396]

company first battalion of Spanish Louisiana troops maintained by the King of Spain, and served as civil and military commandant for the St Bernard parish, and was a member of the *Cabildo* from 1798 to 1803 under the Spanish domination, succeeding his brother-in-law Don Almonester to this post. He was a member of the constitutional convention of 1812, and served on General Andrew Jackson's staff during the Battle of New Orleans, which was fought over his plantation, and later became major general of the state militia.

By his marriage to Eulalie Guerbois he became the father of nine daughters and one son. The daughters of this family were known to the select society of that period as "The Nine Muses," their brother was called "Apollo," and *Versailles*, to continue the application to mythology, was termed "Parnassus," where a lavish hospitality was dispensed.

1.—Eulalie de la Ronde, born February 25, 1789, died in 1858, married René Philippe Gabriel Villeré, son of Philippe Jacques Villeré, the first Créole governor of Louisiana. Twelve children were born of this marriage: (a) Drauzin Villeré, unmarried; (b) Edmond Villeré, who married Odile Cruzat; (c) Denis Villeré, who married Malvina Cruzat, Odile's sister; (e) Gabriel Eréville Villeré, born January 1821, died 1902, who married in 1842, Adèle Ducros, born December 1821, died 1904, and had ten children: Eulalie Valentine Villere, who married George Alfred Lanaux; Loisa, Adèle, Almaide, René, Robert, Lucie, Arthur, Richard, and Almaide, all unmarried. Of the marriage of Eulalie to George Alfred Lanaux, March 19, 1862, issued twelve children, the seven who survived being: Laurence Gabrielle Lanaux, who married Adolphe Faure; Marie Bianca Lanaux, who first married Dr. Sterling Kennedy, and later Philip N. Nott; Alfred Antoine Lanaux, who married Marie Andrett; Valentine Louise Lanaux, who married Clarence Wolf George Rareshide, and later John P. Coleman; Adèle Lanaux, unmarried; Rita Marie Lanaux, who married Percy Howard Brown; and Henri Joseph Lanaux, who married Emilie Hébert, and later Cameola Bienvenu; (e) Héloïse Villeré, who married Alfred Bodin, and (f) Cyrille Villeré, unmarried.

2.—Elizabeth Céleste de la Ronde, born June 15, 1791, died September 1, 1822, who married Maunsell White of Kentucky, born in Ireland in 1784, and died December 17, 1863. He was the son of Lawford White and Anna Maunsell. Elizabeth Céleste had one child, Eliza, who married Cuthbert Bullitt of Kentucky. Their one child died young.

3.—Héloise de la Ronde, born December 11, 1792, died November 14, 1867, who became the second wife of Maunsell White. Of this union were born three children: (a) Annie White, who married Dr. Hugh Kennedy of Louisville, Kentucky, their children being: Héloise Kennedy, who married Malcolm Bullitt; Clara Kennedy, who married Aleck Bullitt, and Nan Kennedy, unmarried. (b) Clara White, who married Carl Kohn, a New Orleans banker, and had six daughters: Hilda Meyer, unmarried; Clara Meyer, who married Louis M. McCaleb; Evelyn Meyer, unmarried; Mildred Meyer, unmarried; Lenora Meyer, who married John Hickey, and Virginia Meyer, unmarried. (c) Maunsell White Jr., who married Elizabeth Porter Bradford, niece of Jefferson Davis, their children being: Sidney Johnson White, who married Elizabeth Tobin; Anna White, who married Thomas H. Anderson; Lucy White, who married Dr. Clement P. Wilkinson; Mary White, who married A. Ringgold Brousseau; Elizabeth White, who married Edwin W. Rodd; Carl White, who married Mary Mitchel, and Maunsel White III, who died unmarried.

4.—Josephine Pépita de la Ronde, born June 21, 1796, died August 11, 1851, who married, first Thomas S. Cunningham, United States Navy, December 22, 1816, by whom she had two sons, both dying young. Her second husband was General Casimir Lacoste, whom she married after the death of her sister Manette.

5.—Marie Manette de la Ronde, born May 1, 1799, died March 1834, who became the first wife of General Casimir Lacoste, born February 1, 1795, died November 9, 1857. General Lacoste owned a plantation near Versailles and distinguished himself at the Battle of New Orleans, while his plantation home was used by General Gibbs and other British officers as a headquarters. There was no issue to either of General Lacoste's marriages.

6.—Pierre Denis de la Ronde III, born June 1, 1801, died March 12, 1840, the only son, who married May 22, 1828, Malvina Roche (her full name was Rosalie Anne Laurence Adolphe Louise Nicolas Palmyre Malvina Roche), a native of Migolasa, Palmyra, and daughter of Don Nicolas Roche and Doña Louisa Sigur.

7.—Adélaïde Adèle de la Ronde, born December 24, 1803, died October 22, 1837, who married, April 15, 1820, Pierre Adolphe Ducros, son of Joseph Rodolphe Ducros and Marie Lucie de Reggio, who was the daughter of François Marie de Reggio and Hélène de Fleuriau. Adèle de la Ronde's children were: (a) Elizabeth Adèle Ducros who married Gabriel Ernéville Villeré (q. v.); (b) Pierre Adolphe Ducros Jr., born March 16, 1827, died June 20, 1905, educated at Harvard, who became one of the leading members of the New Orleans bar, practicing law for fifty-six years. In 1850 he married Coralie Auguste Louise Fernet, daughter of Auguste Louis Fernet and Françoise Victoire Webre, natives of Paris. Seven children were born to this union: Christian Louis Ducros, died young; Victoria Louise Ducros, died young; Delaronde Pierre Ducros, who established himself in Bluefields, Nicaragua, where he died; Louis Henry Ducros, unmarried; Adolphe Victor Ducros, unmarried; Joseph Emile Ducros, born on *Pecan Grove* plantation, February 15, 1865, who married Florence Olivia Patton, and had five children, and Fernet Octave Ducros. The seventh child of Pierre and Coralie Ducros was Marie Coralie Ducros, born July 7, 1869, who married, April 12, 1887, Henri Jules Stouse, and had eight children.

8.—Marie Félicie de la Ronde, born September 28, 1805, died September 29, 1842, became the wife of Pierre

Jayme F. Jorda, son of Jayme J. F. Jorda and Hélène de Reggio, and the mother of nine children.

9.—Isabelle Emilie de la Ronde, born August 6, 1807, died March 18, 1890, who married Pierre de Hôa Cacho, who was born September 16, 1802 and died November 2, 1866. He was the son of Don Manuel de Hôa. Emilie de la Ronde became the mother of three children: (a) Amélie de Hôa, who married Urbain Forestier, their only child being Albert Forestier; (b) Appoline de Hôa, who married Belgarde Lacoste, and (c) Eulalie de Hôa, who married Charles Emile Le Blanc, and had seven children.

10.—Magdalena Azélie de la Ronde, born May 21, 1809, died July 1, 1872, who married Pierre Urbain Forestier, who was born in 1804, and died May 11, 1833. Their two sons were: (a) Urbain Pierre Forestier who married Amélie de Hôa, their only son died unmarried; (b) Louis Forestier, born December 25, 1833, died April 6, 1862, who married Félicie Jorda, and their three daughters were: Amélie, Louise, and Gabrielle Forestier.

Versailles and the de la Ronde oak alley planted in 1783

DIMITRY Family

THE Dimitry family forms an instance of striking genealogy encountered in the annals of three countries. The beginning of the Greek line is from the Island of Hydra, the first of a Macedonian family to settle on the Acropolis of this island seeking refuge from the Turks. This family remained undefiled in the purity of its Grecian strain. The Canadian line begins with Doctor Giffard, who emigrated to Canada prior to 1634, and with the Hébert family, have been declared as the first Canadian families. To this Giffard family was allied the Canadian brothers Chauvin, de Léry, la Frénière, and Beaulieu, who with Lallande connections, came to Louisiana from Canada.

The first Dimitry in Louisiana was Andrea Dimitry, born on the Island of Hydra in the archipelago of Greece, in 1775, who died in New Orleans March 1, 1852. He married, October 29, 1799, Marianne Céleste Dragon, daughter of Michel Dragon and Françoise Chauvin Beaulieu de Monplasir. Dimitry in its original form was "Demetrois."

Andrea Dimitry in emigrating to Louisiana sought on the virgin soil of the New World the freedom that once blessed him in his own classic land and the spirit that once animated his own people. He became a resident of Louisiana, then under the domination of Spain, but when the colony was transferred to the United States he became an ardent republican and at the historic Battle of New Orleans participated in that memorable conflict. He lived to be eighty and to see grown up about him a posterity honored for their culture.

The Dragon family in Louisiana began with the arrival in the French Colony of Michel Dragon. He was a native of Athens, being born in the year 1739. In English his name would be "Drago," the same as that of the great law-giver. His mother's name was Clino Hellen, and Hellen was the name of the son of Deucalion, the Noah of Grecian mythology who gave origin to the Hellenes or Greeks. The exact date of Michel Dragon's coming to America is not known but it was previous to 1764, as can be learned from his warrant of promotion, for he was an officer in the French militia when Louisiana was transferred to Spain. He then entered the Spanish colonial militia and participated in Governor Galvez's campaign against the British in West Florida.

By his marriage to Françoise Chauvin de Monplasir, the Dragons became allied to the Chauvin family (q. v.). Her father was Louis Chauvin de Beaulieu and Charlotte Orbanne Duval d'Epresmenil. The issue of this union was a daughter named Marianne Céleste Dragon, born in New Orleans, March 1, 1777, died April 22, 1856, who married Andrea Dimitry. From this Dimitry-Dragon alliance were born ten children: (a) Euphrosine Dimitry, born September 12, 1800, who married, April 23, 1822, Paul Pandely; (b) Manuella Aimée Dimitry, born January 12, 1802, who married, January 10, 1826, A. Dietz; (c) Alexander Dimitry, born February 6, 1805, died January 30, 1883, who married Mary Powell Mills; (d) Constantine Andrea Dimitry, born May 24, 1807; (e) J. B. Miguel Dragon Dimitry, born May 18, 1809, died January 12, 1873, who married Caroline Sophia Powers; (f) Angelica Clino Dimitry, born March 7, 1811, died July 19, 1882, who married G. Perri; (g) Marie Françoise Athénaïs Dimitry, born February 5, 1813, who married, first, Isidore Michel Ravent-Martainville, secondly, Jean B. Lagarde, and, thirdly, G. A. D. Buel; (h) Mathilde Isabelle Théophanie Dimitry, born November 29, 1816, who married Dr. A. Natili; (i) Nicholas Dimitry, born February 7, 1815, and (j) Antoine Marie Dimitry, born February 8, 1820.

Alexander Dimitry, the oldest son of Andrea Dimitry and Céleste Dragon, was a man of colossal learning and intellect. Noted as a scholar, linguist, orator, lecturer, writer, and diplomat he takes rank as one of the great sons of Louisiana. He was commissioned in 1847-50 as first state superintendent of public education. In 1842, after he had returned from diplomatic service in Washington, he devoted his time and splendid intellect to the organizing of the free school system of Louisiana. President James Buchanan appointed Alexander Dimitry minister plenipotentiary and extraordinary to Costa Rica and Nicaragua. Previously President Martin Van Buren appointed him secretary to a mixed commission which decided the boundries in dispute between Mexico and the United States. During the Civil War Jefferson Davis appointed him chief of the finance bureau of the Confederate post-office. Alexander Dimitry was familiar with eleven languages, ancient and modern, a prominent Odd Fellow, and one of the founders of the Seven Wise Men of Heptasophs.

In 1835 Alexander Dimitry married, in Washington, D. C., Mary Powell Mills, daughter of Robert Mills of Charleston, South Carolina, a leading United States government architect, who designed the Washington Monument, and many of the government buildings in the nation's capital. Her mother was Eliza Barnwell Smith, of Hackwood, Frederich county, Virginia. General John Bull was her great grandfather, and her maternal grandfather was General John Smith, both of distinguished Revolutionary fame. She was also a direct descendant of Abigail Smith, wife of John Adams and mother of John Quincy Adams.

It has been said that the children of the Dimitry-Mills union inherited the towering intellects of their father and the gentleness and beauty of character of their mother. This is best exemplified in the achievements of John Bull Smith Dimitry, and Charles Patton Dimitry, authors, historians, diplomats, and scholars. John Dimitry married Ada Stuart, a relative of General J. E. B. Stuart, the "Plumed Cavelier" of the Confederacy. Other children were: Alexander Dimitry Jr., Robert Andrea Dimitry, Thomas Dabney Dimitry, who married Annie Stone; Eliza Virginia Dimitry, who married Enoch Fenwick Ruth; Elizabeth Linn Dimitry, who married C. McRea Selph, and Mathilda T. Dimitry, who married William Devere Miller of New York.

John Bull Smith, or John Dimitry, as he is known in the world of letters was, like his father, a historian, master of languages, and a statesman. He was born in Washington, D. C., December 27, 1835, and educated at College Hill, Mississippi, a school established by his father. Wounded at the Battle of Shiloh, where his hip was shattered while rescuing his company commander, he entered the Confederate postal service at Richmond where he served until the end of the war. In the early seventies he went to Europe to write of the manners and customs of the peoples of the continent and devoted especial attention to a study of Spain. After his return from Europe he accepted the chair of languages and *belles letters* in the College Caldas, South America. He returned to New Orleans and while secretary to the state superintendent of education, wrote his history of Louisiana, for many years a valuable text-book in the public schools.

Charles Patton Dimitry is renowned as author, historian, journalist, biographer, and veteran of the Civil War. He was born in Washington, D. C. and received his education at Georgetown College. He married Annie Elizabeth Johnston of Alexandria, Virginia, who died shortly thereafter without issue. He served in the Louisiana Cavalry, and upon the cessation of hostilities resumed his studies at Georgetown, graduating in 1867. He took up journalism in Washington, New York, Mobile and New Orleans. For many years he was a constant and prolific contributor to the New Orleans *Times-Democrat*, and in that paper ran his series of short genealogical sketches, *Louisiana Families*, into which he wove with consummate skill and romanticism all the wealth of legends that abound in the research of Louisiana names and their ramifications, which have been abridged and extended and appear in the first part of this present work.

Eliza Virginia Ruth, a daughter of Alexander Dimitry, married Captain Enoch Fenwick Ruth of Baltimore, who served in the Indian Bureau at Washington. Returning to Louisiana a widow, she wrote under the name of Virginia Dimitry Ruth. She was one of the pioneer women writers. Following the trend of her pedagogic family, she was an educator, having her private school for young ladies, an institution recognized for its splendid educational system and culture. She had three daughters: Elizabeth Dimitry Ruth, who married Dracos A. Dimitry, her cousin; Margaret Dimitry Ruth, who married Louis Grey Norwell, and Genevieve Ruth, who married Louis A. Veazey.

J. B. Miguel Dragon Dimitry, best known as M. D. Dimitry, a son of Andrea and Céleste Dimitry, and brother of Alexander, was born May 18, 1809, at the Dimitry home, 24 Ste. Anne street, facing the *Place d'Armes*. He married, January 12, 1836, Caroline Sophia Powers of Waltham, Massachusetts. His wife's father was Theodore Powers and her mother Caroline Elizabeth Françoise Péronne of Charleston, South Carolina. Mlle. Péronne was of a distinguished French family, her father was Charles Adrien Césaire Graville Péronne Sochet des Touches of Lucon, France, and her mother was Elizabeth Francoise de la Salle. She was the widow of Doctor Lafond when she married Césaire Péronne.

The marriage of M. D. Dimitry to Caroline Powers resulted in an issue of several children: (a) Emile Bozzaris Dimitry, who died young; (b) Alice Dimitry, who died young; (c) Theodore John Dimitry, born March 16, 1839, who married March 1, 1871, Irene Mary Scott; (d) Mary Céleste Dimitry, born February 18, 1842, who married, April 26, 1866, John T. Block; (e) Clino Sophia Dimitry, born January 19, 1844, who married Captain James Gale; (f) George Dimitry, who died young; (g) Caroline Dimitry; (h) Robert M. L. Dimitry; (i) Walter Artemere Dimitry; (j) Norbert Dimitry; (k) Alexander J. Dimitry, and (l) Dracos Anthony Dimitry, born September 17, 1858, who married, December 27, 1883, his cousin Elizabeth Dimitry Ruth.

Theodore John Dimitry, who married Irene Mary Scott, daughter of Joel Tomlin Scott and Naomi Josephine Wood of New Orleans, was a student of genealogy. As a result of his family researches he left what is reputed to be one of the most complete uninterrupted genealogical record of a single family. He served the Confederacy. His children were: (a) Joséphine Naomi Dimitry, born January 19, 1872, who married Octave François Desforges; (b) Michael Dracos Dimitry, born August 9, 1874; (c) Clino Sophia Dimitry, born March 1, 1877, who married Louis F. Beauvais; (d) Dr. Theodore John Dimitry, born June 26, 1879, who married Fernande Jacob; (e) Irene Mary Dimitry, (f) John Scott Dimitry, born November 21, 1886; and (g) Caroline Sophia Dimitry, born June 24, 1890, deceased.

Prepared by Lillian Norvell from the Dimitry family records.

DE LA LANDE DE FERRIÈRE Family

NO fiercer contest is recorded on the pages of medieval chivalry than that which took place around the crenellated towers of the *Chateau Fort de Domfront* in Normandy. Among the valorous knights who participated in the battle was one named la Lande, Seigneur de Ferrière, whose ancestral lands stood not far from this beseiged citadel. Froissart, in his Chroniques, mentions a Jean de la Lande, of apparently the same family, who fought at the Battle of Poitiers, as well as another who was an *écuyer* in the days of Richard II.

A member of this ancient family, Louis Guillaume de la Lande de Ferrière, born near Paris, France, came to New Orleans in 1750 as a royal engineer and surveyor. He married there in 1764, Jeanne Catherine du Bois (or Dubois), a native of that city, born in 1748, who died in 1819, being buried in the old St. Louis Cemetery on Rampart street. At his death his surviving widow became in 1776 the wife of Don Manuel Perez, of ancient Hispanic lineage (q. v.).

From the union of Louis Guillaume de la Lande de Ferrière to Jeanne Catherine du Bois issued a son, Nicolas Louis, who became a cadet in the Spanish army and at the age of eighteen participated, under Governor de Galvez, in the surprise of Fort Bute, and the seiges of Baton Rouge and Pensacola. This Nicolas Louis de la Lande de Ferrière married in New Orleans, February 4, 1793, Marie Magdeleine Jacinta Arnoult, born in New Orleans February 28, 1767, daughter of Jean Arnoult (q. v.) (a native of Poitiers, France) and Marie de Lile Dupard (or Dupart). He was murdered at his own doorstep by a pirate.

From his marriage to Mlle. Arnoult, Nicolas Louis de la Lande de Ferrière left several children, among whom Joseph, the youngest, born in 1801. He married in New Orleans,

November 7, 1829, Marie Caroline Roche, then only sixteen years of age, by whom he had several sons who wore the grey in 1861-1865 and fought bravely under the Stars and Bars. Joseph de la Lande de Ferrière inherited the bravery of his ancestors and showed his mettle at the time that the notorious General Benjamin Butler was the military tyrant of New Orleans, in Civil War days, and occupied the elegant Slocum-Urquhart home that stood next to the present City Hall. Joseph de la Lande was his next door neighbor and, undaunted by Butler's tactics of invading private homes with his armed cohorts, prepared to resist the military despot. Being informed that his home was about to be searched for silver, weapons and valuables, he bravely notified Butler that no one would enter his residence except by stepping across his dead body and that he was prepared to shoot to kill any trepasser on his premises. His home was not molested.

At his death, Joseph de la Lande de Ferrière, left several sons and daughters, one of them being John B. de la Lande de Ferrière, well known in cotton circles in New Orleans a few years ago, who married Emma Rathbone, daughter of Henry Alenson Rathbone and Céleste Forstall (q. v.). He left in turn several sons and beautiful daughters, none of whom married. His daughters, Juanita, Ethlyn and Ruby became social favorites in New Orleans and graced several of the Carnival courts of that gay city, one of them being queen of the Carnival. Two of them are now living in Washington, D. C. and the third resides in Paris. Of the sons of John B. de la Lande, one of them, Roy, still lives in New Orleans, and the other, Gayoso, was a resident there until a few years ago. A nephew of John B. de la Lande is Joseph de la Lande, well-known railroad official in New Orleans.

The escutcheon of the de la Lande de Ferrières is described: On a field *argent* a lion rampant *sable*, armed and langued *gules*. The crest is a lion rampant *sable* between two tree stumps *sinople*, and their motto is *Tiens Ta Foy*, or "Keep Thy Faith."

FAGOT DE LA GARCINIÈRE Family

DANIEL François Fagot de la Garcinière, son of François Fagot, mayor of Voiron, St. Nicolas, Dauphiné, France, and Françoise Lemoine, was born in the French town administered by his father in 1731. Entering the army, he crossed the ocean and reached Louisiana where he became an officer in the colonial troops, as well as a planter and fur trader.

While visiting his far-off fur-trading post at Kaskaskia, in the Illinois country, he met and married Geneviève Boucher de Montbrun de Bonacueil at Fort Chartres in 1704-1705. His wife died in that section of Louisiana in 1756, but not before giving birth to a son, André Fagot de la Garcinière, on December 5, 1755. At her death, Daniel François Fagot de la Garcinière married again in New Orleans, August 4, 1766, his second wife being Charlotte Constance, daughter of Pierre François Marie Olivier de Vezin and Marie Josephte Gatineau Duplessis. Before his death on his plantation in St. Bernard parish, April 7, 1776, Daniel François de la Garcinière had discharged the duties of Regidor and Receiver of Fines in the Spanish Cabildo, being appointed to that office February 8, 1774.

By his second marriage to Mlle. Olivier de Vezin, he had four children: Pierre François, Charles Daniel, Pierre Etienne and Louise Fagot de la Garcinière. The second named, Charles Daniel, married and left posterity, but the other three children died young or unmarried. At the death of Daniel François Fagot de la Garcinière, his widow, Mlle. de Vezin, married December 2, 1782, Charles Antoine de Reggio.

Andre Fagot de la Garcinière, only child of Daniel François by his first wife, Mlle. Boucher de Montbrun de Bonacueil, was born in Fort Chartres in 1785, educated in France and served as a Spanish officer in Louisiana. He does not appear to have married. Charles Daniel Fagot de la Garcinière, son of Daniel François de la Garcinièee by his second wife, Mlle. Olivier de Vezin, was born in New Orleans May 27, 1769. He became a district judge and died in St. Bernard parish in 1834. Marrying twice, he had twenty-four children by both of his wives, twelve being born from each. His first nuptials to Adèlaide Bérard, daughter of Jean Baptiste Bérard and Anne Broussard, took place in St. Martinville September 6, 1792. His second marriage, celebrated in New Orleans about 1809, was with Norma Cuvillier.

By his first wife he had, among twelve children, a son, Rosemon de la Garcinière, who married Elizabeth Alpuente, a daughter, Aglaë, wife of M. Rapp, and another daughter, Charlotte Constance married to Evariste Marin. The eldest child from this first marriage was Charles Fagot de la Garcinière, who continued the line.

Among the twelve children born of the second marriage of Charles Daniel Fagot de la Garcinière with Norma Cuvillier, were Auguste de la Garcinière, who married Séverine Cazzeau, Rosine de la Garcinière, wife of Charles Seuzeneau, Anatole de la Garcinière, a Confederate soldier, who did not marry; Théodule de la Garcinière, whose wife was Annette Marin du Gardin de St. Alexandre; Derneville de la Garcinière, another Confederate soldier, who probably died in action, and Ernest de la Garcinière, still another grey-clad soldier of the South who disappeared during this terrible American conflict.

Charles Fagot de la Garcinière, eldest son of Charles Daniel by his first wife, Mlle. Olivier de Vezin, was born in the Attakapas country, at Isle des Cyprès, where his father's plantation stood, August 30, 1793. He died in New Iberia August 13, 1872. It is said that he preferred his American citizenship to a French title and estate and refused to accept a noble heritage in France. In fact, he was so democratic that he dropped the de la Garcinière from his patronymic and signed his name as Fagot. He was an orderly sergeant in the United States forces in 1812 and took part in the Battle of New Orleans. He occupied positions of honor and trust in St. Martinville, but sold his plantation on Isle des Cyprès in 1850 and moved to New Orleans, where he was appointed in 1853 surveyor of customs for the port of Pontchartrain, an office he held until the day of his death. He married in St. Martinville, April 10, 1822, Charlotte Virginie Bienvenu, daughter of Alexandre Devince Bienvenue and Charlotte Uranie de la Barre.

Nine children issued from this union. They were: (a) Marie Célestine Adèlaïde, who married François Théodoric de la Croix, of Puyreaud, France; (b) Charles Jr., who married three times, viz: first Augusta Fagot, second, Elaine Douze, and third, Ellen Terrell; (c) Marie Constance, who married Judge Lucien Adams (or Adam), son of Lucian Adam, from Acadia; (d) Louise Marie, unmarried; (e) Godfroi, husband of Frances Israel; (f) Anna Clara, wife of Gaston Duvigneaud' (g) Pierre Octave, whose wife was Margaret McCleary; (h) John Anatole, who married first Sophie Buisson and second Idéa De Blanc; and (i) Marie Corinne, who married, July 16, 1866, De Witt Clinton Roberts, of Winchester, Illinois, son of Surgeon Major Dr. Clark Roberts and Asenath Adams. From this last marriage issued a daughter, Louise Roberts, wife of Louis F. Anaya, of New Orleans.

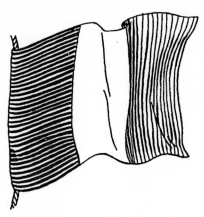

The tricolor of Republican France that floated over Louisiana for only twenty days

OLIVIER DE VEZIN Family

ONE of the earliest iron founderies in Canada was established in 1738 at *Trois Rivières* by Pierre François Marie Olivier, *écuyer*, Sieur de Vezin, a young French nobleman from the Province of Champagne. His foundry, known as *Forge St. Maurice*, resulted from a demand made by the Governor of *Trois Rivières* to the King of France for such an establishment in *Nouvelle France*.

This Pierre François Marie Olivier de Vezin was born in Nancy in 1716 and died in New Orleans April 20th, 1776. Before going to Canada he had been a king's Councillor in his native land. His father, Hugues Olivier de Vezin was *seigneur* of Sionne-en-Bassigny, and his mother was Louise Leroux de Dinjolincour. While exercising the managership of the *Forge St. Maurice* he married at *Trois Rivières* on June 14, 1747, Marie Josephte Gatineau Duplessis (widow Linier), daughter of Jean Baptiste Gatineau Duplessis and Marie Céleste Le Boullanger. His wife was a native of *Trois Rivières* being born there September 4, 1720, and dying in New Orleans December 7, 1772.

Proving himself a valuable French subject, Pierre François Marie Olivier de Vezin was appointed by the Crown, in 1749, *grand voyer, inspecteur des ponts et chaussées et arpenteur général de la Province de la Louisiane* and went to New Orleans to discharge his new duties. Holding the front rank among the French colonial officials, he was also honored by the Spaniards, new masters of Louisiana, in 1769, and took his seat in the Cabildo, on December first of that year, as *regidor perpetuo y alguazil mayor*. His marriage to Mlle. Gatineau Duplessis resulted in the birth of eight children, namely:

1.—Hugues Charles Honoré Olivier de Vezin de St.

Maurice, born in 1748 at *Trois Rivières*, who married Marie Madeleine Philippe de Marigny de Mandeville, daughter of Antoine Pierre Philippe de Marigny de Mandeville and Françoise de Lile Dupart. He left three children.

2.—Charlotte Constance Olivier de Vezin, born 1750 in New Orleans, died there August 11, 1801. She married first Daniel Fagot de la Garcinière (q. v.), and at his death in 1776, married a second time Charles Antoine de Reggio, son of François Marie de Reggio and Helene Fleuriau. She left issue by both marriages.

3.—Pierre Louis Olivier d'Erneville, baptized in New Orleans, October 18, 1752, and died May 9, 1805. He became a lietuenant colonel in the Regiment of Louisiana and served under Governor Galvez.

4.—Charles Frédéric Olivier de Forcelle, born in 1763, who served as a lieutenant under Galvez and became a captain in the Spanish troops. He married February 14, 1777, Marie Françoise la Mollére d'Orville.

5.—Avineent Adélaïde Olivier de Vezin, born February 20, 1755, who married, September 15, 1770, Etienne de la Lande d'Alcour, son of Etienne de la Lande d'Alcour and Marie Josephe Trudeau.

6.—Nicholas Joseph Godfroi Olivier de Vezin, born May 27, 1757, died July 18, 1813, who became a lieutenant of grenadiers under Galvez and married first, on December 3, 1782, Eulalie Toutant Beauregard, daughter of Jacques Toutant Beauregard, and took for his second wife, in 1789, Marie Marianne Bienvenu, daughter of Jean Baptiste Bienvenu and Helene Belet (widow Ducret).

7.—Louise Judith Olivier de Vezin, born about 1758, who married after 1776, the chevalier Augustin de Reggio.

8.—Françoise Victoria Olivier de Vezin, born about 1753, died June 23, 1820. She entered the Ursuline Order in New Orleans at the age of sixteen, being known as Mère Sainte Marie. Eventually, on June 3, 1803, she was made Mother Assistant and before May 1812 became Superioress of the New Orleans Convent. On the memorable January 8, 1815, when Pakenham and his

English Army were advancing against New Orleans, Mère Sainte Marie made a vow to have a solemn high mass and a *Te Deum* sung annually if the Americans were victorious. Up to the present time her promise is being piously carried out by her worthy condisciples.

The children of Hugues Charles Honoré Olivier de Vezin, eldest son of Pierre François Marie Olivier de Vezin and Mlle. Gatineau Duplessis, were Major Charles Olivier de Vezin who married in 1798, in St. Martinville, Céleste Mathilde DeBlanc, daughter of Captain Charles DeBlanc and Elizabeth Pouponne d'Erneville. From this union issued five children, all born in St. Martinville. Another son was Pierre Olivier du Closel de Vezin, whose first marriage, celebrated March 2, 1802, in St. Martinville, was with Jeanne Aspasie Devince Bienvenu, daughter of Alexandre Devince Bienvenu and Louise Félicité Henriette Latil de Tinecour from which were born five children. His second wife was Marie Joseph Latiolais, daughter of Joseph Latiolais and Françoise Nezat, by whom he had one son.

The children of Nicolas Joseph Godfroi Olivier de Vezin, sixth child of Pierre François Olivier de Vezin and Mlle. Gatineau Duplessis from his second marriage with Marianne Bienvenu were: Anastasie, wife of Augustin de Reggio; Eulalie, unmarried; Jean Baptiste married to Alix Duverjé Elmire, wife of Furcy Verret; Henriette, wife of Pierre Réaud; Charles Godfroi, married to Eulalie Duverjé; Eulalie, wife of John Wogan; Victor Bienvenu, whose wife was Pauline Reynaud and Césaire, whose wife was Henriette Lavergne.

Victor Bienvenu Olivier de Vezin married to Pauline Reynaud had in turn eleven children among whom Emma, who became the wife of A. N. Robelot; Valentine, who became Mrs. W. H. Vredenburgh, and Victor, who married on September 10, 1866, Louise Marie Hébrard, and left six children: Albert J., who married Marie Théard; Victor W., who married Cécile Albert; Lucie Marie, unmarried; Christian Louis who married Ida Dreuschke; Pierre D. who married Marie Amélie Minor and Berthe Marie, who married Jacques de Tarnowsky.

D'ESTREHAN Family

JEAN Baptiste d'Estréhan des Tours, founder of the d'Estréhan family in Louisiana, served for many years as Royal Treasurer in that French colony. Born in France, he married Catherine de Gauvrit, daughter of Jean Baptiste de Gauvrit, an officer in the colonial troops, and Jeanne Catherine Pierre. He died in New Orleans after 1759, and his wife breathed her last September 29, 1773. He incurred the enmity of Kerlerec for aiding the Commissaire de Rochemore and was expelled from the colony by the irate governor who declared that he was a too wealthy and dangerous man to remain in Louisiana.

D'Estréhan des Tours, the Royal Treasurer, had three sons and three daughters namely: (a) Marie Marguerite d'Estréhan, born after 1759, educated at the royal school of St. Cyr, who married in Paris, France, September 20th, 1771, Jean Etienne de Boré de Mauléon, born in Kaskaskia, Illinois, December 27th, 1741, who died in New Orleans February 2, 1820; (b) Jean Baptiste Honoré d'Estréhan, who died October 20, 1773, and married Félicie de St. Maxent, leaving no issue by her. At his death, his widow took for her second husband Governor Bernardo de Galvez; (c) Jean Louis d'Estréhan; (d) Jeanne Marie d'Estréhan, born after 1759, who married July 14, 1772, Pierre Enguerrand Philippe de Marigny de Mandeville, son of Antoine Philippe de Marigny de Mandeville and Françoise de Lile Dupart; (e) Jean Noël d'Estréhan de Beaupré, born after 1748, died October 9, 1823, who married in 1786 Marie Claude Céleste Léonore Robin de Logny, daughter of Pierre Antoine Robin de Logny and Jeanne Dreux de Gentilly. His wife was born in 1768 and died in Boston, Mass., September 3, 1824. Her mother, Jeanne Dreux, was the daughter of Mathurin Dreux, one of the earliest settlers in New Orleans, who owned a concession on Bayou St. John, near that city, in 1721, and who married Françoise Hugo. Mathurin Dreux, in turn was the son of Louis Dreux de Brézé (of Angers, Anjou, Maine-et-Loire, France) and Françoise Harand. The Dreux furnished sovereign dukes to Brittany and descend from Robert, fifth son of Louis VI of France; (f) Mlle. D'Estréhan who married Nicolas Favre d'Aunoy. She was born after 1759 and died after 1773.

Jean Noël d'Estréhan de Beaupré, fifth mentioned child of Jean Baptiste d'Estréhan des Tours and Catherine de Gauvrit, had from his marriage fourteen children: (a) Célestine d'Estréhan, born 1787, who married René Trudeau and died in 1811; (b) Guy Noël d'Estréhan who married a Miss Oliver of New York and left two children, Mrs. Chazot and Mrs. Théophile Roussel; (c) Justine d'Estréhan, whose husband was Jean Baptiste de Macarty; (d) Nicolas Noël d'Estréhan, born in St. Charles parish, April 3, 1793, who died there June 16, 1848. He married twice, namely; first, on May 17, 1814, to Victorine Fortier, born April 30, 1799, daughter of Jacques Fortier and Aimée Durel (without issue), and second, on November 12, 1826, to Louise Henriette de Navarre, born in Paris, France, October 10, 1810, died in Louisiana October 11, 1836, daughter of Ange Louis de Navarre and Adélaïde Catherine Clémentine Gabrielle Rose Barthe: (e) Eléonore Zélia d'Estréhan, wife of Stephen Henderson, who died in New York city September 19th, 1830; (f) Louise Odile d'Estréhan, born 1802, died 1877, who married first Pierre Edouard Foucher and second Pierre Adolphe Rost. From her first husband she left among other children, Destours Foucher, who was on the staff of General Taylor in the Mexican War, and Louise Foucher, who married Felix Henri Larue, from which union were born George H. Larue (without issue); Anna Larue, wife of Léon Sarpy (with issue); Odile Larue, wife of Frank O. Minor (with issue); Ferdinand E. Larue, who married Anna LeGardeur de Tilly (with issue); Dr. Felix A. Larue, whose first wife was Lisette Rea (with issue) and whose second wife is Stéphanie Levert (without issue) and Destours P. Larue (without issue). From her second marriage with Pierre Adolphe

Rost, she had five children, one of whom Emile Rost (without issue) owned the Destréhan plantation and was for many years the district judge of the Parishes of Jefferson, St. Charles and St. John; (g) Marie Céleste d'Estréhan, born 1808, died 1885, who married first Prosper de Marigny and second Alexandre Grailhe.

Nicolas Noël d'Estréhan had from his second marriage with Mlle. de Navarre, four children, namely: (a) Louise d'Estréhan, wife of Joseph Hale Harvey; (b) Adèle d'Estréhan, who married Samuel B. McCutcheon; (c) Eliza d'Estréhan, who married Daniel D. Rogers; (d) Azby d'Estréhan, who married Rosa Ferrier. The above mentioned Louise d'Estréhan (Mrs. J. H. Harvey) left nine children namely: (1) Nicolas Harvey, who married Miss Stewart (with issue); (2) Sallie Harvey who married Samuel R. Stewart (with issue); (3) Henriette Harvey who married Horace DeGruy (with issue); (4) Henry Harvey who married Marie DeGruy (with issue); (5) William Harvey (with issue); (6) Laura Harvey, who married James D. Séguin (with issue); (7) Robert Harvey (with issue); (8) Horace H. Harvey (with issue); (9) Jennie Harvey, who married J. E. McGuire (with issue). Joseph Hale Harvey, husband of Louise d'Estréhan, was a grandson of Robert Harvey who with his brothers fought in the Revolutionary War, one of them, William Harvey, being killed at the battle of Guilford Court House, N. C., March 13, 1781. Their granddaughter, Alida Harvey, married Major Guy Brandon Lawrason, U. S. A. The above named Adèle d'Estréhan (Mrs. Samuel B. McCutcheon), left four children, namely: (a) Samuel B. McCutcheon; (b) Amélia McCutcheon; (c) Adèle McCutcheon (without issue), and (d) Azby d'Estréhan McCutcheon who married Mattie Cabaniss (with issue). The above named Eliza d'Estréhan (Mrs. Daniel R. Rogers), left two children: Lucie Rogers, wife of Alonzo Charbonnet (with issue), and Nina Rogers, wife of S. Locke Breaux (without issue). The above named Azby d'Estréhan, who married Rosa Ferrier, left one child, Marie Delphine Louise d'Estréhan, married first to Dupuy de Lome and second to Ernest Richard.

BARROW Family

AMONG the early English settlers in Louisiana were some bearing the name of Barrow. The immediate male ancestor of the large number of descendants who are scattered widely throughout Louisiana, but who himself never came to the state, was William Barrow of Edgecombe county, North Carolina, at one time sheriff of Tarborough county, of that state, who married, July 8, 1760, Olivia Ruffin, daughter of Robert Ruffin and Anne Bennett. William Barrow died at his Tarborough homestead January 27, 1787, and was the father of eight children.

His widow, Olivia Ruffin Barrow, in 1798 left her North Carolina home on a long journey, via the covered wagon, to that far-famed country of *Nueva Feliciana*, then under the domination of the Spaniards. With her on this trek came her three daughters and three of her sons. Her two other sons came to Louisiana a few years later. With these Barrow pioneers came their possessions, their slaves and their wealth. They took up large Spanish grants of land, and soon began the erection of several wonderful plantation homes, most of which are still standing in 1931. The widow of William Barrow did not live long to enjoy her new found home, as she died April 2, 1803, five years after her arrival in Feliciana and lies buried at *Highland* plantation, originally christened *Locust Grove*. Her children were:

1.—William Barrow, born November 29, 1761, died November 27, 1762.

2.—Robert Barrow, born February 18, 1763, died November 9, 1813, who married Mary Haynes. They had no issue.

3.—William Barrow, born February 26, 1765, died November 9, 1823, the second so named, who married

Pheraby Hilliard in North Caolina June 26, 1792. She was born February 10, 1775, and died October 10, 1827. He was the William Barrow who played a most important role in the West Florida rebellion. Although younger than his brother Robert, William was evidently the "head of the family," and in 1799 began the construction of the family home, which became "a mansion in the wilds" and named *Locust Grove*, although later it was rechristened *Highland*. The children of William Barrow were: (a) Robert Hilliard Barrow, born February 7, 1795, died July 21, 1823, who married Eliza Pirrie (q. v.), whose home place was *Prospect* plantation. His posthumous child, Robert H. Barrow Jr., born March 27, 1824, became lieutenant colonel of the Rosale Guards. He married Mary Eliza Barrow, and *Rosale* plantation was a wedding present from the bride's father, David Barrow; (b) Ann, or Nancy, Barrow, born September 17, 1795, died in 1856, married John Benoist and had one child, Rosina E. Benoist; (c) William Ruffin Barrow, born December 21, 1800, died March 22, 1862, who married his cousin, Olivia Ruffin Barrow, born April, 1806, died June 1, 1857, daughter of Bennett Barrow and Martha Hill. They had six children, and built the *Greenwood* plantation home in 1830, one of the finest examples of colonial homes in the Feliciana country' (d) Bennett Barrow, born December 23, 1803, died August 29, 1805; (e) Martha Hilliard Barrow, born September 11, 1809, died 1899, who married Daniel Turnbull, born June 5, 1796, died October 30, 1861, and had three children. One daughter, Sarah Turnbull, married James Pirrie Bowman, born 1832, died August 25, 1927, at ninety-four, and lived at *Rosedown*, the famed Feliciana home which Daniel Turnbull built in 1835 (See page 195); (f) Bennett Hilliard Barrow, born October 21, 1811, died May 29, 1854, who married first, Emily Joor, born July 15, 1815, died May 22, 1845, and by her had six children. His second wife was Mrs. Nancy Joor Haile, by whom he had two children. According to one of his sons, Captain John J. Barrow, it was Bennett

Hilliard Barrow who inherited *Locust Grove* and, after his father's death, renamed it *Highland;* (g) Eliza Eleanor Barrow, born October 18, 1814, died August 6, 1885, who married her cousin, William Hill Barrow, born 1808, died 1870, and had nine children.

4.—Bartholomew Barrow, born October 16, 1766, died February 15, 1852, one of the two brothers who remained in North Carolina until 1820 before migrating to the Feliciana country. He married, first, Elizabeth Slatter, who died in North Carolina; his second wife was Bethier Brantly, born 1777 and died in 1843. He settled what is now known as *Afton Villa* plantation, purchasing the land from his brother, William, May 11, 1820. His children by Miss Slatter were: (a) Ann Barrow, who married Robert Ratcliffe; (b) William Bennett Barrow, died without issue; and (c) Robert Ruffin Barrow, who married Volumnia Hunley, and became the father of R. R. Barrow Jr., who married Jennie Tennant. Barthlomew's children by his second wife, Miss Brantly, were: (d) Mary Ann Barrow, who married Alexander Barrow of Tennessee, and had three children; and (e) David Barrow, born September 15, 1805, died February 9, 1874, who married, first, Sarah Hatch, born February 27, 1808, died January 9, 1846, by whom he had two children, one being Mary Eliza who married Robert H. Barrow Jr. (q. v.). David Barrow bought *Afton Villa* from his father. It was not then so named. When his daughter Mary Eliza, surrounded by gallants, sang so sweetly that tender favorite of that candlelit past, "Flow Gently, Sweet Afton," it became the favorite song of the young bloods of that day, and so came *Afton Villa* by its name. David Barrow married, secondly, Mrs. Susan Wolfork Rowan of Kentucky. David Barrow had two children by his marriage to Susan Wolfork Rowan, one was Florence Barrow, who married Maximillan Fisher, and whose son is David B. Fisher.

5.—Ann Barrow, born September 11, 1768. No further data obtainable.

6.—Mary Barrow, born May 16, 1771, who married William Lane, and had three children: William Lane Jr., died without issue; (b) Ann Lane, who married Frank Ruth and had two children, and (c) Olivia Ruffin Lane, who married, first, William Ratcliffe, and had two children. Her second husband was William Wade. Olivia Ruffin Lane is reputed to have built in 1835, the *Ellerslie* plantation home, another of the Feliciana show places.

7.—Sarah Barrow, born May 14, 1773, who married John Dawson, and whose son was Judge John Barrow Dawson of St. Francisville.

8.—Ruffin Barrow, born April 9, 1775, died December 16, 1799. No further data obtainable.

9.—Bennett Barrow, born June 22, 1777, died July 22, 1833. He did not come to the Feliciana country until 1816, remaining in Edgecombe county, North Carolina, where he carried on a banking business until he joined his brothers and sisters in Louisiana. He married Martha Hill and installed her in a plantation home called *Rosebank*, across the Little Bayou Sara from his brother William's home. The children of Bennett Barrow and Martha Hill were: (a) Olivia Ruffin Barrow, who married William Ruffin Barrow, son of William Barrow and Pheraby Hilliard (q. v.); William Hill Barrow, who married Eliza Eleanor Barrow, daughter of the Barrow-Hilliard union; (c) Margaret Barrow, no information available; (d) Bennet James Barrow, born 1811, died 1873, who married Caroline Hall, and had nine children. One was Stephen Decatur Barrow, whose widow is the present owner of *Ambrosia* and *Independence* plantations. Another son, Nicolas Hall Barrow, at one time owned the old *Live Oak* home, reputed to be one of the oldest in the Felicianas, and (e) Robert James Barrow, born October 5, 1817, died December 16, 1887, who married July 11, 1839, Mary Elinor Crabb, daughter of Judge Henry Crabb of Tennessee. She was born March 23, 1822, and died February 20, 1897. Robert James Barrow was a general in the Confederate army, and was the father of eight children.

PLAUCHE - DART - KERNAN - WALL - WINANS
DU BOSE Families

ON the eighth day of February, 1765, Etienne Henri Plauché married Marguerite Sélam in New Orleans. He was the son of Etienne Plauché and Madelaine Vaderache (or Vaderoche or Vaderaze). The bride, was a daughter of Jacques Sélam and Marie Magdeline Golem (or, possibly, Golure), early settlers who came to the colony on one of John Law's ships. She was born November 6, 1750, and died June 8, 1818, at the age of sixty-eight.

Etienne Henri Plauché was born in the village of Seine, in Provence, France, April 11, 1736, and came to Louisiana when he was only fifteen. He is described as a shipwright, designer and builder of ships, establishing his shipyard on Bayou St. John. His children were:

1.—Marie Madeline Plauché, born July 21, 1769, who married Jean Jacques Chessé, and died in la Rochelle, France.
2.—Charles Martin Plauché, born November 4, 1771, died October 31, 1795.
3.—Louise Marguerite Plauché, born April 1, 1774, who married François Chessé, and died in Saint Yago, Cuba, July 1840.
4.—André Plauchç, born December 16, 1776, assassinated at Pointe Coupée July 21, 1801, by Broudoc Boisdoré.
5.—Emilie Plauché, born January 30, 1779, died November 21, 1785.
6.—Joseph Alexandre Plauché, born February 4, 1782, who married Eugénie Bourgéat, and died in Avoyelles in 1823.
7.—Jean Baptiste Plauché, born January 28, 1785, who married Mathilde Saint Amand and died April 1856 in New Orleans.

8.—Jacques Henri Urbain Plauché, born May 25, 1787, who married Mary Brown in Avoyelles, and died April 1856 in New Orleans.

9.—Marguerite Mélanie Plauché, born June 25, 1785, who married Marius Michel, and died in New Orleans May 1855.

10.—Marie Victoire, born October 30, 1792, who married Marie (Adélie) Boulmay in 1825, and died in May 1857.

Some of the sons became planters in various parts of Louisiana, particularly in the Red River parishes; some became merchants in New Orleans. Among the latter were the two youngest, Jean Baptiste Plauché and Jacques Henri Urbain Plauché.

Louisiana will never forget Jean Baptiste Plauché for it was he who commanded the famous *Bataillon d'Orleans* at the Battle of New Orleans with the rank of major. It was this contingent of Créoles that ran all the way from Spanish Fort along the banks of Bayou St. John into the city when the news of the arrival of the invading British hosts was conveyed to their impetuous commander, and he and his men fought valiantly in every one of the desperate encounters with Pakenham's forces. After the war, J. B. Plauché was elected colonel of the Louisiana Legion and was later made its first brigadier general. In 1850 he was elected lieutenant governor of his native state. He died at the age of seventy-five and was buried with military honors.

His brother, Jacques Henri Urbain Plauché, best known as Urbain Plauché, also fought under General Andrew Jackson. On July 9, 1809, he, a Catholic, was married to Mary (or Polly, as she was called) Brown, a Protestant, the daughter of William and Dicey (or Dacie) Brown of the Red River parish of Rapides. William Brown came to Louisiana from Kentucky with his wife, who was Dicey White of South Carolina, and settled in Rapides in 1800, where the head of the family died in 1820, his wife dying three years earlier. Their children were: (a) James Brown, who married Elizabeth Martin of Rapides, no issue; (b) John Brown, who married Claire Boulong, of Rapides, without issue; (c) Joseph Brown, who married Boulong Lajar, and had a daughter; (d) William Brown, who married a Miss Lajar, without issue; (e) Elizabeth Brown, who married Thomas F. Oliver, and left children; (f) Sally Brown, who married Jean Louis Lacroix, and had a daughter who married a Mr. Bossier of Natchitoches, and (g) Mary Brown, who married Urbain Plauché.

Six children were the result of the marriage of Mary Brown to Urbain Plauché: Stephen Plauché, born March 11, 1811; William Plauché, born 1812, died 1816; Sélam Plauché, born 1813; Euphémia Plauché, who died in 1832; Mary Plauché, born September 23, 1823, died December 30, 1897, who married Henry Dart, and Margaret Plauché, born October 1825.

The fifth child of Mary Brown and Urbain Plauché, named for her mother, who died at the time the last child was born, spent her younger days with her grandmother in Kentucky, but was returned to New Orleans when she was eleven, to finish her education in the Ursuline Convent, although she depended on her Bible in later years for her religious guidance.

When Mary Plauché, just fourteen, was shopping in Royal street, followed closely by her black mammy, she came to a muddy street. She lifted her long skirts to make the crossing. This action revealed such a delicate pair of slender ankles that a jolly, brown-haired. husky young Englishman, standing on the opposite, *banquette*, an engineer, then in the Créole city on business, determined to know her. He found a mutual friend and, on June 22, 1841, the beautiful *demoiselle* Mary Plauché and Henry Dart, a Church of England man, were married.

Henry Dart, born April 5, 1807, in Helston, Cornwall, England, died in his seventy-eighth year, February 4, 1885. He was the son of Richard Dart and Rose Alford, who followed their son to America. Rose Aflord was the daughter of John and Elizabeth Alford. Henry Dart, an engineer by profession, came to Louisiana from New York. After engaging in railroad construction activities he entered the service of the U. S. Engineering department and became an American citizen in 1844.

[423]

Thirteen children were born to Mary Plauché and Henry Dart, but only four attained maturity. They were: (a) Agnes Dart, born in New Orleans February 28, 1854, who married J. Pickett; (b) Isabelle Dart, born January 8, 1856, in New Orleans, who married Robert Preis; (c) Henry Plauché Dart, born at Fort St. Phillip, who married, September 27, 1882, Mary Lytle Kernan, and (d) Emily Dart, born at Fort St. Phillip, December 13, 1859, died October 26, 1906, who married C. C. Matthews.

Henry Plauché Dart, lawyer, historian and archivist, who married Mary Lytle Kernan at Clinton, Louisiana, became the father of (a) Henry Plauché Dart Jr. who married Suzanne Dupaquier, daughter of Dr. Edouard Dupaquier and Eugénie Limongi; (b) William Kernan Dart, married Louise LaPlace, daughter of Albert LaPlace and Paola Gelpi; (c) Mary Winans Dart; (d) John Dart, who married Phyllis Reeves, daughter of Robert Dulaney Reeves and Evelynn Humphries; (e) Benjamin Wall Dart, who married Clara Bell Cromwell, daughter of Nicholas Cromwell and Clara Bryan; (f) Sally Dart, and (g) Edith Thorn DuBose Dart, who married Henry Grady Price.

Mary Lytle Kernan was the daughter of William Fergus Kernan and Sarah Wall. Judge Kernan, born May 10, 1825, died May 13, 1899, was a well known lawyer and planter of East Feliciana parish, the son of John Kernan and Martha Lytle of County Cavan, Ireland. They were the parents of six children: (a) Thomas J. Kernan, who married a Miss Wetherill; (b) William Fergus Kernan Jr., who married Elizabeth Nevill; (c) Mary Lytle Kernan, who married Henry Plauché Dart; (d) Sarah Kernan, who married Dr. Emmett Lee Irwin; (e) Benjamin Wall Kernan, who married Alice Lange, and (f) Elizabeth Kernan, who married Joseph J. Joffrion.

Sarah Culbertson Wall, wife of Judge Kernan, was the daughter of Isaac Wall, an architect of note, born July 31, 1789, near Newark, New Jersey, who married Mary Susannah Winans of Wilkinson county, Mississippi. In later life he became a Methodist minister of the gospel. His wife was the daughter of Bishop Williams Winans and Martha DuBose, and Isaac Wall's second wife, he having first married Sarah Culbertson. Mary Susannah Winans Wall was a widely known and much beloved educator in Louisiana and Mississippi, a profession she adopted after her husband's death. Their children were: (a) Sarah Culbertson Wall, born February 28, 1835, died in 1881, who married William Fergus Kernan, April 13, 1853; (b) William Winans Wall, of the Confederate army; (c) Benjamin Drake Wall, killed in the Civil War; (d) Ira Bowman Wall, a lieutenant in the Confederate army; (e) Westley Winans Wall, who served in the Civil War; (f) Martha DuBose Wall, who married J. Embree; (g) Mary Eliza Wall; (h) Dickson Wall, and (i) Francis Richardson Wall.

William Winans, father of Mary Susannah Winans Wall, was the son of Creighton Winans and Susan Hannah Hopkins, daughter of Captain John Hopkins, colonial governor of Rhode Island and one of the signers of the Declaration of Independence. He was born November 3, 1788, and died August 31, 1857. He married, September 14, 1815, in Charleston, South Carolina, Martha DuBose. William Winans adopted the ministry and became a bishop of the Methodist-Episcopal Church and the founder of the second church of that denomination in Louisiana, and held the first Protestant Sunday school in New Orleans. Bishop Winans was a direct descendant of the first John Winans, or Jan Winants, the Associate, who came to America in 1664, from Holland and settled in the town of Elizabeth, New Jersey, and of Peter Melyn, one of the Dutch patroons who settled in New York. His wife, Martha DuBose, born April 20, 1797, in Darlington, South Carolina, died March 22, 1862, in Centerville, Mississippi, was the daughter of Daniel DuBose, who served in the American Revolution as captain of South Carolina volunteers, and a direct descendant of Isaac DuBose, a French Huguenot, who came from Dieppe, Normandy, France, to settle in South Carolina in 1689. The children of Bishop Winans were: (a) Mary Susanna Winans, who married Isaac Wall; (b) Margaret Winans, who married William Dickson, of Centerville, Miss.; (d) Anna Eliza Winans, who married Nolan Dickson, of Centerville, and (d) Westley Winans, who married Jane Harper of Shreveport, Louisiana.

BRINGIER Family

THE founder of the Bringier family in Louisiana was Emanuel Marius Pons Bringier, a great grandson of Ignace Bringier, judge in the district of Limange, in the present department of Puy-de-Dôme, France. His grandfather, Jean Bringier, related to the Counts of Rochebriant, married Marie Douradou, of the family of Baron Douradou d'Auvergne. This couple had a son, Pierre Bringier de Lacadière, who was the father of Emanuel Marius Pons Bringier, born October 27, 1752.

This last named Bringier disposed of his estate *Lacadière*, near Aubagne, and sailed for the New World accompanied by his young wife, and a cousin named Françoise Durand. He established himself on the island of Martinique where, in partnership with his brother Victor, who later was lost at sea, he became a planter. The Martinique venture was brief and unsatisfactory. Consequently Marius Pons Bringier (he dropped the name Emanuel) determined to set up a new home in Louisiana. Arriving in that colony with abundant means he acquired a plantation near New Orleans.

In the years from 1785 to 1798 Bringier purchased several adjoining plantations in St. James parish, and formed them into one pretentious estate which he named *La Maison Blanche*, a place long famous throughout the South, best known, as "White Hall."

Here the head of the family lived until April 21, 1820, when he was laid away in the plantation burial ground. His children were: Louis, Françoise, Elizabeth, Douradou, Laure, and Mélanie.

The eldest daughter, Françoise, best known as Fanny, was born at *White Hall* March 9, 1786, and died May 10, 1827. In 1801 she married Christophe Colomb of *Bocage*, Ascension parish, a native of Corbeille, near Paris. At the outbreak of the French revolution he fled from Paris for San Domingo and, encountering another revolution there, escaped, disguised as a cook, and came to Louisiana. Christophe Colomb was an artist, poet and musician, and while he dallied with the Muses, Fanny managed *Bocage* plantation.

Elizabeth Bringier, the second daughter, known to intimates as Betsy, was also born at *White Hall*, April 21, 1788, and died November 23, 1873. She married Augustin Dominique Tureaud, born at La Rochelle, France, October 23, 1764. Involved in an amorous scrape, Tureaud's father sent him to manage a plantation in San Domingo, and, when the uprising of the blacks occured, a female slave effected the young man's escape, but he drifted about on the gulf in an open boat for a number of days, until he was picked up by a vessel that landed him at Philadelphia. From there he journeyed to Louisiana and while on a visit to *White Hall* he was detained for days because of rains that flooded the roads. During his enforced stay his hospitable host offered the guest his daughter, Mademoiselle Betsy, in marriage. Tureaud was delighted, accepted, and Betsy, just thirteen, was called to her father's presence and presented to her future husband. The marriage, celebrated a year later, proved to be a very happy one. The bride's father bestowed on the wedded pair *Union* plantation, and for many years Tureaud was judge of St. James parish, and held a like post in the county of Acadia. They had many children.

The fourth daughter of the Bringier household was Mélanie, born August 16, 1793, at *White Hall*. Her first husband was William Simpson, a native of Savannah, Georgia, at that time a New Orleans merchant, and her second was James Fisher Wilson, hailing from Inverness, Scotland.

The eldest son of Marius Pons Bringier was called Don Louis. He was born in the Tchoupitoulas district August 25, 1784, and died in New Orleans October 29, 1860, after a romantic and exciting career, in which he made and lost a tremendous fortune. With his younger brother he managed *White Hall* after their father's death, lost every penny he possessed gambling in New Orleans, wandered into Mexico, discovered mines of fabulous wealth, lost all he had by a revolution, was clapped into prison and sentenced to death, which he escaped by proving he was related to Mgr. Du Bourg, Catholic Bishop of Louisiana, returned to New Orleans, rehabilitated himself and his fortune, and participated in the Battle of New Orleans. In his advanced age he married a young and beautiful girl, who several years after their marriage, became demented, leaving several daughters and a son, Charles Pendelton Bringier, who died unmarried.

The younger son of the first Bringier was Michel Doradou Bringier, born at sea, December 6, 1789, and died March 13, 1847. Despite remonstrance from the French branch of the Bringiers he dropped the first "u" from the ancestral name of Douradou. He acquired *White Hall* from the other heirs, and at the time of his marriage to a niece of Bishop Du Bourg, he built *The Hermitage* in Ascension parish. Other plantations he owned were *Houmas* and *Bruslé*.

Doradou Bringier married, in Baltimore, Maryland, June 17, 1812, Louise Elizabeth Aglaé Du Bourg de Ste. Colombe. This fourteen-year-old girl was born in Kingston, Jamaica, January 4, 1798, being the daughter of François Pierre Ste. Colomb Du Bourg, Chevalier, Sieur de Ste. Colombe, and Elizabeth Etiennette Bonne Charest de Lauzon, whose father was Etienne Charest, last Seigneur de Lauzon. Mme. Bringier survived her husband thirty-one years, dying at the *Melpomène* town residence in New Orleans, June 8, 1878. Their children were:

1.—Marius Ste. Colombe Bringier, best known as "M. S." Bringier, born at *White Hall*, November 3, 1814, and died in New Orleans, August 22, 1884. On his return to Louisiana he married his first cousin, Augustine Tureaud, daughter of August D. Tureaud and Betsy Bringier. They had five children: (a) Louise Bringier, who became the second wife of Dr. James de B. Trudeau (q. v.); (b) Augustine Bringier, who died young; (c) Félicie Bringier, unmarried; (d) Marius Ste. Colombe Bringier, not married; (e) Eda Bringier, who married Thomas Holmes of Baltimore, Maryland.

2.—Marie Elizabeth Rosella Bringier, born at *The Hermitage*, June 24, 1818, died there July 20, 1849, married General Hore Browse Trist of *Bowden*, Ascension parish, born in Washington, D. C., March 19, 1802.

He and his elder brother, Nicholas Philip Trist, became wards of President Jefferson and were reared at *Monticello*. Here Nicholas Trist married Virginia Randolph, daughter of Governor Mann Randolph of Virginia and granddaughter of Jefferson. Hore Browse Trist, on his return to Louisiana, became commander-in-chief of the state troops and married Marie Bringier. He died November 16, 1856. His children were: (a) Nicholas Browse Trist of *Totness* on the Atchafalaya, and later a notary public in New Orleans. Educated at Stuttgart, Germany, he became a captain of artillery in the Confederacy. He married his cousin Augustine Gordon; (b) Julien Bringier Trist, educated with his brother, was killed in the Battle of Murfreesboro; (c) Wilhelmine Trist, who married Colonel Robert C. Wood, a son of Brigadier General R. C. Wood, assistant surgeon general U. S. A., and Ann Taylor, eldest daughter of President Zachary Taylor. Colonel Wood commanded Wood's Cavalry of the Confederacy in the Civil War; (d) Rosella Trist, died young; (e) Nicholas Philip Trist, a lieutenant in the Confederate army, whose first wife was his cousin Marie Tureaud, and his second, her sister Alice.

3.—Louise Françoise Bringier, born in New Orleans, October 6, 1820, died there November 13, 1889, who married Martin Gordon, and whose children were: (a) Aglaé Gordon, who married Guichard Bienvenu; (b) Anna Gordon, not married; (c) Martin Gordon Jr., not married; (d) Bianca Gordon, died young; (e) Loutie Gordon, who married Dr. P. S. O'Reilly of St. Louis; (f) Wilhelmine Gordon, unmarried.

4.—Anne Guillelmine Nanine Bringier, born at *The Hermitage* August 24, 1823, died in New Orleans, November 6, 1911, married Duncan Farrar Kenner of *Ashland* (q. v.), their children were: (a) Duncan Farrar Kenner, who died young; (b) Blanche Kenner, who married Samuel Simpson; (c) Roselle Kenner, who married General Joseph Lancaster Brent, and (d) George Kenner, unmarried.

5.—Louis Amédée Bringier, born February 4, 1828, died

in Florida January 9, 1897. He lived at *The Hermitage*, was a colonel of cavalry in the Confederacy, and married his cousin, Stella Tureaud, their children being: (a) Louis Amédée Bringier Jr. who married Ella D. Threlkeld, widow Hobbs; (b) Louise Bringier, who married William C. Bateman; (c) Julien Trist Bringier, M. D., of *Tezcuco* plantation, Ascension parish, who married Mary Cuthbert Jones; (d) Stella Bringier, who married Robert H. Thach of Birmingham, Alabama; (e) Mather Du Bourg Bringier, married, first, Jennie E. McGalliard, and then Helen Jane Mills.

6.—Marie Elizabeth Aglaé Bringier, born January 17, 1830, who married her cousin, Benjamine Louis Michael Tureaud of *Tezcuco* plantation, their children being: (a) Aglaé Tureaud, who married, first, William Brooks, and later George Parks; (b) Benjamin Tureaud, and (c) Henri Tureaud, both unmarried.

7.—Louise Marie Myrthé Bringier, born January 28, 1834, died at *Melpomème*, New Orleans, March 16, 1875, who married Lieutenant-General Richard "Dick" Taylor of *Fashion* plantation, St. Charles parish, only son of President Zachary Taylor. Their children were: (a) Louise Margaret Taylor, not married; (b) Betty M. Taylor, who married Walter H. Stauffer; (c) Zachary Taylor, died young, and (d) Myrthé Bianca Taylor, who married Isaac Hull Stauffer.

8.—Anne Octavie Marie Bringier, born at *The Hermitage*, January 1, 1839, died in New Orleans November 20, 1917, who married General Allen Thomas of *New Dalton* and *New Hope* plantations, a brigadier general in the Confederacy, and U. S. minister to Venezuela. Their children were: (a) Allen Thomas, who married his cousin, Marie Sauvé; (b) Julien Bringier Trist Thomas, who married Mary Agnes Saal; (c) John Ridgeley Thomas, unmarried and (d) Dall Thomas, who married, first, Elma Bergeron, and then Louise Moret.

9.—Martin Doradou Bringier, born August 3, 1841, lieutenant and aide-de-camp in the Confederate army, who died unmarried.

INDEX

INDEX

CPSIA information can be obtained at www.ICGtesting.com
Printed in the USA
LVOW08s1231260913

354243LV00004B/6/A